DINNER FOR DICKENS

For my father, Thomas A. Rossi, and his never-ending enthusiasm for my culinary adventures and my mother, Josephine M. Palmer Rossi, who let me play with dough when I was very young.

DINNER *for* DICKENS

THE CULINARY HISTORY OF
MRS CHARLES DICKENS'S MENU BOOKS

INCLUDING A TRANSCRIPT OF

WHAT SHALL WE HAVE FOR DINNER?

BY

'LADY MARIA CLUTTERBUCK'

SUSAN M. ROSSI-WILCOX

Susan M. Rossi-Wilcox

PROSPECT BOOKS

2005

First published in Great Britain in 2005 by Prospect Books, Allaleigh House, Blackawton, Totnes TQ9 7DL.

British Library Cataloguing in Publication Data:
A catalogue entry for this book is available from the British Library.

ISBN 1-903018-38-2

Typeset in Adobe Garamond by Tom Jaine.

Printed and bound in Great Britain by the Cromwell Press, Trowbridge.

CONTENTS

ILLUSTRATIONS

Between pages 160 and 161.

1. A study sketch of Catherine Dickens by Daniel Maclise, probably drawn about 1842. Dickens's wedding present acknowledged her talents in the domestic arts, which she put to good use creating beautiful point-laces and needle-worked covers in Berlin wool for their dining-room chairs. (Photograph courtesy of the Charles Dickens Museum.)

2. The marriage certificate of Catherine and Charles. Catherine required her father's consent since she was under age. (Photograph courtesy of the Charles Dickens Museum.)

3. Sketch by Pierre Morand of Catherine on board S.S. *Britannia en route* for America in 1842. (Photograph courtesy of the Charles Dickens Museum.)

4. A daguerrotype of Catherine by Mayall in about 1852. (Photograph courtesy of the Charles Dickens Museum.)

5. Catherine near the time of her first book of menus in 1851. Photographer unknown. (Photograph courtesy of the Charles Dickens Museum.)

6. A studio portrait of Catherine probably taken near the end of her life in 1879. Photographer unknown. (Photograph courtesy of the Charles Dickens Museum.)

7. 'The Toast and Water Club' by Daniel Maclise captured the four Dickens children at play with their toy decanter, glasses and books. From left to right are Katey, Walter, Charley and Mamie, with their pet raven Grip perched behind Mamie. Apple trees can be seen through the window. The sketch accompanied Charles and Catherine on their North American tour in 1842. (Photograph courtesy of the Charles Dickens Museum.)

8. 'The Duet' by the Dickenses' neighbour and friend Frank Stone captures the family, friends and pet in their drawing-room. The use of richly figured silk damask fabric for curtains, seats on the rosewood chairs, couches, pillows and ottomans helped coordinate the room. The piano was made by Cramer & Co. Catherine is thought to be the woman at her needlework. (Photograph courtesy of the Charles Dickens Museum.)

9. The Palazzo Peschiere in Genoa where the family lived from late 1844 to the middle of 1845. The huge rooms of the Palazzo boasted frescoes, high ceilings and marble floors. (Photograph courtesy of the Charles Dickens Museum.)

10. Rosemont Villa, Lausanne, where they lived in 1846, 'with two pretty salons, a dining-room, hall and kitchen.' Charles's study upstairs had breathtaking views; the bowers were covered with roses. (Photograph courtesy of the Charles Dickens Museum.)

11. 1 Devonshire Terrace, Regent's Park, where the Dickens family lived from 1839 to 1851. (Photograph courtesy of the Charles Dickens Museum.)

12. The stable at 1 Devonshire Terrace, photographed in the summer. The groom lived above. Grip the raven is buried in the flower bed on the right-hand side. (Photograph courtesy of the Charles Dickens Museum.)

13. The front exterior of Tavistock House where the Dickenses lived from 1851 until 1858. The photograph shows the communal front garden before the terrace of three houses. The Dickenses' house is the one nearest the railing. (Photograph courtesy of the Charles Dickens Museum.)

14. Tavistock House, seen across the central flower bed. The tops of the kitchen windows, giving onto the area, can just be seen. (Photograph courtesy of the Charles Dickens Museum.)

15. Painting by Augustus Egg, *ca.* 1848, depicting Charles Dickens as Joe the ploughboy and Mrs Cowden-Clarke as Mary in the farce *Used Up*, the source of the pseudonym 'Lady Maria Clutterbuck' used in *What Shall We Have For Dinner?* (Photograph courtesy of the Charles Dickens Museum.)

16. The playbill for Charles Dickens's private theatricals in Montreal, Canada, while they were on their North American tour in 1842. Dickens recorded the names of the casts and he boasted about his wife's performance as Amy Templeton in *Deaf as a Post*, saying 'only think of Kate playing! and playing devilish well, I assure you!' (Photograph courtesy of the Charles Dickens Museum.)

17. Catherine Dickens's formal invitation to dinner at Devonshire Terrace to Harriet Beecher Stowe and her husband, written on 3 May 1853. (Courtesy of the Beinecke Rare Book & Manuscript Library, Yale University.)

WHAT SHALL WE HAVE FOR DINNER?

SATISFACTORILY ANSWERED BY NUMEROUS

BILLS OF FARE

FOR FROM TWO TO EIGHTEEN PERSONS.

BY

LADY MARIA CLUTTERBUCK.

A NEW EDITION.

LONDON:

BRADBURY & EVANS, 11, BOUVERIE STREET.

1852.

Photocopied image of the title-page of the 'new edition' of 1852. The transcript of this edition begins on page 21.

FOREWORD
by Lillian Nayder

Highlighting the social and cultural significance of women's cookbooks as registers of women's lives and communities in her study *Eat My Words* (2002), Janet Theophano argues that such works provide formulae for conduct as well as for cooking, 'constructing, defending, and transgressing social and cultural borders' as they instruct readers in the domestic arts. As Susan M. Rossi-Wilcox demonstrates in the pages that follow, Catherine Dickens's book, first published in 1851, serves as a case in point. Placing Mrs Dickens's cookbook in context, Rossi-Wilcox traces the fascinating history of many food items that appeared on her table as well as their sources and marketing, and outlines the eating habits of middle-class Victorians. But more specifically, Rossi-Wilcox shows how Catherine Dickens's collection of recipes and bills of fare illuminates aspects of Mrs Dickens's life story as well as the social boundaries and expectations of the Dickenses' world. Like their 'Best Dinner Set', the abundant courses, highly-prized food items, and artfully designed desserts served at their table signalled Dickens's professional success and upwardly-mobile social status while their relatively informal style of serving meals marked the limits of their ambition and their comfort within the middle class.

As Rossi-Wilcox suggests, Mrs Dickens's cookbook and its history of revisions are particularly significant because of Mrs Dickens's fate at the hands of Dickens scholars – the way in which she has been unfairly dismissed as an incompetent domestic manager by biographers and critics anxious to justify Charles Dickens's decision to separate from her in 1858 and all-too-willing to uncritically accept Dickens's own word on the subject. Despite Charles Dickens's disparaging remarks about his wife and her incompetence at the time of their separation, Michael Slater and others have rallied to Mrs Dickens's defense, identifying the unjust misrepresentations in Dickens's account of his wife of twenty-two years. Rossi-Wilcox's detailed analysis of Catherine Dickens's cookbook, Catherine's repeated revisions of the text, and her experiences as hostess and domestic manager lends force to such revaluations, casting Dickens's wife as a knowledgeable, engaged, and sympathetic figure in her own right – outlining, for instance, her 'wise use of ingredients', her 'practicality as a menu planner', and her ability to temper extravagance with frugality in serving her guests. Locating Catherine's own voice amid her recipes, Rossi-Wilcox enables us to hear from Mrs Dickens in a new way – in the self-assured Scottish brogue that was largely muffled after 1858.

According to Janet Theophano, women who authored cookbooks not only constructed and defended social boundaries in their works but also transgressed those boundaries, often challenging the authority of those who disparaged the domestic arts or sought to keep women in their 'proper place'. Illustrating her point, Theophano cites the example of Buwei Yang Chao's cookbook *How to Cook and Eat in Chinese* (1945), in which recipes and instructions were translated into English by Chao's linguist husband, whose usurpations of authorship Mrs Chao complains of to her readers and resists. Catherine Dickens did not depend on her husband to translate her work into English, but she undoubtedly relied on his agency and fame as a novelist to get her book into print, using her husband's publishers, Bradbury and Evans, as her own, and allowing him to write the joking introduction to the book, setting its terms for readers. Yet while these elements of *What Shall We Have For Dinner?* suggest Catherine's dependence on her husband and her recognition of his authority, her cookbook also provides a subtle challenge to the claims of its opening pages – to Dickens's conviction, for example, that a woman's cooking is primarily important as a means of keeping her husband happy and at home. Dickens's introduction, as Rossi-Wilcox writes, 'inculcates what became a growing moralistic attitude that husbands should expect their home to be their tranquil castle and their wife the silent keeper of its orderliness.' There can be no doubt that Catherine Dickens took satisfaction in pleasing her husband and their guests, and was a warm and gracious hostess. Yet she also found gratification in applying and recording her knowledge of the domestic arts – in that sense of competence and authority that emerges from her recipes and bills of fare but that has been too often overlooked or denied by Dickens critics receptive to Dickens's portrait of Catherine, rather than to Catherine's own self-portrait, in the pages of her book.

Bates College,
Lewiston, Maine.

ACKNOWLEDGEMENTS

On a December holiday I visited the Charles Dickens Museum and hoped to find a recipe for plum pudding. To my surprise, the gift shop sold neither a recipe card nor Catherine Dickens's work mentioned in the guide book. David Parker, former director of the museum, kindly sent a photocopy of the 1852 edition, which increased my curiosity. The short introduction I proposed to Tom Jaine for a facsimile grew, and when the four other editions appeared as library catalogues came online, the manuscript expanded again.

Along the way, many people offered assistance. First and foremost, I want to thank my sister, Helen M. Rossi DeMaiolo, whose enthusiasm never wavered; and Barbara Wheaton, the 'patron saint of culinary historians', who provided a wealth of insight and discovered the all-important 1854 edition in the recently bequeathed Sophie Coe collection.

I am grateful to the Harvard University Library System, particularly the Botany Library and Judith Warnement, Lisa DeCesare and Gretchen Wade; to the extraordinary culinary collections at the Schlesinger Library with Sarah Hutcheon, as reference librarian, and to Barbara Haber. Florian Schweizer from the Charles Dickens Museum provided access to archival materials, as did Lorraine Ouellette from the Beinecke Rare Book and Manuscript Library, Yale University, and Gayle Barkley from the Manuscript Department of the Huntington Library. The staff of the British Library, the New York Academy of Medicine, the New York Public Library, and the Victoria and Albert Museum provided information or copies of other pertinent documents.

Discussions with Alan Kabat, Karsten Hartel, Alison Pirie, Judy Chupasko, Gustavo Romero, David Boufford and other colleagues from the Harvard Museum of Comparative Zoology and the Harvard University Herbaria were very helpful, as were the historical insights of Leah Price, Michael Slater, Robert Patten, Paul Lewis, Crinan Alexander and Julia Abramson. I am responsible for any mistakes, but am indebted for the critical views of Barbara Wheaton, Sharon Smith Abbott, Joe Carlton, David Parker, Julie Calko, and especially Gary W. Crawford, whose humour and advice were always appreciated, and Karen Krieger who supported the project from the outset of our original visit to London. Glenn Adelson solved nagging editorial issues; Holly Weeks provided guidance in untangling the proverbial web. Lillian Nayder, who wrote the foreword, offered perceptive comments through all the versions of the manuscript. Most importantly, Tom Jaine reorganized the text, making my work look very good – and very English. The Culinary Historians of Boston enthusiastically created a banquet using Catherine Dickens's recipes. The dedicated committee, led by Mark Zanger, included Anne Faulkner, Heather McDonald, Ai Ling Sim, Barbara Kuck, Scott McKay, with the president, Beth Riely. The Vintage Dancers, who added to the gaiety of the event, taught us the 'Sir Roger de Coverly' quadrille, which the Dickenses would have learned in the festivities after she played Lady Clutterbuck to his Sir Charles Coldstream in the farce *Used Up*. To all these people and the countless others who added valuable observations, I raise my glass of vintage port in gratitude.

CHRONOLOGY

1812, 7 Feb.	Charles John Huffman Dickens born to John and Elizabeth Barrow Dickens at 13 Mile End Terrace, Landport (now 396 Commercial Road), Portsmouth.
1815, 19 May	Catherine (Kate) Thomson Hogarth born to George and Georgina Hogarth at 8 Hart Street, Edinburgh.
1834	Hogarth family moves to London. George Hogarth becomes co-editor of the *Morning Chronicle,* soon after meets Charles Dickens who also joins the staff.
1835, May	Charles Dickens and Catherine Hogarth are engaged
1836, 2 April	Catherine's and Charles's marriage ceremony takes place at St. Luke's Church, Chelsea and the Hogarth family gives a wedding breakfast at 18 York Place, their Chelsea residence. The newlyweds honeymoon in Chalk and return to live at 15 Furnival's Inn.
1836, 23 July	Catherine and Charles give their first large dinner party and stage a reading of Dickens's play *The Village Coquettes.*
1837, 6 Jan.	Charles (Charley) Culliford Boz Dickens born; christened on 6 Dec. 1837. (Died in 1896.)
1837, April	Catherine and Charles move to 48 Doughty Street (now the Charles Dickens Museum).
1837, 7 May	Catherine's sister Mary Hogarth dies.
1837, May	Catherine has a miscarriage. Family goes to Collins Farm, Hampstead for her to convalesce.
1838, 6 March	Mary (Mamie) Dickens born. Catherine and Charles go to Richmond for her to convalesce; christened on 7 Jan. 1839. (Died in 1896.)
1839, 29 Oct.	Kate (Katey) Macready Dickens born; christened on 25 Aug. 1840. (Died in 1929.)
1839, Dec.	The Dickens family move to Devonshire Terrace, Regent's Park.
1841, 8 Feb.	Walter Landor Dickens born; christened on 23 Jan. 1841. (Died 1863 in India.)

1841, July	Catherine and Charles travel to Edinburgh and tour Scotland. She visits her family home.
1841, 24 Oct.	Catherine's brother George Thomson Hogarth dies.
1842, 2 Jan.	Catherine and Charles begin their tour of North America leaving London for Liverpool to sail on the S.S. *Britannia* (Jan. 4).
1842, 22 Jan.	Catherine and Charles arrive in Boston for their six month tour of the USA and Canada.
1842, 25 May	Catherine and Charles take roles in a production of *Deaf As a Post* with the Garrison Amateurs at the Queen's Theatre in Montreal.
1842, 7 June	Catherine and Charles sail home from New York City on the *George Washington*.
1842, 29 June	Catherine and Charles arrive at Devonshire Terrace.
1844, 15 Jan.	Francis Jeffrey Dickens born after a difficult pregnancy. (Died in 1886 in the USA.)
1844, 2 July	The Dickens family and staff leave for Italy for a year's stay. Arrive in Albaro at the Villa Bagnerello on 16 July; around 23 Sept. move to Palazzo Peschiere, Genoa.
1845, Feb. 21	Catherine, her sister Georgy, Dickens and party climb Mt. Vesuvius.
1845, 9 June	The Dickens family returns to London, arrives on 3 July. Jane, their cook, remains in Genoa to marry and open a restaurant.
1845, 28 Oct.	Alfred D'Orsay Tennyson Dickens born; christened 21 April 1846. (Died in 1912 in the USA.)
1846, 31 May	The Dickens family leaves for Lausanne, Switzerland. They move into Rosemont on 15 June 1846. They later meet the Watsons and others who become life-long friends.
1846, 28 July	Catherine, Georgy, Charles, and Lausanne party make an expedition to Chamonix.
1846, 16 Nov.	The Dickens family leaves for Paris. They live at 48 rue de Courcelles.
1847, 28 Feb.	The family returns to London. Their house is still rented and they take 1 Chester Place, Regent's Park until 25 June when they move back into Devonshire Terrace.

1847, 18 Apr.	Sydney Smith Haldimand Dickens born; christened around 4 July. (Died in 1872 at sea.)
1847, 26, 28 July	Performances by Dickens's amateur theatrical company.
1847, 29 Dec.	Catherine has a miscarriage.
1848, 19 July	First performance of *Used Up* at the Theatre Royal, Glasgow. Mrs Cowden-Clarke played the part of Lady Clutterbuck.
1848, 2 Sept.	Charles's sister Fanny (Mrs Henry Burnett) dies.
1848, 5 Dec.	Catherine and Charles host the wedding celebration of Dickens's brother Augustus and Harriet Lovell in their Devonshire Terrace home.
1848, 30 Dec.	Dickens disapproves of his brother Fred's marriage to Anna Weller. The wedding is celebrated at Dr James Wilson's home in Malvern. Catherine and Charles do not attend. (Dr Wilson will later become Catherine Dickens's physician at Malvern.)
1849, 15 Jan.	Henry Fielding Dickens born. Dickens arranges to have chloroform administered to ease Catherine's labour; christened on 21 April. (Died in 1933.)
1849, 26 Nov.	Catherine, Charles, and Georgy visit the Watsons again and meet Mary Boyle.
1850, 30 March	First issue of Dickens' magazine *Household Words*.
1850, 16 Aug.	Dora Annie Dickens born; christened 2 Feb. 1851. (Died 14 April 1851.)
1850, 18-20 Nov.	Theatre productions at Sir Edward Bulwer Lytton's estate, Knebworth. Catherine takes a role, but severely sprains her foot and cannot perform. Mary Boyle's friend dies and she also is unable to take part.
1851, 15 Jan.	Performance of *Used Up* at Rockingham Castle. Mrs Dickens plays Lady Clutterbuck, Mary Boyle plays the farmer's niece Mary and Dickens plays the dual roles of Sir Charles Coldstream and Joe the ploughboy.
1851, 13 Mar.–15 April	Catherine is taken to Malvern for treatment.
1851, 31 March	Death of Dickens's father, John Dickens; buried on 5 April at Highgate Cemetery.
1851, 14 April	Death of Catherine's and Charles's daughter Dora Annie Dickens; buried on 17 April at Highgate.

1851, 16 May	Command performance for Queen Victoria and entourage at the Duke of Devonshire's estate (postponed from 30 April due to Dora's death).
1851, 1 May	The Great Exhibition (Crystal Palace) opens in London.
1851, July	Dickens begins negotiations for the purchase of Tavistock House.
1851, Aug.	Extensive renovations of Tavistock House begin.
1851, Oct.	Publication of Catherine's menu book *What Shall We Have For Dinner?* by 'Lady Maria Clutterbuck'.
1851, 20 Oct.	The family moves into Tavistock House.
1852, Feb.	The second revised edition of *What Shall We Have For Dinner?* by 'Lady Maria Clutterbuck' is published.
1852, 13 Mar.	Birth of their last child, Edward (Plorn) Bulwer Lytton Dickens; christened 6 May. (Died 1902 in Australia.)
1852, 26 Nov.	The Duchess of Southerland holds an anti-slavery gathering. Catherine was one of the signatories in support of women against slavery.
1853, 2 May	Charles and Catherine meet Harriet Beecher Stowe and her husband, Professor Stowe, who are invited to dinner on Saturday, May 14.
1853, 13 June –10 Oct.	The family lives at the Château des Moulineaux, rue Beaurepaire, Boulogne.
1854	Catherine revises the menus in *What Shall We Have For Dinner?* and expands the recipe appendix.
1854, 18 June –17 Oct.	The family lives at the Ville du Camp de droite, Boulogne.
1855, 27 Feb.	Mrs Dickens invites Mrs Maria Winter (née Beadell), Dickens's first love, to dinner at Tavistock House.
1855, 16, 18, 19 June	Wilkie Collins's play, *The Lighthouse,* is performed at a theatre built at Tavistock House. Georgy and the Dickens children, Charley, Katey, Mamie, perform.
1855, 16 July–13 Oct.	The family takes a house in Folkestone.
1855, 15 Oct. –May 1856	The family lives in Paris, but returns occasionally to London.
1856	Another edition of *What Shall We Have For Dinner?* is published.

1856, March 14	Dickens purchases Gad's Hill Place in Kent and the family takes possession one year later when the tenant's lease expires.
1856, 7 June –3 Sept.	The family returns to the Château des Moulineaux, Boulogne.
1857, 6, 8, 12, 14 Jan.	Wilkie Collins's play, *The Frozen Deep,* is performed at Tavistock House with the older children as actors.
1857, 1 June–17 July	The family spends summer at Gad's Hill Place.
1857, 4 July	*The Frozen Deep* is performed for the Queen, and again on 11 July to raise funds for Douglas Jerrold's widow and family.
1857, 20 July	Walter, their fourth child and second son, passes his exam and at the age of 16 leaves for regimental service in India.
1857, Aug.	Dickens needs professional actresses for the Free Trade Hall performances on 21–23 in Manchester. He meets Mrs Ternan and her daughters.
1857, Sept. & Oct.	Dickens makes two trips with Wilkie Collins.
1858, May	Catherine and Charles agree to separate. Catherine moves to 70 Gloucester Crescent on May 22.
1860	*What Shall We Have For Dinner?* is reissued.
1870, 9 June	Charles Dickens dies in the dining-room of Gad's Hill Place.
1879, 22 Nov.	Catherine dies and is buried in the same grave as her daughter Dora.
1899	Katey Dickens (Mrs Perugini) gives her mother's letters to the British Museum with the stipulation that they remain sealed until the death of the last surviving child.
1933	The archive of Dickens's correspondence with his wife becomes available to the public.

WHAT SHALL WE HAVE FOR DINNER?

A TRANSCRIPT OF THE 'NEW EDITION' OF 1852

TOGETHER WITH THE ADDITIONAL RECIPES CONTAINED

IN THE APPENDIX TO THE 1854 EDITION

WHAT SHALL WE HAVE FOR DINNER?

SATISFACTORILY ANSWERED BY NUMEROUS

BILLS OF FARE

FOR FROM TWO TO EIGHTEEN PERSONS.

BY

LADY MARIA CLUTTERBUCK.

A NEW EDITION.

LONDON:

BRADBURY & EVANS, 11, BOUVERIE STREET.

1852

LONDON :

BRADBURY AND EVANS, PRINTERS, WHITEFRIARS.

INTRODUCTION.

—◆—

THE late Sir Jonas Clutterbuck had, in addition to a host of other virtues, a very good appetite and an excellent digestion; to those endowments I was indebted [though some years the junior of my revered husband] for many hours of connubial happiness.

Sir Jonas was not a *gourmand*, although a man of great gastronomical experience. Richmond never saw him more than once a month, and he was as rare a visitor to Blackwall and Greenwich. Of course he attended most of the corporation dinners as a matter of duty (having been elected alderman in 1839), and now and then partook of a turtle feast at some celebrated place in the city; but these were only exceptions, his general practice being to dine at home; and I am consoled in believing that my attention to the requirements of his appetite secured me the possession of his esteem until the last.

My experience in the confidences of many of my female friends tells me, alas! that others are not so happy in their domestic relations as I was. That their daily life is embittered by the consciousness that a delicacy forgotten or misapplied; a surplusage of cold mutton or a redundancy of chops; are gradually making the Club more attractive than the Home, and rendering "business in the city" of more frequent occurrence than it used to be in the earlier days of their connubial experience; while the ever-recurring inquiry of

WHAT SHALL WE HAVE FOR DINNER ?

makes the matutinal meal a time to dread, only exceeded in its terrors by the more awful hour of dinner!

It is to rescue many fair friends from such domestic suffering, that I have consented to give to the world

THE BILLS OF FARE

which met with the approval of Sir Jonas Clutterbuck, believing that by a constant reference to them, an easy solution may be obtained to that most difficult of questions,—"WHAT SHALL WE HAVE FOR DINNER?"

M. C.

CONTENTS

—◆—

———————

✱ The Appendix contains Receipts for some dishes, the preparation
of which may not be generally understood.

WHAT SHALL WE HAVE FOR DINNER?

BILLS OF FARE FOR TWO OR THREE PERSONS.

—◆—

Giblet Soup.

Loin of Mutton, rechauffé à la Soyer.   Mashed and
Fried Potatoes.   Beetroot Salad.

Cold Mince Pies.

[Jan. to Dec.]

Fried Whitings.

Roast Loin of Mutton.   Cauliflowers.   Potatoes.

Toasted Cheese.   Water Cresses.

[Jan. to Dec.]

Vegetable Soup

Pork Cutlets, with Savoury Sauce.   Spinach.
Mashed and Brown Potatoes.

Bloaters.

[Jan. to Dec.]

Roast Ribs of Beef, rolled.   Brown Potatoes.
Spinach.

Rice Pudding.

[Jan. to Dec.]

Roast Fowl.   Bacon.   Hashed Mutton.   Mashed and
Brown Potatoes.

Roll Jam Pudding.   Macaroni.

[Jan. to Dec.]

Fried Sole.   Shrimp Sauce.

Haricot Mutton.   Mashed and Brown Potatoes.

Tartlets.   Omelette.

[Jan. to Dec.]

Veal Cutlets.   Hand of Pickled Pork.   Mashed
and Brown Potatoes.   Turnip Tops.

Marmalade Tartlets.

[Jan. to Dec.]

Roast Shoulder of Mutton.   Onion Sauce.
Browned Potatoes.   Spinach.

Toasted Cheese.

[Jan. to Dec.]

Roast Leg of Welsh Mutton.   Spinach.   Mashed
and Brown Potatoes.

Macaroni.

[Jan. to Dec.]

Lobster Cutlets.

Rabbit Curry.   Rice Dumplings.   Mashed and
Brown Potatoes.

Italian Cream.

[Jan. to Dec.]

Vegetable Soup.

Minced Beef with Bacon.   Cold Pigeon Pie.
Potatoes.

[Jan. to Dec.]

Roast Fillet of Mutton, stuffed.   Potatoes.

Currant Pudding.

Toasted Cheese.   Water Cresses.

[Jan. to Dec.]

Soles, with Brown Gravy.

Roast Loin of Mutton.   Rissols of Beef.   Mashed
Turnips.   Potatoes.

Macaroni.   Broiled Mushrooms.

[Jan. to Dec.]

Roast Leg of Mutton.   Mashed Turnips.   Potatoes.

Suet Dumplings.

Toasted Cheese.   Water Cresses.

[Jan. to Dec.]

Sole in Brown Gravy.

Cold Beef.   Salad.   Potatoes.

Batter Pudding.

Toasted Cheese.   Water Cresses.

[Jan. to Dec.]

Ox-Tail Soup.

Minced Mutton, with Bacon.   Cold ditto.
Mashed and Fried Potatoes.

Strawberry Jam Cream.

[Jan. to Dec.]

Mutton Broth.

Roast Fowl.   Boiled Bacon.   Minced Mutton.
French Beans.   Potatoes.

Cold Ground Rice Pudding.

Toasted Cheese.   Water Cresses.

[Jan. to Dec.]

Ox-Tail Soup.

Stewed Veal.   Cold Saddle of Mutton.   Beetroot
Salad.   Mashed and Brown Potatoes.

Eve's Pudding.

[Jan. to Dec.]

Ox-Tail Soup.

Fried Sole.   Shrimp Sauce.

Haricot.   Mashed Potatoes.   Rice.

[Jan. to Dec.]

Giblet Soup.

Minced Mutton, with Bacon.   Cold ditto.   Mashed
and Fried Potatoes.   Beetroot and Celery Salad.

Boiled Batter Pudding.

[Jan. to Dec.]

Vegetable Soup.

Bubble and Squeak.

Cold Beef.   Hashed Hare.   Mashed and Brown
Potatoes.

Rice Pudding.

[Jan. to Dec.]

Broiled Mackerel.

Stewed Rump Steak, with Vegetables.   Mashed
and Brown Potatoes.

Bread-and-Butter Pudding.

[April to Aug.]

Fried Oysters.   Lamb's Head and Minced Liver.
Mashed Potatoes.

Macaroni.

[April to Sept.]

Broiled Salmon.   Shrimp Sauce.

Cold Lamb.   Salad.   New Potatoes.

Rice Blancmange.   Italian Cream.

Toasted Cheese.

[April to Oct.]

Hashed Mutton, with Vegetables.

Roast Duck.   Green Peas.   New Potatoes.
Batter Pudding.   Artichokes.

Water Cresses.

[April to July.]

Pickled Salmon.

Calves' Liver and Bacon.   French Beans.   Potatoes.

Plum Pudding.

Macaroni

[April to Sept.]

Broiled Salmon.   Shrimp Sauce.

Lambs' Hearts.   Cauliflower.   Potatoes.

Cold Ground Rice Pudding, flavoured with
Marmalade.

Toasted Cheese.   Water Cresses.

[April to Sept.]

Broiled Salmon.   Shrimp Sauce.

Roast Fillet of Beef, stuffed.   Cauliflower.   Potatoes.

Baked Bread-and-Butter Pudding.

Cheese.   Water Cresses.

[April to Oct.]

Lamb Stewed with Peas.   Potatoes.

Batter Pudding.

Toasted Cheese.   Water Cresses.

[May to Aug.]

Steak.   Horse Radish Sauce.   Cold Lamb.   Salad.   Mashed Potatoes.

Rice Pudding.

Macaroni.

[May to Sept.]

Broiled Mackerel.

Minced Mutton, with Bacon.   Pork Cutlets.
Turnip Tops.   Mashed and Brown Potatoes.

Roll Jam Pudding.

Toasted Cheese.

[May to Sept.]

Roast Leg of Lamb.   Salad.   Mashed Potatoes.   Sea Kale.

Omelette.

[May to Oct.]

Fried Whitings.   Shrimp Sauce.

Lamb's Fry.   Mashed and Brown Potatoes.

Macaroni.

[All the Summer.]

Fried Soles and Whitings.   Shrimp Sauce.

Mutton Curry.   Potatoes.   Summer Cabbage.

Toasted Cheese.

[All the Summer.]

Broiled Mackerel.

Veal Cutlets.   Bacon.   Salad.   Mashed and Brown Potatoes.

Fruit Pudding.

[All the Summer.]

Roast Leg of Mutton.   Mashed and Brown Potatoes.
Summer Cabbage.

Cold Custard Pudding.

Macaroni.

[All the Summer.]

Minced Beef, with Bacon.   Cold Lamb.   Salad.
Mashed and Brown Potatoes.

Omelette.

[All the Summer.]

Broiled Mackerel.

Cold Lamb.   Patties.   Salad.   Potatoes.
Brocoli au Gratin.

[All the Summer.]

Lamb's Fry.   Fillet of Beef.   New Potatoes.

Baked Rice Pudding.

[All the Summer.]

Fried Sole.   Shrimp Sauce.

Lamb's Fry.   Asparagus.   New Potatoes.

[All the Summer.]

Minced Collops.   Cold Lamb.   Beetroot Salad.
New Potatoes.

Raspberry Jam Sandwiches.

[All the Summer.]

Lamb's Head and Minced Liver.   New Potatoes.

Custard Pudding.

[May to Sept.]

Green Pea Soup.

Roast Leg of Lamb.   New Potatoes.   Asparagus.

Sweet Omelette.   Macaroni.

[May to Sept.]

Roast Leg of Lamb. Asparagus. New Potatoes.

[May to Aug.]

Green Pea Soup.

Minced Mutton. Cold Mutton. Patties. Salad.
Potatoes.

Tartlets.

[May to Aug.]

Green Pea Soup.

Pickled Salmon.

Mutton Chops. Hashed Venison. Cold Bath Chap.
Peas. Potatoes.

Cold Lemon Pudding.

Toasted Cheese. Water Cresses.

[May to Oct.]

Stewed Lamb, with Peas. Potatoes.

Black Currant Pudding.

Sweet Omelette.

[May to July.]

Vegetable Soup.

Fried Oysters.

Mutton Curry. Rice. Cold Beef. Salad.
French Beans. Potatoes.

Apple Pudding.

Macaroni. Water Cresses.

[May to Dec.]

Fried Oysters.

Veal Cutlets. Boiled Knuckles of Ham. Potatoes.
Cauliflower.

Toasted Cheese. Water Cresses.

[May to Aug.]

Brill.

Haricot Mutton.   French Beans.   Potatoes.

Ground Rice Pudding.

Prawns.   Water Cresses.

[May to Sept.]

Pickled Salmon.   Whiting.

Stewed Rump Steak.   French Beans.   Potatoes.

Rice and Apples.

Toasted Cheese.   Water Cresses.

[May to July.]

Roast Shoulder of Mutton.   Onion Sauce.   Browned
Potatoes.   Summer Cabbage.

Omelette.

[June.]

Baked and Stuffed Haddock.

Lamb's Head and Mince.   Summer Cabbage.
Potatoes.

Cream Cheese.

[June to Aug.]

Rump Steaks à la Soyer.   French Beans.
Potatoes boiled.

Macaroni.   Water Cresses.

[July to Sept.]

Cod.   Oyster Sauce.

Rump Steak Puddings, with Oysters and Kidneys.
Potatoes.   French Beans.

Toasted Cheese and Water Cresses.

[July to Feb.]

Mutton Chops.   Broiled Mushrooms.   Grouse.
Potatoes.   Cauliflower.

Omelette.   Water Cresses.

[Aug. to Dec.]

Codling.   Oyster Sauce.

Grouse Pie.   Potatoes.   Mutton Cutlets.

Apples and Rice.

Macaroni.   Water Cresses.

[Aug. to Dec.]

Filletted Sole à la Maître d'Hôtel.

Haricot Mutton.   Potatoes.   Cold Grouse Pie.

Prawns.   Water Cresses.

[Aug. to Dec.]

Fried Oysters.

Irish Stew.

Toasted Cheese.

[Aug. to May.]

Fried Oysters.

Rump Steaks.   Horse Radish Sauce.   Mashed and
Brown Potatoes.   Spinach.

Toasted Cheese.

[Aug. to Jan.]

Fried Sole.   Shrimp Sauce.

Rump Steak à la Soyer.   Hashed Hare.   Potatoes.
Cauliflower.

Prawns.   Water Cresses.

[Aug. to Jan.]

Fried Sole and Whitings.
Roast Leveret.   French Beans.   Potatoes.

Omelette.   Water Cresses.

[Aug. to Jan.]

Roast Hare.   Cold Rump Steak Pie.   Mashed
Potatoes.

Rice.   Roll Jam Pudding.

[Aug. to Jan.]

Cod rechauffé.

Broiled Turkey Legs.   Cold Beef.   Beetroot and
Celery Salad.   Mashed and Brown Potatoes.

Plum Pudding.

[Aug. to April.]

Ox-Tail Soup.

Mutton Chops.   Roast Black-Cock.   Potato Balls.

Toasted Cheese.

[Aug. to Dec.]

Cod.   Oyster Sauce.

Lark Pie.   Potatoes.   Pork Cutlets.

[Sept. to Jan.]

Fried Sole and Whitings.   Shrimp Sauce.

Roast Hare.   Potato Balls.

Macaroni.

[Sept. to Jan.]

Mutton Broth.   Boiled Mutton.   Hashed Hare.
Mashed Potatoes.   Mashed Turnips.

Apples and Rice.

[Sept. to Jan.]

Carrot Soup.

Broiled Legs of Turkey.   Cold Beef.   Mashed
and Fried Potatoes.

Charlotte Brosse.

[Sept. to Feb.]

Mutton Chops.   Mashed and Brown Potatoes.
Roast Larks.

Apples and Rice.

[Sept. to Jan.]

Mutton Chops.   Roast Pheasant.   Fried Potatoes.

Roll Jam Pudding.

[Oct. to Feb.]

Carrot Soup.

Cold Saddle of Mutton.   Beetroot and Celery
Salad.   Fried Potatoes.

Roast Pheasant.

Bloaters.

[Oct. to Jan.]

Rump Steaks.   Roast Pheasant.   Potatoes à la
Maître d'Hôtel.

[Oct. to Feb.]

BILLS OF FARE FOR FOUR OR FIVE PERSONS.

—◆—

Roast Loin of Mutton.   Browned Potatoes.   Salad.

Rice Blancmange, with Strawberry Jam and Cream.

Toasted Cheese.

[Jan. to Dec.]

Fried Oysters.

Haricot Mutton.   Mashed and Brown Potatoes.
Roast Fowls.

Raspberry Puffs.

Stilton Cheese.

[Jan. to Dec.]

Carrot Soup.   Irish Stew.

Savoury Omelette.

Toasted Cheese.

[Jan. to Dec.]

Fried Sole.   Shrimp Sauce.

Mutton Cutlets.   Salad.   Mashed and Brown Potatoes.

Cheesecakes.   Macaroni.

[Jan. to Dec.]

Filletted Soles.   Shrimp Sauce.

Minced Lamb.   Calves' Liver and Bacon.   Potatoes.
Cauliflower.

Pound Puddings.

Water Cresses.

[Jan. to Dec.]

Vegetable Soup.

Fried Soles.

Roast Beef.   Yorkshire Pudding.   French Beans.
Potatoes.

Toasted Cheese.   Water Cresses.

[Jan. to Dec.]

Mutton Chops.   Broiled Fowl.   Potatoes.
Broiled Mushrooms.

Tapioca Pudding.

Bloaters.   Water Cresses.

[Jan. to Dec.]

Fried Oysters.

Roast Beef.   Yorkshire Pudding.   Mashed and
Brown Potatoes.   Brocoli.

Macaroni.   Water Cresses.

[Jan. to Dec.]

Mutton Broth.

Cold Beef.   Minced ditto, with Bacon.   Mashed
and Fried Potatoes.   Salad.

Marrow Pudding.

Bloaters.

[Jan. to Dec.]

Fried Soles.   Shrimp Sauce.

Roast Fillet of Beef, stuffed.   Turnip Tops.
Mashed and Brown Potatoes.

Spanish Pudding.

Toasted Cheese.

[Jan. to Dec.]

Fried Soles.   Shrimp Sauce.

Irish Stew.

Toasted Cheese.

[Jan. to Dec.]

Fried Sole and Whiting.   Shrimp Sauce.

Roast Leg of Mutton.   Salad.   Brown Potatoes.

Mince Pies.

Macaroni.

[Jan. to Dec.]

Vegetable Soup.

Roast Leg of Welsh Mutton.   Pork Cutlets.
Salad.   Mashed and Brown Potatoes.

Roll Jam Pudding.

Stilton Cheese.

[Jan. to Dec.]

Vegetable Soup.

Roast Loin of Mutton.   Spanish Onions.   Mashed
and Brown Potatoes.

Apple Tart.   Macaroni.

[Jan. to Dec.]

Baked and Stuffed Haddocks.

Broiled Fowl, with Mushrooms.   Minced Collops.
Mashed and Brown Potatoes.

Raspberry Jam Sandwiches.

[Jan. to Dec.]

Salt Fish.   Egg Sauce.   Parsnips.

Cold Beef.   Salad.   Mashed and Brown Potatoes.

Marmalade Tartlets.

Toasted Cheese.

[Feb. to May.]

Salmon.   Asparagus Soup.   Smelts.

Fore Quarter of Lamb.   Fricassee Chickens.   New Potatoes.   Peas.

Lobster Patties.

Noyau Jelly.   Ice Pudding.

[May to July.]

Asparagus Soup.

Salmon Curry à la Soyer.

Cold Mutton.   Minced Collops.   Mashed Potatoes.
Salad.   Sweet Omelette.

Brocoli au Gratin à la Soyer.

[May to Aug.]

Asparagus Soup.

Turbot.   Shrimp Sauce.

Roast Saddle of Mutton.   Stewed Pigeons.   Mashed
and Brown Potatoes.   Brocoli.   Salad.

Pound Puddings.   Macaroni.

[May to Aug.]

Baked Haddock.

Roast Leg of Lamb.   Stewed Kidneys.   Peas.
Potatoes.   Salad.

Cherry Tart.   Macaroni.

[May to Aug.]

Fried Soles.   Shrimp Sauce.

Roast Ribs of Lamb.   Peas.   Potatoes.

Roll Jam Pudding.

[May to Aug.]

Codling.   Oyster Sauce.

Beef Steak Pudding, with Kidney and Oysters.
Broiled Fowl.   French Beans.   Potatoes.

Plum Tart.

Toasted Cheese.   Water Cresses.

[May to Aug.]

Salmon.   Shrimp Sauce.

Roast Fowl.   Boiled Knuckle of Ham.   Sheep's
Hearts, stuffed.   French Beans.   Potatoes.

Batter Pudding.

Water Cresses.

[May to Aug.]

Salmon.   Shrimp Sauce.

Roast Beef.   Cauliflower.   Potatoes.

Greengage Tart.   Hominy.

Cheese.   Water Cresses.

[May to Aug.]

Asparagus Soup.

Fried Soles.   Shrimp Sauce.

Pork Cutlets.   Oyster Curry.   Rice.   Cold Lamb.
Salad.   Mashed and Brown Potatoes.

Marmalade Tartlets.

Macaroni.

[May to Aug.]

Brill.   Shrimp Sauce.

Mutton Cutlets.   Brussels Sprouts.   Potatoes.

Boiled Batter Pudding.

Bloaters.

[June to Oct.]

Filleted Soles.   Shrimp Sauce.

Roasted and Stuffed Leg of Mutton.   French Beans.
Potatoes.

Greengage Tartlet.   Macaroni.

[June to Sept.]

Baked Haddock.

Roast Shoulder of Lamb.   Cauliflower.   Potatoes.
Broiled Mushrooms.

Saxe Gotha Pudding.

[July to Jan.]

43

Cod.   Oyster Sauce.

Haricot Mutton.   Roast Hare.   French Beans.   Potatoes.

Apple Tart.

Toasted Cheese.   Water Cresses.

[July to Jan.]

Cod.   Oyster Sauce.

Roast Loin of Mutton.   Stewed Rump Steak.

French Beans.   Potatoes.

Damson Pudding.   Macaroni.

[July to Oct.]

Cod.   Oyster Sauce.

Haricot.   Mashed and Brown Potatoes.

Macaroni.

[Aug. to Feb.]

Cod rechauffé with Potatoes.

Mutton Curry.   Rice.   Mashed and Brown Potatoes.

Apple Pudding.

[Aug. to Feb.]

Fried Whitings.   Shrimp Sauce.

Mutton Chops.   Mashed Potatoes.   Beetroot Salad.

Brace of Partridges.

Apple Pudding.

Bloaters.

[Sept. to Feb.]

Fried Whitings.

Rump Steak à la Soyer.   Brace of Partridges.
French Beans.   Potatoes.

Tapioca Pudding.

Toasted Cheese.   Water Cresses.

[Sept. to Jan.]

44

Roast Loin of Mutton.   Mashed Turnips.   Mashed
and Brown Potatoes.

Woodcocks.

Pancakes.   Toasted Cheese.

[Sept. to Feb.]

Fried Whitings.   Shrimp Sauce.

Roast Leg of Mutton, stuffed with Oysters.
French Beans.   Potatoes.   Partridge.

Apple Pudding.

Toasted Cheese.   Water Cresses

[Sept. to Feb.]

Haricot Mutton.   Roast Hare.   Mashed Potatoes.

Bread-and-Butter Pudding.

[Sept. to Jan.]

Cold Oysters.   Ox-Tail Soup.   Turbot.

Saddle of Welsh Mutton.   Veal Cutlet.   Tomato
Sauce.   Vegetables.

Cabinet Pudding.   Savoury Omelette.

[All the Winter.]

Vermicelli Soup.   Potatoes.   Salmon.   Lobster Sauce.

Saddle of Mutton.   Brocoli.   Potatoes.   Rabbit Pie.

Raspberry Jam Pudding.

Toasted Cheese.   Salad.

[All the Winter.]

45

BILLS OF FARE FOR SIX OR SEVEN PERSONS.

—◆—

Vegetable Soup.

Roast Fillet of Veal.   Boiled Knuckle of Ham.
Greens.   Browned Potatoes.

Apple Tart.   Custards.

[Jan. to Dec.]

Scotch Mutton Broth.

Fresh Herrings.

Roast Shoulder of Mutton, Onion Sauce.
Curried Oysters.

Roll Jam Pudding

Toasted Cheese.

[Jan. to Dec.]

Cod.   Oyster Sauce.

Mutton, stewed with Vegetables.   French Beans.
Potatoes.

Baked Rice Pudding.   Savoury Omelette.

[Jan. to Dec.]

Fried Soles.   Shrimp Sauce.

Roast Haunch of Mutton.   Mashed and Brown
Potatoes.   Brocoli.

Apple Tart.   Custard.

[Jan. to Dec.]

Vegetable Soup.

Filletted Soles.   Shrimp Sauce.

Roast Leg of Mutton, stuffed with Oysters.
Minced Collops.   Spinach.   Mashed and Brown
Potatoes.

Cold Lemon Pudding.   Bloaters.

[Jan. to Dec.]

46

Boiled Mackerel.

Roast Leg of Welsh Mutton.   Minced Collops.
Spinach.   Mashed and Brown Potatoes.

Marmalade Tartlets.   Macaroni.

[April to Aug.]

Broiled Mackerel.

Veal Cutlets.   Bacon.   Cold Beef.   Spanish Salad.
Mashed and Brown Potatoes.   Cauliflower.

Rice and Apples.   Macaroni.

[April to Sept.]

Vegetable Soup.

Filletted Sole à la Maître d'Hôtel.

Roast Fillet of Beef.   Cold Pigeon Pie.   Salad.
New Potatoes.   Spinach.

Raspberry Jam Tartlet.   Custard.

Macaroni.

[May to Sept.]

Asparagus Soup.

Fried Soles.   Shrimp Sauce.

Patties.   Lobster Cutlets.   Curry.   Rice.
Cold Lamb.   Salad.   Potatoes.

Punch Jelly.

Toasted Cheese.

[May to July.]

Salmon.

Roast Loin of Mutton.   Boiled Fowls.   Bacon.
French Beans.   Potatoes.   Salad.

Greengage Tart.   Macaroni.

[May to Aug.]

Asparagus Soup.

Filletted Sole.   Shrimp Sauce.

Saddle of Mutton.   Mayonnaise of Fowl.
Cauliflower.   New Potatoes.

Gooseberry Tart.   Devonshire Cream.

Macaroni.

[May to July.]

Asparagus Soup.

Salmon.   Shrimp Sauce.

Roast Saddle of Mutton.   Rabbit Curry.   Rice.
Salad.   Sea Kale.   Mashed Potatoes.

Cabinet Pudding.   Macaroni.

[May to July.]

Carrot Soup.

Filletted Sole à la Maître d'Hôtel.

Roast Leg of Lamb.   Minced Collops.   Salad.
Mashed and Brown Potatoes.

Cold Lemon Pudding.

Toasted Cheese.

[June to Sept.]

Filletted Soles.   Shrimp Sauce.

Roast Leg of Lamb.   Stewed Rump Steak, with Vegetables.
Cauliflower.   Potatoes.   Salad.

Currant and Raspberry Tart.   Macaroni.

[June to Sept.]

Filletted Soles.   Shrimp Sauce.

Roast Beef.   Cold Pigeon Pie.   Peas.   Potatoes.
Salad.

Raspberry and Currant Tart.   Macaroni.

[June to Aug.]

48

Fried Flounders.   Shrimp Sauce.

Rump Steak Pudding, with Oysters and Kidneys.
Bubble and Squeak.   Cold Beef.
Mashed and Brown Potatoes.   French Beans

Boiled Batter Pudding.

Toasted Cheese.   Water Cresses.

[June to Sept.]

Fried Sole.   Shrimp Sauce.

Roast Leg of Lamb.   Peas.   New Potatoes.

Prince Albert's Pudding.

[June to Sept.]

Brill.   Shrimp Sauce.

Roast Rump Steak, rolled and stuffed.   Boiled Rabbits.
Onion Sauce.   Potatoes.   Brussels Sprouts.

Lemon Pudding.

Toasted Cheese.   Water Cresses.

[June to Dec.]

Brill.   Shrimp Sauce.

Roast Loin of Mutton.   Beef Steak Pudding, with
Kidneys and Oysters.   French Beans.   Potatoes.

Boiled Rice and Apples.   Macaroni.

[June to Dec.]

Vegetable Soup.

Codling.   Oyster Sauce.

Roast Fillet of Mutton, stuffed.   Cauliflower.
Potatoes.

Raspberry and Currant Tart.   Macaroni.

[July to Dec.]

49

Cod.   Oyster Sauce.

Roast Rolled Ribs of Beef.   Roast Fowl.   Bacon.
French Beans.   Potatoes.

Plum Tart.

Toasted Cheese.   Water Cresses.

[July to Dec.]

Cod.   Oyster Sauce.

Roast Loin of Mutton.   Stewed Kidneys.
Mashed and Brown Potatoes.   Stewed Mushrooms.

Apple Pudding.   Macaroni.

[Aug. to Feb.]

Cod Rechauffé, with Potatoes.

Roast Beef.   Pork Cutlets.   Spinach.   Mashed
and Brown Potatoes.

Bread-and-Butter Pudding.

Toasted Cheese.   Water Cresses.

[Aug. to Feb.]

Filletted Sole.   Shrimp Sauce.

Roast Beef.   Haricot Mutton.   Cauliflowers.
Mashed and Brown Potatoes.

Apple Tart.   Custards.

Toasted Cheese.   Water Cresses.

[Aug. to March.]

Vegetable Soup.

Baked and Stuffed Haddock.

Roast Saddle of Mutton.   Hashed Hare.
Brocoli.   Browned Potatoes.

Pound Puddings.   Greengage Tartlet.

Custard.   Macaroni.

[Sept. to Feb.]

50

Fried Soles.

Irish Stew.   Rump Steak à la Soyer.   Potatoes.
Brussels Sprouts.

Raspberry Jam Sandwiches.

Toasted cheese.   Water Cresses.

[Sept. to March.]

Carrot Soup.

Filletted Soles à la Maître d'Hôtel.

Roast Saddle of Mutton.   Jugged Hare.
Spinach.   Mashed and Brown Potatoes.

Beetroot and Celery Salad.

Rice Blancmange.   Cream Tartlets.

Macaroni, with Bacon.

[Sept. to March.]

Pea Soup.

Filletted Soles.   Shrimp Sauce.

Roast Turkey.   Sausages.   Cold Ham.   Mashed
and Brown Potatoes.   Brocoli.

Open Damson Tartlet.   Macaroni.

[Sept. to Feb.]

Fresh Herrings.

Roast Leg of Mutton, stuffed with Oysters.
Stewed Kidneys.
Mashed Turnips.   Mashed and Brown Potatoes.

Greengage Tart.   Macaroni, with Bacon.

[Oct. to Feb.]

Oyster Soup.   Hare Soup.   Cod's Head.   Smelts.

Two Roast Fowls.   Boiled Bacon.
Saddle of Welsh Mutton.   Two Pheasants.

Eve's Pudding.   Raspberry Jam Tart.

Macaroni.

[All the Winter.]

Mock Turtle.   Cod's Head.   Smelts.

Roast Turkey.   Sausages.   Maintenon Cutlets.
Sweetbreads.   Mushroom Sauce.   Vegetables.

Apple Tart.   Orange Fritters.

[All the Winter.]

Turbot.   Lobster Sauce.   Fried Soles.
Shrimp Sauce.

Roast Pig.   Oyster Patties.   Fricandeau of Veal.
Mutton Cutlets.   Curry Rabbit.   Roast Beef.

Apple Fritters.   Macaroni.   Sweet Omelette.
Croquits of Rice.

[All the Winter.]

BILLS OF FARE FOR EIGHT OR TEN PERSONS.

—◆—

Vegetable Soup

Fried Sole.   Shrimp Sauce.

Roast Fillet of Beef, stuffed.   Minced Mutton,
with Bacon.   Browned Potatoes.   Kalecannon.

Savoury Omelette.   Raspberry Jam Sandwiches.

[Jan. to Dec.]

Turbot.   Shrimp Sauce.

Roast Loin of Mutton.   Pigeon Pie.   Brocoli.
Mashed Potatoes.   Salad.

College Puddings.

Macaroni.

[Jan. to Dec.]

Scotch Mutton Broth.

Fried Oysters.   Shoulder of Mutton.   Boiled Fowl.
Bacon.   Mashed and Brown Potatoes.
Stewed Onions.   Salad.

Batter Pudding.   Macaroni, with Bacon.

[Jan. to Dec.]

Filletted Soles.   Shrimp Sauce.

Boiled Beef.   Mutton Curry.   Rice.   Potatoes.
Kalecannon.

Ground Rice Pudding, flavoured with Marmalade.

Cauliflower au Gratin.   Water Cresses.

[Jan. to Dec.]

Barley Broth.

Fried Whitings.   Shrimp Sauce.

Roast Beef.   Minced Veal.   Cold Ham.   Cauliflower.
Mashed and Brown Potatoes.

Bread-and-Butter Pudding.   Macaroni.

[Jan. to Dec.]

Roast Fillet of Veal.   Boiled Knuckle of Ham.
Mutton Pie.   Mashed and Brown Potatoes.
Spinach.

Roll Jam Pudding.

Toasted Cheese.   Water Cresses.

[Jan. to Dec.]

Carrot Soup.

Turbot.   Shrimp Sauce.   Lobster Patties.

Stewed Kidneys.   Roast Saddle of Mutton.   Boiled
Turkey.   Knuckle of Ham.   Mashed and Brown
Potatoes.   Stewed Onions.   Salad.

Cabinet Puddings.   Rice Blancmange, and
Cream.   Macaroni.

[Jan. to Dec.]

Green Pea Soup

Salmon.   Shrimp Sauce.   Cucumber.

Veal and Ham Patties.   Lamb's Fry.   Roast Saddle
of Mutton.   Boiled Fowl and Tongue.   Asparagus.
New Potatoes.   Salad.

Gooseberry Tart.   Devonshire Cream.

Cabinet Pudding.   Macaroni.

[May to Aug.]

Ox-Tail Soup.

Cod.   Oyster Sauce.

Roast Saddle of Mutton.   Stewed Breast of Veal.
Stewed Onions.   Artichokes.   Mashed and
Brown Potatoes.

Eve's Pudding.   Raspberry Jam Sandwiches.
Custards.   Macaroni.

[Sept. to March.]

Green Pea Soup.

Salmon.   Shrimp Sauce.   Salad.

Haunch of Venison.   Boiled Fowl.   Pig's Jaw,
garnished with Beans.   Potatoes.   French Beans.

Lemon Pudding.   Raspberry and Currant Tart.

Devonshire Cream.   Macaroni, with Bacon.

[May to Sept.]

Green Pea Soup

Salmon.   Lobster Sauce.   Cucumbers.

Lamb's Fry.   Patties.   Roast Saddle of Mutton.
Boiled Fowls.   Peas.   Potatoes.   Salad.

Cabinet Pudding.   Raspberry and Currant Tart.   Devonshire Cream.

Dressed Crab.

[May to Aug.]

Carrot Soup

Turbot.   Shrimp Sauce.

Roast Beef.   Turkey Poult.   Tongue.   Patties.
Pork Cutlets.   Stewed Celery.   Mashed and
Brown Potatoes.   Greens.

Hare.   Macaroni.
Ice Pudding.   Clear Jelly.   Cream.

Cheese.   Anchovies.   Celery and Beetroot Salad.

[Aug. to Jan.]

55

Ox-Tail Soup.

Cod.   Oyster Sauce.

Roast Saddle of Mutton.   Pork Cutlets.
Kalecannon.   Mashed and Brown Potatoes.
Roast Pheasants.   Salad.

Soufflet Pudding.   Mince Pies.

Anchovy Toast.

[Oct. to Feb.]

Scotch Mutton Broth.

Roast Goose.   Mutton Curry.   Rice.   Cold Pigeon Pie.

Salad.   Brocoli.   Mashed Potatoes.

Eve's Pudding.

Toasted Cheese.   Water Cresses.

[Sept. to Jan.]

Scotch Mutton Broth.

Roast Leg of Mutton, stuffed with Oysters.
Boiled Fowls.   Knuckle of Ham.   Cauliflower.
Mashed and Brown Potatoes.

Damson Tart.   Macaroni.   Water Cresses.

[Sept. to March.]

Vegetable Soup.

Brill.   Shrimp Sauce.

Roast Saddle of Mutton.   Minced Collops.   Peas.
New Potatoes.   Salad

Currant Tart.   Cream.   Macaroni.

[May to Aug.]

Giblet Soup.

Baked and Stuffed Haddocks.

Roast Haunch of Mutton.   Stewed Onions.
Browned Potatoes.

Roast Pheasant.

Pound Puddings.

[Oct. to Feb.]

Filletted Soles.   Shrimp Sauce.

Boiled Beef.   Roast Hare.   Carrots.   Potatoes.

Swiss Pudding.   Macaroni.

[Aug. to Feb.]

Cod.   Oyster Sauce.

Roast Leg of Mutton with Veal Stuffing.
Boiled Fowl.   Tongue.   Brocoli.   Mashed and Brown Potatoes.

Rice Blancmange.   Cream.   Macaroni.

[Nov. to March.]

Spring Soup.   Ox-Tail.

Salmon.   Lobster Sauce.   Mackerel à la Maître d'Hôtel.
Parsley and Butter.   Soles.   Potatoes.

Two Boiled Spring Chickens.   Asparagus Sauce.
Lobster Curry.   Sweetbreads.
Fore Quarter of Lamb.   Tongue.   Veal Olives.
Oyster Patties.   Two Ducklings.
Peas.   New Potatoes.   Asparagus.

Currant and Raspberry Tart.   Cold Custards.
Lemon Jelly and Charlotte Russe.

[All the Summer.]

Ox-Tail Soup.

Cod.   Oyster Sauce.

Roast Saddle of Mutton.   Pork Cutlets.   Mashed
and Brown Potatoes.   Artichokes.

Cabinet Pudding.   Macaroni.

[Nov. to March.]

Spring Soup.   Mock Turtle.

Salmon.   Fillets of Soles à la Maître d'Hôtel.
Mackerel.   Lobster Sauce.   Potatoes.

Two Spring Chickens Boiled.   Oyster Sauce.
Lobster Patties.   Sweetbreads.   Ham.
Fore Quarter of Lamb.   Stewed Kidneys.   Curry
Rabbit.   Two Ducklings.
Asparagus.   New Potatoes.   Peas.

Currant and Raspberry Tart.   Orange Jelly.
Custards.   Cabinet Pudding.

[All the Summer.]

Oyster Soup.   Vermicelli Soup.

Cod's Head.   Smelts.   Fried Whitings.

Saddle of Mutton.   Curry Oysters.   Veal Olives.
Tongue.   Fricassee Chickens.   Lobster Salad.
Two Boiled Fowls.   Oyster Sauce.
Two Wild Ducks.   Two Pheasants.

Lemon Pudding.   Jelly.   Tart.

[All the Winter.]

Vermicelli Soup.   Ox-Tail Soup.

Turbot and Smelts.   Stewed Eels.   Soles and Cod's Head.

Fricassee Chicken.   Oyster Patties.   Stewed Kidneys.
Roast Sweetbreads.   Two Boiled Fowls.   Ham.   Pigeon Pie.
Saddle of Mutton.
Three Woodcocks.   Hare.   Two Wild Ducks.
Mashed Potatoes.   Brocoli.

Apple Tart.   Orange Fritters.   Charlotte Russe.
Italian Cream.

Macaroni.   Toasted Cheese.

[All the Winter.]

Mock Turtle.   Hare Soup.   Ox-Tail Soup.

Cod's Head.   Oyster Sauce.   Smelts.   Soles.
Shrimp Sauce.   Stewed Eels.   Oyster Sauce.

Roast Turkey.   Sausages.
Brocoli.   Ham.   Sweetbreads.   Curry Lobster.
Haunch of Mutton.   Brocoli.   Brown Potatoes.
Pigeon Pie.   Oyster Patties.

Maintenon Cutlet.   Potatoes.   Brocoli.

Boiled Turkeys.   Oyster Sauce.

Two Woodcocks.   Hare.   Four Snipes.

Cabinet Pudding.   Apple Tart.   Charlotte Russe.
Jelly.

[All the Winter.]

BILLS OF FARE FOR FOURTEEN, EIGHTEEN OR TWENTY PERSONS.

—◆—

White Soup.   Spring Vegetable Soup.

Boiled Salmon.   Lobster Sauce.   Filletted
Lobster.   Shrimp Sauce.   Cucumbers.

Mushroom Patties.   Lobster Cutlet.   Lamb's
Cutlet, with Cucumber Sauce.   Rabbit Curry,
smothered with White Sauce.
Roast Haunch of Mutton.   Boiled Fowl and
Tongue.   Spinach.   New Potatoes.   Salad.
Duckling.   Guinea Fowl.   Asparagus.

Clear Jelly.   Italian Cream.   Marble Cream.
Strawberry Cream.
Lobster Salad.

[April to July.]

Green Pea Soup.

Broiled Salmon.   Turbot.   Lobster Sauce.   Cucumbers.

Mushroom Patties.   Lamb's Fry.   Lobster Curry.   Rissols.
Roast Saddle of Mutton.   Mayonnaise of Chicken.
Brocoli.   New Potatoes.   Roast Duck.   Peas.

Pudding.   Clear Jelly.   Italian Cream.   Macaroni.

Cheese.   Brunswick Sausage, &c.

[May to Aug.]

White Soup.   Asparagus Soup.

Boiled Salmon.   Lobster Sauce.   Cucumbers.
Filletted Soles.   Shrimp Sauce.

Mushroom Patties.   Pork Cutlets.   Oyster Curry.
Lamb's Fry.   Grenadine of Veal.
Fore-Quarter of Lamb.   Boiled Chicken and Tongue.
New Potatoes.   Spinach.   Salad.

Larded Capon.   Roast Pigeons.   Asparagus.

Clear Jelly.   Italian Cream.   Noyau Jelly.
Macaroni.   Ice Pudding.

Brunswick Sausage, with small Salad.   Anchovies.
Cheese.

[April to July.]

Asparagus Soup.   White Soup.

Boiled Salmon.   Lobster Sauce.   Filletted Soles.
Shrimp Sauce.

Patties.   Pork Cutlets.   Lobster Ditto.
Grenadine of Veal.   Rabbit Curry.
Fore-Quarter of Lamb.   Chickens and Tongue.
Spinach.   Potatoes.   Salad.

Guinea Fowl.   Pigeons.   Lobster Salad.   Asparagus.

Cabinet Pudding.   Punch Jelly.   Charlotte
Russe.   Clear Jelly.   Italian Cream.

[June to Sept.]

Vegetable Soup.

Turbot, with Smelts.   Shrimp Sauce.

Roast Saddle of Mutton.   Boiled Fowls.   Tongue.
Oyster Curry.   Rice.   Pork Cutlets.   Spinach.
Mashed and Brown Potatoes.   Beetroot Salad.

Cabinet Pudding.   Marmalade Tartlets.   Custards.
Macaroni.

[Nov. to March.]

61

APPENDIX

USEFUL RECEIPTS FOR DISHES REFERRED TO IN
THE PRECEDING BILLS OF FARE

—◆—

MAÎTRE D'HÔTEL BUTTER.

Put a quarter of a pound of fresh butter upon a plate, the juice of two lemons, and two large table-spoonfuls of chopped parsley, half a teaspoonful of salt, and half that quantity of white pepper; mix all well together, and keep in a cool place for use.

SAUCE À LA MAÎTRE D'HÔTEL.

Put eight table-spoonfuls of white sauce in a stew-pan, with four of milk, boil it five minutes, then stir in three ounces of maître d'hôtel butter, stir it quickly over the fire till the butter is melted, but do not let it boil. This sauce should be made at the time of serving.

POTATO BALLS.

Bake the potatoes, mash them very nicely, make them into balls, rub them over with the yolk of an egg, and put them into the oven or before the fire to brown. These balls may be varied by the introduction of a third portion of grated ham or tongue.

HORSE-RADISH SAUCE.

Stew an onion in a little fish-stock until it will pulp, add a tea-spoonful of grated horse-radish, and one or two spoonfuls of essence of anchovies; beat all together over a fire; thicken it with a little butter, and finish with a spoonful of lemon pickle or lemon juice; vinegar may be substituted, in which case it must be mixed with the horse-radish and boiled with it, while the lemon or lemon pickle (being of a delicate flavour) should only be warmed.

ITALIAN CREAM.

Whip together for nearly an hour a quart of very thick scalded cream, a quart of raw cream, the grated rind of four lemons and the strained juice, with ten ounces of white powdered sugar, then add half-a-pint of sweet wine, and continue to whisk it until it becomes quite solid; lay a piece of muslin in a sieve, and ladle the cream upon it with a spoon; in twenty hours turn it carefully out, but mind it does not break; garnish it with fruit, jelly, or with flowers.

SCOTCH BROTH.

Set on the fire four ounces of pearl barley, with three Scotch pints (or six quarts) of salt water, when it boils skim it, and add what quantity of salt beef or fresh brisket you choose, and a marrow bone or a fowl, with a couple of pounds of either lean beef or mutton, and a good quantity of leeks, cabbages or savoys, or you may use turnips, onions, and grated carrots; keep it boiling for at least four or five hours; but if a fowl be used, let it not be put in till just time enough to bring it to table when well done, for it must be served up separately.

MUTTON BROTH.

The best part of the mutton from which to make good broth is the chump end of the loin, but it may be made excellently from the scrag end of the neck only, which should be stewed gently for a long time (full three hours or longer, if it be large,) until it becomes tender, but not boiled to rags as it usually is; a few grains of whole pepper, with a couple of fried onions and some turnips, should be put along with the meat an hour or two before sending up the broth, which should be strained from the vegetables, and chopped parsley and thyme be mixed in it; the turnips should be mashed and served in a separate dish to be eaten with the mutton, with parsley-and-butter or caper sauce. If meant for persons in health, it ought to be strong or it will be insipid; the cooks usually skim it frequently, but if given as a remedy for a severe cold, it is much better not to remove the fat, as it is very healing to the chest.

LEG OF MUTTON WITH OYSTERS.

Parboil some fine well-fed oysters, take off the beards and horny parts, put to them some parsley, minced onions, and sweet herbs boiled and chopped fine, and the yolks of two or three hard-boiled eggs; mix all together, and make five or six holes in the fleshy part of a leg of mutton, and put in the mixture, and dress it in either of the following ways: tie it up in a cloth and let it boil gently two and a half or three hours according to the size, or braise it, and serve it with a pungent brown sauce.

TO BOIL CAULIFLOWER WITH PARMESAN.

Boil a cauliflower, drain it on a sieve, and cut it into convenient-sized pieces, arrange these pieces in a pudding-basin so as to make them resemble a cauliflower on the dish, season it as you proceed, turn it on the dish, then cover it with a sauce made of grated parmesan cheese, butter, and the yolks of a couple of eggs seasoned with lemon juice, pepper, salt, and nutmeg, and put parmesan grated over it; bake for twenty minutes and brown it.

SWISS PUDDING.

In many parts of the continent, as well as throughout Switzerland, it is customary to put layers of crumbs of bread and sliced apples, with sugar between, till the dish be as full as it will hold; let the crumbs be the uppermost layer, then pour melted butter over it, and bake.

ASPARAGUS SOUP.

Take two quarters of good beef or veal broth, put to it four onions, two or three turnips and some sweet herbs, with the white part of a hundred of young asparagus, but if old or very large at the stem half that quantity will do, and let them all simmer till sufficiently tender to be rubbed through a tammy, which is not an easy matter if they be not very young; then strain and season it, have ready the boiled tops which have been cut from the stems, and add them to the soup; or poach half-a-dozen eggs rather hard, have ready a hundred of asparagus heads boiled tender, boil three quarts of clear gravy soup, put into it for a minute or two a fowl just roasted, then add a few tarragon leaves, season with a little salt, put the eggs and asparagus heads quite hot into the tureen and pour the soup over them without breaking them; the fowl will be just as good as before for made dishes.

SALMON CURRY.

Have two slices of salmon weighing about a pound each, which cut into pieces of the size of walnuts; cut up two middling-sized onions, which put into a stew-pan with an ounce of butter and a clove of garlic cut in thin slices; stir over the fire till becoming rather yellowish, then add a teaspoonful of curry powder, and half that quantity of curry paste; mix all well together with a pint of good broth, beat up and pass through a tammy into a stew-pan, put in the salmon, which stew about half-an-hour, pour off as much of the oil as possible; if too dry, moisten with a little more broth, mixing it gently, and serve as usual with rice separate. Salmon curry may also be made with the remains left from a previous dinner, in which case reduce the curry sauce until rather thick before putting in the salmon, which only requires to be made hot in it. The remains of a turbot may also be curried in the same way, and also any kind of fish.

PRINCE ALBERT'S PUDDING.

Put one pound of butter into a saucepan, with three quarters of a pound of loaf-sugar finely powdered, mix them well together, then add the yolks of six eggs well beaten, and as much fresh candied orange as will add colour and flavour, being first beaten to a fine paste; line the dish with paste for turning out, and when filled with the above lay a crust over as if it were a pie, and bake it in a slow oven; it is as good cold as hot.

CHARLOTTE RUSSE.

Line the bottom of a plain round mould with Savoy biscuits, placing them close together in a star or some device; line the sides, placing the biscuits edgeways to make them form a compact wall, put the mould upon ice, have ready a Crême au Marasquin, adding a glass of brandy; fill the mould as it stands on the ice, and leave it till the time of serving, when turn it over on the dish and take off the mould.

MAYONNAISE.

A cold roast fowl divided into quarters, young lettuce cut in quarters and placed on the dish with salad dressing, eggs boiled hard and cut in quarters, placed round the dish as a garnish; capers and anchovies are sometimes added.

SCOTCH MINCED COLLOP.

Take two pounds of the fillet of beef, *chopped very fine*, put it in a stew-pan, and add to it pepper and salt and a little flour, add a little good gravy, with a little ketchup and Harvey's sauce, and let it stew for twenty minutes over a slow fire; serve up very hot, garnished with fried sippet of bread. This quantity of beef makes a good-sized dish.

COD RECHAUFFÉ.

Take any cold cod that may be left, warm up with mashed potatoes, and serve with oyster sauce poured over.

EVE'S PUDDING.

Take half-a-pound of very finely grated bread crumbs, half-a-pound of finely chopped apples, half-a-pound of currants, half-a-pound of very fine suet, six ounces of sugar, four eggs, a little nutmeg, two ounces of citron and lemon peel; butter the mould well, and boil three hours.

HOMINY.

Boil Indian corn in milk, add sugar or salt according to taste.

KALECANNON.

Boil three or four carrots *tender*, some nice young greens, a few turnips, a few potatoes; cut off the *outsides* of the carrots and chop them up *very fine*, also chop the greens, mash the turnips and potatoes, then place it in a melon shape to form the stripes of colours, filling up the interior of the mould with all the vegetables chopped up together with pepper and salt. Butter the mould, and boil half-an- hour.

LAMB'S HEAD AND MINCE.

Cut a lamb's head in half, boil and then brown in a Dutch oven or with a salamander; mince liver and dish up together.

RICE BLANCMANGE.

Boil rice in milk, put in a mould, and let stand until cold.

SCOTCH MUTTON BROTH.

Make a good brown stock of a small shin of beef, with vegetables, carrots, turnips, onions and celery; when sufficiently boiled the vegetables must be taken out *whole*, and the soup seasoned with pepper and salt and a little cayenne to taste: also a little Harvey's sauce and ketchup; then fry some mutton cutlets, the quantity required for the number, a pale brown, add them to the soup with the vegetables cut up small.

SWISS PUDDING.

Butter your dish, lay in it a layer of bread crumbs grated very fine, then boil four or five apples very tender, add a little butter, nutmeg, and fine sifted sugar, mix all up together and lay on the bread crumbs, then another layer of the crumbs, then add pieces of fresh butter on the top, and bake in a slow oven for a quarter of an hour, until it become a delicate brown; it may be eaten hot or cold.

SPANISH PUDDING.

One pound of flour, and one table-spoonful of good yeast to be put in a basin, melt half-a-pound of butter in a little milk, add it to the flour and yeast, and mix them together; then take three eggs – yolks and whites – with a *little salt*, and well beat them; when well beaten frisk them into the butter, mix the dough well up till it will leave the basin and spoon quite clear, let it stand to rise for an hour, then roll it up with six ounces of powdered sugar, and a tea-spoonful of powdered cinnamon, and half-an-ounce of candied orange-peel, and half-an-ounce of citron cut very fine, to be served with sauce of clarified sugar, with orange-flower water poured over it about half-an-hour before sent to table.

STEAK À LA SOYER.

The rump-steak to be broiled and to be dressed with pepper, salt, cayenne and flour, all in a dredge-box together; keep constantly turning the steak and dredging it; chop up one small shalot, put it in a stew-pan with a little ketchup, when the steak is sufficiently done add a little butter to it, strain the sauce through a small sieve, and serve up very hot.

SPANISH SALAD DRESSING.

One tea-spoonful of water, half a tea-spoonful of pepper, ditto of salt, two wine-glasses of oil, about a dessert-spoonful of very strong vinegar, all well mixed together. To make this salad thoroughly good, some sweet herbs should be added, but chopped very fine.

[RECIPES ADDED TO THE APPENDIX OF THE 1854 EDITION]

COCK-A-LEEKIE.

Make a stock of six or eight pounds of beef, seasoned as for brown soup, and when cold skim off the fat. Wash well a bunch and a half of leeks, and cut them in pieces of an inch length. Put on the stock with two-thirds of the leeks, and a good sized fowl, and boil for an hour. Then take out the fowl, *skin* it, and cut it into small pieces, return it to the soup along with the other third of the leeks, and boil all up for another hour. *If prunes be liked*, throw in a quarter pound half an hour before serving. Some cooks thicken this soup with fine oatmeal, but if the leeks be tender, they boil away sufficiently to make the soup of a proper richness and consistency without this addition.

HOTCH POTCH.
(MEG DOD'S RECIPE.)

Make the stock of sweet fresh mutton. Grate the zest of two or three large carrots, slice down also young turnips, young onions, lettuce and parsley. Have a full quart of these things when sliced, and another of green pease, and sprays of cauliflower. Put in the vegetables, withholding half the peas till near the end of the process. Cut down 4 lb. of ribs of lamb into small chops, trimming off superfluous fat, and put them into the soup. Boil well and skim carefully; add the remaining peas, white pepper and salt, and when thick enough serve the chops in the tureen with the Hotch Potch.

N.B.—As parsley loses its colour in boiling, it should be chopped fine, and be put in just before dishing, which gives a delightful freshness.

ORANGE FRITTERS.

Dip the sections of oranges in thin batter and fry them a nice brown.

ANOTHER WAY.

Dip the sections of oranges in *white of egg only*, dredge them afterwards with flour, and then fry them a nice brown.

POTATOE SOUP.

Mash to a smooth paste three pounds of good mealy potatoes that have been steamed or boiled very dry; mix with them, by degrees, two quarts of boiling broth, pass the soup through a strainer, set it again on the fire, add pepper and salt, and let it boil five minutes. Take off entirely the black scum that will rise upon it, and serve it very hot with fried or toasted bread. Where the flavour is approved, two ounces of onions, minced and fried a light brown, may be added to the above, and stewed in it for ten minutes before it is sent to table.

VERMICELLI AND VEGETABLE SOUP.

5 Pounds Lean Beef.
2 Heads of Celery.
2 Carrots.
2 Turnips.
4 Onions.
1 Bunch Sweet Herbs (in a muslin bag).
$^1/_2$ oz. White Pepper.
$^1/_2$ oz. Allspice.
A little Salt.
5 Pints Water.

To be boiled *six hours*, well skimmed and strained from the vegetables, &c.

Next day, 1 Carrot, 1 Turnip, the hearts of the two heads of Celery, to be boiled in water, after being cut into dice, and added to the soup with $^1/_4$ lb. Vermicelli.

KIDNEYS A LA BROCHETTE.

Let your kidneys steep five minutes in cold water to soften the skin; remove it and split each; through the middle put a wooden or silver skewer, if you have them; when they are skewered, season them with pepper and salt. Dip each into oil or melted butter, and broil them on a gridiron. Before you serve, remove the skewers, unless they are of silver, and serve them on a dish with butter and fine herbs.

FONDUE (SIMPLE METHOD).

Put two ounces of Gruyère and two ounces of Parmesan cheese (grated) into a basin (or if you have not got them use English cheese), with a little salt, pepper, and cayenne, add the yolks of six eggs with a quarter of a pound of butter melted (mix well), whip the whites of the six eggs, stir gently into the other ingredients, fill small paper cases (*or one large paper case*) with it, bake about a quarter of an hour in a moderate oven, and serve very hot.

TENDRONS OF VEAL.

Scald your tendrons of veal, and then put them on to stew with butter, a little flour, some mushrooms, and a bunch of sweet herbs; add some stock to moisten the tendrons, and when done enough skim the sauce in which the veal was dressed, and just before you serve it, add some yolk of eggs well beaten with some cream, and the juice of a lemon, then serve.

STRAWBERRY CURD AND JELLY.

Put twelve pounds of strawberries into a wide pan after having picked them. Mix five ounces of tartaric acid in two quarts of cold spring water: when dissolved pour it over the fruit, cover it with a cloth and let it stand 24 hours, then strain it through a sieve, taking care not to bruise the fruit, and to every pint of juice add $^1/_2$ lb. of good sugar, finely powdered; let it remain undisturbed until the sugar is dissolved, and then stir it for two hours without ceasing, that the sugar may amalgamate with the juice. When done, put it into pint bottles corked tight, and keep it in the cellar.

FOR USE.

Dissolve about $^1/_2$ oz. (*not more*) of isinglass in a small tea-cup, full of boiling water, and when strained, pour *into it* one pint of the acid, and when perfectly stirred together, put it into a mould, in a cool place, till the next day, when it will turn out for use.

STONE CREAM.

Half an ounce of isinglass dissolved and added to a pint of cream, eight lumps of sugar rubbed over a lemon, also put to it and boiled. When half-cold put it into a mould, and serve with preserve round it.

BAKED IRISH STEW.

An ordinary Irish stew, with a little gravy added, and baked until nicely browned; about half an hour.

MAROONED MUTTON.

Stew 6 chalots, 1 cup of mushroom ketchup, and 2 tablespoonsful of vinegar, together for *two hours*; then add slices of cold mutton cut thin, and stew *ten minutes*. Add a little rich gravy.

QUEEN'S PUDDING.

Half pint of cream, one pint of milk, flavour with vanille and white sugar to taste, and boil together for a *quarter of an hour*; add the yolks of *eight eggs*, well beaten. Then place over the shape a piece of thin paper, and boil the pudding *one hour*. Serve it up with sauce made of two glasses of sherry, one pot of red currant jelly, and a white sugar mixed together, heated, and poured *round* the dish with the pudding.

BEEF SANDARS.

Mince cold beef small with onions, add pepper and salt and a little gravy, put into a pie-dish, or scollop shells, until about three parts full. Then fill up with mashed potatoes. Bake in an oven or before the fire until done a light brown. Mutton may be cooked in the same way.

SOUP MAIGRE.

Quarter of a pound of butter placed in a stew-pan, add to it two tablespoonsful flour, half pint milk. Then add cold vegetables chopped very fine, and stew together *a quarter of an hour*. Before sent up, beat the yolks of two eggs, add a quarter of a pint of cream, and a little pepper and salt to taste.

RUMP STEAK BREADED, OR BEEF CUTLETS.

The fillet of beef cut into slices, with bread crumbs, chopped parsley, pepper and salt, placed in a tin with a little butter, and baked a quarter of an hour in a brisk oven.

MACARONI WITH BACON.

Macaroni dressed in the usual way, with cheese. Small thin slices of bacon laid on the top and baked with the macaroni about twenty minutes.

TIMBALLE OF MACARONI, WITH CHICKEN AND HAM.

Simmer $1/2$ lb. macaroni in plenty of water, and a tablespoonful of salt till it is tender; but take care not to have it *too soft;* strain the water from it, beat up five yolks and the whites of two eggs, take half a pint of the best cream, and the breast of a fowl and some slices of ham. Mince the breast of the fowl with the ham; add them with from two to three tablespoonsful of finely grated Parmesan cheese, and season with pepper and salt. Mix all these with the macaroni and put into a pudding mould, well buttered. Let it steam in a stew-pan of boiling water, about an hour and serve quite hot with rich gravy.

It is very good cold.

PALESTINE SOUP.

Wash and pare quickly some freshly-dug artichokes, and to preserve their colour throw them into spring water as they are done, but do not let them remain in it after all are ready. Boil three pounds of them in water for ten minutes; lift them out, and slice them into three pints of boiling stock; when they have stewed gently in this from fifteen to twenty minutes, press them with the soup through a fine sieve, and put the whole into a clean saucepan, with a pint and a half more of stock; add sufficient salt and cayenne to season it, skim it well, and after it has simmered two or three minutes, stir to it a pint of rich boiling cream. Serve it immediately. The palest veal stock as for white soup should be used for this, but for a family dinner or where economy is a consideration, excellent mutton broth made the day before, and perfectly cleared from fat, will answer very well as a substitute; milk, too, may take the place of cream when this last is scarce; the proportion of artichokes should then be increased a little.

Vegetable marrow, when young, makes a superior soup, even to this, which is a most excellent one. It should be well pared, trimmed, and sliced into a small quantity of boiling veal stock, or broth, and when perfectly tender, pressed through a fine sieve, and mixed with more stock and some cream.

COFFEE FOR THIRTY PEOPLE.

Put 1 lb. of best coffee into a stewpan, sufficiently large to hold seven quarts of water; put it on the fire to dry the coffee (be sure to shake it, for fear it should burn); then take it off the fire and put the whites of two eggs into it, stir it till it is mixed, then pour on it six quarts of water, BOILING; let it stand a quarter of an hour, covered closely; then strain it through a jelly-bag, and put it away for use.

THE HISTORY OF CATHERINE DICKENS'S MENU BOOKS

CHAPTER I

LADY MARIA CLUTTERBUCK'S MENU BOOKS:
THEIR PUBLICATION AND AUTHORSHIP

CATHERINE Dickens had been married to the world-renowned author Charles Dickens for nearly sixteen years when the first edition of her menu book was published in 1851. The slender volume, entitled *What Shall We Have For Dinner? Satisfactorily Answered by Numerous Bills of Fare for from Two to Eighteen Persons* by 'Lady Maria Clutterbuck', was evidently well received. In October of that same year, she published a second edition and, four months later in 1852, she produced a revised 'new edition'. By 1854, Catherine updated the menus, doubled the recipe appendix, shortened her pseudonym to 'Lady Clutterbuck' and her publishers, Bradbury and Evans, were able to retain the price of one shilling. Judging from extant copies, the menu book was reissued again after some minor editorial changes in 1856 and 1860.[1]

It is probably not surprising that Catherine Dickens's publication concerns the culinary arts, her husband's writing abounds in culinary references. As one literary critic noted, 'In the richness and variety of his treatment of food and drink Dickens is the indisputable master among the Victorian novelists.'[2] Other critics and historians have widely acknowledged Dickens's use of food as metaphor in his fiction.[3] Yet there is little known about the Dickens family's own table.

As the subject of this culinary history, the bills of fare and recipes from Catherine Dickens's work illuminate the colourful palette of their upper-middle-class life. By their nature, menu books and cookery books are personal documents. While they do not verify that the author actually cooked or served the variety of courses suggested, they do express views of ideal meals under favourable circumstances. As such, these publications become period pieces that unwittingly chronicle attitudes towards food that are cultural, regional, socio-economical, and idiosyncratic. Catherine's publications serve as excellent examples.

Catherine probably wrote her menu books for the same readership as her husband's magazine, *Household Words*, which first appeared the year before.

The majority of the 164 menus in the 1851 edition (and those in the subsequent editions) suggest small family dinners that would have been served from day to day; the few elaborate multi-course bills of fare may reflect the dinner parties the couple hosted at their homes in Devonshire Terrace, Regent's Park and Tavistock House in Russell Square, where they moved in October 1851. The recipes in her appendix provide guidance for cooks, although the quirkiness of the recipe selection and some careless editing by the publishers make her publications somewhat homespun pieces, even if the lively introduction, attributed to Charles Dickens himself, and the humorous pseudonym Lady Clutterbuck, taken by Catherine from a role she played in Dickens's amateur theatrical production of *Used Up*, a farce by Félix-Auguste Duvert, added verve and vitality. Evidence of lax editorial conventions and other mistakes include, for example, 'ditto' and '&ct.' used inconsistently. Spellings like 'brocoli', while used by some cookbook writers, may be overlooked, but others like 'croquits' for croquettes could reflect either Catherine's spelling or the typesetter's, and mistakes like 'Brosse' for Russe and so forth, were never corrected from the original 1851 edition. Complaints about compositors were not new. That very December, Dickens had written to Frederick Evans, the publisher, concerning mistakes in his own work. 'I declare before God that your men are enough to drive me mad!' he railed.[4] In fairness, the men set type under enormous pressure and short deadlines, often working late in poorly lit rooms.[5] To compound the problem, Catherine's handwriting is difficult to decipher.

The Dickenses' progressive outlook flavoured their dining-room. Her publication conforms with her husband's desire to improve the standard of British cooking and his advocacy of famine-relief foods such as American corn meal, nutritious soups, and an increased use of fish. Catherine's Scottish heritage is visible in the recipe section, particularly in the 1854 edition onwards, as are her adaptations of a few foreign dishes gleaned from their travels. Judging from accounts in diaries and letters written by some of the Dickenses' dinner guests, they entertained well and were among the early proponents of a less formal dining style.

In culinary matters, Charles and Catherine must have shared a similar philosophy. 'What shall we have for dinner?' would have been a frequently discussed question in the Dickens household as it continues to be today in our own homes. Their personal favourites, seasonal availability, previous menus, and returning guests would all factor into the conversation. From the individual dishes to the unusual pairings within each course, every detail would have been scrutinized. And just as their daughter Mary (Mamie) Dickens described her father's dinner critiques at Gad's Hill Place after her parents' separation, one imagines that Dickens had previously shared his opinions – humorously or not – with his wife. According to Mamie, when the house was filled with guests, the dinner menu was placed on the sideboard at luncheon:

> And then he would discuss every item in his fanciful, humorous way with his guests, much to this effect: 'Cock-a-leekie? Good, decidedly good; fried soles with shrimp sauce? Good again; croquettes of chicken? Weak, very weak; decided want of imagination here,' and so on, and he would apparently be so taken up with the merits or demerits of a menu that one might imagine he lived for nothing but the coming dinner.[6]

What Shall We Have For Dinner? was in tune with the *zeitgeist* of the 1850s. The social and economic shifts of the Victorian era brought changes to all aspects of publishing. With the increased wealth accruing to the middle classes from manufacturing, colonialism, and other financially lucrative opportunities, a need arose to define their new stations. Even for the less affluent, the effects of industrialization on factory workers and middle managers and their adaptation to city life, were rapid since the upwardly-mobile wanted to develop social graces.[7] Dickens himself requested a copy of *Hints on Etiquette and the Usage of Society, with a Glance at Bad Habits* from his publisher in 1836 when it was issued.[8] He later purchased *Anecdotes of the Manners and Customs of London* in 1841.[9] Dickens's motives for obtaining these books may reflect his interest in manners as an observant novelist, but may also mark his own social ambitions.

Beside etiquette books, household manuals became an important publishing category and reflected changes in women's domestic lives. Dena Attar argues that they set standards for comfort, cleanliness, and behaviour that signified middle-class respectability. As either the mistress of the household, or as domestic servants, women were required to uphold these high standards. By 1851, one in four married women (not widowed) was employed, and they had to juggle both their work lives and family responsibilities. According to Attar, women represented a readership interested in topics that ranged from entertaining guests socially to nursing their babies privately. They 'bought books in the millions seeking advice on household routines, managing servants, provisioning, decorating and furnishing their homes, marketing, planning menus and cooking,' among other topics.[10]

As Richard Altick points out, the general public's desire to read literally inked the presses. The sheer number of publications produced in the nineteenth century rose staggeringly. Meanwhile, groups such as the Utilitarians campaigned for a diet of Christian literature and uplifting, righteous themes in books and other family publications. Even the newly established public libraries fuelled debate over their mission and the appropriate literature for the lower classes whom they served. Passionate discussions centred around the suitability of various genres, from the Bible to cheap novels.[11]

'Democracy of print' was a revolutionary concept espoused by Dickens and his circle that stressed open access to reading materials. They argued that everyone should be able to read for insight, information, and relaxation.[12] *Household Words*, 'A Weekly Journal Conducted by Charles Dickens', was launched a year before his wife's publication. The title was taken from a Shakespearean quote, 'Familiar in their Mouths, as Household Words', and the articles were 'designed for the instruction and entertainment of all classes of readers'.[13] 'A Preliminary Word', which he wrote for the first issue dated Saturday March 30, 1850, outlined his philosophy:

> We seek to bring into innumerable homes, from the stirring world around us, the knowledge of many social wonders, good and evil, that are not calculated to render any of us less ardently preserving in ourselves, less tolerant of one another, less faithful in the progress of mankind, less thankful for the privilege of living in this summer-dawn of time.[14]

His creed assured readers that the articles would be informative, entertaining, or both. Not surprisingly, the magazine also became Dickens's vehicle for advocating pertinent social reforms. He hoped to serve a broad audience, yet *Household Words* became primarily a journal for the middle classes. According to Richard Altick, the publication demonstrated a high literary level and, given the quality, was inexpensive at twopence a copy.[15] Even American audiences enjoyed the articles that were reprinted in anthologies from 1852 onwards.[16]

Dickens generally wrote the serialized fiction, although other authors were solicited. He commissioned nonfiction from professional writers and know-ledgeable specialists to supplement his staff's contributions. Articles on natural history, historical accounts, travel adventures, and topical matters provided engaging, yet instructive reading. Attitudes to wines, cooking, entertaining and English culinary foibles personally respected his views. Soberly or humorously, the articles also brought attention to appalling sanitary conditions, polluted water supply, fetid sewers, filthy meat markets, and problematic foodstuffs. *Household Words* both informed readers and attempted to galvanize legal action.[17] In the years Catherine compiled her menus, Britain reeled from tremendous problems with spurious and adulterated food and beverages. 'Constitution Trials' summarized the extent of the problem:

> The British consumer is a little angry on the subject of adulterations. From one side he is shouted at to mind his milk, and from another to beware of his bread; a sepul-chral voice informs him when he lifts a cup of coffee to his lips that it contains chicory and coffins. In his tea, he is told to look for black-lead, Prussian blue and gypsum; in his wine, he is warned that there are drugs past reckoning; and in his cakes, he is kindly admonished; in his custards, prussic acid lies in waiting to destroy. Whatever the British consumer may feel inclination to devour, let him devour it at his peril.[18]

Other articles, such as 'Death in the Breadbasket', disclosed specific admixtures found in the most basic of foodstuffs.[19] Obviously, *Household Words* was not alone in reporting deleterious conditions in London's (and other cities') food supply, but it reached an important audience.

Anne Lohrli believed that Dickens maintained tight control over the content, authors and editing. Over the years, his assistants included Richard H. Horne, Henry Morley, and Wilkie Collins. Four other journalists were among the regulars, Dudley Costello, Frederick Knight Hunt, Sidney Laman Blanchard, and William Blanchard Jerrold.[20] They contributed articles on culinary topics, as did Charles Knight, Harriet Martineau, and George Sala.[21] (Leigh Hunt, Mark Lemon, and Mary Boyle, all actors in Dickens's amateur theatre productions, submitted work as well.)[22] The food and wine articles have contributed substantially to our understanding of his wife's publication and provide an historical context for Catherine's work.

The editors of Dickens's letters and Michael Slater acknowledge that the introduction to *What Shall We Have For Dinner?* was more likely written by

Dickens than his wife, judging by the clean, witty style.[23] Dickens's prose cleverly used the characters from the farce, *Used Up*. Adopting the pen-name of Lady Clutterbuck, he played humorously with social expectations. The device mimicked a trend, often used by male authors, such as Charles Day in *Hints on Etiquette*, to claim aristocratic respectability.[24] Etiquette manuals were particularly ripe for pseudonymous authorship, and the few writers with actual titles – Lady Campbell, Lady Greville, Lady Howard and Lady Grove – unwittingly lent credibility to the aliases.[25]

The first publication of Catherine Dickens's book in 1851 is still shrouded in mystery, since the only copy that survives from that year is defined as a '2nd Edition'. The 'new edition' of 1852 (from which the transcript in this volume derives), just as all the other printings, is extremely rare. I have so far located only five extant originals and two copies of any of the editions in libraries across the world.[26] Curiously, the few letters from her husband to their publisher Bradbury & Evans contain no references to the writing or the printing of these editions.

******

What can a collection of mid-Victorian menus reveal about its author? After all, there is a vast difference between reading a menu and eating the meal, and a far greater gap between reading Catherine's menus and understanding the social dynamics surrounding their dining-room table.

Did, for instance, Catherine Dickens borrow menus verbatim from other cookery books, or were her meals more personal combinations? One soon realizes the difficulty in answering this question since only odd spellings or other markers would tie Catherine's menus to her contemporaries' publications. Because every culture has well-established dishes, these combinations are difficult to untangle as individual preferences. Some pairings have historic associations. One menu, for example, that was consistently repeated through her editions, opened with cod and oyster sauce, and moved on to roast rolled ribs of beef, roast fowl, plum tart, and a few other flourishes including bacon, French beans, potatoes, toasted cheese, and a watercress salad. This combination was so common that nearly two decades earlier, her then fiancé Charles, who was travelling, ate similar fare: 'I have just ordered dinner in this curious den for five people, cod and oyster sauce, Roast beef, and a pair of ducks, plum pudding, and Mince Pies.'[27] Dickens's meal that evening was probably the wisest choice from the tavern's kitchen. His 1835 dinner and Catherine's 1850s menu mirror enduring British cookery, served on our own tables over a century and a half later.[28] The only noticeable differences today are the proportions; by our standards, the menus were enormous even for the hardiest of appetites.

While bills of fare for both tavern meals and home dinners reflect the chef's, cook's, or homemaker's creativity, the menus also make a statement about the writer's worldliness and financial status. To this end, one wonders what were the Dickenses' food preferences. How did they change over time? And what, if anything, do Catherine's editions disclose about regional foods and agricultural availability?

Fortunately the Dickenses' letters provide supporting commentary on their home, travels, personal preferences, and social conventions. A wider cultural context is opened by Dickens's magazine, *Household Words*, and by contemporary cookbooks and other culinary sources that document Victorian daily life.

In order to identify the patterns and the frequency of foodstuffs represented in Catherine's menus, databases were created for all the editions. Admittedly, an analysis of this type assumes that her menus represent the dinners she would have liked to serve her family and guests or those she actually served. Beside the predictable pairings among the roughly 1,400 entries composing the bills of fare for each edition, Catherine's personal touches are evident. She has graciously pulled back the dining-room curtains, so we may glimpse her family enjoying dinner around their own table.

Not surprisingly, in all the versions of her book, Catherine demonstrates a decidedly British character. She consistently prefers the term 'bills of fare' to 'menus', enlists plain English names for dishes, and only occasionally opts for French terms or spellings (such as rechauffé, Crème au Marasquin, and so forth). She never uses titles in Italian or other languages. She did not necessarily create menus that paired dishes in strict symmetry (as required by the more formal *à la française* service), which suggests that their guests dined in the more 'modern' *à la russe* style. The informality and relative freedom the *à la russe* approach offered was transferred to the actual items Catherine could, and did, choose for the courses. While the family menus are similar to our everyday meals, the larger dinner party menus owed more to precedent and custom so that the combinations Catherine offers may, at first, seem unfamiliar. But as one looks at the courses (grouped by the closer spacing of the lines in the bills of fare), the Victorian meal-pattern emerges and her creativity, or occasionally lack of it, is unveiled.

For anyone who remembers his or her first dinner party, the timing and coordination of the finished dishes were difficult skills to learn, but once acquired, proved invaluable. Catherine's cooking practices and menus reveal an author who knows how much juggling is realistic in a small kitchen with limited personnel. Like any experienced hostess and cook, Catherine writes the larger menus realizing that some items would be made ahead and served cold or at room temperature. For meat cookery, she balances preparations simmered on the stovetop, baked in the oven, or roasted on the bottle-jack (which require less surveillance) with those that demand the cook's constant attention.

To provide an overview of the cooking methods, the more numerous 1852 menus were chosen for the following chart. Since Catherine sometimes included the cooking techniques in the dish's title, it gives insight into the methods she used. Restraint, however, must be exercised when interpreting the relative significance of these cooking methods. For example, she does not mention steaming, braising, and potting, but doubtlessly these methods were used. Moreover, the statistical frequency of baking would soar if pies, tarts, baked macaroni, and so forth were included as they are roughly estimated under the category entitled 'baked desserts'. Since some items, especially desserts, would have been made before or after meal preparation, these would not influence the flow of the kitchen work during dinner service.

Catherine suggests frying half as often as roasting, but one cannot tell if she means pan-frying or deep-frying, except in obvious cases like fried potatoes, fritters, and so forth. Hashed meats were pan-fried, and preparations such as minced collops were so popular with the Dickens family, she provides a recipe in the appendix.

Beside traditional meat stews, vegetables and mushrooms are individually stewed (actually braised). With the exception of boiled puddings, boiling is reserved for meats, predominantly chicken, turkey, mutton, and knuckles of ham, which also provides well-flavoured stocks. While Catherine lists 'boiled' salmon and mackerel, she and her cook most likely poached the fish in an aromatic court-bouillon. The terms 'boiled' and 'boiling', were used similarly by contemporary cookbook writers.

Curries, although not strictly a cooking method, are singled out here since they represent a distinctive style. 'Curry-eating engagements' are mentioned

SUMMARY OF COOKING METHODS IN THE 1852 DISH TITLES

Type	Frequency	Comments
roasted	98	meats
fried & pan-fried	45	usually reserved for certain types of fish and potatoes
boiled	35	meats & desserts
stewed (braised)	32	includes fricassee, fricandeau & stewed vegetables
curried	20	seafood & meats
broiled (grilled)	18	fish, fowl, & mushrooms
hashed	14	including collops
baked	6	for fish
[baked desserts]	82	[estimate]
jugged	1	for hare only

in Dickens's notes to their friends John Leech and Frank Stone. These invitations may refer to a restaurant outing, but it is equally likely that curries featured at Devonshire Terrace.[29] Twenty menus offer curry dishes, and Catherine provides a recipe in the appendix. Unlike the sentiments of 'Mrs. B' in Soyer's cookery book, Catherine has no preference as to the proper season for serving curry, that is, either to help cool in the summer or to warm in the winter.[30] She suggests the dish year round, with seafood curries of lobster or oysters as her most popular, and mutton and rabbit being a close second. In one menu, Catherine serves rabbit curry 'smothered in white sauce' in an over-the-top Victorian treatment, but she drops this combination in the 1854 edition and adds curried skate. Catherine, like most of her contemporaries, offers a curry dish to the menu only for variety. There is no evidence that a traditional ethnic meal with curries and condiments was prepared in the Dickens house.

Catherine broils fish, fowl, and mushrooms. She is also fond of stuffing meat, offal, and fish for menus serving up to ten diners. With few exceptions, she neither indicates the type or ingredients of the farce. In nearly twenty menus, she includes stuffed haddock, sheep's heart, roast fillet of beef or rump roasts and, the most popular, a stuffed leg of mutton.

She offers meat pies, made from rabbit or small game birds in roughly another twenty menus, and about half the time she serves the pies cold. Overwhelmingly, her favourite is pigeon pie, and one assumes she placed the spiky pigeon feet sticking out of the pie crust as was the customary to authenticate the contents. (This garnishing style continued to be shown in the colour-plates of Mrs Beeton's work a decade later.[31])

For especially large dinner party menus (some with over thirty dishes), the middle-class hostess did not necessarily ask her kitchen staff to make or to cook all the dishes at home. Alternatives, like using the local baker's commercial ovens could be arranged for roasting large birds and joints. Elaborate meat pies, pastries, or jellies could also be purchased from the bake shops. Confectioners would provide ices and spectacular desserts, and fancy provisioners, taverns, and hotels also supplied full meals – as Dickens knew very well. On one occasion when he boasted about his punch-making, Dickens extended a dinner invitation in his wife's absence. He wrote to her saying, 'it will become necessary to furnish fully the table with some cold viands from Fortnum and Mason's.'[32] The party, he later reported, was a success, 'Cold collation of pigeon pie, collared red partridge [a red-legged French partridge], ham, roast fowls, and lobster salads. One hot dish, consisting of a most immense heap of asparagus. Considerable quantities of punch were disposed of.'[33] We do not know how often Catherine bought prepared viands, but one suspects from her husband's letter that there were times when it was necessary.

In viewing the menus as a whole, several other generalizations may be made. Catherine designed the majority (roughly 80 per cent) of the bills of fare for small family groups. That is, out of the 164 to 174 menus in the various editions, over seventy were created for two or three persons, nearly forty for four to five diners, and about thirty for six or seven persons. Given the Dickenses' household with three adults (Catherine, her husband, and her sister Georgy), the older children, in-laws, and visitors, these expanding menus could readily accommodate the variable configurations at the nightly dinner table. Invitations for Sabbath meals were extended weekly to family and close friends. 'My sister (being alone just now) usually dines with us on that day, and moreover my brother [Fred] whom I encourage so to do,' Dickens wrote to Mrs William (Catherine) Macready asking her to join them.[34]

The Dickenses probably gave more dinner parties than most middle-class families since they enjoyed entertaining. When her bills of fare switch from an uneven number of diners to those for ten persons or more, Catherine reflects the more formal structure associated with entertaining. The remaining menus, designed for up to twenty persons, may reflect larger family gatherings (for christenings or birthdays), or those to entertain colleagues as celebrations of publications and other benchmarks.

Catherine's practicality as a menu-planner is evident. A third of her menus provide foodstuffs available all year long. These 'January to December' menus for two to ten persons offer convenience by using common pantry items and things easily obtainable at market. Because her household was often on the move from one temporary holiday home to another, she knew how to expand menus or produce meals for a larger company at short notice. Judging by how often pantry lists continue to be given in today's culinary magazines, we still appreciate this approach. Catherine's mainstays include soups from root vegetables, or first courses of sole or salmon, and entrées prepared from beef, mutton, and fowl. Long-keeping vegetables (carrots, onions, turnips, etc.), those with two growing seasons (like spinach), and those raised year-long (like watercress) fill out the courses. In these year-long menus, Catherine relies on steamed puddings, starch-based custards, and jam tarts for desserts. She often ends the meal with a cheese dish.

Sometimes Catherine just wrote 'vegetable' without specification. She also wrote a few menus with just meat, potatoes, and a sweet – with no apparent inclusion of vegetables. This is not unusual. If we compare British and American menus listed in contemporary cookbooks, the American literature, especially if published in New England and the eastern part of the mid-western states, tended to contain more vegetable dishes – albeit the same vegetables – than their British counterparts.

Catherine is not indifferent to the choice of foodstuffs, her bills of fare celebrate the change of seasons: more particularly after the new edition of 1852 which reorganizes all the menus into seasonal groups, adding under each menu the time of year it could be served. (She also provides ten wholly new menus.) Her spring menus feature the first tender asparagus shoots, while

CHANGES IN THE KNOWN EDITIONS

	1851 (2nd ed.)	1852 (new ed.)	1854, 1856, & 1860
Total Menus	164	174	170
for 2–3 diners	74	73	72
for 4–5 diners	36	39	37
for 6–7 diners	29	32	32
for 8–10 diners	20	25	24
for 14–20 diners	5	4	4
Dishes Omitted from Retained Menus	—	15	20
Dishes Replaced or Preparation Changed	—	28	186
Recipes in Appendix	27	27	48

early summer dishes highlight delicate peas, juicy cucumbers, and crisp cabbages before later harvests of cauliflower and broccoli. Only rarely does she suggest vegetables (artichokes and Brussels sprouts) beyond their apparent availability. As one might expect, her husband held strong opinions about foodstuffs out of season. 'I abhor the idea of – whether it be for Winter peaches, Spring lamb, Midsummer ice, [or] unnatural cucumbers,' Dickens commented once while asserting a point.[35]

Even with today's culinary movements promoting fresh ripe local produce, seasonality may be an aspect of Victorian life we fail to appreciate fully. Mid-nineteenth-century cooks had far fewer choices during the off-season, and they maximized each month of the calendar as availability dictated. If the *Epicure's Year Book and Table Companion* may speak for the choices in the Dickenses' time, 'the year opens well for the table. Butcher, fishmonger, poulterer, and fruiterer, present rich stores to the epicure. Butcher's meat is in perfection. Game is plentiful. The fishmonger has his richest show of the year. The garden and the hot-house supply a rare variety of vegetables, salads, and desserts.'[36]

January in London offered ducks, geese, kid, partridges, snipe, teal, and pheasants for those who enjoyed the 'rich variety of game'. Small birds, like plovers and teal, and larger fowl, like wild ducks and geese, were thought to be at their best. Salmon, trout, turbot, sturgeon, cod, crevettes (shrimp), oysters, and smelts were at their peak. Accompanied by spinach, chicory, mallow, celery, cardoons, Brussels sprouts, salsify, and hothouse herbs, the market also held a variety of grapes, pears and apples. 'The weather invites to the solid and succulent' dinners rather than a 'light, dainty diet', the author remarked.[37]

February is 'the month when our neighbours, at any rate, regale themselves the most freely; and when truffled poultry are poured into Paris' for Carnival. The 'perfumed highway from Périgord to Paris' was said to be replete with other succulent fungi, but Londoners had to settle for game and look forward to March when the 'opening spring brings new delicacies – with the violets'. Plump oysters were at their best. There was an abundance of fish, and vegetable gardens yielded fresh young asparagus, artichokes, tender lettuces, radishes and beets.[38]

With the burst of spring in April, dramatic changes were seen in the kitchen. Young lamb and chickens were available with the first green peas appearing in the garden and asparagus coming into perfection. Hams were imported and the sea was bountiful with mackerel, each taking its place upon the table at the end of the month. The store of native fruits was ending, and the cook fell back on imports, forced varieties, or preserves from the pantry. May was a merry month since 'the round of dining seriously begins'. Peas were now plentiful. There were young haricots, cucumbers, and cauliflower in the markets and growing more bountiful. Salmon, oysters, and sole added to the cook's credibility. Young pigeons, turkeys, and duckling invited combinations with asparagus or peas. While few of us realize it today, May was the month when eggs and butter were at their best. A simple omelette was the perfect way to 'wind up a little dinner delightfully'.[39]

For the English epicure, June was described as a 'gracious' month 'to him who will eat in season, and who does not run after strawberries in January'. The garden produce and orchard fruits, particularly from the southern regions, took their honoured places. In June, veal and mutton were excellent. Turkey poult, chicken, duckling, quail, and pigeon were abundant. Whitebait was well in season, along with red mullet, crab, and a variety of vegetables.[40]

July provided pears for the picking and the 'last kiss from the ardent sun' for apricots, peaches, and the orange flowers in bloom. Quail and lark helped an impatient diner wait for the autumn partridges. Tomatoes redden, melons and the greengage fruits ripened, while the 'almond lies like a pearl, in its green shell'. The juicy summer fruits continued to be picked through the month of August. Figs and peaches were now plentiful. The suckling roast pig was in all its glory, and grouse, leverets, young rabbits, and partridges were abundant once again.[41]

September was the month of game, particularly partridge, pheasant, and woodcocks, which were brought to the market with the autumn artichokes. Fishmongers had firm, fine-fleshed trout. October brought the rest of the game birds. Winter fruits such as plums, pears, quinces, apples, and nuts began to appear, and the first frost ripened the medlar. The cold offered abundant fish in fine condition, including mackerel and herrings.[42] The increased cold of November fattened cattle, plumped turkeys and capons, and brought the oyster once again into perfection. December, 'the month of the year when every Englishman is a bon vivant,' put forth an abundance of fish, flesh, fowl, and game with both venison and boar in high season.[43]

The seasonal information that Catherine provides in her menus is helpful in another way. Some of the odd placements of a few menus betray editorial changes that occurred when new menus were added to a succeeding edition. It is likely that two of her seasonal frames, 'All the Summer' and 'All the Winter', may have been inserted into the second printing of the 1852 edition, published as 'a new edition'. This suggests that there were two editions that year, as there had been in the previous year. If these menus were an after-thought, it would help explain why the overly large menus appear under the section for eight to ten persons. These were more likely intended for eighteen to twenty diners. The compositor (perhaps using the previous edition for formatting) may have inserted the menus where they most conveniently fitted the space, rather than where they should have been placed (see the endnote for specifics).[44] Many of these misaligned menus were dropped in the 1854 edition, which tacitly acknowledges the problem of their placement.

Undoubtedly, helpful comments from readers, as well as time to reconsider her work, guided Catherine in her evaluation of the menus in the first edition and allowed her to revise the 1852 and 1854 versions quite heavily. The table on page 88 above summarizes the overall changes. One should note that, as of this writing, neither the first editions of the 1851 or 1852 publications are extant, nor are there known copies for the intervening years: 1853, 1855, 1857, 1858, and 1859. If her work was printed beyond 1860, no copies have been located to date.

For the 1852 editions, Catherine revises the bills of fare as she adds the seasonal time-frames for each, and rearranges the menus by seasons while occasionally substituting dishes. She also changes the title of the group of menus pertaining to banquets, raising the maximum number of diners from eighteen to twenty persons. However, the title page was never amended in any of the subsequent editions.

The single most important overall menu change is the reduction of toasted cheese. If Catherine was unaware that over a third of the 1851 menus ended with her husband's favourite dish, toasted cheese, she must have realized it soon after publication. By the following year, she replaces toasted cheese in twenty-four entries with several other dishes, including macaroni, sweet and savoury omelettes, cheese, fruit pudding, or prawns. She omits toasted cheese altogether in several other menus, and by the 1854 edition (and thence onwards), she eliminates or replaces fourteen more listings for toasted cheese.

The 1854 publication discloses other significant revisions, which were most likely inspired by the Dickenses' experience of living in France. They resided in both Paris and the seaside town of Boulogne. Catherine was clearly influenced by French traditions, particularly the culinary treasures of northern France that shared features with her Scottish heritage. Surrounded by extremely fertile agricultural land, Boulogne's cooking is rich in root vegetables. Stews, much like Scottish hotchpotch, are regional specialities – flavoured with juniper berries. Leeks, cabbages, and tender baby vegetables (known as 'hortillonnages') are abundant. There were rich fish preserves, particularly of herring, which was served fresh, salted, and lightly cured as the legendary regional speciality called *harengs saurs*. Experts, called 'maître saureru', mastered the secret preparation of brining the herring and smoking it over oak and beech. The Flemish wool trade, dating back to the Middle Ages, left its legacy on the food of Boulogne and Picardy. Meat, and plenty of it, dominated the cuisine. Lamb and mutton were particular favourites, with pork and pig's feet running a close second, so to speak. Beef *carbonnade*-style stews, with their heavy, somewhat sweet beers, added to Boulonnais cooking, as did the sweet Flemish tarts using the sugar produced from sugar beets raised in northern France. Champagne was the crowning touch to any meal.[45]

French recipes and food have a long history in British cookery books but, for the Dickens family, living in France made an indelible impression. Catherine adds distinctly French dishes to her 1854 edition. The new titles include *Blauquet* of Veal, *Vol au vent* of Sweetbreads with Cockscombs,

Stewed Tripe, Pig's Feet with Truffles, *à la brochette*, Roast Haunch of Mutton with Laver, Marooned Mutton, Beef *Croquits*, and *Fondue* (which was actually a cheese soufflé). She uses *ramiquins*, *timballes*, and adds more *gratin* dishes to her menus.

Not only did the preparation styles reflect French recipes, but Catherine adds more variety in the foodstuffs. Salmon trout, red mullet, and curried skate make their appearance, as did the larding of both roast pheasant and fillet of beef. Tendrons of Beef, Beef Sandars, Lamb's Feet with Parsley and Butter, Marrow Bones, Broiled Bones, and Kidneys Stewed in Madeira all are added to the menus and recipes in 1854 edition.

Catherine's saucing changes as well. This is not to suggest that she, or their cook, adopted French sauces and the extreme reductions that transform an amalgamation of ingredients into Parisian classics. Her sauces are British with bright, seasonal elements that complement the main dish. With less reliance on shrimp and oyster sauces as standards, she expands her use of flavouring components with capers, fennel, and celery for three new sauces.

Catherine adds a wealth of soups (as well as some recipes for them) to the 1854 edition, including Clear Soup with Poached Eggs, Lettuce Soup, Winter Soup, Potato Soup, Vermicelli Soup, Vegetable Soup, Jerusalem Artichoke Soup, Julienne Soup, Semolina Soups, and a lean Soup Maigre.

In addition, she gives aspic and jellies more prominence in the menus, and for the first time suggests a garnish of plovers' eggs. Condiments, such as lemon juice and cayenne for fried oysters, are not new to the Dickenses, but Catherine adds them for clarification in the 1854 menus. Potatoes are as ubiquitous as in the earlier menus. However, she cites them less often as 'mashed and brown' and simply writes 'mashed potatoes'. Dishes of turkey legs are dropped altogether and there is less boiled fowl mentioned. She concludes meals with more fashionable Continental savouries, such as radishes served with spring onions, 'hung beef' grated on buttered toast, and thin slices of German sausage garnished with a salad of young greens. Anchovies and sardines are now accompanied with chilli vinegar, which may denote a change in personal preferences, dining fashions, or both.

Not only does the 1854 edition profit from the family's residence in France, but Catherine is more willing to promote British dishes as well. Her new entries include Baked Irish Stew, Peas Pudding, Roast Duck with Peas, Small Mutton Pies, and Chicken Salad. She added a few desserts such as Queen's Pudding, Trifle Pudding, Brown Bread Pudding, and Strawberry Jam

Creams. For some of these new entries, she includes the recipes.

Although Catherine's Scottish heritage is subtle in the early editions, by 1854 she confidently adds regional recipes and dishes to her menus. It is surprising that she had taken so long to include these items; not only were they traditional, but they were well known beyond Scotland.[46] The Dickenses had visited Edinburgh early in their marriage, when a public dinner was given in Charles's honour. The opportunity allowed Catherine to visit her birthplace and Dickens to see the sites, taste the foods, and drink the beverages. In his letters to friends, he mentioned 'oatcake, mutton, hotch potch, trout from the loch, small beer bottled, marmalade, and whiskey,' and that they 'dinned on eggs and bacon.'[47] Hotch-potch and trout were not mentioned in Catherine's first two editions, but she adds these two 'comfort foods', along with cock-a-leekie, in 1854.

******

As well as bills of fare, Catherine provided recipes: 'The Appendix contains Receipts for some dishes, the preparation of which may not be generally understood', and 'Useful receipts for dishes referred to in the preceding bills of fare'. Why did she select these particular recipes? How often were the dishes used in her menus? Were they from family receipts or borrowed from published cookery books? If she borrowed recipes, did she record them verbatim or give them an individual spin? Unfortunately the library inventory from Devonshire Terrace does not include cookery books (unlike those of William Makepeace Thackeray and George Augustus Sala).[48] Dickens's letters offered some clues, as does comparison of the recipes with contemporary printed books. The sources of some have been identified, and one expects others will be in time.

Although there is a certain difficulty in identifying a dish in the bills of fare that may go under several names, it is clear that the recipes in the appendix appear infrequently as dishes in her bills of fare. Asparagus soup, one of the most popular, only shows up in nine of the menus and others, like Spanish salad dressing or Scotch broth, are not listed in any menus at all, in any of the editions. Likewise, the sauces that Catherine recommends in the recipes, such as pungent brown sauce with leg of mutton, or caper sauce with boiled mutton, are not given in the bills of fare either. Perhaps she did not subscribe to the combinations herself, but it is more likely that her menus involve much cultural shorthand. Food combinations, then and now, are so embedded that a reader subconsciously supplies the excluded items. Bread(s), butter, condiments, beverages, fresh or dried fruits and nuts may have completed the Dickenses' meals, but Catherine never mentions them. Even her contemporaries rarely provide that information, and often only in their general introductory remarks.

Altogether, Catherine's 1851 '2nd edition' contains an appendix with twenty-six recipes arranged in no apparent order. These are retained without changes for the 1852 editions onwards. They include: Maître d'Hôtel Butter, Maître d'Hôtel Sauce, Potato Balls, Horse-radish Sauce, Italian Cream, Scotch Broth, Mutton Broth, Leg of Mutton with Oysters, Boiled Cauliflower with Parmesan, Swiss Pudding, Asparagus Soup, Salmon Curry, Prince Albert's Pudding, Charlotte Russe, Mayonnaise [of Fowl], Scotch Minced Collop, Cod Rechauffé, Eve's Pudding, Hominy, Kalecannon, Lamb's Head and Mince, Rice Blancmange, Scotch Mutton Broth, Spanish Pudding, Rump Steak à la Soyer, and Spanish Salad Dressing.

With the major revisions for the 1854 edition, Catherine adds twenty-one recipes. These are retained for subsequent editions. A few of the new recipes cater to her Scottish heritage, and some of the others reflect her trips abroad. The additions include: Cock-a-Leekie, Hotch Potch, Orange Fritters, Another Way (to make orange fritters), Potatoe [sic] Soup, Vermicelli and Vegetable Soup, Kidneys à la Brochette, Fondue (Simple Method), Tendrons of Veal, Strawberry Curd and Jelly, Stone Cream, Baked Irish Stew, Marooned Mutton, Queen's Pudding, Beef Sandars, Soup Maigre, Rump Steak Breaded or Beef Cutlets, Macaroni with Bacon, Timballe of Macaroni with Chicken and Ham, and Palestine Soup. She ends with Coffee for Thirty People. If Catherine had organized the forty-seven recipes into categories, there would have been twelve meat dishes, twelve sweets, ten soup-stews, three vegetable preparations, two fish dishes, and seven miscellaneous.

Catherine made some editorial changes in the 1854 edition; Scotch mutton broth is renamed winter soup, which avoids confusion with two similar titles (Scotch broth and mutton broth). She also omits the introductory paragraph for Swiss pudding that was placed six pages before the actual recipe in the 1851 and 1852 editions. Swiss pudding is the first recipe that most directly reflects their experience living in a foreign country. The original recipe's introduction begins with the statement: 'In many parts of the continent, as well as throughout Switzerland, it is customary to…', and then she describes the process of creating the dish. The second part of the recipe (placed six pages later) provides more specific instructions for layering the boiled apples with bread crumbs, sugar, nutmeg, and butter before baking. Only the second section is retained after 1854. The updated appendix probably reflects helpful commentary she received from friends.

Evidence from Dickens's correspondence suggests that family and friends ate the dishes included in her recipe section. In a dinner invitation to Mark Lemon, Dickens declares, 'the baked Irish Stew-time next Monday, is 5'.[49] Was this a test-run for the recipe that found its way into her book that same year? The brief recipe for baked Irish stew is interesting in its own right. It reads more like a reminder of a familiar favourite than an actual set of instructions: 'An ordinary Irish stew, with a little gravy added, and baked until nicely browned; about half an hour.' Why was it necessary for Catherine to include it? The scant recipe seems absurdly simple but, in fact, it highlights a change in technology. In the additions to the 1854 recipe selection, Catherine inadvertently acknowledges an adaptation to the new kitchen ranges that offered experimental cooks more convenient baking ovens. These methods began replacing both stove-top cooking and browning methods that had required more of the cook's attention. True, the oven is recommended in Catherine's 1851 recipes, but she gives the alternatives, such as 'put them into the oven or before the fire to brown' when making potato balls, or her recipe entitled lamb's head and mince was made 'brown in a Dutch oven or with a salamander'. These methods no longer appear in the recipes she chose for the edition published only three years later. In addition, most of the new instructions include the length of the baking time needed.

The 1854 and later editions show other changes. The earlier (1851, 1852) recipes gave less exacting measurements, fewer techniques, and often omit baking temperatures or characteristics of the finished dish, but by 1854 that information is usually incorporated. Furthermore, she now chose recipes that rely on isinglass for moulded desserts like strawberry curd jelly and stone cream, unlike the original edition where Italian cream, for example, was not stabilized with any type of gelatin.

Catherine does not include one recipe for cake. Spanish pudding, a sweet bread enriched with butter and eggs that relies on yeast for leavening, is the closest she comes. Yeast-risen bread-cakes have centuries-long traditions and may reflect the tastes she developed in her childhood. Dried German yeast was available for cooks in the early 1850s, and provided a better alternative to the erratic quality of barm (beer yeast) purchased from breweries. The rich dough in the recipe Catherine offers is rolled with candied orange, finely chopped citron, cinnamon, and powdered sugar. Similar to a *savarin*, a sauce of clarified sugar flavoured with orange-flower water is poured over the bread to form a delicate glaze. Perhaps it was the citrus flavour that prompted the recipe's Mediterranean title.

Catherine's sweets rely on lemon, vanilla, and almond flavourings, orange-flower water, candied and fresh citrus, dried fruits, cinnamon, nutmeg, mace, sweet wines and liqueurs. Her choice of seasoning is typical of Victorian taste, but nutmeg may also reflect her own husband's penchant for the spice. Dickens is said to have carried around his own nutmeg grater – most likely for punch-making.[50] In a few recipes where the garnishes of capers, herbs, fruit, jelly, or flowers are suggested, one appreciates the aesthetic care Catherine must have expected in the presentation of the dishes.

The names of the recipes given in Catherine's appendices add an element of confusion when we try to tie them to other printed sources. Prince Albert's pudding for example, is usually a steamed pudding, but not in Catherine's version. The Prince Consort apparently preferred lighter puddings where suet was replaced with butter and ground rice for some of the flour. A version of Prince Albert's pudding is still popular today.[51] Catherine's interpretation is a luxuriously rich orange-flavoured custard pie baked with top and bottom pastry. The crusts made the pie easy to serve when cold, as the recipe notes. Eliza Acton's recipe with the same title begins in like fashion, but her filling is lightened with beaten egg whites, stabilized with flour, contains raisins, and is boiled rather than baked.[52] Catherine's may have been an old recipe given an updated name. It resembles Hannah Glasse's orange pudding, which was baked between puff-pastry.[53]

Although the exact sources of many of the recipes are not yet identified, there are certainly eleven which she copied almost verbatim from available literature and five others that are close interpretations.[54] To her credit, Catherine acknowledges two authors, Alexis Soyer and 'Meg Dods' (Christian Isobel Johnstone). She also borrowed recipes from at least two other cookbook writers, Eliza Acton and Sarah Hale, whom she did not cite.

The flamboyant chef Alexis Benoît Soyer (1809–58) had the most profound influence on Catherine's work, but that may also be true of his contribution to Victorian cuisine as a whole. In 1830, as an ambitious young man in his early twenties, Soyer left Paris and became the chef to the Duke of Cambridge. Seven years later, he presided over the Reform Club in London. His interest in improving British cooking generally, and his desire to help the poor specifically, culminated in a government request for him to oversee the famine-relief soup kitchens in Dublin in 1847. By 1851, Soyer had already written three successful cookery books and was currently involved in opening his London restaurant called The Symposium, which catered to visitors attending the Great Exhibition.[55]

Catherine openly acknowledges borrowing three of his recipes: cod rechauffé à la Soyer, salmon curry à la Soyer, and steak à la Soyer. Two other menu items (without recipes in her appendix) also use the appellation 'à la Soyer', suggesting she used his book *The Gastronomic Regenerator* for preparations of broccoli au gratin and loin of mutton rechauffé. In addition, she copied three other classic recipes from Soyer without specific acknowledgement: maître d'hôtel butter, sauce à la maître d'hôtel, and fondue. A popular accompaniment, maître d'hôtel butter flavoured meats, fish, and vegetables, and it is the base for the sauce à la maître d'hôtel. Catherine copied the sauce recipe nearly verbatim from Soyer, only replacing his white stock with white sauce, begging the question whether she or the compositor copied the recipe correctly. Three years later for the 1854 edition, Catherine returned to Soyer's work and pinched the recipe for fondue (simple method), which was actually a preparation for a cheese soufflé.[56]

Catherine also appears to have interpreted (rather than copied) Soyer's recipe for rump steak from the summary of cooking techniques that describe broiling. Soyer wrote the technique using the immodest voice of his alter ego 'Mrs. B' who says: 'I have latterly, in broiling rump-steaks, added that which, by a great many, is considered an improvement.' Catherine obviously felt the same way, but she deviates from Soyer's original recipe by using seasoned flour for dredging the steak, rather than the powdered biscuits and other seasonings such as shallot powder or mushroom powder with which he coats the cooked steak. When done, he places the steak on 'a very hot dish, with a little mushroom-ketchup, [and] a small piece of butter'.[57] Catherine chops shallots, which are sautéed in the pan juices with the addition of [mushroom] ketchup and a little butter, before the sauce is strained and served over the steak. Catherine's changes reflect practical adaptations for home cooks who relied on common pantry items rather than the expensive products available in a professional kitchen.

'Made-dishes' (essentially leftovers that repackaged yesterday's meal into today's repast) were praised by Soyer. He thought these entrées were 'dishes upon which, in the high class of cookery, the talent of the cook is displayed.'[58] Part of the skill was to create delicious, well-prepared food, the other was an equally valid quest for economy. As he put it, these dishes were clever creations made 'out of those parts which are rarely or never used in this country by the middle classes.'[59] Having emigrated from France, the contrast and wastefulness of English practices continually prompted him to target British attitudes. He hoped his suggestions, espoused in the enlightened letters of 'Mrs. B' to her formerly extravagant friend 'Mrs. L', would gently guide readers toward reducing the housekeeping expenses while serving more imaginative meals.

His view found an echo *chez* Dickens. Expensive cuts of meat were special fare reserved for special occasions. In Catherine's small menus, most likely family meals, she suggests more economical cuts, such as the shoulder, three times as often as she uses premium joints and roasts. In the 1851 and 1852 editions, she also includes turkey legs for these family meals. Like Soyer, Catherine combines the expensive cuts with made-dishes in fairly even ratios in meals designed for up to five diners, but for parties of six or more, she serves roasts and joints to save preparation time for the kitchen. Here her made-dishes fill out the menus and add more choice for the guests. For these company-dinners, the large saddle-cut that Soyer introduced was a favourite. In harmony with Soyer's sentiments, Catherine rarely serves joints or roasts as cold dishes thus avoiding 'the domestic crime' of offering inappropriate dishes to guests in the winter.[60]

Another author whose influence extended to Catherine's kitchen was Eliza Acton (1799–1859), from Tonbridge in Kent.[61] Miss Acton had probably never met them, judging from Dickens's rather formal letter of 11 July 1845:

Dear Madam

I beg to thank you cordially for your very satisfying and welcome note of the tenth of January last; and for the book that accompanied it. Believe me, I am far too sensible of the value of a communication so spontaneous and unaffected, to regard it with the least approach to indifference or neglect – I should have been proud to acknowledge it long since, but I have been abroad in Italy.

Dear Madam/ Faithfully Yours[62]

Presumably she had sent him a copy of her new publication, *Modern Cookery in All its Branches*, issued that January. Her book included regional Kentish recipes and a recipe attributed to Dickens's fictional character, which she entitled 'Ruth Pinch's beefsteak puddings, à la Dickens'. The 'cheerful, tidy, bustling, quiet little Ruth,' who kept house for her older brother Tom, in *Martin Chuzzelwit*, was a popular persona. Acton's recipe accommodates Dickens's version of the dish as he described it:

And when she [Ruth] asked him [Tom] what he would like to have for dinner, and faltered out 'chops' as a reasonably good suggestion after their last night's successful supper, Tom grew quite facetious and rallied her desperately.

'I don't know, Tom,' said his sister, blushing, 'I am not quite confident, but I think I could make a beef-steak pudding, if I tried Tom.'

'In the whole catalogue of cookery, there is nothing I should like so much as a beef-steak pudding!' cried Tom: slapping his leg to give the greater force to this reply.

'Yes, dear, that's excellent! But if it should happen not to come quite right the first time,' his sister faltered; 'if it should happen not to be a pudding exactly, but should turn out a stew, or soup, or something of that sort, you'll not be vexed, Tom, will you?'

The serious way in which she looked at Tom; the way in which Tom looked at her; and the way in which she gradually broke into a merry laugh at her own expense; would have enchanted you.

'Why,' said Tom, 'this is capital. It gives us a new, and quite an uncommon interest in the dinner. We put into a lottery for a beef-steak pudding, and it is impossible to say what we may get. We may make some wonderful discovery, perhaps, and produce such a dish as never was known before.'

'I shall not be at all surprised if we do, Tom,' returned his sister, still laughing merrily, 'or if it should prove to be such a dish as we shall not feel very anxious to produce again; but the meat must come out of the saucepan at last, somehow or other, you know. We can't cook it into nothing at all, that's a great comfort. So if you like to venture, I will.'

'I have not the least doubt,' rejoined Tom, 'that it will come out an excellent pudding; or at all events, I am sure that I shall think it so. There is naturally something so handy and brisk about you, Ruth that if you said you could make a bowl of faultless turtle soup, I should believe you.'

And Tom was right She was precisely that sort of person.[63]

After returning with a choice steak from the butcher, Ruth set out to make the beefsteak pudding without guidance of a recipe:

> First, she [Ruth] tripped down-stairs into the kitchen for the flour, then for the pie-
> board, then for the eggs, then for the butter, then for a jug of water, then the
> rolling-pin, then for a pudding-basin, then for the pepper, then for the salt: making
> a separate journey for everything, and laughing every time she started off afresh.
> When all the materials were collected, she was horrified to find she had no apron on,
> and so ran up-stairs, by way of variety, to fetch it…Such a busy little woman she was!
> So full of self-importance, and trying so hard not to smile, or seem uncertain about
> anything! It was a perfect treat to Tom to see her with her brows knit, and her rosy
> lips pursed up, kneading away at the crust, rolling it out, cutting it up into strips,
> lining the basin with it, shaving it off fine round the rim, chopping up the steak into
> small pieces, raining down pepper and salt upon them, packing them into the basin,
> pouring in cold water for gravy, and never venturing to steal a look in his direction,
> lest her gravity should be disturbed; until, at last, the basin being quite full and only
> wanting the top crust, she clapped her hands all over with paste and flour, at Tom,
> and burst out heartily into such a charming little laugh of triumph, that the pudding
> need have had no other seasoning to commend it to the taste of any reasonable man
> on earth.

As Ruth rolled out the top crust, John Westlock, whom she had not yet met but who would figure prominently in her life, walked into the apartment to talk to her brother concerning some business. When the men returned for dinner, Ruth already had set their humble table, but it 'wanted neither damask, silver, gold, nor china: no, nor any other garniture at all.' Ruth's 'first experiment of hers in cookery' was so successful they insisted 'she must have been studying the art in secret for a long time past and urged her to make a full confession of the fact.' Discussion of the pudding resumes later in the novel, but at the conclusion of this chapter, a cookery book with the page turned down for beefsteak pudding, was left anonymously as a present in the Pinches' parlour.

Dickens's use of butter and eggs to make the pastry crust, rather than suet and water, anticipated (or picked up on) the humour he unfolded six chapters later for his readers. John, smitten with Ruth, contrived to see her and invites the Pinches to an impromptu meal (albeit one which he had carefully arranged in his apartment beforehand). John refers to the ingredients in Ruth's pastry crust:

'If I had known a little sooner,' said John, 'I would have tried another pudding. Not in rivalry; but merely to exalt that famous one. I wouldn't on any account have had it made with suet.'

'Why not?' asked Tom.

'Because that cookery-book advises suet,' said John Westlock; 'and ours was made with flour and eggs.'

'Oh good gracious!' cried Tom, 'ours was made with flour and eggs, was it? Ha, ha, ha! A beefsteak pudding made with flour and eggs! Why anybody knows better than that. I know better than that! Ha, ha, ha!'

It is unnecessary to say that Tom had been present at the making of the pudding, and had been a devoted believer in it all through. But he was so delighted to have this joke against his busy little sister, and was tickled to that degree at having found her out, that he stopped in Temple Bar to laugh.[64]

Dickens's description in *Martin Chuzzelwit* was accurate enough for Eliza Acton to create a one-and-a-half-pint pie that both acknowledged Dickens's humour and provided a butter-egg pastry recipe in place of the standard.[65]

The overwhelming popularity of Acton is easy to understand, her work is thoughtful, well written, and comprehensive. The mayonnaise recipe Catherine uses gives directions for assembling a cold dish rather than instructions for making the emulsified dressing and should have been entitled mayonnaise of fowl, or mayonnaise of chicken, as they appear in her menus. The preparation was most likely borrowed from Acton's recipe entitled 'fowls à la mayonnaise'. Catherine's directions simplify Acton's arrangement of cold roast fowl, wedges of lettuce and hard-boiled eggs, and she adds capers and anchovies as extra garnish.[66]

For the expanded 1854 appendix, Catherine again turned to Acton for both Palestine soup (also called Jerusalem artichoke soup) and potato soup.[67] The directions were copied verbatim, only omitting the original list of ingredients. (The recipe title in Catherine's 1854 edition is misspelled as 'potatoe' but was subsequently corrected.) There are other recipes, for instance for potato balls, cauliflower, and kidneys à la brochette, with much affinity to Acton's own, although Catherine may have taken them from other works – if she did not write them herself – for they were widely popular.[68]

Catherine also borrowed recipes from an American cookbook writer whom they met while touring North America in 1842. Sarah Josepha Buell Hale (1788–1879) was a women's rights activist and the literary editor of

Ladies Magazine in Boston and later of *Godey's Lady's Book* in Philadelphia. She edited the American edition of Eliza Acton's *Modern Cookery*, and produced at least five of her own cookbooks and a book on etiquette.[69] Hale was among those who established Thanksgiving as a nationally recognized holiday, but she is probably best known for her verse 'Mary Had A Little Lamb'. To honour the Boz, she prepared a poem entitled 'The Welcome of Philadelphia to Charles Dickens', for which he thanked her, writing from the Fuller's Hotel in Washington, DC:

My Dear Madam,

I left Philadelphia so hurriedly, that I had not time to reply to your earnest and gratifying letter.

Believe me, that I did not read your beautiful lines unmoved; and that you could not have devised a mode of pleasing me more, than by the production of such a tribute. I scarcely know how to thank you for it. As I am in that condition, however, wherein we are apt to feel that we cannot say enough, but in which a very little may be very expressive, I will only add that I thank you with my whole heart.

On second thoughts though, I must couple with these latter words, one assurance, no less truthful and sincere. It is, that you will never find me departing from those sympathies which we cherish in common, and which have won me your esteem and approval.

Catherine unites with me in cordial regards and best wishes. And I am always. Dear Madam/ Faithfully/ Your friend[70]

It is likely that Hale later sent some of her books, including cookbooks, to the Dickenses. Catherine took three recipes from her publication *The Ladies New Book of Cookery: A Practical System for Private Families in Town and Country*. Catherine copied verbatim the recipes for leg of mutton with oysters, mutton broth, and a partial recipe for charlotte russe, a popular dessert. Oddly, the portion of the charlotte russe recipe that Catherine selected only included the directions for arranging the savoy biscuits and filling the mould with the crème au marasquin. She omitted the vanilla cream recipe that substituted the cherry liqueur for vanilla extract.[71] The complete recipe was never added in any of the subsequent editions.

Mutton broth is a misleading title since the recipe, in the manner of a *pot au feu*, creates a rich broth garnished with fresh parsley and thyme, as well as a second course of boiled mutton and mashed turnips, which was served with caper or parsley butter sauce. Catherine even repeated Hale's instructions for serving the broth to invalids – that is, 'persons in health'.

Sarah Hale's recipe for leg of mutton with oysters is by far the most intriguing. The unusual combination prompted the title for Sarah Freeman's book *Mutton and Oysters: The Victorians and Their Food*. Freeman highlights the recipe given by Catherine and provides an updated version.[72] The combination of oysters and mutton has a long history. Mutton stuffed with oysters may be an adaptation from mid-seventeenth-century recipes for mutton sausage enriched with plump oysters.[73] The tradition carried over with the popular eighteenth-century cookery book writers who provided several variations on that theme.[74] However, the recipes 'a shoulder of mutton stuff'd with oysters' in Charles Carter's *The Complete Practical Cook*, and 'to make a shoulder of mutton eat like venison' written six years later in *Receipts for Cookery and Pastry-Work* by the Scots cook, Mrs McLintock, come closest to Mrs Hale.[75] Catherine may have grown up with a preparation similar Mrs McLintock's in Scotland and added Hale's recipe to her appendix because it was more 'modern'. There is a certain irony in her selection of an American recipe, especially if Hale's was originally borrowed from a British source.

This dish does represent one of the few which we can link directly to Catherine's own dinner table. She served the stuffed mutton to family and friends. Charles particularly enjoyed it. A letter extends an invitation to Daniel Maclise:

> I have been writing all day, and mean to take a great, London, back-slums kind of walk tonight, seeking adventures in knight errant style. Will you come with me? And as a preparation, will you dine with us *at a quarter before 5*? – Leg of mutton stuffed with oysters.
>
> Reply 'Yes'.[76]

The combination runs full circle since it was also included in *Little Dorrit* where John Chivery, the son of the prison's turnkey, was invited to dinner by Mr Agent Rugg, the debt collector: 'The banquet was appointed for a Sunday, and Miss Rugg with her own hands stuffed a leg of mutton with oysters on the occasion, and sent it to the baker's.' Although their guest did not eat much, Miss Rugg 'took kindly to the mutton, and it rapidly diminished to the bone. A bread-and-butter pudding entirely disappeared, and a considerable amount of cheese and radishes vanished by the same means. Then came the dessert.'[77]

Judicious use of food may have reflected Catherine's Scottish training, but undoubtedly it humoured her husband's desire for household economy. Two recipes for made-dishes, Cod Rechauffé and Salmon Curry (already attributed to Soyer), among others such as Potato Balls, Marooned Mutton, Beef Sandars, Soup Maigre, and Timballe of Macaroni with Chicken and Ham, for example, followed the same principles of using leftovers. Likewise, Kalecannon was an artful assembly of chopped vegetables arranged in stripes and unmoulded from a melon-shaped tin.

Catherine's Scottish preferences are not evident until her revisions of 1854, although the first edition does include a Scotch broth that gives measurements first in Scotch pints and then in English quarts. In the recipe, Catherine succumbs to the use of pearl barley, which was readily available in London, rather than the preferred Scottish variety known as pot-barley. The Edinburgh author 'Meg Dods' states 'with her usual sagacity' that one capital defect of barley-broth cooked by 'Englishers and other unqualified persons, is produced nine times out of ten by the bad quality of the barley often used in England. Nor does *pearl-barley* give the same consistency as *pot-barley* [italics hers].'[78] 'Bere', that is barley to a Scot, is an invaluable grain used whole and milled for porridge, bread and baked goods or malted for beer and whisky making. If pot-barley held a place of honour in the Dickens household, it is not promoted in Catherine's book.

'Mistress Margaret Dods', the pen-name used by Christian Isobel Johnstone (1781–1857), was taken from the feisty cook in Sir Walter Scott's novel *St. Ronan's Well*. Scott based the character on Marian Ritchie, the brilliant cook at his local inn, The Cross Keys. According to Catherine Brown, Mrs Johnstone was a retiring person who had more success as the author of *The Cook and Housewife's Manual: A Practical System of Modern Domestic Cookery and Family Management* than with her novels. The Edinburgh cookery book was published in 1826 and went through numerous editions over the next century.[79] Johnstone preserved old Scots dishes and the traditional cuisine in succinct recipes with a passionate and authoritative commentary. It is possible that Catherine was given (or purchased) a copy before her marriage.

Catherine adds two well-known Scots recipes, hotchpotch and cock-a-leekie, to her 1854 edition. She acknowledges using 'Meg Dod's recipe' in the title for hotchpotch and makes only a few minor changes to the classic. The recipe, originally entitled 'Scotch hotch-potch' by Johnstone to distinguish it from 'winter hotch-potch', is modified by Catherine, who changes the spelling of 'peas' to 'pease', adds 'sprays of cauliflower' to the vegetables, and writes 'chops' rather than 'steaks' – although the terms were interchangeable.[80] Catherine also includes Johnstone's note under 'N.B.' with advice on keeping the parsley's colour.[81]

The source for cock-a-leekie has not yet been identified. The name for this thick soup of chicken and leeks came into use in the eighteenth century, but the preparation dates easily to medieval times when it was known to contain onions, prunes, and sometimes raisins. Cock-a-leekie may have been originally served as two dishes, chicken and a broth. By Catherine's time, the onions were retained, the raisins were lost, and the prunes remained controversial.[82] In her 1833 edition, Johnstone observed that 'Prunes used to be put to this soup. The practice is obsolete.'[83] Evidently Catherine did not agree with her countrywoman. The recipe she chose states in italics: '*If prunes be liked*, throw in a quarter pound half an hour before serving.' The recipe notes that some cooks thicken with fine oatmeal, but if the leeks boil down, they provide the richness and consistency desired.

Henry Dickens recalled a joke his mother often told of a Scotswoman's view of Eve and the Garden of Eden. The story began with the woman patiently listening to a discourse on the beauty of Paradise. In broad Scots, Catherine would retort: 'Eh mon, it would be nae temptation to me to gae rinning aboot a gairden stairk naked 'ating green apples.'[84] This story comes to mind when looking at Eve's Pudding in Catherine's recipes. A very common title on both sides of the Atlantic, the dessert combines apples, currents, citron, lemon peel, and nutmeg with breadcrumbs and suet for a hardy steamed pudding. Though stretching the point, one wonders if the title was part of the attraction since Catherine was known to have such a lively sense of humour.

Catherine may have written a number of recipes, particularly the shorter ones. The recipe for lamb's head and mince was probably Catherine's. Although the directions are scant, they are reminiscent of a traditional dish from her home town. In the eighteenth century, so-called sheep's-head clubs were fashionable in Edinburgh where the jellied head was prepared as it had been for centuries.[85]

North American foods had a strong attraction to both Charles and

Catherine. They each helped promote cornmeal in their own way. Catherine's recipe 'Hominy' says simply, 'Boil Indian corn in milk, add sugar or salt according to taste.' These are the shortest and most versatile set of instructions in the entire appendix, yet they represent one of the most historically significant entries in her publication. Although Catherine uses the term 'hominy', it is unlikely that she is referring to the regional speciality of the American south-west. Hominy, a Native American food made from dry corn kernels soaked in a lye solution to remove the seed coat, is boiled as a starchy vegetable called *pozole* in Latin cultures. Grits are made from boiling the roughly ground hominy. The Dickenses would have tasted them while visiting Fredericksburg and Richmond, Virginia. The Indian corn in her directions more likely refers to American cornmeal. The versatile cornmeal was, and still is, used as either a sweet porridge, as in New England Indian pudding, which the Dickenses would have tasted in Boston, or as a starch like polenta that they may have eaten in Italy.

In Britain, Indian corn (also called 'Indian-corn flour', 'Indian meal' or 'yellow meal') was imported in the late 1840s as a substitute for potatoes.[86] The British thought it was tasteless and dubbed the flour 'Peel's brimstone' after the government's initiative.[87] To counteract this aversion, wealthy, influential English liberals like Thomas Carlyle experimented with cornmeal recipes, but publicly declared the product unpalatable. Even Thomas Webster, who thought corn 'the noblest of the cereal grasses', stated that 'there are great differences of opinion as to its merits' in his 1847 edition of *The Encyclopædia of Domestic Economy*.[88] The negative reports prompted Dickens to published 'A New Plea For A New Food' in *Household Words*.[89] The article by Harriet Martineau discusses the advances made in milling corn flour (cornmeal) and suggests that for English taste, it may be best to replace half to two-thirds of the meal with 'wheaten flour'. One wonders if Catherine neglected to write a full recipe because her husband's magazine had already provided the information several months earlier to potentially the same readers. Martineau's version of 'American pudding' (New England Indian pudding) is:

Six table-spoonfuls of Indian-corn flour; one pint of milk scalded with an ounce of butter (or suet); stir in the milk and butter to the flour, and also two table-spoonfuls of molasses, and a very little salt; lemon-peel or citron is an improvement. Tie up in a basin, with a thick cloth, and boil four hours. If baked, it will take two hours. Eat with butter, molasses, or lemon. The flour should always be worked up with boiling water or milk.[90]

Martineau did not cite her sources, but it is likely that she was familiar with Eliza Leslie's booklet, *The Indian Meal Book*, published first in London around 1847. The Dickenses had met Miss Leslie in Philadelphia and occasionally saw her father in France.[91] Whether or not they exchanged publications cannot be determined, but the Dickenses would have known of her work.

'Common Cookery', another article in *Household Words*, gave 'stir-about' recipes using cornmeal: one sweetened with treacle (molasses) or sugar and butter, and a savoury porridge with red herring and herbs. Clearly cornmeal was a difficult sell for the English palate:

> These are modes of preparation in high repute in America; but here, although Indian meal is cheap and plentiful – and were there the demand, it would be more plentiful still – we doubt if the poorest person in the kingdom would touch them.[92]

Catherine gave but one recipe for a drink. Why she added 'Coffee for Thirty People' in the 1854 edition is unclear. The make-ahead preparation creates a concentrate that may have been reheated or diluted with hot water when served. Although odd by our standards, the logic is apparent. Since the lightest part of the grounds float as a suspension in the water, the addition of egg white would act like a particulate-filter – just as beaten whites clarify a broth for a consommé. Perhaps the Dickenses found that serving coffee to a house-full of dinner-guests required a foolproof preparation for the kitchen staff. As an article in *Household Words* implied, making good coffee was more than just an art form: 'A coffee-pot is not a coffee-pot now: it is a mechanical pneumatico-hydrostatic piece of apparatus. Let us not for one instant imagine that making a pot of coffee is a trifling affair, beneath the dignity of scientific cookery.'[93]

******

In the chapters which follow, I attempt to put *What Shall We Have For Dinner?* into the broader contexts of Victorian food supply and kitchen practice as well as relating it the narrower concerns of Catherine Dickens's own life and the circumstances of her household and marriage. So many factors may be brought to bear on what is, on the surface, an ephemeral and frivolous production. For example, there may have been some economic factors in the equation. On 19 April 1851, Dickens had written to Thomas Mitton, as his solicitor, to express financial concerns. The expenses covering Catherine's ill-health, the medical and burial costs for both his father and youngest daughter, and the 'great vexation' from his brother Frederick, were mounting. Dickens sublet their London house in Devonshire Terrace as soon as the family left for Broadstairs for the summer months. The older children were reaching their teens; Charley was fourteen, Mamie – thirteen, Katey – twelve, Walter – ten, Francis – seven, Alfred – six, Sydney – four, and little Henry was nearly three years-old. Money was tight. Dickens asked Mitton to recall a loan he had made.[94]

Dickens's balance with his publisher was skimpy, according to Robert Patten's assessment. There were no funds from two of the Christmas books, and no current book under way. The back-numbers of *David Copperfield* were the only consistent show of profits, but even a portion of those was put towards the reprinting of three other numbers. Dickens had been preoccupied with the renovations for their new home, Tavistock House, and had a psychological need to be settled in order to write. Money was quite literally going down the drain with the bathroom, kitchen and sanitation system upgrade for the new house. Modernization and redecoration left him with a balance of £6, deposited on October 1851. Dickens apparently had predicted as much.[95]

While one would hesitate to suggest that Catherine's work was undertaken specifically to bring in income, it is fair to assume that any profits from the two 1851 printings would certainly have been welcome. It may also explain why the work was issued again several months later in February 1852 as another revised edition. Dickens's first number of *Bleak House* was published on the 28 February of that year and the novel quickly became a resounding success. This relieved the financial pressures.[96]

Given the complexity of the Dickenses' lives in the 1850s, it is remarkable that Catherine managed to compile the menu book, let alone produce so many editions. She began the project when her husband was working feverishly as editor and co-owner of *Household Words*, finishing *David Copperfield* and preliminarily shaping *Bleak House*. In addition, social reform issues, the founding of the Guild of Literature and Art, and a theatrical production for Queen Victoria occupied Dickens's time and added social obligations for his wife. Catherine's first edition was published in the early part of 1851, and the second edition was produced in October while she was in her first term of pregnancy. She managed to completely revise the work for a new edition just a month before she gave birth to their tenth and last child.[97]

In 1854 she incorporated her experiences abroad in a revision of the menus and an expanded recipe appendix. She republished her book with minor changes for at least two more editions, even as her life entered the difficult period of marital breakup. This apparent stoicism in the face of adversity is belied by such recollections as her daughter Katey's, 'my poor mother was afraid of my father. She was never allowed to express an opinion – never allowed to say what she felt,' speaking more probably about the period before the separation. One of her mother's faults, she noted, was showing 'anxiety in regard to her husband's health,' and for her children's wellbeing. Like Lady Clutterbuck, Catherine was especially concerned if her punctual husband did not touch his meals when he was passionately engaged in his work.[98]

Little has been written about Catherine Dickens's preparation of the manuscripts, but her great-grandson Cedric Dickens has enshrined anecdotal evidence in a recreation of the event:

> In 1851 Dickens took his wife to the Great Exhibition in Hyde Park, and then visited the fashionable restaurant of M. Alexis Soyer, the famous ex-chef of the Reform Club, established at Gore House, formerly the residence of his friends Lady Blessington and Count d'Orsay. In contrast to the extremely frugal fare provided within [the Exhibition], where no cooking was permitted, the cuisine at this unique establishment was of a definitely elaborate order, and Mrs Dickens, encouraged by M. Soyer's example, decided to collect and print some of her own bills of fare and recipes.[99]

Using a copy of *What Shall We Have For Dinner?* Cedric Dickens added a few family recipes and his own favourites to make his own book. More recently, *The Times* reported the discovery of papers belonging to Mark Lemon's family which suggest that Dickens may have more fully participated in writing the book. A note, purportedly written by Betty Lemon, the young daughter of their friends, indicated that 'Charles and Catherine paid visits to the Lemon household and often helped to cook supper.' According to the article, sprats, tripe, and stewed oysters were the favourite dishes 'they cooked themselves in the kitchen,' apparently to the annoyance of the Lemon family's cook. Afterwards, 'the couple would retire to the study to jot down the recipes.'[100] This certainly presents a charming picture of the Dickenses as a working couple, and could well be accurate, but one should realize that Betty Lemon was only about nine years old at the time, and that these documents have not yet been opened for scholarly review.

Catherine Dickens, by her own daughter Katey's description, was a 'sweet, kind, peace-loving woman, a lady – a lady born.'[101] A woman who could tell an amusing story herself and always enjoyed a good joke. Surely she laughed heartily at her husband's colourful descriptions of places and people.[102] While the Dickenses' marriage was still settled, they must have both agreed that a wife should be a knowledgeable cook, that the kitchen run efficiently, and that healthy, well-prepared meals be served. When entertaining, they may have professed the same philosophy as one of Dickens's authors who advised:

> A good rule in giving dinners is never to have more guests or more dishes than you know how to manage. A roast saddle of Welsh mutton, two sorts of vegetables, and a tart, is a dinner for a prince; but then there should not be more than four princes or princesses to eat it. It is the best dinner a young housewife whose husband had five hundred pounds a year can, or ought, to put upon the table, and much better than any possible abominations contrived by the pastry-cook round the corner.[103]

In retrospect, using the pseudonym from the play *Used Up* was prophetic. Dickens's roles and the female roles of Lady Clutterbuck and Mary almost characterized his own life's drama during that period. The yearning references to the simple, contented life as Joe, the estate-owning ploughboy, were prevalent in Dickens's letters to cast members. Dickens alluded to other plays, novels and poems, but *Used Up* had a particular resonance for him, particularly in 1851, when he wrote the introduction to his wife's book. Repetition of lines about a blasé life poignantly acknowledged the quiet unhappiness smouldering in middle age, compared to the electrifying drama of a youthful performance. Yet Catherine was tolerant.[104] She had long acknowledged his genial persuasiveness or, as he described it to her, his 'winning manner which you know of.'[105] And when the marriage became rocky, particularly when Dickens's infatuation with a young actress steered it towards separation, his ability as 'supreme dramatizer of his own past, adept at organizing its incidents into a coherent plot' created a fiction that helped him view his wife as ill-fit and undesirable.[106] Until relatively recently, biographers unquestioningly followed Dickens's assertions.

CHAPTER II
CATHERINE THOMSON HOGARTH DICKENS

In the sixteen years of married life before Catherine Dickens's first menu book was published, she was pregnant twelve times and successfully delivered of ten healthy babies. Catherine has been ridiculed by historians and critics for hosting Dickens's table in this condition, but from her social engagements while pregnant, to her children's etiquette training at the adult table, Catherine played a vital role. Like her own mother, she became pregnant immediately after her wedding. Catherine's delicate health was often affected by both difficult births and postpartum depression. She may have begun her book, in part, as a constructive focus away from her ill-health and the traumatic events of 1851.

As a middle-class woman, Catherine juggled the management of servants, a large household which shifted seasonally, and a demanding social schedule. Although there are notes among her extant correspondence that declined invitations, she was active even late-term in her pregnancies.[1] Her husband joked, 'I suppose you have been eternally at the opera, and whirling in a round of dissipation – Paris, and my letters, are tame in comparison,' in a letter from France during her seventh month.[2] As a couple, they declined invitations that required more extensive travel when Catherine was nearly at full-term, but local engagements were accepted even in her ninth month. 'Mrs. Dickens is out,' he wrote to Angela Burdett Coutts, 'I can answer for myself, and I think for her, for tomorrow,' in accepting an invitation very near her due date.[3]

With each birth came the family celebrations.[4] As succeeding babies were christened, Dickens's amusing invitations to special friends became more light-hearted and irreligious. 'A babby [sic] is to be christened and a fatted calf killed on these premises on Tuesday the 25th. Instant,' he wrote in 1840 to John P. Harley, the Shakespearean comedian to whom he had dedicated *The Village Coquettes* years earlier. 'It (the calf; not the babby) is to be taken off the spit at 6. Can you come, and gladden the heart of the indignant,' signed 'Boz'.[5]

This is not to suggest that Dickens was pleased with the number of pregnancies – even though he loved his children. Angus Wilson suggested that Dickens was concerned about the financial pressure.[6] Over half of his married life was affected by nurses and increasing expenses for the growing family. Dickens's letters showed this weighed more and more heavily with each birth. 'I am happy to say that Mrs. Dickens and the seventh son – whom I cannot afford to receive with perfect cordiality, as on the whole I could have dispensed with him,' he disclosed to Miss Burdett Coutts, while adding that they 'are as well as possible, and in a most blooming state'.[7]

By the last christening, Catherine wrote to Sir Edward Bulwer Lytton, one of the godfathers, saying simply, 'We are to have no party, only a family dinner with your fellow sponsors after the christening.'[8] Catherine, who was nearly thirty-eight when the tenth child was born, may have also decided the family was large enough.[9]

The Dickenses' marriage ended badly. Although it was not publicly known until decades after Dickens's death, their separation was triggered by his desire for the young actress Ellen Ternan.[10] Ultimately Catherine and her husband agreed to live apart, and she took residence at 70 Gloucester Crescent in Camden Town (not far from Regent's Park) on 22 May 1858, three days after her forty-third birthday.[11] She was given a fairly generous annual household allowance of £600.[12] Charley, their eldest at twenty-one, lived with his mother. The other eight children, who ranged in ages from twenty to six years, were free to visit, but stayed with their father as was the custom.[13] Catherine's unmarried sister, Georgina Hogarth, remained loyal to Dickens and stayed with him to look after the children: which created a rift in the Hogarth family and added to the gossip. Even by today's standards, the media frenzy was massive.

The editor and writer John Forster, one of the Dickenses' close friends who acted on Dickens's behalf during the separation, was the first to write a comprehensive biography of Dickens after his death. Forster glossed over Catherine's role and generally began the disparaging dynamic that Dickens's apologists have repeated for well over a century and which unfortunately is still found today. Elizabeth Gitter suggests that being a family intimate and literary confidant, Forster positioned himself as the ultra-protective gate-keeper of Dickens's reputation, but as an experienced biographer and a loyal friend, he placed himself in an untenable position. He could either follow Dickens's lead by blaming Catherine for all the ails of the marriage and thus sacrifice his own credibility, or be more truthful and expose his friend's callous behaviour. Many people had known the Dickenses as a relatively content couple in a twenty-two-year marriage in which they raised nine children. They had even combined their own wedding anniversary celebration with Forster's birthday in a yearly dinner party. Since Catherine was still very much alive when Forster wrote her husband's biography, if he was critical of her or made false assertions about the marriage, her son Charley certainly would have defended his mother publicly.[14]

Gitter believes Forster must have felt his only option was to squeeze Catherine Dickens's part in the marriage into 'parenthetical phrases' in which he 'almost entirely effaces' her. Once Forster established his authoritative position as biographer, he was 'able to impose himself between Dickens and the messy historical realities that might spoil the nobility of Dickens' life story.'[15] In the intervening decades, scholars have scrutinized Dickens's work and personal life with publications that represent every major philosophic movement in literary criticism. Loyalists pounced on any evidence that would make Catherine Dickens appear as an albatross around the genius's neck, and from whom he finally had to free himself. She has been faulted for being an incompetent homemaker, a lacklustre companion, and a poor mother by many, including Dickens himself.

Except for demeaning remarks, Catherine Dickens, her work and her activities, have generally been neglected by historians. Judgements like, 'A fondness for some of her [Catherine's] own recipes alone would account for the monstrous alteration in her appearance by the end of the Devonshire Terrace period,' are typical. This comment, by Margaret Lane about the recipe for Italian Cream in the appendix of Catherine's publication, misses several points.[16] For one, Catherine's size was comparable to middle-aged, middle-class Victorian women but, more to the point, Lane fails to appreciate what the recipe could disclose. Italian Cream was such a well-known Victorian dessert that Dickens had once described his legs after an operation as 'two pillars of jelly, or tremulous Italian cream'.[17]

When one compares Catherine's directions to those of Mrs Beeton, whom Lane beatified, or for that matter to other contemporary recipes on either side of the Atlantic, the differences in culinary techniques are evident. Cookery book authors relied on gelatine (isinglass) to stabilize the cream, but the unusual recipe Catherine chose used lemon juice as a curdling agent to produce a thick soft cheese. Was this an adaptation learned by Jane, their cook, during the Dickenses' 1844–45 residence in Italy? And since the kitchen inventory of their Devonshire Terrace home listed a cheese pan and cover, did this indicate that the Dickens family enjoyed Italian Cream often?[18] If Catherine's menus are any indication, the dessert, colourfully garnished with fruit, jelly, or seasonal flowers from their garden, was usually reserved for large dinner parties, sharing a place with both shimmering architectural jellies and stodgy old-fashioned standards.

Another fallacy concerning her alleged incompetence is that her younger sister Georgina (Georgy) Hogarth was the glue holding the Dickens household together. Aunty Georgy's role before the separation appears to have been inflated. Judging by Dickens's own letters, Georgy added generally to the service of the family, performed some household tasks, and to a limited extent helped with the children's education. Even in letters written just before the split, Georgy does not appear to supplant her sister as has been so often implied by Dickens scholars. In fact, there are times when Dickens explains why he asked his sister-in-law, rather than his wife, to do something.[19] Being less soft-hearted, Georgy often dealt with the disagreeable people like their Paris landlord.[20] Catherine, on the other hand, often represented the graciousness of the household, courteously receiving visitors in their homes or while they travelled.[21] Even late in their marriage, Catherine acted as emissary when a special touch was required for her husband's projects.[22]

Historians have been slow in acknowledging Catherine's role.[23] In 1983, Michael Slater recognized that, unlike most Victorian husbands, Dickens felt 'his wife should share very fully in his literary career and the social life connected with it whilst he himself shared very fully in the organization of their domestic life – the two spheres "work" and "home" were not to be sexually segregated.' Slater effectively argues that, as Dickens's pretty fiancée, Catherine was talented, 'game' for adventures, had a sense of humour, and possessed 'everything that the age demanded a young lady should be – gentle and amiable in manner, possessed of some proficiency in music and in French.' As they grew into their marriage, she held Dickens's confidence, discussed his work, and very capably oversaw the housekeeping and social duties.[24]

Lillian Nayder's publications and forthcoming biography of Catherine Dickens will provide a comprehensive study of her life, not simply as Dickens's wife and cast-off, but as a middle-class Victorian woman facing the dynamics of her situation. As Nayder points out and Dickens's voluminous correspondence reveals, through the majority of the marriage, Catherine played a significant role.[25] Dickens often peppered his letters to his wife with humorous observations which spoke to their shared histories and sensibilities. Even in letters to other family members, Dickens sent tantalizing messages for his wife: 'Tell Catherine that I have the most prodigious, overwhelming, crushing, astounding, blinding, deafening, pulverizing, scarifying secret of which Forster is the hero, imaginable by the united efforts of the whole British population.'[26] At the risk of labouring this point, it is important to acknowledge the strength of the Dickens marriage before 1857/8 and Charles's reliance on Catherine as a valued partner.

Of the thousands of extant or published letters written by Charles and Catherine Dickens, their friends, associates and acquaintances, some provide candid commentary on the Dickenses' social activities while others offer historical context for this culinary study. Take, for example, the delicate situation concerning the French actress Pauline Denain, a respected member of the Comédie-Française, for whom the Dickenses gave a dinner party while the company was in London performing at the St James's Theatre. Soon afterwards, Dickens relayed his discovery to his wife:

> I have been a good deal vexed by something [John] Poole has told me about Madlle Denain. It seems that she made a small faux pas, some indefinite time ago, and had a child. Poole did not think it necessary to mention this to [Samuel] Rogers, thinking that only [John] Hardwick and I were going to dine there; and he says he was amazed to see you – and then was afraid to say anything. At this point of the story I stopped him, and said it was no matter. I had said at the time that virgins were not usually to be found in French Theatres; that it was no business of ours after Rogers had presented her; and that we knew nothing and wanted to know nothing. But then it came out that she is now Lord Normanby's mistress (Poole is monstrously chivalrous and absurd concerning Lord Normanby) and that this is very well known in Paris. Now I cannot remember what ladies dined with us that day, but I am satisfied you ought to call upon them, and, without making too much of it, just say 'that her history is not quite correct, you find, and that Rogers was mistaken in presenting her, but you never mean to tell him so – though you feel you owe this explanation to them, whom you asked to meet her.' *This you must do at once.* Of course I said nothing to Poole, in our relative situations, and would on no account make it known to Rogers – who is so revengeful, that I think if he did know it, he would instantly bowl Poole out of any chance of a pension. And we must not do anything to starve *him*, whatever we do.[27]

One may assume that they extricated themselves cleanly from what would have been a sticky social situation. Fortunately, other letters Dickens wrote to his wife recorded information about food. While in Manchester, for example, he glowed over the Bradburys' dinner: 'The young B's did not dine. We had a dinner, without pretension, but the very best cooked dinner I ever sat down to in my life.'[28] One assumes he could make this claim without wounding his wife's feelings. Other letters mention meals, often with his characteristic humour. 'We have had for breakfast,' he reported from Yorkshire for example, 'toast, cakes, a yorkshire pie, a piece of beef about the size and much the shape of my portmanteau, tea, coffee, ham and eggs.'[29]

******

Eight Hart Street in Edinburgh, was a flurry of activity on 19 May 1815, when the first child, Catherine Thomson Hogarth, was delivered.[30] Catherine, called Kate by her family, was the eldest of ten children and as a young woman, she shouldered more than her share of responsibility. Her mother, Georgina Thomson Hogarth (1783–1870), 'was an excitable, not to say somewhat hysterical lady,' Michael Slater suggests; Kate may have had 'to help her gentle father cope' with crises as they presented themselves in the household.[31]

Catherine's father, George Hogarth (1793–1863), remembered as a 'personally cultivated, genial, and attractive' gentleman, studied law in Edinburgh, and practised there as a Writer to the Signet from 1810 to 1830. He was the eldest son of Robert Hogarth, a prosperous Berwickshire farmer. George was interested in the arts, and through his sister's marriage to James Ballantyne, he became a friend and confidant of Sir Walter Scott. With Scott and Ballantyne, he jointly purchased the *Edinburgh Weekly Journal* when Kate was two years old. However, he continued his law practice until 1830, when financial difficulties forced him to turn to journalism for his livelihood. The family moved several times as he accepted different editorial positions, first in London, and then Exeter in 1831. They returned to London in the summer of 1834, where he joined the staff of the liberal newspaper the *Morning Chronicle*. He soon became a music critic for the *Morning Chronicle* and the *Illustrated London News*, and also published his own songs. By January of 1835, he had been appointed co-editor of the *Evening Chronicle* that was created by the owners of the *Morning Chronicle* as a new publication issued three times a week.[32] Among George Hogarth's own credits are a substantial series of articles and several major books on music, including *Memoirs of the Musical Drama* (1838), *Musical History, Biography, and Criticism* (1845), *Memoirs of the Opera in Italy, Germany, and England,* a new edition of *Musical Drama* (1851), and *The Philharmonic Society of London, from its Foundation, 1813, to its Fiftieth Year, 1862* (1862).[33]

Charles Dickens, who had already published several short stories, including 'The Bill of Fare' and 'A Dinner at Poplar Walk', left the *True Sun* as a parliamentary reporter and joined the *Morning Chronicle* in August of 1834, around the same time as George Hogarth. Soon afterwards, Dickens's 'Street Sketches' were published in the *Morning Chronicle* and Hogarth favourably reviewed the work.[34] Catherine's father was enthusiastic about the young man's writing, and invited Dickens to contribute work to his newspaper.[35] From January 31 to August 20, 1835, the *Evening Chronicle* featured twenty articles by Dickens entitled 'Sketches of London'.[36]

Hogarth invited the youthful author to his home at 18 York Place, Fulham, situated among a 'row of substantial houses' with colourful front yards that faced 'orchards and gardens extending as far as the eye could reach'.[37] Dickens met the pretty nineteen-year-old, 'plump and fresh-coloured' Kate. Her 'large, heavy-lidded blue eyes so much admired by men,' according to one woman, were so 'slow-moving' that they gave Catherine something of a 'sleepy look'. Her nose was 'slightly *retroussé*…mouth small, round and red-lipped, with a genial smiling expression of countenance.'[38] Judging from the descriptions, she was open-minded, fun-loving, and active. Like her father, she enjoyed music.[39] Charles also met Catherine's two sisters who would figure prominently in their lives, fourteen-year-old Mary and six-year-old Georgina.[40]

To Dickens, a twenty-three-year-old bachelor, the Hogarths may have represented the well-connected, loving, and unpretentious middle-class family he had always wanted.[41] Yet, parents of the day guarded their daughters' social position and respectability. Accordingly, young women had less access and more constraints to a life outside the home than did their brothers. The Hogarths' interest in the arts, however, allowed their daughters to attend theatrical performances, concerts, and other social activities. In an 1835 letter to her cousin, young Kate briefly described Charles's birthday celebration: 'Papa – Mamma and I were at a Ball on Saturday last and where do you think at Mr. Dicken's [sic].' Although his sisters and other family members were in attendance, she referred to it as 'a bachelors party at his own chambers…it was a delightful party I enjoyed it very much – Mr. Dickens improves very much on acquaintance he is very gentlemanly and pleasant.'[42]

In what may seem like a whirlwind courtship to us today, but typical of the time, Catherine and Charles were engaged a few months later in May of 1835. He gave her a lovely gold ring mounted with seven turquoise stones as a symbol of his intentions, just as Dickens, the novelist, later described David Copperfield's presentation of a similar band to his fiancée Dora. To mark the engagement, Charles had a miniature of his likeness painted on ivory by Rose Emma Drummond as a present for Catherine.[43]

Life, however, was not always bliss. His oldest extant letter to Catherine contained a sweet and sour portent of their married life: he was detained by work, expressed concern about her health, and asked her to give him credit and time 'to prove the sincerity and devotion of his affection'.[44] Catherine and her family obviously had faith in the relationship. By June, Charles had already moved to 11 Selwood Terrace (now Old Church Street, Chelsea), only 200 yards from the Hogarth household.[45] Catherine's mother or her sister Mary would escort her to breakfast with Dickens when he was not spending time at their house. 'I don't live there,' he wrote to Catherine's cousin, 'but somehow or other can be found there at any time without difficulty.'[46]

From Charles's letters to Catherine, one realizes that as a young woman, she knew her way around the kitchen. His June 1835 note, written on Saturday morning at 6 a.m., exemplifies his appeals:

> It's a childish wish my dear love; but I am anxious to hear and see you the moment I wake – Will you indulge me by making breakfast for me this Morning? It will give me pleasure; I hope will give you no trouble; and I am sure will be excellent practice for you against Christmas next. I shall expect you my dearest, and feel quite sure you will not disappoint me.[47]

Judging from the correspondence, she must have prepared breakfast for him routinely. In another note, written at 5 a.m., he wished 'to be awakened' in the morning by her tapping at his door. 'I look forward on making my appearance in the sitting room, to find you heading my breakfast table – you might without difficulty head a more splendid one my dear girl, through life,' he predicted.[48] Undoubtedly, chaperoned by a family member, Catherine whipped up hearty breakfasts for the sleepy reporter, who stumbled into mid-morning after his late-night chase to cover a story.

In time, nightlife entered their courtship.[49] Catherine's interest in music and theatre paralleled those of her fiancé. Dickens sought tickets for Covent Garden and Drury Lane. 'My Dearest Love', 'Dearest Wig', 'Dearest Pig', 'Dearest Mouse', as he affectionately addressed her, 'consult your Mama, dear, about the possibility of there being any fear of your being out after dark.'[50] Mrs Hogarth may have been less concerned about propriety than Catherine's health. Her daughter was just recovering from scarlet fever.

In preparation for married life, Dickens searched for a house, but he could find nothing affordable. Regardless, he was determined to marry.[51] In December of 1835, he signed a lease for a modest third-floor apartment at 15 Furnival's Inn that had been advertised as 'three-pair front, south, at £50 a year for three years certain.' It had two critical advantages – the landlord allowed children and a basement kitchen was included.[52] 'I am very glad to hear your Mama is pleased with the Report of the kitchen.'[53] Succeeding letters in early 1836 update his progress in transforming the Spartan suite into their future home. Eager to please his beloved, Dickens even wrote to her grandfather in Scotland, and asked him to send a special hot-water kettle:

> Catherine is very anxious to have for her Establishment, a little-Toddy-water kettle, I suppose it should be called, like the one they have in York Place [her parents' home]. Now such things can be got in London with great ease, but it appears that it *must* be bought from Scotland, or it's of no value. – Will you do me the favour to put one of these desirable kettles in your Portmanteau, and 'charge the same to my account'?[54]

As his former bachelor apartment filled with various furnishings in anticipation of a comfortable married life, Dickens invited the Hogarth women for a gleeful inspection:

> As your Mama has not seen the sideboard, and as there are a great number of new purchases which even *you* have not seen (!) I think the best way will be, for you, and she, and Mary, to spend the day here, on Saturday. I will ask your Mother to tea…I have bought today, a pair of quart Decanters, and a pair of pints, a chrystal [sic] Jug, & three brown dittos with plated tops, for beer and hot water, a pair of Lustres, and two *magnificent* china Jars – all, I flatter myself, slight bargains.[55]

Finally, after a ten-month engagement, Catherine Hogarth and Charles Dickens were married on 2 April 1836. The 'bright, pleasant bride', as Catherine was described by Dickens's brother-in-law, Henry Burnett, was neatly dressed. The brief ceremony took place at St. Luke's Church in Chelsea conducted by the curate, W. Morice.[56] Presumably Catherine's sister, Mary Hogarth, served as her maid-of-honour. Thomas Beard acted as best man.[57] Beard came from an old Sussex family of brewers. When his family moved to London around 1832, Thomas Beard joined the *Morning Herald* as a reporter, where he probably met Dickens's father who was also on the staff. In August 1834, Beard transferred to the *Morning Chronicle* and recommended Dickens for a position.[58] As reporters, Dickens and Beard covered many politically steamy stories together and remained close friends throughout their lives.

Among the wedding guests were Mr and Mrs John Macrone. Like Hogarth, Macrone came to London from Scotland in the early 1830s. He had jointly published the *Monthly Magazine*, where Dickens's *Sketches* appeared, but in September 1834 he went into business alone. He was introduced to Charles Dickens by W. Harrison Ainsworth, whose novel *Rookwood* he had just published.[59] Originally Macrone was invited to be the second best man, but 'the unanimous voice of the ladies, confirms the authority of Mrs. Macrone,' Dickens informed him. 'They say, with her, that I *must* be attended to the place of execution, by a single man,' and his publisher was released from the duty.[60] Macrone's wedding gift, inscribed to 'Mrs. Charles Dickens, with sincere good wishes of her Friend, the Publisher. April 1836,' was a six-volume set of Milton's *Poetical Works* that he had published.[61] The wedding breakfast took place at the Hogarths' home. Years later, Thomas Beard referred to the wedding as 'altogether a very quiet piece of business'.[62]

For his bride's wedding present, Charles gave Catherine an ivory-fitted workbox with the inscription 'From Chas. Dickens to Kate, April 2nd, 1836.'[63] The gift acknowledged her talents in the domestic arts, which she certainly put to good use through the years. Among her accomplishments were beautiful point-lace pieces and the needlework covers in Berlin wool that she made for their dining-room chairs.[64]

The newlyweds spent a few weeks honeymooning quietly in a cosy little cottage they rented in the village of Chalk. A modest parlour-bedroom served as Dickens's study where he wrote several early chapters of *The*

Pickwick Papers. A bronze portrait plaque of Dickens identifies Craddock Cottage. However, Dickensian topographers have since determined that the couple stayed in another cottage that has since been demolished.[65]

After the honeymooners returned and were settled, her sister Mary spent a month visiting. Writing to their cousin, she reported that the young Mrs Dickens 'makes a most capital housekeeper and is as happy as the day is long – I think they are more devoted than ever since their Marriage if that be possible.' Mary regarded her brother-in-law as 'a nice creature and so clever he is courted and made up to by all the literary Gentleman, and has more to do in that way than he can well manage.' She described the Furnival's Inn apartment as 'a suite of rooms opening from one to another' that were furnished 'most tastefully and elegantly, the drawing-room with Rose-wood the dining-room with Mahogany furniture.' Catherine and Charles had kept his bachelor quarters as a 'prudent way of beginning by staying out the expiration of his time' on the lease.[66]

Just as they had in courtship, the newlyweds continued to attend the opera, concerts, theatre productions and dine with friends. By the first month of marriage, Catherine was pregnant. It is difficult not to interpret Dickens's cancellations of their engagements as evidence of her pregnancy.[67] However, she aptly assumes her roles as wife, home-maker, and hostess. Dickens even bragged to her grandfather about their first dinner party:

> Catherine is extremely well, and has got up a most admirable stock of good looks.
> She has not yet quite recovered the high and mighty satisfaction she derived from a
> supper of her own invention and arrangement which we gave to our first little party
> a week ago, but with this exception she is quite herself.[68]

Dickens had collaborated with the composer John Pyke Hullah on *The Village Coquettes*, a sentimental comic opera set in Georgian England. Hullah, the Macrones, and a few other friends were invited for the celebration. Catherine oversaw the five o'clock dinner, which was followed by a seven o'clock reading of the libretto. These evenings may have resembled those she had known growing up. Her father took a prominent part in the cultural activities of the small towns where they lived. In Halifax, George Hogarth was one of the founders of the Halifax Orchestral Society, and had often arranged for musical performances in their home.[69] Thus began the pattern for the Dickenses' social engagements, his fertile literary activities provided occasions to entertain, and the frequently pregnant Mrs Dickens oversaw their memorable dinner parties.

George Hogarth had introduced Dickens to the proprietor of the St James's Theatre where the operetta was produced.[70] *The Village Coquettes* met with some success, but *The Pickwick Papers*, published not more than four months after their wedding, dramatically and permanently changed the Dickenses' financial and social position.[71] Charles left the *Morning Chronicle* to take the editorship of *Bentley's Miscellany* in November 1836, while he continued to write monthly instalments of *Oliver Twist*.[72] By the end of 1837, Dickens's work had acquired an international reputation. Consequently, his relatively sheltered twenty-two-year-old wife faced the challenges of being married to a public figure. The psychological complexity of accommodating Dickens's strong personality, and the steadily increasing expectations of the general public, would have been challenging for anyone. Having been catapulted into the demanding position of wife of one of Western literature's most popular writers, Catherine adjusted admirably, to judge from her husband's letters.

Their housing situation, however, soon required change. The three-room apartment quickly become too small for the baby, Charles's work, and their social obligations. They did not serve out the three-year lease. In March of 1837, with their two-month-old, they moved into temporary lodgings at 30 Upper Norton Street. A month later, they occupied the spacious and elegant townhouse at 48 Doughty Street, where they remained for two and a half years.[73] Their home has been preserved as the Charles Dickens Museum, the house meticulously restored as closely as possible to its appearance when the family lived there.[74] According to its guidebook, the still-room next to the kitchen 'was also evidently the room from which the housekeeping was directed. Possibly fitted in the late 1830s at Dickens's orders, the handsome fireplace suggests the mistress of the household spent time here.'[75]

Dickens at Doughty Street, John Greaves's publication, provides the most comprehensive account of this period. Although Greaves included a chapter on dining, one regrets his perpetuation of the disparaging myth about Catherine's culinary skills: 'It seems rather doubtful whether she had brought her catering up to that standard at Doughty Street. According to letters written by Dickens they appear to have lived mostly on chops!'[76] Greaves's remarks were based on a partial menu from the 1852 edition of *What Shall We Have For Dinner?* Had he looked carefully at Dickens's letters, he would have realized that the invitations for eating chops were often 'bachelor meals' (when Catherine was out) before the men worked together later in the evening.[77] These casual meetings, often with close friends such as William Macready, Daniel Maclise, and John Forster, offered the informality and comfort to 'dine in a blouse'.[78] In other cases, chops were quick meals before an early theatre or other outing. In fact, Catherine only offered chops in eight out of 174 menus printed in her menu book.

The young couple did not take long to turn the Doughty Street house into a hospitable setting for social gatherings. As soon as they had moved into their new home and had unpacked, they invited Thomas Beard and another parliamentary reporter for dinner.[79] Later in the month the prominent publisher Richard Bentley, who owned *Bentley's Miscellany*, the periodical that Dickens edited, dined with the family.[80] The party included one of Dickens's sisters, Catherine's sisters and her father (who had introduced Dickens to Bentley). As 'the only stranger', Bentley recorded his impressions of the festive April 29th dinner party twenty years later – because of Mary Hogarth, whom he referred to as Hebe, the goddess of youth and spring.

> It was a right merry entertainment; Dickens was in force, and on joining the ladies in the drawing-room, Dickens sang two or three songs, one the patter song, 'The Dog's Meat Man', and gave several successful imitations of the most distinguished actors of the day. Towards midnight, it was Saturday, I rose to leave, but D[ickens] stopped and pressed me to take another glass of Brandy and water. This I w[oul]d gladly have avoided, but he begged Miss Hogarth to give it me. At the hand of the fair Hebe I did not decline it.[81]

After a lively week of theatre and other activities, eighteen-year-old Mary Hogarth died suddenly on 7 May 1837, of an asymptotic heart condition. By all accounts, she was a vivacious, beautiful and frequent addition to her sister's household. 'Our constant companion since our marriage,' Dickens exaggerated.[82] The family was devastated.[83] Mrs Hogarth collapsed and remained in the Dickenses' home 'in a state of insensibility'.[84] With each letter notifying family, friends, and colleagues, Dickens's description of Mary's virtues grew. To Beard he wrote, 'I solemnly believe that so perfect a creature never breathed. I knew her inmost heart, and her real worth and value. She had not a fault.' He confessed, 'Thank God she died in my arms, and the very last words she whispered were of me.' While acknowledging

Catherine's close relationship to her sister, and the strength she mustered to deal with both Mary's death and Mrs Hogarth's alarming health, Dickens neglected to mention that his own wife suffered a miscarriage as a result of the shock.[85] In her own letter later that month, Catherine briefly recounted the events to her cousin. (The emphases are hers.)

> On the Saturday following, she was out with us to see some friends. I never saw her look so lovely and the *next* morning she was dead! You may imagine the *awful* shock, but never shall I forget that dreadful night. We were with her all night, and dear Mama whom we sent for. We almost feared for *her* reason but she is now more resigned. I have not seen her for nearly ten days as I have had a miscarriage and have been obliged to keep very quiet.[86]

Charles, Catherine, and perhaps other family members retreated to a peaceful cottage at Collins's Farm, on the western edge of Hampstead Heath for several weeks to recover after Mary's funeral.[87] Dickens's grief remained with him throughout his life. Mary Hogarth is said to have inspired the angelic child character of Little Nell in *The Old Curiosity Shop*. Charles wished to be buried in the grave next to Mary, but the untimely death of her younger brother, required that George Hogarth be laid to rest there instead. Dickens wore Mary's ring on his finger throughout his life.[88] Little is known about the management of Catherine's grief, although she did have a traditional keepsake bracelet fashioned from Mary's hair.[89]

******

Nearly three years into the marriage and with an adventurous two-year old, two babies in diapers, a wet nurse and other servants, the Dickenses found their once spacious home in Doughty Street cramped. On the 1 December 1839, they took over the remaining lease on 1 Devonshire Terrace, Regent's Park and it remained their principal residence until 1851.[90] Marked only by a plaque today, the handsome brick mansion was located opposite York Gate on Marylebone Road with the entrance around the corner on Marylebone High Street. A drama critic who visited the family commented on the dreariness of the street and frontages that resembled 'a badly whitewashed sepulchre,' although he thought the Dickenses' home 'the most respectable.'[91]

Their stately front door opened into a spacious square hall with a staircase.

Mahogany doors led into the ground-floor library, dining-room, and a breakfast-room (which was later converted into a bedroom, and served as the sitting-room).[92] The library, 'an oval room, simply furnished', occupied the back of the house and contained 'splendid bookcases, filled with fine books, beautifully bound'. The outer glass door of the library opened onto a balcony and an iron staircase that wound down to the garden.[93]

The drawing-room, two bedrooms, and a water closet were located on the first floor. The 'best bedroom, which Charles and Catherine occupied', was situated at the front of the house and had a large side window overlooking the garden. The children's day and night nurseries, and the female servants' bedroom were on the second floor, and a male servant's room was in the attic. The large kitchen, butler's pantry, still-room and cellars located in the basement were collectively known as 'below stairs'.[94]

As usual, the Dickenses refurbished the house before taking residence. The water closet was installed by Mr Chapman, 'a genius in houses'. Mr Snoxell, the decorator from Chancery Lane, was summoned to measure the dining-room windows for white spring-roller-blinds under the drapery.[95] Judging from the counterfoils in Dickens's cheque book, they purchased new dining-room chairs from Mr Ayling, other furniture from Mr Price, and two decorative China jars from Unsworth's china shop.[96]

The dining-room took shape splendidly. Underfoot was a lush Turkish carpet and rug resting on a large oilcloth painted to imitate oak flooring fitting the expanse of the room. Crimson-coloured damask curtains hung in a sweep with fringe and trimmings accenting the recess under the gilded cornices of the three windows. The room was well lit with a gilded bracket and candelabra, a three-burner lamp, and a pedestal table-lamp. The handsomely carved mahogany sideboard was fitted with a mirror in the recess. Their mahogany table stood proudly. The table's five leaves, which accommodated their large, uproarious dinner parties, were tucked neatly away, as was the hand-painted cover that protected the surface when the house was closed. Twelve comfortable mahogany chairs with green leather seats stood like well-polished sentinels around the table. A cane armchair, an easy chair, and an iron rocking chair all found their place. The rosewood teapoy, an ornamental table with three legs, awaited equipment for serving the hot brew. A pair of footstools was carefully placed by the steel fender, irons, and screen near the fireplace. The three-shelved French-polished mahogany whatnot probably displayed sentimental family objects. On the walls hung ten pictures in gilt frames, but Daniel Maclise's 'Girl at a Waterfall' was the only work set off by a lamp with a fitted shade.[97]

Charles and Catherine transformed Devonshire Terrace into a stylish place that allowed them to entertain in comfort. With an ever-widening circle of friends and acquaintances, they frequently opened their home for dinners and small evening performances. At the same time, Charles Dickens's increasing reputation meant that invitations from other cities and countries poured in, and they began travelling farther from the familiar.

Through the years, Charles and Catherine modified Devonshire Terrace to reflect their changing status and Victorian fashion.[98] More substantial home improvements were made before they returned from Italy in 1845. Although they thought the estimate was 'what Mr Swiveller calls, a Staggerer', they seem to have undertaken the project.[99] The interior was freshly painted and the drawing-room was remodelled. Dickens's letters to Thomas Mitton, their friend and solicitor who oversaw the work, reveal their taste and marital dynamics. Dickens had originally proposed green paint for the hall and the staircase up to the attic, until Catherine objected. She advised choosing a colour complementary to the adjoining rooms. 'Not so cold as to be dull, and not so warm as to suffocate the prints,' Dickens reported after discussions with his wife. The wall colour chosen is unknown, but the ceilings were painted white.[100]

The drawing-room ceiling was more dramatically transformed by a 'faint pink blush' colour decorated with a 'little wreath of flowers to be painted round the lamp,' perhaps influenced by Italian design. The wallpaper 'must be blue and gold or purple and gold,' they recommended, to enhance the furniture and curtains. 'I should wish it to be cheerful and gay,' he directed Mitton, trusting his judgement. The paper was hung to the skirting board, which was repainted to imitate the yellowish close-grained 'Satin-Wood' (*Chloroxylon* spp., an Asian hardwood). Gold moulding crowned the wallpaper and the removal of the 'ugly hand rail' completed the drawing-room's walls.[101]

When the drawing-room was completed, a Brussels carpet covered the floor. Like the dining-room, richly-figured damask curtains, trimmed in fringe, hung under carved gilded cornices from the three windows. A green-wire stand with earthenware pots held a profusion of flowers that added more colour. Silk damask co-ordinated the six covered rosewood chairs, two high-backed praying chairs, as well as a pair of couches, the pillows, and ottomans. Catherine's embroidery covered two smaller high-backed praying chairs and a pedestal screen. A highly polished rosewood table accompanied the sofa while four nesting tables, two card tables, and a green 'japanned table' held their appointments. Bell ropes summoned the household.[102]

The walls were adorned with six watercolour drawings, a sketch by Sir David Wilkie, two by Clarkson Stanfield, Daniel Maclise's early drawing of the first three children, and two drawings from *The Old Curiosity Shop* by George Cattermole. A French clock kept time, and various ornaments, marble and enamelled vases, and stuffed American birds in glass cases added character to the décor. Gleaming under a highly polished surface, the rosewood cottage piano by Cramer & Co stood near a matching music stand waiting for the evening's entertainment. To light the cosy room, there were pairs of gilded and china candelabras, a hanging lamp, and table lamps with glass shades. As he did in all their homes, Dickens enhanced the luminosity by hanging large and small mirrors in gilded frames.[103]

The use of gas lights had been exhibited in London as early as 1802. Street lights and the lighting of buildings, like *The Times* printing office and Drury Lane Theatre, were initiated by 1825, but home installation posed more problems. The purification of gas was imperfect, and burning the fuel produced an unpleasant odour and sooty ceilings until the newly-invented atmospheric burner was introduced around 1840. With the reservoir gaso-meter (filled twice a week), gas became more practical and less expensive for home use. The glaring light it produced, however, was harsh compared to candles.[104]

The Dickenses had gas installed in the late summer of either 1842 or, more likely, in 1847. In August of 1842, he had written to his brother, 'Will you tell Chapman and Hall…that I want to know what it would cost to have gas carried into the Hall, and to have the Hall Lamp altered, for burning it.' He suggested 'their gas-fitter would perhaps be the best workman to survey the job'.[105] Dickens's letter a month later stated that the house was dismantled except for a few rooms.[106] While construction would have required installation of the pipes and fixtures, Mr Handisyde and Sons were reupholstering the dining-room furniture, and there were other small projects that may account for the disruption in 1842.[107] In a letter to Mitton five years later, Dickens stated with exasperation, 'I have just put Gas into the hall, staircase, and kitchen'. At the time, he believed that the Devonshire Terrace lease was two years longer than it was.[108] Considering the overall expense and inconvenience of installing gas, he would not have invested so heavily in 1847 unless the work was undertaken before he formally checked his lease agreement. He did cancel a costly room-building project in a letter to the contractor written ten days later.[109]

For either date, the Dickenses were among the earlier users of domestic gas lighting. They obviously enjoyed the advantages, because they installed gas in their next house. Gas lighting in general (and that installed later for their home-theatre specifically) required special care. Highlighted in a note for their servant, Dickens's instructions insisted that 'the Inner Hall Doors must be closed as soon as the Gas is lighted, and must be kept closed all night. They must never on any account be opened while the street-door is open. The Dancing-Room Curtains are to be drawn, when the gas is lighted.'[110] Presumably this prevented the gas flames from being blown out.

Intermittent with the Devonshire Terrace renovations were the family's extended residencies abroad. Some of the home-improvements to change their English décor reflected elements they loved in Europe.

******

As much as the Dickenses loved living and entertaining at Devonshire Terrace, it had become too small for their growing family and his literary status. In 1851, Dickens had expressed interest in purchasing a freehold, since they could not renew their lease. 'I am a going to "make an effort", (like my friend Mrs. Chick) to buy a little place to live in.'[111] Experiencing a few false starts, purchasing a lease became more practical, and Tavistock House on the east side of Tavistock Square seemed ideal. After their daughter Dora's funeral, Dickens wrote: 'I am anxious to direct Kate's attention to our removal [to Tavistock House], and to keep it engaged.'[112]

Tavistock House was a large mansion originally built in 1801 and 1805 by James Burton on a land lease from the Duke of Bedford. The second owner divided the structure into three: Russell House, Bedford House, and Tavistock House, still sharing a landscaped front garden and circular carriage-sweep behind a simple yet handsome cast-iron fence and gates. After viewing the house, Dickens commented to his brother-in-law Henry Austin that 'it is in the dirtiest of all possible conditions,' although 'decidedly cheap – most commodious – and might be made very handsome.' Austin helped inspect the house with Dickens and the surveyor, as he had done Devonshire

Terrace nearly twelve years earlier. Dickens valued his advice, and asked questions like whether the walls would turn into 'a brick and mortar minced veal, on any early occasion,' and the extent of the repairs needed.[113]

After the inspection, Dickens began negotiations.[114] The artist Frank Stone, who had originally occupied Tavistock House, moved into Devonshire Terrace while the Dickenses escaped to Broadstairs, at the seashore, so the renovations could begin. Stone and his family later moved into Russell House, and the wine merchant Nathaniel Powell occupied Bedford House. With Dickens's lead, the three families shared the expenses of improvements to and maintenance of the surrounding grounds.[115]

Dickens had elaborate changes in mind but soon abandoned his plans to build a conservatory and front balcony after he received the contractor's estimates. Stone's studio ('painting room') became the Dickenses' drawing-room and was soon reconfigured 'to carry the entrance passage right through the house to a back door leading to the garden.' The original drawing-room became the younger children's school-room.[116] As the old furnishings were torn down and the space opened up, his letters to Catherine, who was at Broadstairs with the children, grew in anticipation and anxiety over the expenses and schedule. Dickens sought her judgement on various aspects of the renovations. In one note he wrote, 'I almost begin to doubt whether the back room on the second floor' intended for their daughters' bedroom 'will not be the best room for us....You shall decide'.[117]

The drawing-room, on the first floor and at the back of the house, overlooked the garden. It was wallpapered and decorated in green damask. A sliding door was cut between the drawing-room and the study, and was disguised (on the study's side) by an imitation bookcase and books with facetious titles embossed on fine-grain leather spines.[118] Among the titles were: four volumes of *The Quarrelly Review*, *Jonah's Account of the Whale*, *Drowsy's Recollections of Nothing* in three volumes, *Teazer's Commentaries*, *Captain Cook's Life of Savage*, *Orson's Art of Etiquette*, six volumes of *History of the Middling Ages*, *Kant's Ancient Humbugs* in ten volumes, three volumes of *Heavisides Conversations with Nobody*, *Paxton's Bloomers* in five volumes, *Lady Godiva on a Horse*, *The Art of Cutting the Teeth*, *Growler's Gruffology* with an appendix in four volumes, and countless volumes of *Hansard's Guide to Refreshing Sleep*, among many others.[119]

The wallpaper in the study had two designs, a larger pattern on the walls and a smaller one in the spaces behind the books. A 'good sensible' sturdy stove for the study was installed for warmth.[120] They had mirrors placed in the recesses of the mahogany bookcases to highlight the symmetry of the architectural features and to provide more light. Fixtures from Devonshire Terrace were regilded and hung, which added to the room's fashionable decoration.[121]

The bathroom had a shower bath that Dickens designed and a water-closet toilet box somewhat hidden in the corner. Dickens made a small sketch of the shower alcove and waterproof curtains in order to explain the relatively new concept to his brother-in-law and the carpenter. He may have been influenced by the cold-water treatments at Malvern, where Catherine once recuperated, when he wrote, 'what I want is, a *Cold Shower of the best quality, always charged to an unlimited extent,* so that I have but to pull the string, and take any shower of cold water I choose.'[122] By late October, he finally reported, 'faint streaks of civilization dawn in the Water Closet – the Bath Room is gradually resolved itself from an abstract idea into a fact – youthful – extremely youthful – but a fact.'[123]

Their dining-room was splendid. The mahogany table was repaired, a mirror was installed over the console table, and other framed mirrors were regilded and hung. 'A charming little collection of pictures adorned the dining-room, to which a very few additions were made in later years,' explained Marcus Stone, the artist's son who became an illustrator in his own right. His own father's drawing of the four oldest Dickens children was among them, with Daniel Maclise's portraits of Dickens and his wife, the 1842 pencil drawing of the children, and a subject painting with Georgy as the model, William Frith's drawings of 'Dolly Varden' and 'Kate Nickleby', Augustus Egg's painting of Dickens as Joe the ploughboy in *Used Up*, smaller works by Clarkson Stanfield and David Roberts, a sketch by David Wilkie, Webster's 'Mrs. Squeers administering brimstone and treacle to the boys', three or four watercolours by George Cattermole, an early work by Callow, 'a lovely William Hunt, "Moss Roses",' and 'a very charming Little Nell & her grandfather by Topham', he recalled. 'These art treasures were arranged on the wall with great discrimination.' Dickens, he thought, 'showed himself to [be] an excellent "hanger".' A similar arrangement had been used in Devonshire Terrace and much later was repeated at Gad's Hill Place.[124]

Bells to the front nursery were hung outside the dining- and drawing-room doors to summon the children and servants.[125] The flowery ornamentation painted around the lamp at Devonshire Terrace was repeated in the hallway.[126]

Catherine planned the pantry, shelving, and kitchen.[127] As the construction came to an end, the kitchen was whitewashed to give it a light, clean appearance. The kitchen range was scheduled for installation, but after waiting for several weeks neither the heating stoves in the upper rooms, nor the kitchen range were in place. 'O the perjured, beastly, odious, and incompetent Burton! The Imbecile pretender!!' Charles railed at the contractor. With equally inflamed comments, or as a colourful exaggeration of their situation, Dickens complained about everything including his wife: 'Catherine is gradually falling into a state of feverish imbecility as Monday [the scheduled moving day] draws on.'[128] The children were left at Broadstairs, as the Dickenses attempted to keep the work moving along. '[Catherine] is all over paint, and seems to think that it is somehow being immensely useful to get into that condition,' Dickens exclaimed with facetious overtones. 'We sit in our new house all day, trying to touch the hearts of the workmen by our melancholy looks, and are patched with oil and lime and haggard with white lead.' Desperate to have the work completed so he could begin his next novel, he lamented, 'We sit upon a ladder. All the doors are always open; and there is no repose or privacy, as Irish Labourers stare in through the very slates.'[129]

His confidence in his wife was fully restored as Catherine soldiered on with the workmen and he travelled with his amateur acting troupe to raise funds for the organizations he favoured. '[I] am quite delighted to find that all is going on so vigorously,' he praised, 'and that you are in such a methodical, business-like, and energetic state.'[130]

The garden was renovated as well. The paths around the newly designed space needed to comply with the new drainage system for the house. They relied on his brother-in-law's expertise as a member of the Board of Health for this.[131] Two of the cellars were removed, which they later realized 'left but poor cellarage as to space' and restricted wine purchases when abroad, since the small cellar had 'no place to lay down' a quarter-cask of Port offered by their local merchant.[132]

We do not know if gas was installed during the renovations, but ultimately gas jets were placed in the fanlight, kitchen, wash-house, bathroom, and over the chimney piece in each bedroom so that 'no light would ever be carried about the house.'[133]

From cistern to gold urns, the house renovations were finally completed, and the family moved in by mid-November 1851. Rumour, or perhaps gossipy enthusiasm, about the modernization and furnishings had circulated, and Dickens wrote to Mrs Elizabeth Gaskell, the novelist, joking about 'all the plate glass [mirrors] and Californian bullion-fringe on these premises,' adding that 'the kitchen – an apartment painted in an Arabesque manner, with perfumes burning night and day on tripods of silver – crimson hangings of silk damask concealing the saucepans – and melodious singing-birds of every country, pendant in gilded cages from the fretted roof.'[134] Again, in late December, after complimenting her on a piece written for his magazine, Dickens provoked her with the postscript, 'We have just brought a neat little dinner service of pure gold for common use. It is very neat & quiet.'[135] Mrs Gaskell had heard about 'the splendour of Mr Dickens' house' from a Lancaster gentleman, who lived 'in a capital circle in London', and repeated the story that they had 'bought a dinner-service of *gold* plate'. She reported, 'My informant dined with the Dickens the very day when he wrote to me, and told me this.'[136] Most likely the gold service was only an amusing tale that took on a life of its own, but since no inventories of their home were made after 1845, it is difficult to determine. An article on the electroplating process was printed in *Household Words*, however, and a number of 'plated articles' (with only some distinguished as being silver-plate) were among the dinnerware auctioned after Dickens's death.[137]

With or without gold-plated dishes, their informal, yet personal entertaining style carried over to their new surroundings. Henry Morley, an English writer who worked on Dickens's magazine, was invited to Tavistock House for a 'pleasant evening party'. Writing in 1851 to his fiancée, he observed that 'literary people do not marry learned ladies' and Catherine Dickens's attentiveness to new guests was apparently more noteworthy than the room's fastidious furnishings:

Dickens has made evidently a comfortable choice. Mrs. Dickens is stout, with a round, very round, rather pretty, very pleasant face, and ringlets on each side of it. One sees in five minutes that she loves her husband and her children, and has a warm heart for anybody who won't be satirical, but meet her on her own good-natured footing. We were capital friends at once, and had abundant talk together. She meant to know me, and once, after a little talk when she went to receive a new guest, she came back to find me when I moved off to chatter somewhere else. Afterwards, when

I was talking French politics on a sofa, she came and sat down by me, and thereupon we rattled away; and I liked her, and felt that she liked me, and that we could be good friends together, and that she would like you very much. You will be just according to her own heart, and will like each other in five minutes.[138]

******

While the family lived in France in 1853, the nursery and the lavatory in Tavistock House were renovated. Over the years other projects reconfigured the rooms as their needs changed and as the boys went off to private school. They enjoyed the house and its location, but in early February 1855, Dickens learned through Wilkie Collins's former 'charmer Miss [Eliza] Lynn', that her father's home, Gad's Hill Place, would be sold. Dickens had admired the house, built in 1779, located near Gravesend in Kent, from the time of his boyhood. Although he did not mention his interest to his wife at first, he successfully purchased the estate on 14 March 1856 after a few false starts.[139] The property allowed the family to 'have country air and change all through the fine weather; the railway enabling him to go up for business, and come down for dinner.'[140] In February of the following year, when the tenant's lease on Gad's Hill Place expired, their brother-in-law assessed the structure for the repairs as he had for their other places. Although originally considered an investment rather than a permanent home, Dickens had large-scale improvements in mind but, as before, these were slimmed down once he received the estimates. More modest changes turned the china closet into Dickens's study, and new furniture, like a mahogany dining-table, transformed the space.[141]

While Gad's Hill Place was being prepared, Dickens planned a party for his wife's forty-second birthday in May. As he explained to Lord Stanhope:

I feel exceedingly obliged to you for your second kind note. We are very unfortunate in not being able to come. But our engagement is just this; – I have a little old-fashioned house in the country, near Rochester, which I have just now been altering and polishing, to live in in the summer-time. The Nineteenth being Mrs. Dickens's birthday, I gave a promise that she should make her first appearance there on that occasion, and asked some of her friends to come down for two or three days. Hence we are engaged on the nineteenth, exactly as on the twentieth.[142]

As the time neared for the celebration, the 'Inimitable Kentish Freeholder', as Dickens referred to himself, informed their friend Tom Beard that 'the train which will bring down the compact body of attackers of cold meat for the first time, "on the premises", will leave London Bridge Station on Tuesday afternoon at 3:40.' The same message was relayed to Wilkie Collins about the 'main body of the small and noble army who inaugurate Gad's Hill Place with cold meat'. William Wills apparently was responsible for leading the couples and single ladies to Gravesend.[143] The menu is unknown, but there was plenty of champagne. Ellis, their wine merchant, supplied the sparkling wine at 54 shillings a dozen, although the price had 'been steadily rising and [the wine] becoming more difficult to get.'[144]

The refreshing country-living in Kent made Gad's Hill Place a family retreat. The railway offered several options for getting there, and the Dickenses invited friends for visits as soon as they opened the house for the season. In 1857, Dickens even sent instructions to Hans Christian Andersen, whose English language and travelling skills were marginal.[145] It had been years since the Dane had visited the family: 'The two little girls you saw at Broadstairs when you left England, are young women now, and my eldest boy is more than 20 years old. But we have children of all sizes, and they all love you. You will find yourself in a house full of admiring and affectionate friends, varying from three feet high to five feet nine.'[146]

Andersen's visit began well enough, but these were troubled times. Staying for more than a month, though not expected for more than a fortnight, he became an annoyance. Catherine alone remained a conscientious hostess, and Andersen described her as having 'a certain soft womanly repose and reserve'. He associated Catherine with Agnes in *David Copperfield*. 'Whenever she spoke,' he said, 'there came such a light into her large, gentle eyes, such a genial smile upon her lips, and there was something so attractive in her voice' that he thought of her as that character.[147] Andersen became disillusioned with the rest of the family. Although they showed kindness in Dickens's presence, it was remarkably absent when he was not there. 'Miss Hogarth is not at all attentive, nor are the sons; there is altogether a great difference between the whole family and Dickens and his wife. Not in good spirits,' Andersen wrote in his diary for 29 June 1857.[148] Neither this diary nor his letters suggested that he suspected that the marriage was doomed. He appears to have learned about it two months later from the Danish newspapers. Andersen thought that Dickens was 'an exceptionally lovable person,' but confessed that 'he had heard from many quarters that he was a rather sensual nature.' In retrospect, Andersen remembered:

> Mrs. Dickens was a beautiful, though plump woman, rather indolent. He had occasionally met her crying, and he had also seen her come out of a room together with her mother with her eyes full of tears. Her sister was piquante, lively and gifted, but not kind. The reason for the break between them was that D[ickens] had sent a bracelet with a poem to an actress; it got lost, and D. advertised for it in the papers. It was sent, his wife received it, thinking it was a present for her; she put it on, the poem fell out – and she never forgave him that after having been married to her for 25 years he could enter into a understanding with another.[149]

Considering the timing, it is more likely that Catherine's apparent despondency was due to her son Walter's imminent cadetship with the East India Company.[150] Although she had already experienced an emptying nest with the boys attending boarding school, at least they returned home for the holidays. Walter was scheduled to leave for India, where only two months earlier the Mutiny had erupted. Walter, whose hearing impairment had only recently been noticed, faced far different circumstances to his older brother Charley, who studied in Leipzig and had returned to work in London. Accompanied by his father and brother, the sixteen-year-old bravely boarded ship on 20 July to join his regiment.[151]

Meanwhile, Dickens continued to organize performances, including a private production in the Gallery of Illustration for Queen Victoria and her entourage as well as public charity performances. The eldest children were cast in Wilkie Collins' play *The Frozen Deep*.[152] Dickens was heavily distracted with the arrangements, and soon realized that the performance on 17 August at the Free Trade Hall in Manchester required some changes when he saw the size of the hall. Professional actresses needed to be engaged if their voices were to be heard, and Dickens replaced 'our Tavistock girls' with the Ternan family.[153] Mrs Ternan took parts formerly performed by Mrs Wills and Mamie Dickens. Her older daughter, Maria Ternan, to whom Dickens seems to have been first attracted, played the heroine in *Frozen Deep* and also replaced Georgy in another part. Ellen Ternan, a year younger than Dickens's own daughter Katey, played Katey's role.

Within the heart of the hardworking Dickens was a restlessness, which he dubbed a 'Collinsian state' for his confidant Wilkie Collins.[154] Even if

Catherine could have foreseen the storm that accompanied her husband's theatre projects – from the organizing frenzy beforehand, to the 'party's over' disquiet afterwards, she would not have predicted the upheaval of this drama. Catherine was unwell and 'still very poorly' on 13 August, but she did attend the Manchester performance a few weeks later.[155] Had she observed the flirtatious father of her nine children showing interest in an actress barely older than his own daughter?

In his biography of Dickens, John Forster claimed to have received Dickens's letter around that time confessing that:

> Poor Catherine and I are not made for each other, and there is no help for it. It is not only that she makes me uneasy and unhappy, but that I make her so too – and much more so. She is exactly as you know, in the way of being amiable and complying; but we are strangely ill-assorted for the bond there is between us.

Dickens claimed that Catherine would have been better off if she never met him and that they were incompatible. 'Nothing on earth could make her understand me, or suit us to each other. Her temperament will not go with mine.'[156] This time there was little hope for repairing the damage to their marriage, or at best, redirecting Dickens's desires to his family responsibilities.

By the middle of October, Dickens wrote from Gad's Hill Place to Mrs Cornelius (formerly Anne Brown, Catherine's maid) to instruct her on permanently closing the door between his dressing-room and what was his and Catherine's bedroom at Tavistock House, in order to create a separate bedroom for himself.[157] As symbolic and irreparable as that was, their marriage still limped along. Had Catherine been able to see her husband's cheque book for September through November, she would have realized that Dickens paid the manager of Haymarket Theatre to encourage Ellen Ternan's performance there.[158] Meanwhile, Dickens's letters closed with the perfunctory 'Mrs. Dickens, Miss Hogarth, and all the house, send a thousand kind loves.'[159] But by April, Dickens wrote, 'Mrs. Dickens very rarely dines out, and I had best not include her in my answer to your heart-breaking note. I myself am as free as I ever can be,' which certainly summarized their status.[160] All the while, Gads Hill Place was being fully outfitted for the season, the wine-cellar stocked, and sister Georgy even brought down the silver from Tavistock House.[161]

Middle-aged Dickens's attraction to the youthful and beautiful actress, Ellen Ternan, forced Catherine to consider separation on 7 May 1858, as a more desirable alternative. Although the scandal was immense, a divorce, while legally possible, was out of the question. Despite the myths that portrayed Catherine's remaining life as empty, Lillian Nayder shows that the estranged Mrs Charles Dickens remained active.[162]

CHAPTER III

CATHERINE AND CHARLES IN THE WIDER WORLD

Travel in Britain, Europe and North America left its mark both on Catherine Dickens's bills of fare and the recipes collected in the appendix. During the years of their marriage, she routinely set up house in new places to accommodate her husband's restless spirit. Judging even from the limited list provided by J.W.T. Ley, the couple occupied at least twenty-seven homes in three countries.[1] This excludes their extensive travels, the short-term rentals while they waited to return to their primary residence, some of the retreats for recuperation, and many of their seaside holidays. While Dickens's letters mention his penchant for rearranging the furniture to use space more efficiently and stylishly, Catherine and the cook took on the challenge of operating in unfamiliar kitchens and finding local suppliers.

Typically, the family and some of the servants relocated from the beginning of August to the end of September at the beach. Although they explored seaside towns such as Brighton, Bonchurch, and Folkestone, they favoured Broadstairs.[2] In 'Our Watering Place', Dickens described the place for his magazine.[3] The casual pace and ocean breeze made the escape from the city a welcome change. Myriad visitors, summer neighbours including the poet Samuel Rogers, and other local characters, helped create a stimulating refuge. Dickens's lively account of the family's summer activities at the beach were relayed in a letter to an American friend. It was one among at least a dozen letters he wrote daily.

This is a little fishing-place; intensely quiet; built on a cliff whereon – in the centre of a tiny semicircular bay – our house stands: the sea rolling and dashing under the windows. Seven miles out, are the Goodwin Sands (you've heard of the Goodwin Sands?) whence floating lights perpetually wink after dark, as if they were carrying on intrigues with the servants. Also there is a big lighthouse called the North Foreland on a hill behind the village – a severe parsonic light – which reproves the young and giddy floaters, and stares grimly out upon the sea. Under the cliff are rare good sands, where all the children assemble every morning and throw up impossible fortifications which the sea throws down again at high water. Old gentlemen and ancient ladies, flirt, after their own manner, in two reading rooms and on a great many scattered seats in the open air. Other old gentlemen look all day through telescopes and never see anything. In a bay-window in a one pair, sits from nine o'Clock to one, a gentleman with rather long hair and no neck-cloth who writes and grins as if he thought he were very funny indeed. His name is Boz. At one, he disappears, and presently emerges from a bathing machine, and may be seen – a kind of salmon-coloured porpoise – splashing about in the ocean. After that, he may be seen in another bay window on the ground floor, eating a strong lunch – after that, walking a dozen miles or so – or lying on his back in the sand, reading a book. Nobody bothers him unless they know he is disposed to be talked to; and I am told he is very comfortable indeed. He's as brown as a berry, and they *do* say, is a small fortune to the inn keeper who sells beer and cold punch. But this is mere rumour. Sometimes he goes up to London (eighty miles or so, away) and then I'm told there is a sound in Lincolns Inn Fields at night, as of men laughing: together with a clinking of knives and forks and wine-glasses.[4]

In 1837, the young couple had taken their first trip outside the country to visit Belgium. Several years later, Catherine's hometown of Edinburgh warmly welcomed them, as did the rest of Scotland, when they visited in July of 1841. In these early years, however, nothing forged as heavy an impression as their six-month experience touring North America in 1842.[5]

Prompted by an invitation from the American writer Washington Irving, Dickens immediately realized the overall importance of the trip. He was keen to promote his work, to discuss international copyright issues, and to experience Yankee culture, but he had to convince his wife. Should he go alone? Or should they take the children and a few servants? Dickens schemed to win Catherine's approval and confided in his younger brother Fred: 'Kate and I are going to America for five or six months (but I don't tell her how long) – and we sail on the Fourth of January.'[6] She feared for the children's health.[7] Since Catherine believed that the tour would be a relatively short one, she agreed to leave the children at home; Fred was delegated the responsibility of living with 'the darlings'.[8]

As their plans were being made, her twenty-year-old brother, George Hogarth, died suddenly of a heart condition similar to their sister Mary's.[9] Dickens continued planning the North American tour that would take them as far west as the prairies of Missouri, as far north as Quebec, and as far south as Virginia (see endnote for itinerary).[10] About two weeks before leaving, Dickens began declining invitations away from home, so that they could stay close to their 'household Gods', and not suffer 'from too much dining' out.[11] The five-month-old baby, Walter, was christened at the end of the year, but was not yet weaned (from the wet-nurse) before Catherine had to leave him.[12] With their affairs in order, the mounds of luggage delivered, Charles and Catherine Dickens inspected their little box of a cabin and watched the ship's crew 'taking in the Milk', that is, an enormous cow was coaxed aboard. 'Bread, boxes, greens, and bullocks-heads for soup, were strewn about the deck,' Dickens reported. After a jolly send-off party at the Adelphi Hotel, he rejoined his wife and her maid, Anne Brown, who travelled with them. Dickens nearly missed re-boarding the S.S. *Britannia* as the ship left the Liverpool dock.[13] But with Daniel Maclise's sweet sketch of the children at hand, they settled in for the voyage.[14]

A fairly grim Atlantic crossing was punctuated by sea-sickness and finished with the ship actually running aground, yet Catherine still managed to impress. The librarian Charles Coleman Sellers, a fellow-passenger, recalled that she 'was far more socially inclined' than her aloof husband. She and another Scottish lady 'held an informal after-dinner *levée* over a glass of punch or sherry, the quality of which, no less than the dearth of female society on board, usually secured a respectable attendance from acquaintances of the other sex.' Sellers described Catherine as 'of robust, florid, English appearance and amiable manners.'[15]

Once disembarked, Catherine wrote to her sister-in-law Fanny of a face swollen from toothache, yet:

> To turn to the brighter side of the picture, the reception Charles has met with is something not to be described. He is perfectly worshipped, and crowds follow him in the streets even. It will be the same, they tell us, all through America....we shall both be killed with kindness.[16]

The Bostonians were the first to anticipate their arrival, but the curiosity, adulation, and expectation from city to city never paled. The Dickenses commented on their hosts' behaviour just as the Americans wrote about the flamboyant young English writer and his wife. 'We are on tiptoe to see who shall catch a first view of Dickens above the wave,' wrote Charles Sumner, the statesman and Harvard law professor.[17] Some Boston acquaintances quickly became life-long friends, as they did in New York, the next major city they visited. There the press coined the term 'Boz Mania' for the frenzy his visit created. A poem in the *Journal of Commerce* ridiculed the hyperactivity.

> They'll tope thee, Boz, they'll soap thee, Boz –
> Already they begin!
> They'll dine thee, Boz, they'll wine thee, Boz,
> They'll stuff thee to the chin!
> They'll smother thee with victuals, Boz,
> With fish and flesh and chickens,
> Our authorlings will bore thee, Boz,
> And hail thee 'Cousin Dickens.'
> While ladies, spite thy better half,
> Blue, yellow, foul and fair,
> Will coax thee for thy autograph,
> And likewise locks of hair.
> Beware, Boz! Take care, Boz!
> Of forming false conclusions;
> Because a certain sort of folks
> Do mete thee such obtrusions;
> For they are not the people, Boz,
> These templars of the cork,
> No more than a church steeple, Boz,
> Is Boston or New York.[18]

Plans for the Boz Ball, the most ostentatious event of the tour, escalated as did the guest list. Originally limited to 800 'gentleman's tickets' with 'a corresponding number of ladies', the total count reached 2,500. That is, 500 over the maximum that the multiple floors and green room of the theatre could comfortably serve. Undaunted, the hosts transformed the theatre into an oak-panelled Pickwickian saloon. Paintings and wreaths surrounding the titles of Dickens's books decorated the walls. A small stage, built in the back of the hall, had a curtain that rose and fell at intervals to exhibit 'a series of *tableaux vivants*' with groups of Dickens's fictional families from *Pickwick Papers, Nicholas Nickleby, Oliver Twist, The Old Curiosity Shop, Barnaby Rudge*, and his other work.[19] Finally, in the wee hours of the morning, the event was over, 'The Boz ball, the greatest affair in modern times, the tallest compliment ever paid a little man, the fullest libation ever poured upon the alter of the muses, came off last evening in fine style,' wrote the self-satisfied Philip Hone, one of the organizers.[20] He was probably not exaggerating.

The ball, as described in the *Extra Boz Herald*, gave the bill of fare as including 50,000 oysters, 10,000 sandwiches, 40 hams, 76 tongues, 50 rounds of beef, 50 jellied turkeys, 100 chickens and 50 ducks, 2,000 fried mutton chops served cold, and 12 floating swans, 'a new device'. For dessert, there were 350 quarts of fancy jellies and blancmange, 300 quarts of ice-cream, '300 pound of Mottoes' (cookies with messages), and '2,000 Kisses' (lemon-flavoured meringues with currant jelly),[21] 25 pyramids decorated with a scene from *The Old Curiosity Shop* on top (costing an exorbitant $30.00 each), as well as almonds, raisins, apples, oranges, cakes and ladies' fingers in the thousands. To wash the banquet down, no less than 2 hogsheads (126 gallons) of lemonade, 60 gallons of tea, $1 \frac{1}{2}$ barrels of Port, 150 gallons of Madeira, and 'unspecified quantities of Claret and coffee' were drunk.[22] Several days later, a more intimate dinner for 230 people was given at the City Hotel in New York. As custom dictated, the ladies were not seated with their husbands for dinner, but rather 'stowed away in a small room at the upper end of the hall' that 'commanded a view' of the gentlemen's tables and, when it was time for the speeches to begin, they filed in to occupy the vacant seats. Some, a 'group of charming women' including Catherine Dickens, edged onto the stage behind the speakers and Washington Irving, who nervously presided.[23] Expectations by the who's-who of every town made remarkable demands on Charles's and Catherine's time and privacy. The ritual of public meetings, dinners, and hand-shaking levees in their hotel drawing-room became exhausting and problematic.

Catherine elicited much favourable, though never sensational, comment. In Harvard, her 'mild, unexacting character and manners will only make you the more disposed to be kindly and useful to her.'[24] Longfellow, who became a life-long friend of Charles, characterized her as 'a good-natured – mild, rosy young woman – not beautiful, but amiable.' His observations of Dickens were more glowing: 'a glorious fellow…a gay, free and easy character' with 'a good constitution'.[25] Philip Hone said Charles was 'a small, bright-eyed, intelligent-looking young fellow, thirty years of age, somewhat of a dandy in his dress with "rings and things and fine array".' On the other hand, he thought Catherine was 'a little, fat, English-looking woman, of an agreeable countenance, and, I should think, a "nice person".'[26] Richard Dana observed that Catherine Dickens 'appears to be an excellent woman. She is natural in her manners, seems not at all elated by her new position, but rests upon a foundation of good sense and good feeling.'[27] Another portraitist thought her 'a splendid woman, with a handsome, intelligent, happy face and a voluptuous figure' dressed in a white gown.[28] Sentiments were not quite so generous in the capital, Washington DC. Here the air was thick with anti-English feeling due to disputes over the border between Canada and Maine, and the abolition of slavery in America. John Calhoun, an ardent defender of slavery and a South Carolina Senator, was not impressed with Dickens and 'His Lady is quite homely and somewhat countrified in her manners.' But he admitted that she was 'amiable and sensible, of which I think she gave proof by continuing at her needle [work] all the time, when I visited them in the morning, except when she took part in the conversation.'[29] The President's daughter-in-law, Priscilla Cooper-Tyler, confided that Dickens was 'rather thick set,' and 'very English in his appearance, and not the best English.' He wore 'entirely too much jewelry,' she remarked. Mrs Dickens was 'quite a sweet-looking, plump woman,' the Washington socialite condescended, but she was 'tastelessly dressed, and more English looking than Boz himself.'[30] Not everyone felt that way. Much to their amusement, a woman from St Louis complimented Catherine on her voice and manner of speaking, assuring her that she never would have 'suspected her of being Scotch, or even English.' She 'would have taken her for an American, anywhere.' Dickens commented in a letter to John Forster that the Americans believed they 'have greatly refined upon the English language!'[31] Although Dickens was appalled at the Toryism in Toronto, they generally felt more at home in Canada. 'English kindness is very different from American,' he wrote to Forster. 'People send their horses and carriages for your use, but they don't exact as payment the right of being always under your nose.'[32]

Dickens was impressed by his wife's ability to rally for the various events and to meet public expectations during the trip, despite her being ill during portions of the tour.[33] Michael Slater points out that just as Catherine endeared herself to many distinguished men during their trip to Scotland early in their marriage, 'she repeated this success on a much larger scale during their punishing six months' tour.'[34] Dickens even considered his wife 'heroic' when she waited an hour and a half for him to return to the hotel so they could read the packet of letters from home together.[35] The often-quoted passages from Dickens's letters to John Forster usually described Catherine's ineptitude, yet Forster sometimes omitted those passages extolling her participation and Dickens's own acknowledgement of being too harsh a critic:

> I say nothing of Kate's troubles – but you recollect her propensity? She falls into, or out of, every coach or boat we enter: scrapes the skin off her legs; brings great sores and swellings on her feet; chips large fragments out of her ankle-bones; and makes herself blue with bruises. She really has, however, since we got over the first trial of being among circumstances so new and so fatiguing, made a *most admirable* traveller in every respect. She has never screamed or expressed alarm under circumstances that would have fully justified her in doing so, even in my eyes; has never given way to despondency or fatigue, though we have now been travelling incessantly, through a very rough country, for more than a month, and have been at times, as you may readily suppose, most thoroughly tired; has always accommodated herself, well and cheerfully, to everything; and has pleased me very much, and proved herself perfectly game.[36]

With the ease of travel today, we forget the often primitive conditions that existed in the early 1840s. The transportation systems, from dank, cramped canal boats to coaches without shock absorbers, made travelling a rough sport. The wilderness roads had few inns and limited facilities to break the long stretches of difficult travel. Even George Putnam, their American assistant, commented on the brace Dickens rigged to help stabilize Catherine's carriage ride from Columbus to Sandusky, Ohio. To reduce the jolting, Dickens tied handkerchiefs to each of the door posts and made loops for Catherine's wrists, which 'enabled the kind and patient lady to endure the torture of the "corduroy road".'[37]

Despite the complications, the opportunity of travelling in Ontario, Quebec, New England, the Mid-West, and the deep South introduced the Dickenses to regional cuisine and local customs. Their new acquaintances sometimes joined them as travel companions, making the journey more enjoyable, but the company and accommodations were not always agreeable.[38] The men's cabin on the canal boat from Harrisburg to Pittsburgh was challenging. In the morning, the bedsteads were used as tables and seats. 'The atmosphere of the place is, as you may suppose, by no means fresh,' Dickens relayed, 'upon the table tea and coffee, and bread, butter, and salmon, and shad, and liver, and steak, and potatoes, and pickles, and ham, and [black] pudding, and sausages' for about thirty-three tobacco-chewing, alcohol-swigging passengers.[39] However, the picnic on Looking Glass prairie outside St Louis was far more to Dickens's liking and it introduced him to local delicacies. 'We had brought roast fowls, buffalo's tongue, ham, bread, cheese, butter, biscuits, sherry, champagne, lemons and sugar for punch, and abundance of ice,' Dickens listed. 'It was a delicious meal.'[40]

Among American innovations, Dickens was impressed by the mint julep.[41] In Baltimore, he dined with Washington Irving and Philip Hone, who travelled south from New York City to see them. Apparently word of Dickens's newly acquired appreciation of the mixed drink had spread, and William Guy, the proprietor of the Monument House hotel, made a drink that was so enormous 'it filled a respectably-sized round table…it was quite an enchanted julep.' The men drank it through the evening as Dickens expressed their delight in a note of thanks.[42] Others in the Dickens circle knew the classic drink. The actor William Macready encountered it in the deep South when he toured two years later. Although no self-respecting American would drink this version, his sentiments echoed Dickens: 'At supper took a gin mint-julep by way of experiment,' he wrote in his diary on 21 March 1844, 'the most deliciously cunning compound that ever I tasted; nectar could not stand before it; Jupiter would have hobnobbed in it.'[43]

Evidence suggests that the Dickenses served mint juleps to their guests after they returned home. In Georgina Hogarth's 1859 'penny notebook' of drink recipes that was handed down to Cedric Dickens, her great-grand-nephew, there is an entry for the mint julep among other cocktails served in the Dickens household. The assumption is that 'Aunty Georgie' compiled the recipes after the separation when she remained with Dickens to keep house and raise the children. The recipe Cedric Dickens provides for 'two strong or four plain mortals' has the bartender first chill the tankards, silver teaspoon, and a bottle of Kentucky bourbon for twenty-four hours. To make the drink, he adds about five mint leaves bruised to release the aromatics, a little powdered sugar, and a teaspoon of water to the tankard, and then fills it with crushed ice. He pours bourbon to the top, and stirs hard to produce frost on the outside of the tankard. Cedric Dickens suggests that a little more sugar could be added according to taste, before garnishing with a sprig of mint.[44]

In *American Notes*, Charles Dickens mentions other cocktails of which 'the stranger is initiated into the mysteries' and cites the gin-sling, sangaree, sherry-cobbler, timber doodle 'and other rare drinks' that the Dickenses also continued to serve after they returned home.[45] The family's fascination with American concoctions was not singular, the chef Alexis Soyer offered mint juleps among the forty American summer drinks served in his short-lived South Kensington restaurant at Gore House during the Great Exhibition of 1851. According to Sarah Freeman, American mixed drinks were still considered oddities.[46] Perhaps this had to do with the cocktails being prepared individually, unlike large batches of punch, but more probably because the drinks were created from new combinations of ingredients and they required a lot of ice compared to their English counterparts.

Inspired and repelled by their diverse experiences, Dickens's letters home became the basis of *American Notes*, which he published in October 1842, only four months after they returned. Although his book was not well received by some of their American hosts, it remains a fascinating period piece.

******

After the American adventure and informal summers at Broadstairs, the family found it benefited from a change of scenery and a more carefree environment. Dickens began arranging for more varied experiences. By November 1843, he was formulating plans to spend a year on the Continent. Ostensibly to reduce household expenses, he also wanted to feed his fiction and, if nothing else, to produce a travel memoir similar to *American Notes*. He confided to Forster about renting out Devonshire Terrace and taking the family along with two or three servants to a 'CHEAP' and 'delightful climate, in Normandy or Brittany'. This was stymied by Catherine's pregnancy, but by March the next year travel was again in the air.[47] 'Bag and baggage, children and servants, I am coming to Italy for twelve months,' he announced to Angus Fletcher, their artist-friend who was already living there.[48]

On 2 July 1844, Charles and Catherine set out with the baby and four children, sister Georgy (who had been living with them), and three servants: Catherine's maid, Anne; Jane, the cook; and Charlotte, the nurse-governess. Even the family dog Timber came along with them. Fred Dickens and John Forster accompanied the caravan to Dover, where it boarded a steamer for Paris, then travelled to Marseilles and some sightseeing before arriving in Albaro, a picturesque town near Genoa. The flea-ridden Villa di Bagnerello that they contracted had little charm. Dickens described it as the 'most perfectly lonely, rusty, stagnant old staggerer of a domain that you can possibly imagine,' and dubbed it the 'pink jail'. The Mediterranean vistas, however, captivated them: 'green – green – green – as flutters in the vineyard down below the windows, *that* I never saw; not yet such lilac and such purple as float between me, and the distant hills.'[49] The warmth of the sun and depth of the sky's colour were remarkable; sitting under the vineyard's shade, in a letter to Daniel Maclise he teased, 'I am as lazy, however, as – as you are, and do little but eat, drink, and read….Green figs I have already learnt to like. Green almonds (we have them at dessert every day) are the most delicious fruit in the world. And green lemons, combined with some rare Hollands that is to be got here, make prodigious Punch, I assure you.'[50]

The household routine was quickly set. They breakfasted between 9:30 and 10 a.m., dined at 4 p.m., and retired at 11 p.m. Dickens made himself scarce when the many local visitors called, but Catherine cordially received them.[51] In preparation, they had both taken language lessons twice a week, beginning in early April. Dickens thought Italian was difficult, but by the end of August, he felt more confident reading and speaking the language.[52] Catherine, whose father encouraged familiarity with the language in order to appreciate opera, probably gained a similar level of proficiency.[53]

For the rest of the party, the process was slower: 'Our servants answering with great fluency in English,' Dickens observed, 'very loud: as if the others were only deaf, not Italian.'[54] Jane their cook, however, was a marvel; 'she had so primed herself with the names of all sorts of vegetables, meats, soups, fruits, and kitchen necessaries' by talking to the Genovese laundress, that the house was well supplied with 'even such small essentials as the commonest saucepans' she used in London.[55] Perhaps influenced by her, the other servants began 'to pick up scraps of Italian,' and attended 'weekly conversazione' with the Governor's servants on Sunday evenings. 'I think they begin to like their foreigneering life,' Dickens relayed avuncularly.[56]

By the beginning of September, Dickens found a much more accommodating apartment in the Palazzo Peschiere, Genoa, and by the end of the month they moved in for the remaining six months of their sojourn. The huge rooms boasted three-hundred-year-old frescos, dramatic high ceilings, black and white tessellated floors, and the balconies overlooked groves of camellias and orange trees.[57]

As always, the Dickenses encouraged and expected friends to visit. 'If you were disposed to give Mrs. Douglas Jerrold a Christmas Holiday,' Dickens suggested, 'I will warrant my Wife to be as gentle a little woman, and as free from affectation or formality of any kind, as ever breathed. And it would delight her very much to have an opportunity of confirming my judgment.'[58] The Dickenses had already bonded with the English expatriates. In early November, they gave a large dinner party for fourteen guests. Timothy Y. Brown, the British consul and his wife; Charles Gills, a banker; Sir George Crawford (Craufurd) and his wife; Mr and Mrs de la Rue; and Thomas Curry, a merchant, were among the guests. The day began with the Governor's two cooks in immense paper caps, who were friends of the Dickenses' new assistant Louis Roche, knocking on the door at 9 o'clock 'to dress the dinner!' Jane, their English cook, 'wouldn't stand this, however; so we were obliged to decline.' At half-hourly intervals, 'six gentlemen having the appearance of English clergymen' arrived as waiters, and their services were accepted; 'you never saw anything so nicely and quietly done.'[59]

At dinner, Roche, with a case of toothpicks at the ready in his pocket, oversaw the servers as he stood behind Catherine's chair and handed platters around. Roche had asked 'as a special distinction, to be allowed the supreme control of the dessert' by having Italian ices made to resemble fruit. These remarkable, labour-intensive replicas were made by specialist confectioners.

According to W.A. Jarrin's recipe 'Ices in Fruit Shapes' from *The Italian Confectioner*, the preparation required much attention, an eye for colour combinations, and specially hinged lead moulds in the shape of the fruits. After making the sweetened fruit purées, the mould was filled. A stem with leaves could be inserted in the small hole at the top of the mould so the fruit would appear to be attached to branches. To heighten the illusion, the seeds of stone fruits such as apricots and peaches could be placed in the centre of the ice before it was frozen. To complete the task, the confectioner removed the ices from their moulds and applied powder or paste colours. Light and dark shades combined mixtures of cochineal, indigo, carmine, gamboges, burnt sugar, chocolate, fresh cream, and saffron to create the confectioner's palette.[60] 'In colouring your fruit,' Jarrin proudly advised, 'Nature must be your guide.'[61] Only the confectioner's imagination limited the presentation at table. The ices could be arranged as mundanely as a compote or staged as fanciful set-pieces. Dickens described theirs as an arrangement with 'pieces of [edible] crockery turned upside down so as to look like other pieces of crockery non-existent in this part of Europe.'[62] No doubt the sweet creation was a dazzling sight and a delicious, refreshing treat.

When the Dickenses were not entertaining guests, they often took part in outings. For a middle-aged women with five children, Catherine retained her sense of adventure, and her husband planned their escapades accordingly. 'I have notions of taking you with me on my next journey (if you would like to go!),' he wrote to her. Perhaps he was already thinking about trekking up to the crater of Mount Vesuvius. They arranged for Georgy to join them to 'top and cap all our walks'.[63] The ascent was treacherous. Even Dickens confessed that the hike was 'anything but agreeable'.[64] The sunset was spectacular, however. Since they had started out at 4 p.m., they witnessed dusk when they were halfway up the volcano, and raging fire from the crater greeted them at the top. 'It was an inexpressibly lovely night without a cloud…the moon (within a few hours of the full) came proudly up,' Dickens wrote, 'showing the sea, and the Bay of Naples, and the whole country, in such majesty as no words can express.' They were particularly lucky that rare night. A new cone had erupted. 'The fire was pouring out, reddening the night with flames, blackening it with smoke, and spotting it with red-hot stones and cinders that fell down in showers,' as the smoke and sulphur choked breathing. The eruption, the first in five years, added chaos when the party waited for a missing member swallowed in the smoke and feared lost.[65] 'My ladies were now on foot, of course; but we dragged them on as well as we could (they were thorough game, and didn't make the least complaint),' Dickens boasted. Descending through the cinders, the precipitously steep slopes, and slick icy patches were tricky. Catherine and her sister were in and out of their litters. Forsaking propriety, 'with a half-a-dozen men hanging on to each' so they did not fall, the women picked their way carefully through the narrow paths. The trip was not without incident. Mr Le Gros (referred to as Mr Pickle of Portici in *Pictures from Italy*) plunged headlong into the black night and landed five hundred feet below, as did one of the young guides. They were rescued, but another guide, who carried the basket with their spare cloaks, was not found that night. Singed, covered in dust and ash, the party emerged as a bedraggled bunch at the bottom of the mountain. 'My ladies' cloths were so torn off their backs that they would not have been decent, if there could have been any thought of such things at such a time.' The audacious sisters were 'the wonder of Naples' according to Dickens, 'and everybody is open-mouthed'.[66] Whether or not Catherine revealed her secret to her husband before the excursion, we do not know, but she was at least three or four weeks pregnant.[67]

If the year in Italy introduced the Dickens family to a wealth of cultural experiences, it had an equally significant impact on their servants, and changed the dynamics of life below stairs. 'Would you like to know a piece of domestic news,' Dickens chirped in a letter to Maclise:

> You recollect our Cook, our nice Cook, our good-looking Cook; the best Servant as ever trod (excuse my being nautical) 'twixt stem and stern your Honour? Yesterday she came up to her Mistress, and announced that she was not going to return to England, but intended to be married, and to settle here!!! The Bridegroom is the Governor's Cook: who has been visiting in the kitchen ever since our first arrival. The Governor's servants have a weekly ball in the Summer, and there they first met – 'twas in a Crowd, I believe. He is a Frenchman by birth, but has been here a long time. They have courted in Italian, as he knows no English, and she no French. They are to be married as soon as her Baptism Certificate can arrive from England (at Leghorn; they must go there, for the purpose; it is not legal here: she being a Protestant) – and intend opening a Restaurant in Genoa. It is great venture on her part, for she is well brought-up: quite delicate in her ideas: full of English notions of comfort and cleanliness and decency – and must, for some time at all events, live in some miserable rooms in some miserable neighbourhood, of which you can form no idea, without seeing the ordinary residences of an Italian Town. I do not remember a single English person of her own station who will be here, after we have left. But she is resolved. And all I can do, is to take care that the Marriage is lawfully and properly solemnized before we depart.[68]

The ceremony took place in Lord Holland's villa in Florence. The marriage was recognized only under English law; Jane held no legal rights by marriage in France, her husband's native country, nor in Italy, where they planned to live. We only know Dickens's reaction – that he was pessimistic about her future. Obviously, the Dickenses were distressed by having to replace their congenial and accomplished cook. Dickens's anti-papist views made him distrust the priests and worry about their treatment of the couple. And as far as opening a 'nice clean restaurant in Genoa – which I don't believe there is,' he stated with all prejudice, 'for the Genoese have a natural enjoyment of dirt, garlic, and oil': a restaurant, he predicted, would be 'a very hazardous venture'.[69]

The Dickens family left Genoa on 9 June 1845. Jane remained in Italy under the care of the de la Rues and the Dickenses ensured that she would have financial support if ever she decided to return home.[70] The group slowly made its way through the St Gothard Pass to Mainz, Cologne, Brussels and other areas for a little sightseeing. They arrived at Devonshire Terrace on 3 July. A month later, the family was wading in the ocean at Broadstairs for the summer. Dickens finished *Pictures from Italy* which recaptured their experience and it was published on 18 May 1846.

The Continent continued to allure them. Feeling pinched for money in 1846, they planned another season abroad, this time dividing their time between Lake Geneva for the warm months, and Italy or France during the winter. In June, they took a house, Rosemont, in Lausanne.[71] Wise from their experience in Italy, or perhaps without a cook willing to travel, they hired both a cook and coachmen 'taken at hazard from the people of the town'. The new servants were unrivalled for being clean, obliging, orderly, and punctual to the moment, the traits Dickens most expected.[72] That is not to say that Fanchette, the new cook, was obliging to everyone. Louis Roche, whom they again hired and nicknamed 'the Brave', squabbled over the purchasing of duck and 'a battle of life ensued between those two powers.' The cook had been distracted by the political revolution that quietly changed the government. 'She seems calm to-day; and I suppose won't poison the family,' Dickens joked.[73] Being a native French speaker, Roche may have also helped Catherine, although she already had 'a good command at least of the written language' as a young woman.[74] Whatever her skill, by the time they left Lausanne, Dickens at least purports to have spoken French with some fluency.

Georgina, now a permanent member of the household, was nineteen. She assumed more responsibility in Lausanne, helping with Alfred, the nine-month-old baby, and the youngest children Walter and Francis. The Dickens girls, Mamie (now eight) and Katey (a year younger) had 'a little French Governess'. Charley, the oldest child, left the family for the first time to attend Eton late that June. Years later, Mamie lovingly recalled their life in Lausanne where they 'thoroughly enjoyed the place, and made many pleasant and lasting friends.'[75]

The Dickenses were introduced to the inner circle of Lausanne's English residents and seasonal visitors at a dinner party given by their neighbour William Haldimand, a retired banker and prominent philanthropist whose hospitality to English travellers was well known.[76] Guests included William

W.F. de Cerjat and his wife Maria; her sister Elizabeth, who was married to George Goff; and the Hon. Richard Watson and his wife Lavinia. Watson recorded his first impressions in his diary, 'Met Boz, Mrs. Dickens and her sister Miss Hogarth, Liked him altogether very much as well as his wife.'[77] The Watsons had three children roughly the same ages as the Dickens children, including a twelve-month-old baby. Lavinia Watson, a year younger than Catherine, was also interested in the arts.[78] The dinner party and subsequent gatherings cemented lifelong friendship. The two families, but particularly Dickens and Mrs Watson, would later organize a performance of *Used Up* at Rockingham Castle, the Watsons' estate in Northamptonshire, where Catherine would take the role of Lady Clutterbuck.

Lausanne provided a wealth of experiences and at least one recipe for Catherine, Swiss Pudding, an apple dessert. As winter approached, they made plans to move to Paris. For all the stimulating company and activity, Dickens had experienced ill health and had problems overcoming writer's block. The household set out in November 1846 in three overloaded carriages.[79] Up at 5 a.m. and on the road before 7 a.m., they faced fog and frost crossing the Jura, but towards the French border the climate warmed. House-hunting in Paris was 'frightfully severe'. After several days they found 'the most preposterous house in the world' at 48 rue de Courcelles, in the Faubourg St Honoré. 'The bedrooms are like opera boxes,' but the huge dining-room defied description. It was 'a sort of cavern, painted (ceiling and all) to represent a Grove, with unaccountable bits of looking-glass sticking in among the branches of the trees.'[80] Apparently the 'mere midsummer madness' of the interior had been transformed by Henry Bulwer 'in a fit of temporary insanity' when he rented it from the Marquis de Castellane.[81] They remained in Paris until February 1847, while Dickens worked on the early numbers of *Dombey and Son*. They attended the theatre, entertained guests and met friends to 'dine tete a tete at the trois freres or the Café de Paris, or some such over-priced establishment.'[82]

******

After their return from Paris, the Dickenses did not indulge in foreign jaunts for more than six years. Much journalism, writing, amateur dramatics, moving house, building works, childbirth and, on Catherine's part, ill-health kept them fully occupied. In the summers of 1853, 1854 and 1856, however, they took houses in Boulogne and the winter of 1855–56 was spent largely in Paris. 'My study is dismantled, the carpet taken up, the curtains taken down,' Dickens wrote of the ritual chaos as the family prepared for Boulogne.[83] It seemed as if living graciously on the Continent while maintaining one's business back home had become surprisingly feasible. Dickens extolled to his brother-in-law, 'Port every night, parcel communication every day, electric telegraph every minute.'[84]

The family rented the Château des Moulineaux on the rue Beaurepaire in both 1853 and 1856. The 'doll's house' and the grounds, they thought, were only rivalled for charm by Genoa. 'As to the comforts in the house, there are all sorts of things,' Dickens wrote to William Wills, who continued to manage *Household Words* and affairs in London, 'beginning with no end of the coldest water and running through the most beautiful flowers down to English footbaths and Parisian Liqueur-stand.'[85] Perched on a hillside with a long front stairway, the split-level house was surrounded by terraced gardens and a forest beyond.

> On the ground floor there is a very pretty hall, almost all glass; a little dining-room opening on a beautiful conservatory, which is also looked into through a great transparent glass in a mirror-frame over the chimney-piece, just as in [Joseph] Paxton's room at Chatsworth, a spare bed-room, two little drawing-rooms opening into one another, the family bed-rooms, a bath-room, a glass corridor, an open yard, and a kind of kitchen with a machinery of stoves and boilers. Above, there are eight tiny bed-rooms all opening on one great room in the roof, originally intended for a billiard-room. In the basement there is an admirable kitchen with every conceivable requisite in it, a noble cellar, first-rate man's room and pantry; coach-house, stable, coal-store and wood-store; and in the garden is a pavilion, containing an excellent spare bed-room on the ground floor. The getting-up of these places, the looking-glasses, clocks, little stoves, all manner of fittings, must be seen to be appreciated. The conservatory is full of choice flowers and perfectly beautiful.[86]

When it rained, 'a great sea-fog' rolled in, and on bright sunny days, the 'swelling hills' dazzled the eye.[87] Other pleasures beckoned guests: 'excellent light wines on the premises, French cookery, millions of roses, two cows (for Milk Punch), vegetables cut for the pot and handed in at the kitchen window…and winkles are to be obtained in these parts.'[88]

The following spring of 1854, Catherine and her sister travelled with

Dickens to prepare a house ahead of the children. William Makepeace Thackeray and his family were in town when the Dickenses arrived to occupy the Ville du Camp de droite. Dickens described the new abode they rented at five guineas a week: 'The rooms [in the Villa] are larger than those in the old house, and there are more of them; but the oddities are almost as great, and the situation – on top of this hill, instead of three parts down it – is most beautiful.' Shortly afterwards, the children came with their nurse and a well-dressed French governess, who was so small that Dickens thought 'a hat box might have contained her entire wardrobe,' rather than the 'prodigious chests' that accompanied her.

They all enjoyed the location, which had one other feature – a view of the military camp housing several thousand soldiers who were building thatched, mud huts for the troops being assembled for the Crimean campaign. The family monitored the military activity.[89]

If Boulogne brought relaxation, their visit to Paris in the winter of 1855–56 stimulated the family's appetites. Dickens forewarned his wife to be prepared for 'a regular continental abode' at 49 avenue des Champs Elysées, which he and Georgy had found before Catherine arrived. 'There is only one window in each room, but the front apartments all look upon the main street…the view is delightfully cheerful,' he reported, knowing she, her sister, and the children would enjoy watching 'the busy life outside'. There were plenty of rooms and, with Dickens's instincts for interior decorating, their tiny apartment would be comfortable.[90] All the rooms required cleaning to meet his strictures, and afterwards a few new furnishings were purchased to enhance the dwelling, but when it was finished he wrote to Wills: 'You must picture it as the smallest place you ever saw, but as exquisitely cheerful and vivacious – clean as anything human can be – and with a moving panorama always outside, which is Paris itself.' More to the point, the apartment had 'a really slap-up Kitchen near the stars!'[91]

Although they invited friends and associates to luncheons and dinners, the dining-room was so small that jokes continued to be made about it.[92] 'I live in terror of asking Adelaide Kemble to dinner (she lives near at hand), lest she should not be able to get in at the dining room door. *I think* (am not sure) the room would hold her, if she could be once pressed in,' Dickens exaggerated about inviting the rather rotund soprano. 'Nevertheless,' he added, 'we manage our own family dinners very snugly there, and have good ones.'[93] The real challenge came in April. In an invitation to the nieces of his late friend Lady Blessington, Dickens chortled, 'I have asked the Epicurians of La Dressa. You know the beastly dimensions of our dining table (to say nothing of dining-room), and how we have had the cramp in this apartment for 6 months. I have told my trembling wife to write another note with this, and to rest assured that it will explain itself.'[94]

Beyond even the most sumptuous home banquets, Parisian restaurants offered some of the world's most rarified cuisine. Among the Dickenses' favourites was Trois Frères Provençaux (sometimes referred to as 'les Provençaux').[95] Accompanied by their daughters and Georgy before they all attended the theatre, Dickens dutifully reported that 'Mrs. Dickens nearly killed herself, but the others hardly did that justice to the dinner that I had expected.'[96] The elaborate dishes they enjoyed here and at other restaurants, while not research for her own dinner menus, did leave an indelible mark on the couple's entertainment style.

They were asked into French homes. Pauline Viardot-Garcia, the celebrated mezzo-soprano, held memorable dinner parties and, at one, the Dickenses were introduced to 'the illustrious [George] Sand'.[97] And the writer, journalist and politician, Émile de Girardin, threw banquets that taxed even Dickens's powers of description. The dinner given in their honour was recalled in a letter to Forster:

No man unacquainted with my determination never to embellish or fancify such accounts, could believe in the description I shall let off when we meet, of dining at Emile Girardin's – of the three gorgeous drawing-rooms with ten thousand wax candles in golden sconces, terminating in a dining-room of unprecedented magnificence with two enormous transparent plate-glass doors in it, looking (across an antechamber full of clean plates) straight into the kitchen, with the cooks in their white paper caps dishing the dinner. From his seat in the midst of the table, the host (like a Giant in a Fairy story) beholds the kitchen, and the snow-white tables, and the profound order and silence there prevailing. Forth from the plate-glass doors issues the Banquet – the most wonderful feast ever tasted by mortal: at the present price of Truffles, that article alone costing (for eight people) at least five pounds. On the table are ground glass jugs of peculiar construction, laden with the finest growth of Champagne and the coolest ice. With the third course is issued Port Wine (previously unheard of in a good state on this continent), which would fetch two guineas a bottle at any sale. The dinner done, Oriental flowers in vases of golden cobweb are placed upon the board. With the ice is issued Brandy; buried for 100 years. To that succeeds Coffee, brought by the brother of one of the convives from the remotest East, in exchange for an equal quantity of Californian gold dust. The company being returned to the drawing-room – tables roll in by unseen agency, laden with Cigarettes from the Hareem of the Sultan, and with cool drinks in which the flavour of the Lemon arrived yesterday from Algeria, struggles voluptuously with the delicate Orange arrived this morning from Lisbon. That period past, and the guests reposing on Divans worked with many-coloured blossoms, a big table rolls in, heavy with massive furniture of silver, and breathing incense in the form of a little present of Tea direct from China – table and all, I believe; but cannot swear to it, and am resolved to be prosaic. All this time the host perpetually repeats 'Ce petit dîner-ci n'est que pour faire la connaissance de Monsieur Dickens; il ne compte pas; ce n'est rien.' And even now I have forgotten to set down half of it – in particular the item of a larger plum pudding than ever was seen in England at Christmas time, served with a celestial sauce in colour like the orange blossom, and in substance like the blossom powdered and bathed in dew, and called in the carte (carte in a gold frame like a little fish-slice to be handed about) 'Hommage à l'illustre écrivain l'Angleterre.' That illustrious man staggered out at the last drawing-room door, speechless with wonder, finally; and even at that moment his host, holding to his lips a chalice set with precious stones and containing nectar distilled from the air that blew over the fields of beans in bloom for fifteen summers, remarked 'Le dîner que nous avons eu, mon cher, n'est rien – il ne compte pas – il a été tout-à-fait en famille – il faut dîner (en vérité dîner) bientôt. Au plaisir! Au revoir! Au dîner!'[98]

At another of Girardin's dinners for upwards of eighteen guests in April, the host served 'every possible, impossible, conceivable, and inconceivable, dish,' including little red flower-pots 'out of a basket being set before every guest, piled to the brim with the ruddiest fresh strawberries.' After the women retired to the drawing-room, Girardin showed Dickens his mahogany cigar chamber that was literally bursting with 'inestimable and unattainable Cigars, tied up in bundles of about 1000 each.'[99]

1856 was the last year the whole family took up residence abroad. A close reading of the various editions of *What Shall We Have For Dinner?* shows clearly enough that from the first trip Catherine's culinary horizons were extended, just as were those of her domestic staff and her domestic arrangements, to which we now turn.

CHAPTER IV
THE DICKENS HOUSEHOLD

Catherine Dickens addressed *What Shall We Have For Dinner?* to readers like herself: prosperous members of the bourgeoisie. The organization of her own household was doubtless on her mind as she composed her menus for family dinners, dinners with company, or for celebrations. The tremendous industrial and urban growth of England supported a wave of domestic employment by the middle classes until the economy slowed towards the middle of the nineteenth century. According to Theresa McBride, women servants were more numerous, and their responsibilities more diverse, than their male counterparts. General domestics, known as a 'maid of all work' (*bonne à tout faire*), constituted roughly two-thirds of all the female positions.[1] In homes across England, caring for an increased number of furnishings accompanied the general economic upswing: no small task, considering the amount of indoor soot from coal fires and outdoor smog from air pollution. Victorian homes were far dirtier than those of previous eras: not only was there more dust and grime, but more draperies, coverings, furniture, equipment, manufactured goods, and clothing to attract them.[2] A wife's duty was the seamless management of all domestic activities in her husband's home: it was only with the passage of the Married Women's Property Act in 1870 that she might dream of acquiring ownership rights to counterbalance the duty of care.[3]

Dickens had a particular penchant for cleanliness. Mamie, their oldest daughter, described her father as 'the most tidy and orderly man ever born. He could not bear to see a chair out of its place.' Before sitting down to write, he would inspect the house and garden 'to see that everything was in its place and in order.' He invented 'all sorts of neat and clever contrivances, and was never happier than when going about the house with a hammer and nails doing some wonderful piece of carpentering.'[4]

Heavy cleaning was undertaken by seasonal labour. Typical arrangements were outlined by Dickens in a letter from abroad to his solicitor Thomas Mitton in 1845. Topping, a trusted servant, would oversee the work in Catherine's absence. Henry Rudkin, the carpenter, took 'up the carpets: beat them: and put all of them down' and Josephine was 'to clean the house from top to bottom including paint and wainscoating,' as she did every year. Josephine would begin cleaning after the workmen finished, so that the family 'may find her work all fresh and bright' on their return.[5] A thorough job usually took about eight to ten days, unfortunately the renovations and cleaning that year took longer than planned. 'Once more in my own house!' Dickens grumbled when they arrived, 'if that can be called mine, which is such a heap of hideous confusion, and chaos of boxes.'[6] Three days later, he continued complaining to Forster, 'The "cleaning" &c &c is in that advanced stage of damnability....Will you let our engagement for today – having reference to this dining-room – stand over until tomorrow?' In fact, he proposed eating out.[7] One suspects that full-scale house-cleaning met predictable annoyance from most Victorian husbands.

With spring-cleaning complete, staff returned to routine duties within the household hierarchy. Cooks and upstairs servants held higher status than the 'maids of all work', but were less frequently hired according to McBride's study. In larger or wealthier households, the cook usually had a young assistant, who apprenticed as the 'kitchen maid' or 'scullery maid' (*aide de cuisine*). The assistant often undertook the heaviest work in the kitchen and, if diligent, could emerge one day as a cook herself. In wealthy English homes, a 'lady's maid' and 'gentleman's groom' might also be employed. For infant care and the children's education, there were a variety of positions for hire. Wet nurses were retained for about six months to nurse the newborn. A 'monthly nurse' helped with both the baby and the mother during confinement, and a nursery maid was employed for toddlers. A governess or instructress, usually a daughter of a 'professional man', was recruited from the middle classes and was responsible for the education of young ladies. A governess, however, was not considered a servant.[8]

McBride noted that by 1861 one in every three women employed in London between the ages of fifteen and twenty-four worked as a servant. Domestics were a status symbol, and the expectation of the rising middle class was to hire help to run the household. While this may have been a goal, social historians have corrected the misconception that middle-class households had a large staff in operation. Although manuals like Mrs Beeton's declared an annual income of £150–200 was enough to hire a servant, McBride found the reality was different.[9] The London census for 1851 and 1871 showed that thirty-four per cent of the servant-employing households had only one servant, and only a quarter of those households employed two servants. In fact, when she defined the households strictly by income-level, McBride found that some middle-class families did not employ even a single servant, let alone the three servants per household implied by the manuals.[10]

Comparing McBride's data with the Dickens household, one begins to appreciate its extravagance. Although it is difficult to determine the extent of their staff, Dickens's cheque book and his correspondence occasionally mentioned servants or hired positions. His discussion of employees, favourite or not, and their life-changes provide a sketchy, yet fascinating record. For example, in 1842 when he and Catherine were touring the United States, Dickens arranged for payment of 'the weekly bills of my [four] children and servants'. He allocated £10 a month for their lodging, servants' wages, rent, and taxes on Devonshire Terrace.[11] A washerwoman regularly took care of the laundry.[12] As the family grew, more staff were employed and each servant needed to learn the expectations and schedule of the household. There were always the inevitable vexations, such as friends being turned away because of a 'new servant – unlearned in the privileged faces'.[13]

Through the years, Dickens employed a number of secretaries who accompanied them on their travels. As temporary employees, they had marginal impact on the household and have not been included here. Others, like their servant Tom, accompanied the Dickenses to Scotland in July of 1841. Not much is known about him, but in a note to his brother-in-law Dickens joked, 'Young Methusaleh will put the initiatory dish on, at half past five, sharp' in preparation for their casual bachelor dinner together.[14]

In 1845, Dickens stated that he could not afford an 'upper servant'.[15] However, John Thompson became Dickens's manservant sometime in the 1840s. When Thompson planned to leave in 1850, Dickens wrote to his publisher about reserving the 'post for my man John' if Bradbury and Evans ever decided to employ someone at their Wellington Street office. 'He has been with me ten years, and is an excellent servant and a most ingenious fellow, and I should be very sorry indeed to lose him,' he lamented. 'But he has spoken to me on the subject (with a view, I suppose, to get married), and I feel that I have no right to stand in his way, but am bound to reward him with what he likes best, if I can.'[16] Thompson ended up working for Dickens until 1867.[17]

Dickens's groom, Henry, was hired at least from the end of 1837, but probably earlier. Judging from the letters, Henry presented a number of problems. Dickens's most humorous note about him, written to Forster, said

1 (above). A study sketch of Catherine Dickens by Daniel Maclise, probably drawn about 1842. Dickens's wedding present acknowledged her talents in the domestic arts, which she put to good use creating beautiful point-laces and needle-worked covers in Berlin wool for their dining-room chairs.

2 (left). The marriage certificate of Catherine and Charles. Catherine required her father's consent as she was under age.

3 (above). Sketch by Pierre Morand of Catherine on board S.S. *Britannia en route* for America in 1842.
4 (below). A daguerrotype of Catherine by Mayall in about 1852.

5 (above). Catherine near the time of her first book of menus in 1851. Photographer unknown.
6 (below). A studio portrait of Catherine probably taken near the end of her life in 1879. Photographer unknown.

7 (left). 'The Toast and Water Club' by Daniel Maclise captured the four Dickens children at play with their toy decanter, glasses and books. From left to right are Katey, Walter, Charley and Mamie, with their pet raven Grip perched behind Mamie. Apple trees can be seen through the window. The sketch accompanied Charles and Catherine on their North American tour in 1842.

8 (below). 'The Duet' by the Dickenses' neighbour and friend Frank Stone captures the family, friends and pet in their drawing-room. The use of richly figured silk damask fabric for curtains, seats on the rosewood chairs, couches, pillows and ottomans helped coordinate the room. The piano was made by Cramer & Co. Catherine is thought to be the woman at her needlework.

9 (above). The Palazzo Peschiere in Genoa where the family lived from late 1844 to the middle of 1845. The huge rooms of the Palazzo boasted frescoes, high ceilings and marble floors.

10 (below). Rosemont Villa, Lausanne, where they lived in 1846, 'with two pretty salons, a dining-room, hall and kitchen.' Charles's study upstairs had breathtaking views; the bowers were covered with roses.

1 (above). 1 Devonshire Terrace, Regent's Park, where the Dickens family lived from 1839 to 1851. (Twentieth-century photograph.)

2 (below). The stable at 1 Devonshire Terrace, photographed in the summer. The groom lived above. Grip the raven is buried in the flower bed on the right-hand side. (Twentieth-century photograph.)

13 (above). The front exterior of Tavistock House where the Dickenses lived from 1851 until 1858. The photograph shows the communal front garden befor the terrace of three houses. The Dickenses' house is the one nearest the railing. (Twentieth-century photograph.)

14 (left). Tavistock House, seen across the central flower bed. The tops of the kitchen windows, giving onto the area, can just be seen. (Twentieth-century photograph.)

5. Painting by Augustus Egg, *ca.* 1848, depicting Charles Dickens as Joe the ploughboy and Mrs Cowden-
Clarke as Mary in the farce *Used Up*, the source of the pseudonym 'Lady Maria Clutterbuck' used in *What
Shall We Have For Dinner?* This picture hung in the dining-room at Tavistock House.

Private Theatricals.

COMMITTEE.

Mrs. TORRENS.   Mrs. PERRY.
W. C. ERMATINGER, Esq. | Captain TORRENS.
THE EARL OF MULGRAVE.

STAGE MANAGER—MR. CHARLES DICKENS.

QUEEN'S THEATRE, MONTREAL.

ON WEDNESDAY EVENING, MAY 25TH, 1842,
WILL BE PERFORMED,

A ROLAND FOR AN OLIVER.

MRS. SELBORNE. _____ *Mrs. Torrens*
MARIA DARLINGTON. _____ *Miss Griffin*
MRS. FIXTURE. _____ *Miss Ermatinger.*

MR. SELBORNE. _____ *Lord Mulgrave*
ALFRED HIGHFLYER. _____ *Mr. Charles Dickens*
SIR MARK CHASE. _____ *Honorable Mr. Methuen*
FIXTURE. _____ *Captain Willoughby.*
GAMEKEEPER. _____ *Captain Granville*

AFTER WHICH, AN INTERLUDE IN ONE SCENE, (FROM THE FRENCH,) CALLED

Past Two o'Clock in the Morning.

THE STRANGER. _____ *Captain Granville*
MR. SNOBBINGTON. _____ *Mr. Charles Dickens*

TO CONCLUDE WITH THE FARCE, IN ONE ACT, ENTITLED

DEAF AS A POST.

MRS. PLUMPLEY. _____ *Mrs. Torrens*
AMY TEMPLETON. _____ *Mrs. Charles Dickens!!!!!!!!*
SOPHY WALTON. _____ *Mrs. Perry.*
SALLY MAGGS. _____ *Miss Griffin*

CAPTAIN TEMPLETON. _____ *Captain Torrens*
MR. WALTON. _____ *Captain Willoughby.*
TRISTRAM SAPPY. _____ *Doctor Griffin*
CRUPPER. _____ *Lord Mulgrave*
GALLOP. _____ *Mr. Charles Dickens.*

MONTREAL, May 24, 1842.   GAZETTE OFFICE.

16 (left). The playbill for Charles Dickens's private theatricals in Montreal, Canada, while they were on their North American tour in 1842. Dickens recorded the names of the casts and he boasted about his wife's performance as Amy Templeton in *Deaf as a Post*, saying 'only think of Kate playing! and playing devilish well, I assure you!'

17 (right). Catherine Dickens's formal invitation to dinner at Devonshire Terrace to Harriet Beecher Stowe and her husband, written on 3 May 1853.

simply:

My man's an Ass. We dine

> at 4
> at 4 !
> at 4 !!
> at 4 !!!
> at 4 !!!!![18]

In early 1839, Henry 'kicked up his heels very high indeed in cold blood, and was instantly cashiered' after showing impudence to Catherine.[19] Within the week, William Topping replaced him and remained with the household for at least twelve years.[20] Dickens's portrait created a memorable character:

Since I have written this, the aforesaid groom – a very small man (as the fashion is) with fiery red hair (as the fashion is not) has looked very hard at me, and fluttered about me at the same time, like a giant butterfly. After a pause, he says, in a Sam-Wellerish kind of way – 'I vent to the Club this mornin' Sir. There vorn't no letters Sir' – 'Very good, Topping' – 'How's Missis Sir?' – 'Pretty well, Topping' – 'Glad to hear it Sir. *My* Missis an't wery vell, Sir' – 'No!' – 'No Sir – She's a goin', Sir, to have a hin-crease wery soon, and it makes her rather nervous Sir; and ven a young 'ooman gets at all down upon her luck at sich a time Sir, she goes down wery deep Sir.' – To this sentiment, I reply affirmatively. And then he adds, as he stirs the fire (as if he were thinking out loud) 'Wot a mystery it is! Wot a go is Natur!' – with which scrap of philosophy, he gradually gets nearer to the door, and so fades out of the room.

This same man asked me one day, soon after I came home, what Sir John Wilson was. This is a friend of mine, who took our house and servants, and everything as it stood, during our absence in America. I told him, an officer – 'A wot Sir?' – 'an officer' – and then, for fear he should think I meant a Police officer, I added – 'an officer in the army'. 'I beg your pardon Sir', he said touching his hat, 'but the club as I always drove him to, wos the United Servants'.

The real name of this club is the United Service, but I have no doubt he thought it was a High Life Below Stairs kind of resort, and that this gentleman was a retired Butler, or superannuated Footman.[21]

Charles French was Dickens's servant from around 1854. French had 'a very fair business capacity and a good address, can write and keep plain accounts correctly, and has a fair smattering of French – enough to get on easily, with any one,' but could not lift or carry items, and had trouble going up and down stairs. Dickens had sent him to his publishers at Whitefriars in the hope that they could use him. Dickens also talked to William Wills about other jobs for French at the office.[22] He later joined Edward Bulwer Lytton's household.[23] Benjamin Cooper began service as the coachman and groom around 1854. Dickens described him candidly as a 'steady stupid sort of highly respectable creature' with seven children of his own, but in an official letter of reference in 1858, he recognized him as 'an excellent servant, honest, sober, industrious, and obliging.'[24] Cooper was probably let go when the Dickenses ceased renting a stable.

Pregnancies and births presented different staffing needs, 'nurses, wet and dry; [and] apothecaries' were the personnel Dickens listed in the aftermath of delivery.[25] Nurses were probably hired after each birth to help during the weeks of confinement, and they continued afterwards to care for the baby.[26] Counterfoils in Dickens's 1838–9 cheque book show payment on 16 October 1838, for 'nurse wages' amounting to £3.10.6, after Mamie's birth on 6 March 1838. A year later, the 28 December 1839 counterfoil, amounting to £4.11.0 for 'Mrs. Havercombe (Monthly Nurse)', recorded convalescent care after Kateu was born on 29 October 1839.[27] The arrangements are not known for the other children. Catherine had problems nursing as disclosed by her sister Mary writing to their cousin on 26 January 1837:

> I know your kind heart will be anxious to hear of my dearest Kate, who I am sorry indeed to say has not gone on so well as her first week made us hope she would. After we thought she was getting quite well and strong it was discovered she was not able to nurse her Baby so she was obliged with great reluctance as you may suppose to give him up to a stranger. Poor Kate! it has been a dreadful trial for her. I have been staying with her since her confinement and have only returned home today it is really dreadful to see her suffer. I am quite sure I never suffered so much sorrow for any one or any thing before. They are going into the Country whenever she is able to be moved, and I am in great hopes the change of scene may do much for her. Every time she sees her Baby she has a fit of crying and keeps constantly saying she is sure he will not care for her now she is not able to nurse him. I think time will be the only effectual cure for her – could she but forget this she has everything in this world to make her comfortable and happy – her husband is kindness itself to her.[28]

Wet nurses were employed for at least the first three children, and probably for the rest of the infants as well. Although Dickens's cheque book is incomplete, the counterfoils showed payments for 27 September 1838 (£4.5.0), and for 21 November 1838 (£3.18.6), recording payment to Mamie's wet nurses for at least eight months.[29] Walter was not weaned until after Catherine and Charles were in Washington DC, suggesting that the baby had a wet nurse like his older siblings.[30]

As the children grew, a nursery maid and a governess were added to the household staff. Their nurse, Charlotte, accompanied the family to Italy and fell in love with Sir George Crawford's servant, whom she married.[31] Dickens wrote to his publishers, '[if] you should want a couple to keep house (having no older servant with a prior claim) I think he and his Intended would suit your purpose excellently well.' He said of her, 'she is a most respectable young woman, of a very nice appearance and good manner.'[32] The following year in Lausanne, the Dickenses hired 'a little French Governess who can't speak a word of English' to educate their two young daughters.[33] (Charley boarded weekly.) Governesses typically held part-time positions, and their association with the family was more social. Charles Knight's letter testified to the cordial relationship in the Dickens household:

> I have been talking with Mrs. Dickens about your governess plans; and the conversation arose from Mdlle. St. Amand, the governess of her daughters, dining with us on Sunday. She has lived some years in England, speaks English well, has a perfect French accent, is a lady of most varied accomplishments, and can undertake the entire charges of education. She is just now in want of an afternoon engagement, attending at Tavistock house in the morning.[34]

When the family was living in France again in 1856, their youngest child's nurse provided Charles with an amusing tale for friends, and also highlighted the extra work required of Catherine to manage the staff in a foreign country. As Dickens told the incident:

> The Nice little Nurse who goes into all manner of shops without knowing one word of French, took some Lace to be mended the other day, and the Shopkeeper impressed with the idea that she had come to sell it, *would* give her money; with which she returned weeping, believing it (until explanation ensued) to be the price of shame.[35]

Anne Brown was probably with the household the longest, accompanying them on their North American and other tours. She served as Catherine's maid for about sixteen years until 1855 when she married Edward Cornelius.[36] Adjusting to her new life was difficult. Through her tears she confessed that 'she thought she should never "quite" settle down' to marriage, but eventually did.[37] Two years later, she returned to work for Dickens after he and Catherine separated.[38] This helped maintain some continuity for the younger children during this difficult period.

The true extent of their kitchen staff in England is not known. Catherine may have cooked some, or all, of the meals during the early years of their marriage and when they first moved to Doughty Street in 1837.[39] From at least the end of 1838, they began employing a cook. 'Cook's Wages' (recorded on 26 October 1838 as £3.13.6) appear in Dickens's cheque book and may represent her monthly salary. It is not clear when Jane's employment as their cook began, but she travelled with them to Genoa in 1844. As discussed earlier, Jane married and remained in Italy after the family returned to London. In Lausanne the following year, Charles and Catherine hired a Swiss woman named Fanchette. Although cooks may have come and gone through the years, the only others mentioned are in 1856 when they appear to have taken an English cook to Paris, but she thought Boulogne, their next destination, was not for her. 'Our cook's going. Says she an't strong enough for Boo Lone. I don't know what there is particularly trying in that climate,' Dickens reported to Wilkie Collins.[40] Once they had settled, he discussed her replacement:

> Our Cook, growing infirm, has left us for a smaller family, and so arranged her departure as that we might have a Frenchwoman during our stay here. We have accordingly got a cook from the Prefect, of whom I think you will approve. She is at present (while we are alone), going gravely through her performances. She has an immense number: having been a fortnight at it, and showing no signs of exhaustion. I take my seat on the Bench every day at half past five, and try a new case. If I find any prevalent offence in the Calendar, I should say it was butter, but on the whole the state of the kitchen is highly gratifying.[41]

The Dickenses' 'chateau continues to be the best known, and the Cook is really special,' he wrote in a July letter updating Collins,[42] but by November the cook became such a problem Charles wrote to discuss the situation with his wife. At the time, Catherine was visiting the Macready family and received his 'bits on news' from Boulogne: 'I don't think the Cook will do. She seems too sulky a woman to tolerate in a house where the other servants deserve anything but mortification of spirit,' was his indictment and, undoubtedly, she was replaced.[43] After the Dickenses separated, they each employed cooks.[44]

The cook and kitchen staff provided breakfast, lunch, tea, supper, a host of special meals and other refreshments in addition to dinner. With a household full of children, and a new-born to care for nearly every year, the cook also had to make baby foods and nursery meals. Root vegetables were puréed and cooked meats were pounded before being put through hair sieves to produce the creamed textures desired. Children's meals were usually less spicy versions of adult foods, but sometimes they were special preparations such as less rich cakes without currants, raisins and other enhancements. In addition, meals were needed for the servants: often ungarnished and leaner versions of soups and other dishes sent upstairs.

When needed, the kitchen prepared 'invalid meals' and home remedies for the convalescent.[45] Meals for 'persons in health' were usually lighter and easier to digest. In the Dickens household they followed a prescribed pattern and the course of an illness could be charted by the progression of meals, beginning with 'a whiting for his dinner'.[46] Improvement was assured a day later by 'a boiled fowl for his dinner'.[47] Dickens projected his own wife's progress during her confinement in the same way: 'Fish yesterday – boiled fowl to-day – up to dinner tomorrow – drawing room by the middle of next week.'[48] Or after another birth, 'Kate is wonderfully well – eating mutton chops in the drawing room,' which held special significance since this was a very difficult birth.[49]

******

Unfortunately there are no descriptions of any of the kitchens in their various homes, but Dickens envisioned one for Eugene Wrayburn, the upper-class idler who was changed by the love of a good woman in *Our Mutual Friend*, and perhaps we may use it as a model:

> ...the little narrow room – which was very completely and neatly fitted as a kitchen. 'See,' said Eugene 'miniature flour-barrel, rolling-pin, spice-box, shelf of brown jugs, chopping-board, coffee-mill, dresser elegantly furnished with crockery, saucepans and

pans, roasting-jack, a charming kettle, an armoury of dish-covers. The moral influence of these objects, in forming the domestic virtues, may have an immense influence upon me.'[50]

The Dickenses' kitchen was likewise well furnished, to judge from the 1844 inventory of Devonshire Terrace (see appendix) and by comparison with Soyer's list of necessary utensils and equipment recommended for the British housewife.[51] The inventory appears to have been written systematically, giving the impression that the shelves and contexts could be reconstructed, with the scale and weights, tin items, moulds, and covers listed together, while the iron pots, pans, and covers were neatly lined up on other rows of shelves. One can imagine the speciality equipment like vegetable cutters and a paste brush (often a favourite hen's feather) sitting in dresser drawers, or the housemaid's boxes, broom, dustpan, and 'turk's heads' (round-headed brooms) standing in a corner. Candles, candlesticks and shades are scattered through the inventory in locations where they would have been used. Deal tables and chairs prescribed work areas. The flat irons and stands for pressing clothes indicated other household chores, while the pewter inkstand may identify the area where Catherine and the cook kept the household accounts with purveyors. A Dutch clock in the kitchen prominently displayed the time to ensure that the household ran as promptly as Charles would have it. Items such as tea plates, rope mats, foot-warmer, foot-bath, and shaving pot represented personal items used by the staff. And a black-beetle trap attested to the universal problem of controlling invaders in the larder.[52]

Their cook had a wide range of iron spoons – thought to be better than pewter since they did not break as easily. Iron pots, pans, and even an iron 'footman' (a stand for a kettle placed before a fire), as well as an assortment of large and small saucepans, stew-pans with covers, frying-pans, a Dutch oven, a gridiron, and salamander were listed. A copper stew-pan, tin saucepans, and a number of other speciality pieces including a fish kettle, warming-pan, dripping-pan, steamer, cheese-pan, covers, and the all-important cheese toaster lined the shelves. The kitchen also had a variety of metal tea kettles, tea pots, tea urns, and coffee pots, but the inventory did not include a coffee-roaster or coffee-mill, as one might expect. Plate baskets, trays, and an assortment of 'block tin' and 'common' covers (for sending the hot serving dishes upstairs to the dining-room) were also recorded. Activities like butchering meat were well provided for with chopping boards, 'choppers', and a saw. For delicate work, 'vegetable cutters' and an egg-slicer appealed to the cook's creativity in making garnishes, yet the two pails and water can remind us of the necessity of carting water, particularly hot water from the boilers, for routine tasks.[53]

The family enjoyed a variety of home preserves, to judge from Catherine's recipes and menus where they are used to decorate desserts and fill tarts. The still-room was considered the domain of the housekeeper or the lady of the house rather than that of the cook. The importance of preserving food for the household, and the expense of the ingredients, had originally dictated this status. Catherine's still-room at Doughty Street had a handsome fireplace that implied her presence. She would have continued to oversee the preserved fruits and vegetables, the making of jams, jellies, syrups, sauces, fruit cheeses, wines, liqueurs and cordials, sugared flowers, shelled nuts, candied and dried herbs for flavourings, anchovy sauces, fruit and vegetable ketchups, pickles, chutneys, and the condiments often suggested in her menus and recipes. In the Devonshire Terrace inventory five years later, a copper preserving-pan, numerous preserving pots and bottles were prominent. The stone[ware] jars which were listed were preferred by housewives over earthenware containers since a greater variety of foods could be stored in them.[54]

The butler's pantry was equipped with a bath, board, trestles, a press or cabinet for drying glassware and china, butler's tray, sandwich tray, and complete fittings. A pair of steps for reaching equipment from the higher shelves and a clothes horse were stored there as well. The rooms below stairs must have been cosy; a green curtain and roller blind even framed the window.[55]

The inventory is not complete in every detail.[56] Routinely used equipment such as a toasting fork, bread grater, colander, hair sieves, pestle and mortar, lemon squeezer, mustard pot, salt cellar, pepper box, and canisters were deemed worthy of listing, but the indispensable sugar-nippers and mallet for cracking the sugar loaf were omitted. Brooms were listed, brushes were not. Although one would not expect the wide variety of kitchen cloths to be noted, the expensive dining-room linens, tablecloths, napkins, and finger doilies or, for that matter, the silver service and tableware were not listed either.[57]

The fire guard, fire basket, water can, fender, poker and tongs probably indicated a fireplace similar to the one Catherine had at Doughty Street, which was used for warmth during damp weather rather than for routine cooking. The types of kitchen ranges installed in the Dickenses' homes are unknown, but gas kitchen ranges were available. James Sharp began selling his gas cookers as early as 1837. New designs and the many patented inventions filled trade journals and popular magazines. Dickens even included an article by George Dodd called 'Pot and Kettle Philosophy' in *Household Words*. As a 'pyrotechnic philosopher', Dodd reviewed ovens, stoves, and other advances in cooking appliances.[58] Although gas ranges eliminated disagreeable tasks like early-morning lighting of the fire, daily blackening to make the range look presentable, and the frequent cleaning of the flues, they did not gain general popularity until the end of the century.[59]

In the early 1850s when Catherine first wrote her book, there were two distinct types of cooking ranges (open and closed) and many transitional forms in common use. In the late eighteenth century, 'open ranges' were fitted into the brickwork of the fireplace, and through the decades they had been modified to shield the cook from some of the fire and to create heated compartments such as ovens and water boilers. 'Closed ranges', completely enclosing the fire, began to be manufactured around the 1830s. More commonly known as a 'combination range' or a 'kitchener', closed ranges used more fuel but were more efficient since many items could be cooked simultaneously.[60] They had an iron plate that could block heat from going up the chimney and divert it into a series of flues that warmed the ovens and water boilers. The temperature was controlled by the register and damper.[61] According to Caroline Cookson, closed ranges remained popular until the 1880s.[62]

Catherine's kitchen probably had a closed range. Although gas was installed in the kitchens of both Devonshire Terrace and Tavistock House, it seems to have been restricted to lighting. The copper scuttles, coal shovel, and other equipment listed in the inventory attest to the cook's use of a coal-burning cast-iron range.[63] It also listed both a bottle-jack and meat screen as well as a dripping-pan, which further suggests that they did not have a gas range.[64] The bottle-jack apparatus had traditionally been used with open ranges, but was converted when closed ranges became popular. The jack device had a metal bottle-shaped frame (the screen) with a wheel and chain attached at the top, which turned the meat suspended from its hook. The jack hung from the handle of the semicircular shiny screen that was called a 'hastener'. The jack had a clockwork mechanism winding the roast in one direction and then in the other. Since the closed range had less fire exposed, the screen reflected the heat to reduce the cooking time dramatically. The screen had a back door that allowed the cook to baste the meat from the drippings she scooped up from the well in the screen's base. The jack required some attention since it needed rewinding, and an uneven fire could cook the joint unevenly if it was not shifted.[65]

The type of ice-box refrigerator or ice cave in Catherine's kitchen is unknown but the menus would imply that the cook had routine access to refrigeration. A £5 entry in Dickens's 1850 account book was made for ice purchased at Wenham Lake Ice Company. The company, founded by Frederic Tudor, exported ice from Wenham Lake, Massachusetts and opened a store in London at 164A Strand in 1846. They sold ice, patent refrigerators, ice-cream machines and other speciality equipment. But ice still remained a luxury.[66] An 1851 *Household Words* article entitled 'Ice' argued for a larger harvest of domestic ice: 'We have abundant use for ice; yet, its use, instead of being general, is exceptional.' Home use in England was far less than in other countries, particularly Russia and the United States. 'Folks at Boston talk about the state of the ice crops, as we talk about the state of wheat,' the authors reported about the Wenham Lake workers. 'Except at pretentious dinner-parties, and in confectioners' shops; with a lump of two to be met with now and then as a preservative for fish and meat, we see little of it in England.'[67]

******

Catherine's little book was not designed to address wider problems of culinary philosophy or education, but there is ample evidence that such matters were weighed and discussed around the dinner table. With two teenage daughters to train when she first set pen to paper, she was certainly aware of her role in instructing Mamie and Katey in the domestic arts. Like most young Victorian women from the middle class, the girls would have been less likely to embrace these skills than their parents' generation. Catherine and Charles separated when their daughters were just reaching their twenties, and the motherly role was wrenched from Catherine and given over to her sister Georgy. As a stand-in for what many families faced then (and now), with late-blooming offspring who are only motivated to learn cooking skills after leaving their comfortable nest, Dickens's sentimental passage about Bella Wilfer, the vivacious oldest daughter in *Our Mutual Friend*, rings bells of recognition. During Bella's visit home, she decides it is time to learn to cook:

> 'Now, Ma' said Bella, 'you and Lavvy [Bella's sister] think magnificent me fit for nothing, but I intend to prove the contrary. I mean to be Cook to-day.'
>
> 'Hold!' rejoined her majestic mother. 'I cannot permit it. Cook, in that dress!'
>
> 'As for my dress, Ma,' returned Bella, merrily searching in a dresser-drawer, 'I mean to apron it and towel it all over the front; and as to permission, I mean to do without.'
>
> '*You* cook?' said Mrs. Wilfer. '*You* who never cooked when you were at home?'
>
> 'Yes, Ma,' returned Bella; 'that is precisely the state of the case.'
>
> She girded herself with a white apron, and busily with knots and pins contrived a bib to it, coming close and tight under her chin, as if it had caught her round the neck to kiss her. Over this bib her dimples looked delightful, and under it her pretty figure not less so. 'Now Ma,' said Bella, pushing back her hair from her temples with both hands, 'what's first?'
>
> 'First,' returned Mrs. Wilfer solemnly, 'if you persist in what I cannot but regard as conduct utterly incompatible with the equipage in which you arrived –'
>
> ('Which I do, Ma.')
>
> 'First, then you put the fowls down to the fire.'
>
> 'To–be–sure!' cried Bella; 'and flour them, and twirl them round, and there they go!' sending them spinning at a great rate. 'What's next, Ma?'
>
> 'Next,' said Mrs. Wilfer with a wave of her gloves, expressive of abdication under protest from the culinary throne, 'I would recommend examination of the bacon in the saucepan on the fire, and also of the potatoes by the application of the fork. Preparation of the greens will further become necessary if you persist in this unseemly demeanor.'
>
> 'As of course I do, Ma.'
>
> Persisting, Bella gave her attention to one thing and forgot the other, and gave her attention to the other and forgot the third, and remembering the third was distracted by the fourth, and made amends whenever she went wrong by giving the unfortunate fowls an extra spin, which made their chance of ever getting cooked exceedingly doubtful. But it was pleasant cookery too.[68]

The burgeoning number of cookery books and other domestic arts publications found their readership because, unlike Bella, women had taken jobs in the cities and could not return home easily to receive personal instruction from their own mothers or other family members.

Waste in the English kitchen, as contrasted with the more economical practice of French cooks, was a recurring topic in the 1850s and later.[69] Dickens addressed these issues in *Household Words* and other writers, such as Alexis Soyer, promoted sound home practices. In *The Modern Housewife or Ménagère*, Soyer offered advice from the mature voice of his alter-ego 'Hortense', known simply as 'Mrs. B.' The book included eighty-seven pages and two hundred recipes for 'made dishes' to use efficiently leftovers, offal, and less popular cuts of meats and seafood. He listed 'Dishes with the Remains of Lamb and Pork' separately in the table of contents, lest there be a problem finding these handy receipts.[70] His other cookery books followed suit.

Around the same time, Soyer had proposed the founding of a College of Domestic Economy and appealed to the philanthropist, Angela Burdett Coutts. Devoted to social reform, Miss Coutts asked Dickens's opinion of Soyer's project to train upper- and middle-class girls in household management, and less affluent girls to work as 'improvers' (servants). The musical training, overlapping schedules, boarding, and kitchen facilities seemed impractical to Dickens even though he believed fervently in the concept. 'Soyer's scheme, like everything he does,' Dickens wrote, 'has a certain amount of good sense and good purpose in it, with a considerable infusion of puffing and quackery.' He agreed that culinary instruction was important for fashionable young women, 'and I am sure I should send my own daughters to acquire it, if they were old enough.'[71] Perhaps influenced by Soyer's sentiments, Miss Coutts established an award for good housekeeping years later. The 'Prize for Common Things', as it was entitled, was awarded to young women who had entered the teaching profession at the Whiteland's Training Institution and who did well in their written examination.[72] The student teachers answered questions like: 'Give an account of the different grains used for making bread; and give a good receipt for making a quartern loaf, naming the weight of flour, &c.' Miss Coutts added a few of her own 'ideas about cottage cookery' to their prizewinning answers, and distributed the pamphlet to schoolmistresses for instruction of their female pupils.[73]

Soyer's ideas were highlighted in William Wills' article 'A Good Plain

Cook' for *Household Words*. Wills reviewed the educational issues and pointed out the cruel irony of Soyer's cookery book, written for, and dedicated to 'The Daughters of Albion'. The sad gastronomic truth was that most young ladies of the leisured class felt apologetic if they knew anything about the culinary arts. As a result, English brides were overwhelmed by the challenge of running a household effectively and, as a result, healthy home-cooking (not to mention digestion) suffered in the process.[74]

Harriet Martineau's article, 'The New School for Wives', argued for more evening schools like those held in Birmingham, which taught the domestic arts to female factory workers:

> It is a dreary thought – how few of them can make bread or boil a potato properly; how few can make a shirt, or mend a gown; how few can carry an intelligent and informed mind to their own firesides, and amuse their children with knowledge, and satisfy their husbands with sympathy.[75]

Five years later, Wills wrote 'A School for Cooks' as a direct plea for reversing the 'innutritious, wasteful, and unsavoury cooking, [which] is our national characteristic.' Middle-class prosperity was a bad school indeed, he thought: 'The roasting-jack and the saucepan, with an occasional mess or two out of the frying-pan, so thoroughly satisfy their desires,' he reported, 'that they make it a boast not to like soup, nor made-dishes, nor stews, nor any of the more wholesome and succulent modes of enlarging their narrow range of taste.' Briefly he compared English and French attitudes, and those that led a 'few ladies of rank' to establish their small experimental School of Cookery and Restaurant in Regent's Park.[76] The prospectus outlined the school's mission:

> First: To open a kitchen for the poor, where they may buy their food at little more than cost price, and go themselves or send their children for instruction in the elements of cookery.
>
> Secondly: A class of girls desirous of service will be educated under an experienced man cook, and at the same time receive moral training from the matron and ladies connected with the institution.
>
> Thirdly: a special class will be taught cookery for the sick, to qualify them to become sick nurses.[77]

The tuition was lower than that charged at clubs, and the school gave certificates to those who distinguished themselves by completing the programme. Benefactors could send their own cooks (or nominate a girl) for training, and could contract for the instructor's aid 'when wanting help at their own houses' for special occasions. The poor were fed the meals made by the students. Neighbourhood families could order whole meals or complicated preparations such as jellies. Even physicians could arrange for invalid meals to be delivered to their patients.[78] The *Household Words* article informed readers about the school, in part to help raise funds, and other articles provided specific suggestions for home improvements. 'Common Cookery' by William Wills and Eliza Lynn stated flatly, 'It has been too long an English fashion to despise cookery: not the pleasure of good living, but the art of making good food out of unpromising material – of rendering the less tempting and the less nutritious parts of meat, palatable and nourishing by scientific treatment.'[79] They proposed the seven following rules, which hold true today:

Make use of every material possible for food – remembering that there are chemical affinities and properties by which nutriment may be extracted from almost every organic substance, the greatest art being in proper cooking

Make soup of every kind of flesh, fish, farina, and leguminosæ. Everything adds to its strength and flavour. Bones, fish, stale bread, vegetables, nettle-tops, turnip-tops, and water-cresses growing for the gathering, dandelion bleached, and other wild herbs and weeds – all will turn to account in a skilful housewife's hands, more especially in soup.

And remember that even pure vegetable soup, accompanied with bread fried in fat, is the best article of food to be had after solid flesh or meat soup; and that you can make this diet nourishing and savoury out of the material you could not otherwise eat.

Cook your food in closed vessels; and when possible in close stoves. Cook slowly and thoroughly, and abjure, as wasteful and baneful, those fierce caverns of flames, which simply heat the chimney – which does not do much good...

Make stews slowly.

Make soup with cold water, increasing the heat gradually.

Cook boiled meat by plunging it into boiling water, then let the heat decrease, and simmer it till ready.[80]

Other articles such as 'Uncommon Good Eating' by Eliza Lynn provided an overview of the wealth of delicacies world-wide.[81] 'Obsolete Cookery' reviewed Robert May's *The Accomplisht Cook* and pointed out that his 'lordly lavishness…somewhat shames the smaller, if more elegant hospitality of to-day,' yet the moral core of the article remained 'how to make use of every available article of food'.[82] William Hardman's 'The Roll of Cookery', looked at the 1390s manuscript written by the cook for Richard II and humorously gave credit to both the style of former ages and the lost secrets that 'could make a turbot or an ortolan out of hog's flesh'.[83] Viewing Victorian meals through our calorie-conscious eyes and our attempts to simplify lifestyles, we might say the same thing. More to the point, however, in the Dickens household, frugality, knowledge, and culinary skill were evident, although extravagance also had its place.

CHAPTER V

DINNER *CHEZ* DICKENS

To vast numbers of us, Dickens means Christmas. *A Christmas Carol* and his other seasonal stories are uncomfortably close to all that is secular about the season and seem imbued with holiday foods, drinks, smells, and nostalgia *ad nauseam*. Even those who have not read his work since middle-school can recite with authority the trappings of a Dickensian Christmas. Fortunately, a great deal has been written about Victorian holiday celebrations and does not need to be elaborated here.[1] Dickens appears to have lived as he wrote. Mamie, his oldest daughter, recalled: 'Christmas was always a time which in our home was looked forward to with eagerness and delight.' For her father, 'it was a time dearer than any other part of the year, I think. He loved Christmas for its deep significance as well as for its joys.' On 24 December, when they were children, he took them to a toy shop in Holborn to select their Christmas presents, but when they were older, gift-giving was mostly limited to their birthdays.[2] During the holidays the house was usually full, in fact overflowing with guests, especially for New Year's Eve and Twelfth Night. At midnight on New Year's Eve, Dickens traditionally stood with his pocket watch in his hand, and waited for the chime. 'A few minutes of breathless silence, and all eyes fixed upon him as he stood by the open door – whatever the weather might be – then a beautiful voice saying, "A Happy New Year. God bless us all!"' his daughter remembered. With that, came a flurry of kissing, hand-shaking, and toasts of hot mulled wine.[3] Or, as Dickens described the activities to his American friend, Cornelius Felton, 'such dinings, such dancings, such conjurings, such blindmans-buffings, such theatre-goings, such kissings-out of old years and kissings-in of new ones, never took place in these parts before.'[4] Even their servants 'had their own "treat" down-stairs.'[5]

To keep everyone abreast of fashion, Mamie and Katey taught their brothers the latest dance steps when the boys returned home on their school vacations. These lessons had begun when they lived in Genoa and they recreated their British Christmas holidays.[6] In 1850, the girls even taught their father a polka.[7] Celebrations at Tavistock House were so lively, the children's schoolroom became known as the dancing-room, which 'we have danced pretty nearly down,' Dickens boasted, before asking his brother-in-law for advice about stabilizing the floor with 'a pillar or two' in the kitchen below.[8]

Charley's birthday, on 6 January, prompted a dual celebration for Twelfth Night. 'Our boy's birth day – one year old. A few people at night – only Forster, the Degex's, John Ross, Mitton, and the Beards besides our families – to twelfth Cake and forfeits,' Dickens jotted in his diary.[9] The festivities were originally billed as a party for the youngsters, but the 'older boys and girls' were encouraged to 'make a merry evening of it'.[10]

Beginning around 1844, Angela Burdett Coutts began sending an elaborate Twelfth Night cake to Charley for his birthday. Dickens once joked the immense cake weighed ninety pounds.[11] The spectacularly decorated confection displayed humorous scenes fashioned from coloured sugar paste and white royal frosting. The Twelfth Night characters were also printed on cards for a party game.[12] Even when the Dickenses lived in Genoa, Miss Coutts sent the cake, but when it arrived a corner of the icing was chipped and they sent it to the Swiss pastry chef to be repaired. The bakery staff were so enchanted, they showed it to the principal townspeople before returning it.[13] The Twelfth Night character-cards, which she also sent, suffered a worse fate. They were held in the custom house for inspection by Jesuit priests.[14] The Twelfth Night suppers concluded with the cutting of the cake and distribution of pieces with bonbons and Christmas crackers. This made Dickens popular with the young guests as he 'waited upon the children like some good fairy, paying attention to all, and making the little cheeks blush, and the eyes sparkle with pleasure, at some kind or funny remark.'[15]

From the first, Catherine's invitations suggested that the families arrive at 7 p.m. 'as Charles is going to exhibit a magic lantern for the amusement of the children.'[16] The popular Victorian entertainment used hand-painted glass slides that were projected on the wall to illustrate the story being narrated. Mamie later described her father's performance: 'Never such magic lanterns as those shown by him. Never such conjuring as his: when dressed as a magician, he would make the children scream with laughter at the funny things he said and did.'[17]

Dickens's dramatic flare developed into the conjurer known as 'The Unparalleled Necromancer Rhia Rhama Rhoos' who was 'educated cabalistically in the Orange Groves of Salamanca and the Ocean Caves of Alum Bay.' Among Dickens's parlour tricks was 'The Pudding Wonder', a family favourite, where a trusting gentleman from the audience would loan Dickens his hat, underneath which he lit a fire and in minutes a plump plum pudding emerged from this 'magic saucepan'. Pieces of the pudding were then distributed to the delighted audience and apparently no hats needed to be replaced.[18]

Dickens could not only conjure up plum puddings, he also knew their correct ingredients. When Charles Knight sent his article, 'A Christmas Pudding', for the 1851 holiday issue of *Household Words*, Dickens noticed the salt was missing from the recipe.[19]

As the Dickens children grew up, the Twelfth Night party evolved from Dickens entertaining them to the older children joining the adult cast to perform plays before parents and guests. By 1852, the schoolroom at Tavistock House was reconstructed and gas footlights were installed to transform the space into an auditorium for the performance of the *Guy Fawkes* burlesque. The following year's play, *William Tell*, showcased the young talent and Dickens wrote a note to Mark Lemon about his friend's nine-year-old daughter: 'Betty, my dear Sir, is – I say it emphatically – an Actress !!!'[20] They believed that the strict rehearsal schedule and final performance were beneficial for their children's development and sense of responsibility.

******

The Dickenses entertained colleagues, friends, acquaintances, theatre and opera stars, literary figures, and myriad other guests the year round. Some occasions became steeped in tradition, such as toasting the completion of a novel. The dinner for *Master Humphrey's Clock* was held on 20 October 1840. To his friend and illustrator, George Cattermole, Dickens wrote simply:

> All the Clock Corps dine here on Tuesday next, at Six for half past exactly, to celebrate the completion of the first Volume. You have shewn your interest in the matter too well to leave me in any doubt of your joining us, and joining us heartily. Therefore I count upon you.[21]

To the illustrator Charles Gray, whom the Dickenses did not know as well, he issued a formal invitation:

Mr. Charles Dickens sends his compliments to Mr. Gray, and if he has no better engagement for next Tuesday, begs the favour of his company to dinner (at Six o'Clock for half past punctually) to meet their fellow-labourers in the Clock, and celebrate the completion of the first Volume.[22]

For 'Master Humphrey's dinner', William Macready brought Merrick, his servant in livery, to lend 'a hand in waiting at dinner, he will be of great service'.[23] Eliza Franklin, Catherine's friend from when the Hogarths lived in Exeter, gave news of the event: 'on Tuesday next there is to be a grand dinner here, a splendid affair from what I hear.' She had been staying with the Dickenses and wrote to her brother George that she felt 'quite at home with these folks'.[24] Afterwards, she reported:

the dinner I told of went off in style 16 guests…I was quite grand & feel assured I was honoured to move among *the great*. After dinner we retired, he [Dickens] had the folding doors, in the dining room, closed & we heard the speaker. Sergeant T— is a tremendous speaker. I enjoyed this dinner very much…'twas as you may imagine very stylish…4 men waiting besides their own.[25]

Invitations and replies for all types of occasions flew back and forth, sometimes daily, from the Dickens home. Although fewer of Catherine's invitations have survived, they show a socially active woman, both when married and after the separation.[26] Some of her notes are formal, others more lighthearted, 'We have settled to shop then venison on Thursday, and hope you will come and help us to eat it.' Charles's, of course, might run the full creative gamut of wordplay and facetiousness.[27]

The 'fashionable dinner hour' had been pushed back 'no less than ten hours in the course of three centuries!' George Dodd commented, 'for our own time [*circa* 1856] the higher the rank the later the hour for dinner.'[28] The dinner hour in the Dickens household reflects their changing circumstances. It was usually served at 5:00 p.m. when Charles and Catherine were first married. By 1840, it changed to 5:30 or 6:00, and Dickens cajoled John Forster to 'dine at half-past five like a Christian'.[29] When they planned an evening out an early dinner at 4:30 or 5:00 was necessary: 'My Missis says that we dine at 5, not half-past – otherwise it is such a struggle and bustle to reach the Theatre in time.'[30]

Three years later, the timing was less rigid, probably as a result of

Dickens's increased activities. They still issued invitations asking guests to come 'at Six exactly…That is our dinner-hour',[31] but sometimes quarter hours such as 6:15 or 6:45 were given. A stickler for promptness, Dickens often wrote 'sharp', 'precise', or 'exactly', and underlined it to remind their less punctual friends. By 1843 and afterwards, larger dinner parties began as late as 7:00. They, or at least Dickens, disliked eating later than that, and declined invitations for 8:00, referring to the hour as being 'in the Indian Manner'. Perhaps an adaptation from the sun-drenched realm of the British Empire, the late hour was apparently only followed by the unconventional in London.[32]

For friends, dinner time was set earlier so the children who had eaten with their nurse or governess could make an appearance around dessert. 'If we dine so late as 6, it is their bedtime when the [table] cloth is removed,' Dickens explained, 'and I don't like to deprive them of the opportunity of coming down.'[33] At informal gatherings, they sometimes allowed their children to greet guests in the drawing-room before dinner. One guest remarked, 'seldom have I seen more lovely boys, or sweeter or more graceful little girls.'[34]

Sunday dinner was reserved for the extended family and close friends. As the children grew up, the dinner hour accommodated them: 'We generally dine early on Sunday, because of our two girls dining with us.'[35] At the time, Mamie was fourteen and Katey was a year younger. The social training allowed the children to ease into formal situations as they came of age. By 1856, Mamie and Katey joined the adult world and even dined at the famous Trois Frères Provençaux with their parents and aunt.[36]

Fortunately, many guests jotted down accounts of their visits.[37] When Longfellow came shortly after the Dickenses returned from North America in 1842, Charles invited his brother-in-law, Henry Austin, to meet the poet, and enticed him with a 'plump brace of partridges and a stewed steak' that were 'on table today' as part of Catherine's menu.[38] Longfellow recalled simply, 'We had very pleasant dinners, drank Schloss-Johannisberger, and cold punch.'[39] The Dickenses gave a dinner party for Dr and Mrs Samuel Gridley Howe, the Director of the Perkins Institute and Massachusetts Asylum for the Blind in Boston, when the newlyweds were in London in May 1843. 'We shall be quite a family party,' Dickens wrote invitingly to another guest.[40] Julia Ward Howe, the doctor's attractive young wife, described the evening to her sister:

We had a pleasant dinner at Dickens's on Saturday – a very handsome entertainment, consisting of all manner of good things. Dickens led me in to dinner – waxed quite genial over his wine, and was more natural than I ever saw him – after dinner we had coffee, conversation and music, to which I lent my little wee voice! We did not get home until half past eleven.[41]

In a later memoir, Mrs Howe reminisced, 'Of the dinner, I only remember that it was of the best so far as concerns food, and that later in the evening we listened to some comic songs.'[42]

The Dickenses' continuing interest in the theatre and his management of an amateur acting company continuously added fascinating personalities to their social circle. To coordinate the myriad details of the performances, they hosted dinner-meetings. 'The Company dine here to-day, in a body; and I will then settle these points,' he informed one member.[43] When Dickens recruited a new member, or there were changes in the roles, he often invited the players to his home. 'I enclose your part in *Used Up*,' he wrote to Mark Lemon. 'Could you come up and dine with us (alone) at half past 5 today? We could fix Rehearsals then.'[44] 'Will you meet the rest of the Dramatis Personae here, to read the play and compare the parts on *Monday Evening* at 7,' Dickens wrote to Mary Cowden-Clarke, slated to play Lady Clutterbuck.[45] She dined with them the evening after their first Haymarket Theatre performance. Afterwards she and Catherine attended the opera, *La Sonnambula*, which starred Jenny Lind.[46] On another occasion, Mrs Cowden-Clarke was invited to help edit the farce *Two o'Clock in the Morning* that was being added to the second Birmingham performance. She recalled:

A charming little dinner of four it was, – Mr. and Mrs. Dickens, Mark Lemon, and myself; followed by adjournment to the library to go through our scenes in the farce together. Charles Dickens showed to particular advantage in his own quiet home life; and infinitely more I enjoyed this simple little meeting than a brilliant dinner-party to which I was invited at his house, a day or two afterwards [Monday 3 July 1848], when a large company were assembled, and all was in superb style, with a bouquet of flowers beside the plate of each lady present.[47]

Mary Boyle, who later performed with the company, observed that the dinners provided an opportunity where 'guests vied with each other in brilliant conversation, whether intellectual, witty, or sparkling.' There were evenings devoted to music, theatricals, dancing, 'fun and frolic'.[48]

Pliny Earle's letter to his sister described a dinner party in July, 1849. Like Dickens, he was a punctual man, and when he arrived at Devonshire Terrace 'two white-gloved men-servants' met him in the entrance hall before showing him into the library where he was greeted by the Dickenses. In time, the other guests arrived. 'Conversation ran briskly for half an hour,' and just as Dickens was announcing that it was time for dinner, Samuel Rogers, the elderly renowned poet, arrived. Earle did not recite the menu, unfortunately, but merely commented: 'At our dinner there was no learned or literary talk, but Dickens's readiness and fund of anecdote were always at hand to fill any gap in the conversation.'[49]

Samuel Rogers was a relatively frequent guest. The banker-poet had written *Pleasures of Memory* and knew most writers of importance. The Dickenses probably had met him at Holland House in 1839, and Rogers quickly warmed to Catherine Dickens.[50] 'How much I value your friendship,' Rogers once wrote to her.[51] Catherine was invited to his celebrated breakfast parties often given in honour of women writers and artists.[52]

Another of the Dickenses' dinner parties (on 18 April 1849) with Rogers in attendance, made its way around the gossip circuit at Dickens's expense. Rogers became ill, and was taken out of the dining-room. Catherine may have attended him and learned of the practical joke on her husband which continued to unfold as Jules Benedict, the German composer and conductor of the English Opera at Drury Lane, next fell prostrate on the carpet. Albany Fonblanque, the editor, tactfully hinted at food-poisoning as Dr Frederic Quin, Edwin Landseer, and Lord Strangford (Rogers's friend) lent credibility to the joke by collapsing also. Dickens became alarmed. The remaining guests soon learned of the deception, as did the host. The dinner party ended 'in uproarious mirth', apparently with Dickens laughing the hardest for being so gullible.[53]

With sardonic insight, the bald, blue-eyed Rogers was known as a trouble-maker even in his old age. He delighted in needling the acerbic Jane Welsh Carlyle, who remarked that the poet 'ought to have been buried long ago, so old and ill-natured he is grown.'[54] Dickens respected Jane Carlyle's wit and intelligence and with her husband, Thomas Carlyle the historian, she was often part of the inner circle.[55] In turn, Thomas Carlyle enjoyed Catherine's parties. On one occasion when the Carlyles were 'poor sickly creatures' too ill to go out, Thomas wrote to her expressing his regret at having to 'deny themselves the pleasure of dining out, at your house on Saturday – one of the agreeablest dinners of that human ingenuity could provide for us!'[56]

The Dickenses held at least two dinners in the spring of 1849 to introduce the author Elizabeth Gaskell to their friends, including the Carlyles. Mrs Gaskell described the May evening:

We dressed and went to dine at Mr. Dickens's…We were shown into Mr. Dickens's study; this is the part, dear Annie, I thought you would like to hear about. It is the study where he writes all his works; and has a bow-window, is about the size of Uncle Holland's drawing room[.] There are books all round, up to the ceiling, and down to the ground; a standing-desk at which he writes; and all manner of comfortable easy chairs. There were numbers of people in the room. Mr. Rogers (the old poet, who is 86, and looked very unfit to be in such a large party,) Douglas Jerrold, Mr. and Mrs. Carlyle, Hablot Browne, who illustrated Dickens's works, Mr. Forster, Mr. and Mrs. Tagart, a Mr. Kenyon. We waited dinner a long time for Lady Dufferin; (*the* Hon. Mrs. Blackwood who wrote the Irish Emigrant's Lament,) but she did not come till after dinner. Anne sat between Carlyle & Rogers, – I between Dickens & Douglas Jerrold. Anne heard the most sense, and I most wit…After dinner we went upstairs I sat next to Mrs. Carlyle, who amused me very much with her account of their only servant who comes from Annandale Scotland, and had never been accustomed to announce titles…In the evening quantities of other people came in. We were by this time up in the drawing-room, which is not nearly so pretty or so home-like as the study. Frank Stone the artist, Leech and his wife, Benedict the great piano-forte player, Sims Reeves the singer, Thackeray, Lord Dudley Stuart, Lord Headfort, Lady Yonge, Lady Lovelace, Lady Dufferin, and a quantity of others whose names I did not hear. We heard some beautiful music, Mr. Tom Taylor was there too, who writes those comical ballads in Punch; and Anne said we had the whole Punch-bowl, which I believe we had. I kept trying to learn people's faces off by heart, that I might remember them; but it was rather confusing there were so very many. There were some nice little Dickens's children in the room, – who were so polite, and well-trained. We came away at last feeling we had seen so many people and things that day that we were quite confused; only that we should be glad to remember we had *done* it.[57]

Other guests, like Harriet Beecher Stowe and her husband, were more of a chore. Although her sister Catherine Beecher is better known in culinary circles as an evangelist for domestic economy, the author of *Uncle Tom's Cabin* exemplified that same puritanical New England attitude.[58] The Dickens household paralleled the Beecher sisters' management philosophy – albeit relying on servants. Like the Beechers and Stowes, they held anti-slavery views. Only six months earlier, Catherine had attended the Duchess of Sutherland's to sign a petition sent to Mrs Stowe to show English women's support for the American women who opposed slavery.[59] The Dickenses officially met the Stowes in May 1853 at the Lord Mayor's Banquet where Harriet and Charles were honorary guests. Mrs Stowe was presented to Catherine and the other ladies when the women retired to the drawing-room. She recalled:

> Mrs. Dickens is a good specimen of a truly English woman; tall, large, and well developed, with fine, healthy colour, and an air of frankness, cheerfulness, and reliability. A friend whispered to me that she was as observing, and fond of humour, as her husband. After a while the gentlemen came back to the drawing room, and I had a few moments of very pleasant, friendly conversation with Mr. Dickens. They are both people that one could not know a little of without desiring to know more.[60]

She obviously got her wish; the very next day Catherine wrote to invite them to their dinner party (the emphasis is hers): 'Mr. and Mrs. Charles Dickens request the pleasure of Professor and Mrs. Beecher Stowe's company at dinner on Saturday, May 14th, at $^1/_4$ *before* 7 o'clock. Tavistock House May 3d. 1853.'[61]

Professor Stowe (at least) had dined with Dickens ten days earlier, with another American, Cornelius Felton, and John Forster. Charles commented, 'We have all been so bored by that amiable personage', but he apparently felt duty bound to invite Stowe again. He and Catherine later called on the Stowes in their lodgings in Walworth.[62] Ultimately, Dickens's verdict was that Mrs Stowe, like the letter she sent, was pleasant but 'a little conceited in its affectation of humility'. He observed, 'Her Moony Memories are very silly I am afraid. Some of the people remembered the most moonily are terrible humbugs – mortal, deadly incarnations of Cant and Quackery.'[63]

******

Dickens prided himself on being informal, and doubtlessly Catherine was grateful to be spared the most rigid forms of social etiquette. 'Pray do not imagine from this length of notice that we have a formal party; for I hold such things in unspeakable abhorrence,' he stated flatly in an invitation.[64] According to W.A. Fraser, Dickens was uncomfortable when surrounded by upper-class rigmarole and could shrink into shy uneasiness when the ghosts of his own boyhood made him feel out of place. Even eating and drinking in Dickens's fiction was all about middle- and lower-class lifestyles, which he knew first-hand.[65] Although his wife's childhood had moments of financial stress, she was not haunted by debtor's prison or a stint as a child labourer. In the early years of their marriage, her family may have provided an overlay of day-to-day middle-class respectability while the couple developed a style of entertaining that was comfortable for them and manageable in their situation.

Whether formal or pot-luck, their dinners were eventful and welcoming. Some guests admired their beautifully set table as much as the food. Wilkie Collins, for one, described a memorable meal as 'The Grand Dinner…a banquet to make a classical epicure's mouth water,' in 1853 when he visited the Dickenses abroad. 'The table was charming, decorated with flowers, and a nosegay was placed by each guest's napkin,' he observed. 'As for the dishes, I say nothing; having preserved my Bill of fare, as a memorable document for my family to peruse when I come home,' he promised his mother.[66] Wilkie Collins and Dickens had met in 1851, and within a few years became fast friends. Collins, who wrote fiction, plays, and co-authored articles for *Household Words*, was a regular visitor when the Dickens family resided in France 'and dines with us every day'.[67]

Although most accounts by guests commented on the Dickenses' ability to make new acquaintances feel included, some noticed class differences and Jane Welsh Carlyle was among those who spotted the discrepancies. While her letter appears rather damning, she herself was not particularly adept at pulling dinner parties together. Her letters recorded her own husband's impromptu expectations and the resulting calamities.[68] However, in an often-cited letter about the Dickenses' dinner party to introduce Elizabeth Gaskell, she wrote somewhat judgmentally:

> Such getting up of the steam is unbecoming to a literary man who ought to have his basis elsewhere than on what the old Annandale woman called 'Ornament and grander'. The dinner was served up in the new fashion – not placed on the table at all – but handed round – only the desserts on the table and quantities of *artificial*

flowers – but such an overloaded dessert! pyramids of figs raisins oranges – ach! At the [Lady] Ashburton dinner served on those principles there were just *four cowslips* in china pots – four silver shells containing sweets, and a silver filigree temple in the middle! but here the very candles rose each out of an artificial rose! Good God![69]

The 'new fashion' referred most likely to the *à la russe* style of serving dinner. Clearly the Dickenses did not adhere to the formality imposed by *à la française* service to which many clung. What are the differences in these serving styles and why does it matter? *À la française*, the older, more formal style, was originally developed at the French court during the seventeenth century. Symmetry was all important. The table was divided into imaginary quarters which mirrored each other. The centre was dominated by an elaborate '*surtout*', which often remained until the dessert course. The *surtout* could take the form of an ornamental building with figures, and often held the salt, pepper, vinegar, oil, and lemons (if they were not placed on the sideboard). The *surtout* could be replaced by a large platter of food itself sometimes elevated on a stand in the centre of the table. All the accompanying dishes were in even numbers or matched pairs. Twelve dishes of prescribed food types was the typical number for a large dinner party and these were strategically placed to create a balanced arrangement.[70]

The first course, that is the *hors-d'oeuvre*, soups and *entrées*, were put in place before the guests entered the dining-room. When the hostess was notified dinner was ready, the guests informally sorted themselves by rank and entered the dining-room after the host and guest of honour. Unfortunately, by the time all the dishes for the first course were completed, arranged on the table, and the guests were seated – the food had cooled.[71] As the guest ate the first course, 'removes' (*relevés*) were brought in to replace the empty dishes. The second course of *rôtis*, that is, large roasted joints of meat and fowl, were set in the places formerly occupied by the empty soup tureens and fish platters. Ideally the host was skilled at carving, and he supplied each guest with a piece of meat done to his or her preference. Replacement of salty or sweet dishes, called *assiettes volantes*, were brought in as the main serving platters emptied.[72] The integrity of the table's arrangement for *à la française* service was religiously upheld – from the moment the guests entered the dining-room and beheld the banquet table, to the removal of the white linen tablecloth, and the symmetrical placement of the dessert course on the well-polished board. Conversation during the meal was limited since guests were required to serve each other from the side dishes in front of them if there were few or no servants.[73]

The *à la russe* service replaced this rigidly formal style.[74] The change was introduced in 1810 at a reception in Clichy (near Paris) that was hosted by the Russian diplomat Prince Kourakine. Although it took a while to catch on, the style had many advantages. Guests entered the dining-room to see a large well-ironed white damask tablecloth, place settings, and a forest of flowers or greenery decorating the table's centre.[75] The symmetry of large platters was no longer the objective. There were fewer dishes on the menu, and they were brought into the dining-room piping hot and placed on the sideboard or dinner wagon. As 'The Real Cook's Oracle' explained, 'the service [took] place with extraordinary rapidity, …the viands being eaten at the precise instant they ought to be.'[76] The dishes under silver covers were flanked by footmen in wealthy homes, with one footman assisting every three guests. In more humble middle-class circumstances, the kitchen staff generally served the food, but for larger dinner parties with healthier budgets, men could be hired. In addition, servants could be brought by the guests to attend them or to help out generally, as when William Macready provided his man Merrick, who served with three men plus those from the Dickenses' own household.[77]

With *à la russe*, seating arrangements became more flexible as men and women could face each other across the table, rather than in alternating pairs. The guests no longer had to see to each other's needs, or ask for 'potatoes with his fish'.[78] The fast-paced conversation, which was so important to the Dickenses when entertaining, was more easily facilitated.

With smaller serving platters in use, the food was scaled down. Meat and vegetables were cut into equal serving sizes.[79] The hostesses could now be liberal rather than extravagant since the guests only noticed the portion on their plates. Dinners began fostering lightness in the cuisine and variety in the menus. With fewer large brown joints of boiled or roasted meats, meals became more colourful. Smaller garnishes, such as the white and yellow slices of eggs, became popular, as did the associated kitchen gadgets.[80] For the cook and her mistress, the quantity of food was easier to calculate and to handle in both kitchen and dining-room. Individual portions, especially of meat, could be cooked to perfection and served immediately.[81]

Except for formal occasions, dinners in the 1850s had slimmed down to a mere four or five courses. The principal courses often retained their French names: *potage, poisson, hors d'oeuvre, entrée, rôti,* and *entremets.* Speciality courses, such as *relevé, sorbet, salade, entremets de fromage* and so forth, were interchangeable. The courses could also be referred to simply as the soup, fish, or 1st, 2nd, 3rd courses, etc. – as was more typical in the *à la russe* bills of fare.[82]

Mrs Carlyle's letter that mentioned 'the new serving style' was written about three years before Catherine's own book was first published. Her bills of fare, particularly those serving up to eighteen diners (in 1851) and up to twenty persons (in all the other editions), indicate that the Dickenses did not adhere to the strict dictums of *à la française.* The spacing of the bills of fare, particularly in the 1851 edition, between the soup(s), fish, entrée dishes, roasts, and desserts, is slight but noticeable, and appears to demarcate the courses. In addition, the numbers of dishes in each course are not always even, which would create asymmetry on the table. Altogether, the evidence would suggest that the Dickenses were among the earlier proponents of the *à la russe* style.[83]

With the change in serving styles, Dena Attar notes that the ornamentation of the table became a focal point, and the hostess needed to develop different skills. A plethora of specialized books taught women that artful napkin folding, among other aesthetic instructions, contributed gracefulness.[84] Arranging flowers and greenery became an important table art. In the Dickens household, Mamie became the flower arranger as she grew older; her father bragged that she was acquiring an 'immense reputation' by decorating the table at dinner every day.[85]

If Catherine Dickens followed Alexis Soyer's philosophy for entertaining guests, she was well organized beforehand, and remained vigilant through the evening by seeing to her guests' needs. As 'Mrs. B', Soyer's *alter ego* in *The Modern Housewife,* patiently explained to her feckless friend Eloise, 'I have always been of the opinion that the arrangements and serving of a dinner table have as much to do with the happiness and pleasure of a party as the viands which are placed upon it.' Punctuality, bright clean china, sparkling cut glass, accessible salt cellars, warmed soup plates, two knives, two 'prongs', two tablespoons, two wine glasses, and a napkin should greet the guests at each place. This special care added to the *savoir-faire* of the dinner's management.[86]

As to the service, the key words were hot and timely. The formality of the dinner, Soyer professed, was determined by the number of staff who could wait at table. While twelve diners were the ideal number for most middle-class homes, it required at least two manservants – one on each side of a six-foot table – to properly serve the food, quickly change the plates, and fill the wine glasses. To begin the meal, the hot tureens of soup, and possibly the fish carefully laid on its drain-platter, made up the first course. The accompanying potatoes, sauces, cruet-frames, and 'other requisites' were placed on the sideboard until needed. Catherine, as hostess, would have served the soup while her husband later helped guests to the fish. This allowed the hostess to see to her guests, and also give her 'the leisure of taking wine with any gentleman who challenges' her to a toast. As the diners enjoy the first course, the cook had time to prepare the 'removes', and send them up on heated platters under dish-covers so they were waiting outside the dining-room door with a change of warmed plates.[87]

Properly cooking succulent roasts, and handsomely arranging them on garnished platters, only set the stage. Deftly sliced portions were the real performance art. 'As evidence of the pitiable ignorance in which a large number of the inhabitants of this intelligent country are at present languishing,' warned an article in Dickens's magazine about 'the most essential branch of the social duties of life' – that is, the art of carving – 'The Carver's College' recited the horrors of innumerable blunders and butchered attempts. [88]

The art of carving had long been considered a 'part of the education of the well-bred youth of both sexes'. As Georgian civility evolved, men were generally expected to know how to carve all types of large joints, roasts, fowl, and game.[89] Yet Dickens gave credit in 'The Nice Little Couple' to Mrs Chirrup, not to her spouse, who swiftly dismantled the most challenging of all meats – the roast goose.

> To Mrs. Chirrup the resolving a goose into its smallest component parts is a pleasant pastime – a practical joke – a thing to be done in a minute or so, without the smallest interruption to the conversation of the time. No handing the dish over to an unfortunate man upon her right or left, no wild sharpening of the knife, no hacking and sawing at an unruly joint, no noise, no splash, no heat, no leaving off in despair, all is confidence and cheerfulness.
>
> The dish is set upon the table, the cover is removed; for an instant, and only an instant, you observe that Mrs. Chirrup's attention is distracted; she smiles, but heareth not. You proceed with your story; meanwhile the glittering knife is slowly upraised, both Mrs. Chirrup's wrists are slightly but not ungracefully agitated, she

compresses her lips for an instant, then breaks into a smile, and all is over. The legs of the bird slide gently down into a pool of gravy, the wings seem to melt from the body, the breast separates into a row of juicy slices, the smaller and more complicated parts of his anatomy are perfectly developed, a cavern of stuffing is revealed, and the goose is gone.[90]

To provide guidance, many nineteenth-century carving manuals, books on household management and cookery books included descriptions and diagrams to help visualize the process. These publications had become popular around the 1830s, and proliferated along with other etiquette manuals to the end of the century.[91] Although superstitious about knives, carving was a conceit Dickens valued, but not a talent everyone possessed.[92] Dickens enjoyed the showmanship of carving so much that even when they converted to the *à la russe* style where meats were more often disassembled at the sideboard, he continued to carve at the table. Exemplifying the goal of 'the carver's college', Dickens undoubtedly could 'define "joints innumerable in the smallest chick that ever broke the heart of a brood hen," and supply fourteen people handsomely from a single pheasant, still retaining the leg for himself.'[93]

This part of dinner required the most attention and, according to some, a sixth sense by the servants as well. 'A first-rate butler,' Soyer remarked, 'should know almost by the look what this lady and that gentleman require, and what kind of vegetables to hand them…should be able to judge by the physiognomy to whom he should offer mint sauce with the lamb, and who prefers cayenne.'[94] Servants handed around the side-dishes of vegetables, but the guests were also free to pass them around, or help each other. As soon as Catherine observed that all the guests were served, she (as hostess) would have signalled the servants to open the bottles of champagne and serve the filled glasses from a salver. Guests could request refills and offer toasts. The sparkling wit and conversation, so notable a part of their dinners, bubbled forth. As the platters of food emptied, others replaced them, and the plates at the top and bottom of the table were often removed when the game was placed on the table. Timing was everything, as Dickens once remarked about an unsuccessful dinner he attended, 'We wallowed in an odd sort of dinner which would have been splashy if it hadn't been too sticky. Salmon appeared late in the evening, and unforeseen creatures of the lobster species strayed in after the pudding.'[95]

Catherine's first bill of fare for a large party of up to twenty people is helpful for both visualizing the service and appreciating her wise use of ingredients. Admittedly over-the-top by our standards, it does in fact show her frugality in serving twenty diners well. Seasonality dictated the items she suggested. New potatoes, asparagus, salad greens, and mushrooms (most probably morels) in the main course, and strawberries at dessert, heralded the spring. Hothouse cucumbers added extravagance without breaking the budget. Following Soyer's advice, Catherine demonstrated how 'to dispose of those delicacies to the best advantage that friends may appreciate them'.[96] She incorporated lobster into three dishes, but without real duplication. The tail meat was used for the cutlets, the claws for the lobster salad, and the scrap and shells went into a sauce. Guests might take none, one, or all of the offerings.

Catherine's menu opened with a creamily almond-based white soup served to those who preferred a richer start, while the colourful, lighter vegetable soup accommodated leaner appetites. As the tureens were removed, the coral-coloured boiled salmon (actually poached) was arranged on a long platter napped with lobster sauce. A garnished plate of lobster fillets was paired with shrimp sauce, and a festive arrangement of cucumber slices accompanied them. When the seafood was eaten, the entrées appeared: crisp puff-pastry shells stuffed with a mushroom filling, lobster cutlets, lamb cutlets served with cucumber sauce, and rabbit curry smothered with white sauce. While these dishes appeased the diners' appetites, the second course was being readied in the kitchen: a roasted haunch of mutton, and an artistically arranged platter of boiled fowl and tongue. With these were served spinach, new potatoes, and a salad. Then succulent duckling and guinea fowl were taken off the spit, to be offered as removes (or the third course) with plump, fresh asparagus. Guests remained in the dining-room for dessert, rather than moving to another place as might happen in more spacious houses. Dishes with rose-water may have been passed round by the servants so that the diners could dip a corner of their napkin to clean their hands and mouth. But the Dickenses did have fourteen cut-glass finger bowls in their inventory, and could have added them to the table arrangement for smaller groups.[97]

At the conclusion of the third course, the servants carefully lifted and folded the tablecloth, cleaned any crumbs, and placed the dessert on the mahogany. Standing proud were the glories of the confectioner's art: a glistening, clear moulded jelly, an Italian cream garnished with many-hued flowers, a delicate rose-scented marble cream, and a sumptuous pink strawberry cream made with a purée of the fresh fruit. As an adept hostess, Catherine ensured that chilled dessert plates were available for the creams, which she may have served herself.[98]

Liqueurs were handed around with the sweet dishes. When a cheese course was provided, the servants placed the platter for the host to serve. Macaroni, toasted cheese or, in our chosen menu, lobster salad would have been set in front of the hostess to serve those who preferred a savoury finish. An *étagère* piled high with fruits and sweets decorated the centre, flanked by candles and flowers, as Jane Carlyle had described.[99] Perhaps Catherine even filled her silver flower-stand with a small bouquet of flowers from their garden. The elegant stand was given to her by the Birmingham Institute when they honoured her husband.[100]

While it is possible to recreate the dinners from Catherine's many menus, setting her table is more challenging. The Dickenses owned much china, but their inventory did not list the pattern or the manufacturers. For everyday use, there was a 'green dinner set', probably a service for twelve, including 'six water dishes' that could keep food hot by filling the basin underneath with boiling water, a variety of serving platters, soup and butter tureens, and a special dish for hash. Her 'blue dinner set' had a few missing dishes (and may have been older), but was probably a service for sixteen with individual pie dishes. 'Two common blue dishes', which may not have belonged to the original set, were listed with the service.[101]

Their 'Best Dinner Set' undoubtedly was brought out for more elaborate dinner parties. Since the Dickenses served *à la russe*, there were fewer demands on the number of individual place settings, because the plates did not need to be changed as frequently. Fewer large serving platters were required as well. 'The Real Cook's Oracle' explained this advantage: 'have you twelve or twenty guests, all that is to be done, is to reinforce each plate as required, there being no necessity for extra dishes.'[102]

The best china was a service for twenty with various plate sizes, serving platters in graduated sizes and a variety of speciality dishes, such as pie dishes, a 'well dish' that had a depressed area on one side to capture juices from larger birds or roasts, a fish drain for serving fish poached whole, a salad bowl, and cheese stand.[103]

They owned three dessert services which appear to belong to the services already described; the 'common green' set probably matched the everyday dishes. The 'centre' dishes listed would have held fruits, nuts, or sweetmeats. The second dessert service may have belonged to the blue china or could have been a special set of porcelain painted with landscapes or natural history motifs, which guests often admired before they were served.[104]

There was also a 'Blue Tea-Set' that probably matched the blue china and doubtless was kept for afternoon tea, then becoming popular. Sugar bowls were not listed, but were usually included among the silverware. The 'Best Tea Set', as it was labelled, may have matched the dinner service.[105]

Glassware was a separate category in the 1844 inventory. The manufacturers are not known, but an article in the 1852 issue of *Household Words* discussed the Birmingham Glass Works.[106] Table pieces, such as a celery glass vase, cut-glass salts, glass butter dishes with stands and covers decorated with silver cows, and an épergne graced their table. Cut- and frosted-glass 'ice plates' were used for serving ice-cream or other frozen confections at dinner parties, and individual custard cups were among the glass dishes most likely reserved for family meals.[107]

******

Needless to say, the Dickenses did not favour the growing temperance movement. When Lydia Marie Child, the abolitionist, activist, and author of *The American Frugal Housewife*, commented on his description of the Temperance Convention in Cincinnati, Ohio, Charles replied:

> You hardly give me credit, I think, for being as good a friend to Temperance as I really
> am. As to denying myself my cheerful glass of wine because other men get drunk, I
> see no more reason for doing so, than I do for recognizing no distinction between
> Use and Abuse in any other commodity, temporal or spiritual. I am a great friend to
> Temperance, and a great foe to Abstinence.[108]

In fact, Ralph Waldo Emerson's impression of Dickens was of 'a gourmand and a great lover of wines and brandies'.[109] Emerson observed this first-hand, but might have presumed it from Dickens's fiction. Dickens, Thackeray and other contemporaries, in part defined a character's background, nature or situation by mentioning the type of alcohol imbibed and how it was drunk. In *Dombey and Son*, Dickens did not need to say that the wealthy merchant

Paul Dombey lacked human warmth. At his son's christening, when he asked his sister's friend, Lucetia Tox, to 'do me the honour of taking some wine', readers understood his cold-heartedness when Dickens wrote: 'There was a toothache in everything. The wine was so bitter cold that it forced a little scream from Miss Tox.'[110]

In 'First Fruits', perhaps written more from personal experience, Dickens and his co-author George Sala recalled, 'the first time we were ever treated as a man!' After dinner, the host said to the young chaps:

> 'Mr. Bud, will you help yourself, and pass the wine?'
>
> We did it, and felt that we had passed the Rubicon too. We helped ourself feebly, awkwardly, consciously. We felt that they were thinking 'Will he take more than is good for him? Will his eyes roll in his head? Will he disappear beneath the table?' But we did it, and bashfully sipped our wine, and even made impotent attempts to close our left eye critically, and look at it against the light. We have been promoted twice or thrice since, and have even sat in high places, and received honour; but our host has never said, with the same deep significance
>
> 'Mr. Bud, will you help yourself, and pass the wine?'[111]

For Charles Dickens, wine appreciation may have begun when he was a young reporter with a little money in his pocket. But his and his wife's enjoyment of imported wines paralleled the changes in middle-class drinking habits in Britain. Catherine had grown up in a convivial household and not only would have drunk wines and spirits and used them in cooking, but would also have learned to ferment beverages at home. The Edinburgh cookery book that was popular when Catherine and her sisters were growing up included an entire chapter on wines, cordials and beer-making – as did many other contemporary culinary and medical publications.[112]

There were recipes for home-made wines from flowers, such as elder; English fruits like elderberries, gooseberries, raspberries, and red currants or imports such as citrus fruits and ginger stems; garden herbs such as wormwood; and root vegetables like parsnips, horse-radish, and turnips. These sweet non-grape wines tended to appear at ladies' luncheons, and cordials were poured for women in their after-dinner retreat to the drawing-room, or were served at special teas. The Pecksniffs laid out their festive table with 'two bottles of currant wine, white and red; a dish of sandwiches (very long and very slim); another of apples; another of captain's biscuits (which are always a moist and jovial sort of viand); a plate of oranges cut up small and gritty with powdered sugar; and a highly geological home-made cake.'[113] Because they were less expensive, these country-style wines continued to be served by the lower classes well after grape wines were more widely available in Britain.

Certainly Charles and Catherine's appreciation of fine wine flourished as his literary reputation grew and they gained access to the privileged, their habits, and their homes. There was also a distinct change in the country at large while Catherine was setting pen to paper. For her parents, the term 'wine' would have meant the fortified Iberian wines: port, sherry, and Madeira. By the 1850s, Catherine and her husband would have begun serving table and vintage wines imported from Germany and France. Although the wine industry was plagued with adulteration, high tariffs, shifting political alliances and restricted production, middle-class Victorians were buying more varieties of imported wines than had their parents. Articles in *Household Words* and *All Year Round* began using the term 'light wine' to designate these non-fortified wines as a new commodity.[114] However, the 'art' of pairing 'the right wine with the right dish' was a relatively new concept even in France.[115]

With the greater variety of wines available, the equipment for serving and drinking them also increased. Whether swirling the wine to admire the jewelled hues of a claret, or smelling the fruity notes of a Sauterne, the Dickenses, like other wine enthusiasts, drank from the appropriate glassware. In their 1844 inventory, besides the tumblers and goblets for water, they owned wine, hock, sherry, liqueur and claret glasses, and two types of champagne glasses, oval and tulip-shaped. For decanting, there were quart and pint decanters, cut-glass claret jugs, and also water bottles for the table.[116] The Dickenses enjoyed sharing discoveries and often sent friends bottles of wine for them to try. When a vintage was particularly good, his comments were simple: 'The wine exhausts the language in its approving adjectives.'[117] Dickens could suggest reliable merchants in different regions. 'I forgot to tell Mrs. Macready to bear especially in mind at Broadstairs in connection with the bottled stout, ale, punch, wines and spirituous liquors, Mr. Ballard of the Albion Hotel,' Dickens recommended, 'one of the best and most respectable tradesmen in England.'[118]

A few wines became life-long favourites. Hock, champagne, Sauterne, Chablis, claret, dry golden sherry, rare old Madeira and vintage port were served with their 1850s dinners. Metternich hock, a white Rhine wine from Johannisberg for example, was ordered in 1842 as 'three dozen yellow seal, and three red. I have a dinner party on Saturday, and am out of both Wines.'[119] He continued to drink hock twenty-two years later. Forty-two bottles were among the cellar contents auctioned at Gad's Hill Place after his death.[120] However, the wine he evidently most prized in his later years was Château Brane Mouton, now known as Château Mouton Rothschild.[121] Some wines mentioned in Dickens's correspondence may have been difficult to purchase, or passed out of favour. Zeller-Baden was a hearty red wine Dickens described effusively. He sent six bottles for trial to Alfred Count D'Orsay in 1846, declaring it 'perfectly pure and genuine'.[122] On their return from Genoa and while only twelve miles from Strasbourg, the Dickenses purchased wine from an enormous cask under the Offenburg Town Hall from a merchant famous for his Zeller wine.[123] At a time when spurious concoctions flooded the market, part of its attraction may have been its unadulterated state. Liebfraumilch was supplied by the dealer Joseph Valckenburg of Worms while the Dickenses were living in Lausanne. Joseph and his brother, Francis, were partners in the firm founded by their grandfather Peter Joseph. The brothers became growers and shippers of a variety of wines, and they developed a client-base in England.[124] In reply to Joseph's inquiry, Charles verified that the wine arrived safely and 'its flavour is quite wonderful'.[125]

They continued to enjoy the vintage when the poet Alfred, Lord Tennyson and his party arrived unannounced in Lausanne, and the hospitable Dickenses 'gave them some fine Rhine wine, and cigars innumerable' as they visited in the open air of the garden.[126] Tennyson also recalled the biscuits that they served with the wine, since they were difficult to find. Unlike English ones, the biscuits were not 'sweet and soft, but hard and unsweet,' and accompanied 'a flask of Liebfraumilch, interpreted as "Virginis lac", as I dare say you know,' he reported.[127] The Dickenses introduced others to the wine: 'dine together here on Sunday…when we broach some of the Rhine Wine to its success, and wreathe the bowl, etc. etc.' stated the invitation to Thomas J. Thompson and the Weller family, 'firstly, because the Rhine Wine will give him an immensely improved taste for the Rhine water,' Dickens mused. Afterwards it would help Mr Weller sleep in the coach as he travelled home.[128]

Hermitage was a rich full-bodied red or white wine from vineyards on the left bank of the Rhône. It was another favourite and when Dickens travelled, he would give a tumbler of 'whatever I may have', Sauterne or Hermitage, to Louis Roche, his European servant, as a reward after dinner.[129]

Sauterne and shrimps were a cherished combination.[130] 'A bottle of Chablis, or Sauterne, at *déjeûner* is looked upon merely as a bottle of water, just serving to wash down a few shell-fish, or other little preliminary whet, before the serious business of the meal begins,' stated the article in *Household Words*.[131] While sweet wines like Sauterne were banished to the end of the meal by the twentieth century, they had earlier been thought to entice the guest's palate in anticipation of dinner. Dickens had two small decanters of Barsac on the refreshment table for guests as they came into the drawing-room.[132]

Dickens frequently extended invitations to drink port to his comrades. 'Chops and Cheerfulness are impossible of connection, but Joints and joy are clearly related; and Port and peace go hand in hand,' he professed.[133] 'Will you come and dine with us (alone) at 5 on Sunday? We can then crack a peaceful bottle of *the* Port,' he often enticed Thomas Beard.[134] 'I have made a purchase of port which I should like you to taste. It is *rayther* uncommon.'[135] Dickens mentioned two makers by name: 'Twenty', a famous vintage that they 'kept a few last lingering caskets with the gem enshrined therein,' and 'Croft's London Particular', which was actually a Madeira. Port, predominantly a gentleman's drink, was usually brought out with the cigars after dinner while the ladies gathered in the drawing-room.[136] Savouries, or classic combinations such as Stilton cheese, biscuits, fruit and nuts, enhance the flavour of a glass of port and often accompanied it. In the Dickens house-hold, toasted cheese or macaroni and cheese were informal favourites judging from a decade of Catherine's menus.

Sherry was frequently ordered from the Ellis family, usually from six to a dozen bottles at a time, and combined with requests for port.[137] Ever versa-tile, sherry was drunk before, during, or after dinner. Two large decanters were available in the drawing-room as Catherine greeted guests.[138] Since Ellis continued to supply Dickens after the separation, we can surmise the types of sherry purchased in earlier years. In the 1870 cellar inventory, four cate-gories were listed: twelve dozen 'brown Sherry, dry, golden', two dozen 'Solera Sherry', and a dozen 'Amontillado'. Golden Sherry was purchased in magnums. There were thirteen 'very old, full flavoured, dry' bottles, nearly forty-eight bottles of 'rare old Madeira', and five bottles from the 1818 vintage.[139] However, Spanish Manzanilla was disliked. Dickens wrote to the

Countess of Lovelace, who had recommended it: 'I find, on further consideration, that I don't like Manzanilla! People who dine with me won't hear of it. I have been horribly reproached for offering it.' Dickens thought the wine, so highly publicized by Richard Ford in *A Hand-Book for Travellers in Spain*, was too bitter and explained 'I find that weak chamommile [sic] tea is a wonderful imitation of this wine.'[140]

'And let me have, if you please, four dozen of Sparkling Champagne,' Dickens requested from Ellis, along with six dozen bottles of Metternich hock. 'I have a dinner party on Saturday, and am out of both Wines. I want them, therefore, with all speed.'[141] Edmund Saul Dixon dubbed champagne 'the confectionary [sic] of wine-making' in his article 'A Bottle of Champagne'. He admitted that the French reserved their sparkling wine for desserts while the English drank champagne with dinner.[142]

Dickens instructed their servant, 'at Supper, let there be a good supply of Champagne all over the table.' They did not want champagne served before the meal, there were other wines for that.[143] Perhaps they were in agreement with Soyer about serving champagne. Soyer suggested maximizing the experience by opening two bottles (rather than one) after the guests were seated. He argued that sparkling wine not only 'prepares the palate for entrées', but by opening the bottles together, the wine goes farther, can be served more quickly when poured in glasses and passed on salvers, to give the appearance of being generous. In addition, there was enough champagne for 'challenges', a tradition lost from Victorian times where a gentleman lifts his glass to a specific lady and asks her to drink a toast with him. This obviously added a distinct liveliness to the dinner party.[144] Of course the Dickenses always lifted a glass of champagne in celebration of finished projects.[145] The bubbly did not have to be French, when in Italy a sparkling 'Vino d'Asti' substituted nicely.[146]

The Dickenses served a number of different liqueurs, particularly after they expanded their repertoire by living abroad. Kirschwasser and Curaçoa were drunk, and in later years a case of Eau d'Or, the French equivalent of Goldwasser with a flavour of anise and caraway, was brought home. Since it was Mrs Lemon's favourite, they sent a couple of bottles to her.[147]

For suggestions in buying, storing, and using wines, *Household Words* published other well-written articles for their readers. 'Our Wine Merchant' provided helpful information and a recipe for French champagne salad, a bowl full of fresh fruit 'covered thickly with pounded loaf-sugar' and bathed in champagne. To keep the fruit salad chilled, 'some small globules of transparent ice are placed about in the Salad.' The writer declared 'nothing can be more delicious and refreshing and all the ladies like it.'[148] This is a recipe that periodically resurfaces.

Dickens observed wine-making first-hand in Genoa and he remained fascinated by the process.[149] *Household Words* published a series of eight wine articles for armchair travellers, which highlighted walks over the chalky soils and through the fragrant harvests of the best vineyards. 'The Hill of Gold' rambled over the Côte-d'Or following 'Jean Raisin' through the process of wine-making. Since the best Burgundy stayed in the area, the author recommended purchasing a barrel and ageing it in one's own cellar.[150] 'A Dash Through the Vines' compared Bordeaux with the other French wine regions.[151] 'Claret', 'Cognac', and 'Sherry' rounded out the series.[152] 'The Hall of Wines' described a Parisian paradise, that is, a shopping area retailing wines, vinegars, liqueurs, and accompanying paraphernalia.[153]

Unlike his fellow countrymen, Charles drank more wine than beer. Statistics gathered in 1851–2 reported that each person drank $22\frac{1}{2}$ gallons of alcoholic liquor annually, that is, $21\frac{1}{4}$ gallons of beer, one gallon of spirits, and only a quart of wine.[154] The low wine consumption reflected the high duties, roughly 5s 9d per bottle in 1852. Dickens argued for repeal. Articles like 'Really a Temperance Question', and three years later, 'Strictly Financial', voiced strong criticism.[155] Even for those who were willing to pay the exorbitant duty, there was less wine available. Fungal disease, which preceded phylloxera, had begun to destroy the French vineyards.[156] As a result, adulteration became rampant. 'Wine Wizards' concocted spurious potions with aged corks to reinforce the deception. *Household Words* alerted readers to these tricks.[157]

Dickens, who was raised in the hop-growing region of Kent, certainly appreciated well-crafted beers, ales, stouts, and porters. He assigned the article 'The Chemistry of a Pint of Beer' to Percival Leigh for the second volume of *Household Words*. The cleverly written piece was based on Michael Faraday's lectures.[158] Adulteration of beer was as rife as of wine, and Leigh's article disclosed the practices found in the beer industry.[159] 'Bitter things have been lately said concerning beer,' opened Wills's article, entitled 'Constitutional Trials', also written about the scandalous practices of brewers and beer sellers.[160] It is unlikely that the Dickens household made its own beer since brewing tubs and gear were not listed in the inventory, but casks of beer were always at the ready in their cellar. A portion of the cask would have been allotted to the servants. It was not uncommon for the cook to be allowed to drink beer as a way of combating the hot conditions of the kitchen. According his journal, three eighteen-gallon casks were delivered fresh to Charles on 16 January 1841. The first would be 'fit to tap' in a month, he noted.[161] Even when they were in North America, he organized deliveries. Dickens wrote to his brother from Cincinnati, Ohio, asking him to be sure 'to have two strong men in, to roll the casks out, and stand them on the horse in the old place,' and to time this about a month before their return or 'it will not be in drinking trim when we arrive'.[162]

To Thomas Beard, whose family were brewers, Dickens once confidently announced, 'the beer is in a high state of perfection' in a dinner invitation.[163] He favourably contrasted the barrels of 'meeker and gentler, and brighter ale' they had in the cellar to Harrison Ainsworth's supplies.[164] When Dickens planned a train trip, he arranged to carry lunch and reported to Beard that he 'ordered a box of cold mutton sandwiches, some Captains' biscuits, and a pint and a half of Mild Porter in a bottle. These we shall take with us. And I think – with sich [sic] a basket – we shall be as nearly as possible all right?'[165]

Beers, wines, and punch accompanied meals, picnics, 'gypsy outings', and other excursions. Learning to drink responsibly was a worthy lesson passed on from father to son, although not without its anxieties. Fortified with two immense Fortnum and Mason hampers, Dickens and Thomas Beard, Charley's godfather, visited Charley at school and, along with 'three other Etonian Shavers', the party proceeded by boat down river where they ate outdoors. The tobacco and champagne 'in the starn of the wessel' were ostensibly for the men until the rules were relaxed.[166] 'What I suffered for fear those boys should get drunk – the struggles I underwent in a contest of feeling between hospitality and prudence – must ever remain untold,' he wrote to Mrs Watson before disclosing that the boys were very good, but 'the speech of one became thick, and his eyes too like the lobster's to be comfortable.' The boy recovered and later that evening they were returned to the school after tea and rashers of bacon at a public house.[167]

Dickens was known as a fabulous punch maker. Occasionally they purchased a commercial milk punch, most likely Chichester Punch, with other purchases of brandy, rum, and hollands (Dutch gin), which were ingredients for his own recipe.[168] The Dickenses served punch casually in a 'cool green glass', and probably enjoyed drinking it outdoors in the refreshing breeze of the summer garden.[169] For dinner parties, they usually had a bowl of gin-punch on ice waiting under the refreshment table, later ladled out by Dickens or a close friend like Mark Lemon.[170] Certainly no holiday festivity would be complete without a decorated bowl of Dickens's punch. He shared his recipe with Mrs Watson after they left Switzerland in 1846.[171] Two recipes have been published, and are reproduced here from articles in the *Dickensian*. K.F. Yapp provided the following recipe in 1905:

> To Make Three Pints of Punch
>
> Peel into a very strong common basin (which may be broken, in case of accident, without damage to the owner's peace or pocket) the rinds of three lemons, cut very thin, and with as little as possible of the white coating between the peel and the fruit, attached. Add a double-handfull [sic] of lump sugar (good measure), a pint of good old rum, and a large wine-glass full of brandy – if it be not a large claret glass, say two. Set this on fire, by filling a warm silver spoon with the spirit, lighting the contents at a wax taper, and pouring them gently in. Let it burn three or four minutes at least, stirring it from time to time. Then extinguish it by covering the basin with a tray, which will immediately put out the flame. Then squeeze in the juice of the three lemons, and add a quart of *boiling* water. Stir the whole well, cover it up for five minutes, and stir again.
>
> At this crisis (having skimmed off the lemon pips with a spoon) you may taste. If not sweet enough, add sugar to your liking, but observe that it will be a *little* sweeter presently. Pour the whole into a jug, tie a leather or coarse cloth over the top, so as to exclude the air completely, and stand it in a hot oven ten minutes, or on a hot stove one quarter of an hour. Keep it until it comes to table in a warm place near the fire, but not too hot. If it be intended to stand three or four hours, take half the lemon-peel out, or it will acquire a bitter taste.
>
> The same punch allowed to grow cool by degrees, and then iced, is delicious. It requires less sugar when made for this purpose. If you wish to produce it bright, strain it into bottles though silk.
>
> These proportions and directions will, of course, apply to any quantity.[172]

The second recipe, also believed to have been sent to Mrs Watson, was published a year later. To make gin punch, just replace the brandy with gin. They are well worth the effort.

Pour into a jug in this proportion: –

Ten wine-glasses of Madeira,

Two-thirds of a wine-glass of brandy,

Four wine-glasses of water.

Add the peel of a small lemon, cut very thin.

Sweeten to taste. Plunge into the whole a brown [slice of] toast.

Grate a little nutmeg over the surface.

Tie a cloth over the jug, and stand it in a cool place, or in cold water until you are

ready to drink the contents.[173]

Other traditional concoctions, like negus, were disdained by the upper classes in the nineteenth century, according to Edward Hewett and W.F. Axton.[174] In an often-repeated passage from Dickens's letter, Forster described a mangled request for negus to warm himself and Catherine one chilly evening in Scotland. Dickens had given the directions to a young Gaelic-speaking servant who worked in the private house near Loch Leven where they stayed.[175] We cannot be sure they ever received their negus that blustery night, but the drink would have been a welcome antidote for the damp Scottish weather. Hot toddy drinks warmed the body in homes without central heating. A considerate host served steaming beverages to their guests at the end of the evening to brace them for a cold carriage-ride home.[176]

CHAPTER VI
AMATEUR DRAMATICS AND LADY CLUTTERBUCK

The theatre was a natural outlet for Charles Dickens's boundless energy. Playwrights, actors, the excitement of the green-room, the brightness of the footlights, and the thunderous applause of the audience were woven into the day-to-day fabric of his being. It is not surprising that he enticed his wife to take a role early in their marriage, or coached his children for Twelfth Night performances, and perhaps least of all, that his involvement with a young actress irreparably changed all those relationships. *Used Up: A Petit Comedy in Two Acts*, from which the pseudonym Lady Clutterbuck was taken, was adapted by Dion Boucicault and Charles Mathews from Félix-Auguste Duvert's farce *L'homme blasé*. The work had enough personal resonance for Dickens to base the fictional introduction he wrote for his wife's menu book on the role she performed. Lillian Nayder makes a case that the play, like other farces, 'ridicules the institution of marriage, which it represents as a matter of money rather than love.' Dickens, in effect, set up the dynamic between Lady Clutterbuck and the character of Mary, the farmer's sweet young niece, which left Catherine Dickens as the 'unattractive and undesirable wife' on and off stage. By choosing the pen name of Lady Clutterbuck, 'possibly at her husband's prompting, Catherine plays along with a joke told at her own expense.'[1]

Dickens had begun organizing theatrical performances to raise money for causes he championed by the late 1840s.[2] But earlier (1842) he had talked Catherine on to the stage when they visited Montreal and took roles in several well-received productions. 'The audience, between five and six hundred strong, were invited as to a party; a regular table with refreshments being spread in the lobby and saloon,' he recounted. The 23rd Royal Welch Fusiliers made up the orchestra and the Garrison Amateurs performed comedic works. Catherine took her place as Amy Templeton in John Poole's farce *Deaf as a Post*. 'But only think of Kate playing! and playing devilish well, I assure you!' the stage-managing Dickens boasted.[3] She did not take the stage again until the 1851 production of *Used Up*, although she often participated in the activities of her husband's amateur acting companies. Nor was she the first to play Lady Clutterbuck in his troupe. The role fell to Mary Cowden-Clarke when the comedy was presented in July 1848, at the Theatre Royal in Glasgow as an untested replacement preceding two other farces, *Love, Law, and Physic* and *Two O'Clock In The Morning*.[4] On the night, Dickens reduced the admission price to attract a larger audience. They cleared an impressive £210–10s for the Relief Fund to assist unemployed actors and the Shakespeare Fund, to endow a curatorial position for Shakespeare House.[5]

Mrs Cowden-Clarke described the enthusiasm of the cast as they travelled that summer from London to Manchester, Liverpool, Birmingham, Edinburgh and, finally, Glasgow.[6] They included the editor of *Punch*, Mark Lemon; the artists, Augustus Egg and Frank Stone; the illustrators, George Cruikshank and John Leech; Dickens's youngest brother, Frederick; a professional actress, Anne Romer; the author G.H. Lewes; and Charles's friend John Forster.[7] Catherine toured with the group and provided comfort and support. In almost schoolgirlish tones, Mrs Cowden-Clarke portrayed Dickens as 'ever present, superintending, directing, suggesting, with sleepless activity and vigilance.' His punctuality, methodical precision, and 'incessant watch that others should be unfailingly attentive and careful throughout,' made him, she simpered, anything but dictatorial.[8] The company addressed him as 'Dear Dickens' or 'Darling Dickens', while he referred to himself as 'The Implacable Manager.' Dickens created rules for rehearsal still in use today.[9] As a result of the 'diligent rehearsals', she recalled that the performance of *Used Up* 'went with such extraordinary smoothness' that even the manager of the Glasgow Theatre complimented them.[10] She candidly disclosed Dickens's 'free-and-easy familiarity of a lawyer patronizing an actress.' She gushed, 'it is something to remember, having been tucked under the arm by Charles Dickens, and had one's hand hugged against his side! One thinks better of one's hand ever after.'[11] It was a gay time for all. Lemon developed a falsetto giggle for his character, which never failed to provoke hilarity. An Edinburgh man commented that he had never seen 'anything like those clever men; they're just for all the world like a parcel of school-boys.'[12]

Probably in consultation with his wife, Dickens planned dinners for the troupe when they first arrived in a new town and following the last performances. As host, he assumed the head of the table and carved the roasts. Mary Cowden-Clarke sat next to him. Because she ate so little, he catered to her 'kindly and persuasively, tempting my appetite by selecting morsels he thought I should like.' After serving her a piece of chicken on one occasion, she acknowledged it in Captain Cuttle's words from *Dombey and Son*. 'Liver wing it is!' she said, much to his amusement. Dickens had a 'peculiar grace in taking any sudden allusion of this kind to his writings.'[13] She thought no one could better make ' "a party for pleasure" truly pleasant and worthy of its name than he. There was a positive sparkle and atmosphere of holiday sunshine about him.'[14] All the while, Catherine tolerated his flirtatiousness.

******

The plot of *Used Up* works well as a frame for our menu book's fictional introduction. That little piece of prose begs recollection of the characters in the play. Lady Clutterbuck is the twice-widowed neighbour of Sir Charles Coldstream, a wealthy, but bored baronet. The first scene opens with Coldstream's servant James and Ironbrace the blacksmith discussing the construction of a window balcony that would overlook the river below. Farmer Wurzel's niece, Mary, who embodies 'some of the finest qualities that belong to her sex,' enters.[15] Mary intends to repay her mother's £20 debt to Coldstream, formerly her childhood playmate. While she waits, Ironbrace, who had once been a wealthy foundry owner, tells her his sad tale about his wife's kidnapping and his own reduced circumstances.

Meanwhile, in the salon, a melancholy Coldstream is being entertained by his *bon vivant* friends, Sir Adonis Leech and the Honourable Tom Saville, who propose adding some excitement to his life. 'My dear Leech,' Coldstream laments:

> You began life late – you are a young fellow – forty-five – and have the world yet before you – I started at thirteen, lived quick, and exhausted the whole round of pleasure before I was thirty. I've tried every thing, heard every thing, done every thing, know every thing and here I am, a man at thirty-three – literally used up – completely *blazé*.[16]

Coldstream, played by Dickens, is wearied by all their suggestions and offers £1,000 for any event that would make his pulse beat 'ten to the minute faster.' After exhausting other options, they advocate marriage. He likes the idea's novelty, but soon realizes he would be bored with the exertion of making a choice. 'If a wife now could be had like a dinner – for ordering,' he moaned, before his companions, in a moment of practicality, urge him to simply ask the next woman he sees.[17]

Enter the matronly Lady Clutterbuck soliciting donations for the school. With a lifeless finger on his pulse, Coldstream asks about her two previous husbands. The poor widow recounts her blissful three-month marriage to her true love Ironbrace, whom she believed had died, and her subsequent marriage that provided a title and financial security. Indifferent, Coldstream proposes marriage, and gives her ten minutes to decide while he takes a nap.

Meanwhile Mary, anxious to repay her mother's debt, shows herself into the salon and learns of Coldstream's proposal. Ever helpful, Mary offers the older woman advice about Coldstream's melancholy moods, but is soundly rebuffed with 'Heyday, child! – are you going to instruct me how to take care of a husband?'[18]

Sir Adonis Leech then recognizes Lady Clutterbuck as the former Mrs Ironbrace. She, in turn, realizes Leech was the very person who told her of Ironbrace's death and then took advantage of her, but before she is able to attend to the business at hand, that is, accepting Coldstream's marriage proposal, Ironbrace arrives. He sees his wife and concludes that it was Sir Charles Coldstream who had kidnapped her. Feeling his pulse elevate, Coldstream delights in the mayhem. The infuriated Ironbrace attacks him, and in the fight they fall out of the window and are presumed drowned. Each is held liable for the other's death.

The second act opens in Farmer Wurzel's modest but cosy kitchen. Unbeknownst to the others, Mary's uncle has hidden Ironbrace in the secret passage under the house, and she has transformed Sir Charles Coldstream into 'Joe, the Plough Boy'. As they sit in the kitchen, Mary lovingly serves 'Joe' a comforting bowl of hot soup, some bacon, cabbage, and a piece of 'nice white bread' she had made herself.

A few comic twists keep the plot lively. Coldstream's companions claim his estate, he secretly adds a codicil leaving everything to Mary, and predictably, they propose marriage to her. But pure sweet Mary chooses 'Joe', whom she adored since childhood. He is elated both for his quickened pulse and the realization that Mary loves him for himself, and not, as he phrased it, 'for my dinners.'[19] His true identity is recognized, however, and he is held under house-arrest awaiting the authorities. Remembering the cottage's secret passageways he knew as a boy, 'Joe' opens the trap door and sees the hidden Ironbrace, whom he believes to be a ghost. When Mary's uncle returns, he admits that Ironbrace is also alive. After explanations and forgiveness, Sir Charles Coldstream ends the play with a most Dickensian sentiment:

> I've found within this lowly farm what I've sought in vain amidst the dissipation of Europe – a home – yes, I've had a good lesson – a man's happiness, after all, lies within himself – with employment for the mind, exercise for the body, a domestic hearth, and a mind at ease, there is but one thing wanting to complete his happiness – the approbation of his friends, without which there is nothing in it.[20]

The next performance of *Used Up* did not occur for two and a half years but, in the meantime, Dickens's amateur dramatics found new pastures. Richard and Lavinia Watson had met the Dickenses in 1846 in Lausanne. The men shared views on social reform and they developed a friendship, as did their wives.[21] The Dickenses first visited the Watsons at their Northamptonshire estate of Rockingham Castle in November, 1849.[22] 'Picture yourself,' Dickens wrote to John Forster, 'a large old castle, approached by an ancient keep, portcullis, &c, &c, filled with company, waited on by six-and-twenty servants' parodying Henry Coleman's recent publication *European Life and Manners in Familiar Letters to Friends*. 'The slops (and wine-glasses) continually being emptied; and my clothes (with myself in them) always being carried off to all sorts of places, and you will have a faint idea of the mansion in which I am at present staying.'[23]

Mary Boyle was a distant cousin of Lavinia Watson. Since she was a great fan of the Boz's work, she wanted to visit when the Dickenses were at Rockingham. Of the family of the earls of Cork, her broad social network seemed to make her the 'universal cousin' of everyone.[24] Her nephew described her as a 'light-winged butterfly' (she stood barely five feet tall) who 'flits from flower to flower, resting long on none.' According to him, her 'brilliant wit and imperturbable good nature' made her welcome in the homes of many distinguished families.[25] As a boy, Henry Dickens remembered her as 'full of life and with a strong sense of humour.'[26] Eschewing gossip and scandal, she became friends with many of the literati, including Tennyson, Mrs Browning, James Russell Lowell, Walter Savage Landor, and Wordsworth.[27] The blue-eyed blonde was two years Charles's senior and herself the author of two historical novels, a poetic drama, and a book of poetry.[28] Accomplished, independent and well-bred, she willingly conspired in Dickens's ventures. The novelist was smitten.[29]

Mary Boyle and Charles maintained their friendship. Other theatricals occupied them. At first there was the performance at Knebworth, the home of Sir Edward Bulwer Lytton, but both Mary and Catherine had to withdraw from their roles.[30] However, a reprise of *Used Up* at Rockingham Castle in 1851 cast Catherine as Lady Clutterbuck and Mary Boyle as the farmer's niece Mary. The contrast of Catherine Dickens, although five years younger than Mary Boyle, must have been sharp in both their roles and their personalities. In a bizarre way, the dull, plodding character of Lady Clutterbuck and her charity work with the ragged school may have more closely fit the kindly, but lacklustre Mrs Dickens – or at least in Dickens's perceptions. The fresh-faced farmer's niece in the character of Mary, found a willing personification in the exuberant and sprightly Miss Boyle. Even her costume, a perky pink muslin frock with short sleeves, overlaying apron with pockets and ribbons, and a little mop cap on her pretty head, provided theatrical simplicity for a sophisticated woman.[31]

Oddly, in her memoirs, Mary omitted any mention of the performance or of her brother Cavendish Boyle's, who took the part of Farmer Wurzel. But the old-world splendour of the Tudor architecture of Rockingham Castle that she described must have added immeasurably to the scenery designed for the oak-panelled dining-room already emblazoned with heraldic shields.[32] *Used Up* was particularly challenging since two of the characters were required to be in hiding for one of the scenes. The minutest details were all important to Dickens, who declared: 'It cannot possibly be a success, if the smallest pepper-corn of arrangement be omitted.'[33] On 15 January 1851 the stage was set, the actors dressed, and a successful performance was delivered with Catherine as Lady Clutterbuck, Mary as Mary, and Charles in the dual lead roles.[34]

The day of the performance, he wrote a note to Mary Boyle from the 'Loft over Stable' referring to scenes from *Used Up*.[35] His command of the language allowed him to juggle angst, illusion, disillusionment, and humour, but the specific issue was obscured by his clever prose. If their relationship was ripe for a dalliance, he appears to have been unable or unwilling to submit at that point. Nine days after the Rockingham performance, his letter to Lavinia Watson moved to a personal note. 'Kate will have told you, I dare say, that my despondency on coming to town' was lifted at a mutual friend's dinner party, but his slow recovery was still 'liable to sudden outbursts of causeless rage, and demoniacal gloom.' In his inimitable style, Dickens predicted:

'What a thing it is, that we can't be always innocently merry, and happy with those we like best, without looking out at the back windows of life!' He continued more ominously, 'Well – one day perhaps – after a long night – the blinds on that side of the house will be down for ever, and nothing left but the bright prospect in front.'[36]

What did Catherine make of Charles's relationship with Miss Boyle? Although he provided no evidence, Georgina Hogarth's biographer Arthur Adrian stated that from the first, Catherine 'seems not to have entered happily into the group at Rockingham Castle.' His assertion that Catherine was 'on the brink of a nervous collapse and pathetically insecure as to her own charms,' perpetuates the same myth.[37] Perhaps Adrian would have still held his disparaging, yet unfounded view, and interpreted what he called a 'mock flirtation' differently had he had access to the extensive archive now available.[38] In another study, Michael Slater suggests that Catherine took her husband's flirtations in her stride and that his relationship with Mary Boyle was based on 'affectionately friendly terms', retained until his death in 1870.[39] Others, including myself, argue that none of Dickens's biographers has fully assessed the depth of the Boyle-Dickens friendship.[40] Earlier attractions to young girls like Christiana Weller and married women like Mary Cowden-Clarke had been relatively safe. Mary Boyle, on the other hand, was a spirited woman, financially independent and a worldly aristocrat. Was she willing to have an affair? We will never know what transpired, but the intrigue, intensity, and emotional spillover had an impact on the Dickens home and would most directly affect his wife. Only two months after the Rockingham production, Catherine was admitted to Great Malvern spa with Charles writing to Dr James Wilson in these terms:[41]

I am anxious to place Mrs. Dickens under your care. As her case is a nervous one and of a peculiar kind, I forbear to describe it… As I think it may be advisable for Mrs. Dickens to remain at Malvern some time, and as I shall come with her, and her sister also, (several of our children probably following) I do not contemplate her living in your house. Indeed, under any circumstances, I should have my reasons (founded on my knowledge of her) for desiring to settle her in some temporary home of her own. With this view, I purpose sending down a trusty female servant, who has been with her many years and accompanied her in all our travels.[42]

The next day he wrote to Lavinia Watson, 'Don't appear to know it, but

I am rather uneasy about Kate, who has an alarming disposition of blood to the head, attended with giddiness and dimness of sight.' He added, 'I am inclined to believe that it is not at all a new disorder with her.'[43] Catherine's own letter to Fanny Kelly at the same time said, 'I have been suffering for some time from fullness in the head, which has lately increased so much, & caused me such violent headaches &c.,' that she was 'ordered to go at once to Malvern and try what change of air and cold water will do' for her.[44] Her 'nervous illness', probably 'migraines combined with post-natal depression', required 'repose, and the absence as much as possible from worry or domestic cares.'[45]

Accompanied by her maid and sister, Catherine took up residence and Charles spent a considerable amount of time with her. One would like to believe he was being supportive of his wife yet the treatment and location would have had their own appeal. Dickens referred to the picturesque town of Great Malvern as 'a most beautiful place.'[46] The old church, white houses with colourful gardens, rose-covered parterres, and the surrounding lush green fields dotted with pear and chestnut trees must have been a welcome refuge from the drab grey of London.[47] The Dickenses had known many people who were treated there.[48] Six years earlier, he had congratulated Douglas Jerrold for returning from Malvern as 'discharged cured', when Jerrold's bent stiff body returned to a happy light-stepping figure.[49] The spa attracted other famous patients, including the Carlyles, Huxley, Ruskin, and Darwin.[50]

For Catherine, the depression and any psychological distancing by her husband could be dealt with outside their social obligations. Sheltered from her household routine and other demands, Catherine would have been pampered by an understanding staff and empathetic fellow patients at Malvern – if she wished to socialize. Janet Brown makes the case for Charles Darwin, which may well have been true for Catherine Dickens, that 'alternatively, or simultaneously, his [Darwin's] illness may well have acted as a mediator in married life.'[51] We do not know if Catherine began compiling her menus for the book while at Malvern, but by the 20 March 1851, she wrote to Joseph Howe saying that she was feeling a great deal better.[52] Dickens's letters confirmed her progress. Unfortunately, five days later, Dickens had to write to his wife about his own father's sudden death.[53] Catherine's peaceful world at Malvern was shattered again two weeks later by the death on 14 April 1851, of their eight-month-old daughter, Dora Annie, whom she had left in the care of the family and nurse. Catherine had had a difficult pregnancy and delivery the previous August. The baby's health was not strong. In February, Dickens wrote that 'Our poor little Dora is very ill – with something like congestion of the Brain. She was taken with it on Saturday at midnight, and, though better this morning, is not out of danger.' He confessed 'the little thing was so ill yesterday, that we thought it right to have her baptized by [The Rev. James] White, who was here.'[54] A few days later he wrote to Forster, 'Little Dora is getting on bravely, thank God!'[55] She had been doing well and 'was quite charmed to see me', Dickens reported to Catherine, by this time at Great Malvern, on 26 March.[56] Dora died three weeks later.

Forster, who accompanied Catherine home from Malvern, reported to Dr Wilson that they 'had a sorrowful journey enough, but I really think that Catherine is somewhat better since her return. She grieves bitterly, of course – but I fancy the grief & suffering less morbid than it was for the first twelve hours.'[57] To Fredrick Evans, his publisher, Dickens wrote, 'Mrs. Dickens is as well as I could hope. I am not without some impression that this shock may even do her good.'[58] To Edward Bulwer-Lytton, he said the same and added, 'I do not yet know what the effect of such a shock may be on her nervous condition, but she is quite resigned to what has happened and can speak of it tranquilly. She is so good and amiable that I hope it may not hurt her.'[59] To his sister Letitia (Mrs Henry Austin), he confided, 'I write hastily…and to tell you that Kate has borne her shock as well as I could hope, but that she is very far from well. We have buried our poor little pet [Dora],' in Highgate Western Cemetery near John Dickens's grave.[60]

******

Afterwards, various domestic duties occupied Catherine, including the move to Tavistock House and the finalizing of the menu book. The play *Used Up* was revisited, at least as a subtext, in the introduction to and apparent authorship of *What Shall We Have For Dinner?* By providing the given name of Maria to the pseudonym during the first two years that Catherine's book was published, they added a personal dimension to the fiction. In the 1854 edition, the author's name was shortened to 'Lady Clutterbuck', although the initials 'M.C.' remained at the end of the introduction, which itself was unchanged. 'Lady Clutterbuck's' mission was to help her 'many fair friends' with the universal problem of deciding what to serve one's husband for the evening meal.[61]

Sir Stephen Clutterbuck's given name was changed from the play, and became Jonas for the introduction – perhaps conjuring up images of the biblical Jonas, here not swallowed by, but swallowing the whale. Like the play, Clutterbuck was probably 'a little wizened old gentleman' of fifty-five years who wore powder, whose family was good, and 'his name a pretty one'.[62] Sir Jonas Clutterbuck may have had more than a sixpence, unlike his poor counterpart in the play, but he likewise liberated his spouse:

> *Lady Clutterbuck:* He soothed my indignation – for he had a good heart withal – by making me the only atonement in his power.
> *Sir Charles Coldstream:* I see – he left the country.
> *Lady Clutterbuck:* No, he died.
> *Sir Charles Coldstream:* Better still.
> *Lady Clutterbuck:* Yes. However, notwithstanding his behaviour, I mourned him the regular time.[63]

After the 1848 performance, lines from *Used Up* expressed Charles's mood in letters to the cast, particularly to Mary Cowden-Clarke. Amidst a dizzying schedule, he wrote to her from Devonshire Terrace quoting lines from the play. 'I have no energy whatever – I am very miserable. I loathe domestic hearths. I yearn to be a Vagabond,' as they had been when travelling to the various theatres. 'Why can't I marry Mary! Why have I seven children,' he stated somewhat facetiously, 'I am deeply miserable. A real house like this, is insupportable after that canvass farm wherein I was so happy.' Reflecting on his role as Joe the ploughboy, he continued, 'What is a humdrum dinner at half past five, with nobody (but John) to see me eat it, compared with *that* soup, and the hundreds of pairs of eyes that watched its disappearance [during the performance]!'[64] 'I am completely blasé – literally used up,' his next letter confessed, 'I am dying for excitement. Is it possible that nobody can suggest anything to make my heart beat violently, my blood boil, my hair stand on end – but no. Where did I hear those words (so truly applicable to my forlorn condition) pronounced by some delightful creature?'[65] Meanwhile Catherine was three months pregnant with their eighth child and not very well.[66] But three days before the baby was born, he wrote to Clarke again and, although his focus was redirected, the references persisted:

But had you seen him in 'Used up',
His eye so beaming and so clear,
When on his stool he sat to sup
The oxtail – little Romer near
   &c &c
— you would have forgotten and forgiven all.[67]

With the birth of Henry Fielding Dickens, the household returned to its regular activities, including Charles's birthday celebration, but the consistent pattern for the ageing Dickens was evident. He threw himself frenetically into projects that had socially worthy goals, provided self-expression, and stretched the boundaries of social mores. When the performers took their last bow and the party was over, there were fewer adoring fans to provide Charles with undivided attention, leaving Catherine, the family, and their friends to help him make the transition until the next project took hold.

In maintaining the play's farcical tone, the late Sir Jonas Clutterbuck had 'a host of other virtues, a very good appetite, and an excellent digestion' to which his widow was indebted 'for many hours of connubial happiness' – hours apparently, rather than years. Although he was not considered a gourmand, he had 'great gastronomical experience', and he certainly attended his share of banquets and corporation dinners having been an alderman for thirteen years.[68] An alderman's love of feasts was an easy target and certainly a useful device for the introduction. 'The Garrickers and the Alderman are wonderful temptations, so are the Vintages, if not the Vintners,' Dickens once wrote to Rev. Richard H. Barham when declining an invitation by the Vintners' Company where Barham, as the chaplain, would say 'grace over their turtle'. Dickens deliberated, 'On one side I perceive a clear head, looking forward to the end of Chuzzlewit. On the other, a blear-eyed (but amiable and prepossessing) Youth, drinking Soda Water and incapable of any greater mental exertion than ordering it. On the one side, a solitary chop. On the other a Gregarious and Aldermanic spread.'[69] If 1839, the year Sir Jonas Clutterbuck became an alderman, had significance to Dickens other than moving into Devonshire Terrace, that is not made clear.

According to 'Lady Maria Clutterbuck', the ideal arrangement for happy 'domestic relations' was to make home-dining more attractive than the popular men's clubs. Apparently the road to a rocky marriage, or worse still, more frequent business in the city, was 'a surplusage of cold mutton or a redundancy of chops'. She confessed 'a delicacy forgotten or misapplied' can embitter a husband's daily life. The unfortunate wife begins dreading the 'matutinal meal', which is 'only exceeded in its terrors by the more awful hour of dinner' itself. With the spirit of public service, she 'consented to give the world' the bills of fare approved by her late husband. Consoled as she was, her 'attention to the requirements of his appetite secured [her] the possession of his esteem until the last.'[70] Perhaps the relationship indicates a respectful, if loveless, marriage for 'Lady Clutterbuck', but it certainly implies a childless one. The introduction also inculcates what became a growing moralistic attitude that husbands should expect their home to be their tranquil castle and their wife the silent keeper of its orderliness. Dena Attar's comprehensive overview of British household books noted that there were many popular references to the 'disorganized home as the cause which drives a man to his club or to the alehouse,' particularly after John Ruskin's influential, *Sesame and Lilies,* was published.[71]

******

The years 1850 and 1851, the very time when Catherine must have been preparing her menu book, seem to mark a subtle shift in the dynamics of her marriage. For example, by late August 1850 Dickens began entertaining business guests at the *Household Words* office rather than exclusively at his home. At the time, Dickens was incredibly busy writing, editing, and managing his magazine in addition to other political and social activities. Was there a weakening of the bond between husband and wife at this juncture? That same month, leaving his wife in confinement with her mother and a nurse the very afternoon that his daughter Dora Annie was born, he joined the rest of the family at the beach.[72] His letter to his wife the following day was full of news of the children and their impressions of their new baby sister. He was looking forward to Catherine coming to Broadstairs as soon as she was able.[73] Nearly a week later, he wrote two letters from Broadstairs. In one, he asked his wife to have the maid 'make my bed in the night-nursery where I can have air' in case he was able to get home by 11 or 12 p.m. on Thursday. One assumes this was to avoid waking Catherine, who was recovering and 'will have shut up shop then'. His contingency plan was to return to London on Friday, and work all day at the *Household Words* office. 'I shall not come back [to Devonshire Terrace] until Saturday morning in any case. And of course come when I may, I shall come straight home.'[74] Dickens would not return until Saturday, because he had issued invitations for 'dinner on Friday at 6' to Downing Bruce, a barrister whom he interviewed for a series of articles. In the second letter, he made arrangements with his business manager, William Henry Wills, to 'have a roast loin of mutton for one thing'. Dickens commented on the lack of cutlery and other necessities for serving the food at a previous office dinner saying, 'we had nothing to cut and come again at, last time'.[75] Forster, Leech, Stone, Thackeray, and Wills made up the rest of the guests for an apparently successful dinner party. Bruce enjoyed the get-together remarking that 'the gloryfications of last night or rather this morning' included 'a first rate dinner Wines of every kind'.[76]

The office dining-room continued to be well stocked. Another note alerted Wills to a parcel with clean curtains and glass-cloths, and a delivery of cases with 'two dozen champagne and two dozen claret,' which 'had better be put in the top room'. [77] George Augustus Sala remembered the 'Noctes' hosted by Dickens. 'The repasts were not suppers, but dinners – substantial dinners sent in from an hotel close by: in York Street, Covent Garden. How often these social gatherings were held, I do not know. … There were ladies' nights, too; but to these fêtes I never had the honour of being bidden.' Writers such as Elizabeth Gaskell, Adelaide Procter, and Dinah Mulock (Mrs Craik) were among the first women writers for *Household Words* who were guests. [78] The dinner group usually included Charles Knight, Leigh Hunt, Richard H. Horne, and Dickens's 'young men' (William Blanchard Jerrold, Sidney Blanchard, W. Moy Thomas, Walter Thornbury), with William H. Wills, his business manager, who sat as second chair especially on the evenings before publication and after the half-yearly audits.[79] Conversations were sometimes 'welded into an article' for *Household Words*.[80]

One does not want to draw exaggerated conclusions from what is literally Lady Clutterbuck's warning about 'rendering "business in the city" of more frequent occurrence than it used to be in the earlier days of their connubial experience.'[81] No doubt there were many factors influencing Dickens's decision to entertain at the office, rather than socialize at home. Perhaps these first dinners began when their dining-room was closed up in anticipation of Catherine's removal to Broadstairs for the late summer months, or possibly he did not want to disturb his wife during her confinement, however, he did invite Frank Stone over for an 8:15 breakfast of kidneys, eggs, and ham the morning after the dinner for Downing Bruce.[82] Whatever the impetus, the dinners at the office continued, but they certainly were not the only business to have them. *Punch* magazine held in-house dinner-meetings, referred to as 'The Punch Table', on Wednesday nights for the editor, proprietors, and staff.[83]

Although Dickens met colleagues and friends at gentlemen's clubs and taverns, his office may have offered the privacy and informality necessary for frank discussions of highly sensitive subjects. Certainly it allowed him to entertain well beyond any club's closing-time. But whatever the reason, no matter how honourable or considerate, when Dickens held dinner parties in the office, it changed the social role of his home and more directly of his marriage. By limiting or eliminating his wife's participation on any level, Dickens (consciously or not) freed himself psychologically by redefining social and business functions. Neither Catherine's role as wife and house-keeper, nor her limited presence as hostess, was required. Dickens and his wife continued to entertain friends at home, but the office provided an exclusive venue, and one which could function outside the scrutiny of his family and their servants.

But 'Lady Clutterbuck' again dusted off her pen around 1854. Charles had just completed another major work, but at a price. 'Why I found myself so "used up", after Hard Times, I scarcely know,' he wrote referring to the Rockingham Castle performance of three years earlier.[84] The play may have been a fresh reminder of his introduction again being used for his wife's new edition of the menu book. Theatrics within the Dickens household main-tained a pulsating undercurrent. For one, Charles celebrated his forty-third birthday, and connived to see Mrs Henry Louis Winter (née Maria Sarah Beadnell) his boyhood heart-throb. Before travelling to Paris with Wilkie Collins, he wrote, 'When I return, Mrs. Dickens will come to you, to arrange a day for our seeing you and Mr. Winter (to whom I beg to be remembered) quietly to dinner,'[85] which sounds innocent enough, except that the nostalgic letters that followed suggested they meet secretly beforehand.[86] Several days later, Catherine dutifully called on the Winter family and invited them for dinner. [87] They were guests several times through the years, but soon after that first dinner, Dickens's ardour cooled faster than the leg of mutton.[88]

In addition to the personal drama, Charles staged public readings of his work to raise money, yet there was time to coach the children who 'have got up our Annual Fairy Play at home' for Twelfth Night.[89] By 1857, the Twelfth Night productions became so elaborate Dickens renovated their home for

Wilkie Collins's production, *The Frozen Deep*.[90] Catherine set the table for friends and workers, who were persuaded to 'take your mutton with us'.[91] And on performance night, some guests were invited to 'join the Green Room Supper after the play, and be jovial for an hour or so'.[92] Catherine did not take a role in the play as did her sister, but she had written invitations, acted as emissary, consulted on the crinoline problem (squeezing the large dresses becoming fashionable into the seating plan), and held fast on the number of attendees.[93] With the children dressed and the gin punch chilled, Catherine greeted their arriving guests and circulated during the intermission before helping the audience depart after the performance. When the 'last atoms of the theatre' were smashed at home, Catherine dealt with the predictable gloom and bad temper that always hung about her husband after these ventures.[94] Little did she realize that the impending public production of the play would dismantle their private lives.

THE INGREDIENTS OF
WHAT SHALL WE HAVE FOR DINNER?

CHAPTER VII
SOUPS AND SEAFOOD

As far as Lady Clutterbuck's civic-minded alderman-husband knew, and Catherine's real husband was aware when he wrote the introduction to *What Shall We Have For Dinner?* – turtle soup began the first course of a great banquet. Dickens was no stranger to these menus, he organized events with flare. On Saturday, 1 September 1843, for example, his inner circle honoured William Macready before the actor embarked on a tour of America. A colourful account of the event, published as 'A Dickens Dinner Party', chronicled the food: 'Turtle and Venison and Lamb and Ham and Goose and at least fifty other dishes…Hock, Sherry, Moselle, Madeira, Champagne, Port etc…Ices and Creams and Pine apples Melons and sundry other fruits.'[1]

Turtle feasts were traditional for important civic occasions or, as Soyer opined, 'turtle has been esteemed the greatest luxury which has been placed upon our tables.'[2] Green turtle, named for the colour of its fat, was the most prized. In 1852 , it was reported that the passive five- to six-foot reptiles were being caught at a rate of fifty a week off Ascension Island, the British victualling station in the Atlantic. Turtles could weigh as much as six hundred pounds, captured along the coasts of China and the East and West Indies, but the live turtles which were brought from the West Indies for the London taverns generally averaged between thirty-five and one hundred and twenty pounds. Only a third of the reptile was edible.[3] The beef-like meat was boiled, stewed or pan-fried as steaks. Soup, the most popular preparation, was usually served during the autumn or winter. [4]

In 1849, Soyer recommended that if one 'received the fine green turtle as a present', it should be sent to a place where they were accustomed to preparing it. 'I will, therefore, give you no receipts for cooking it,' but if one was curious, his previous cookbook, *The Gastronomic Regenerator*, provided instructions.[5] By 1865, when Mrs Beeton compiled her cookery book, home preparations for turtle meat and turtle soup were not even mentioned since the work was so laborious. Thomas Webster describes the process: the turtle's head had to be removed, and the body hung to drain overnight. The next morning, the meat from the calipash and calipee (upper and lower shields) and the fins were removed, cut into pieces and scalded before being added to the stock pot with the bones. Whole onions and sweet herbs were added and, when the meat was nearly cooked, it was cut into serving pieces. Forcemeat balls were made from the scrappier pieces, which were finely chopped and seasoned with sweet herbs, black pepper, mace, allspice, salt, and fortified with Madeira wine. The stock was reduced, strained, thickened, and seasoned with lemon juice, cayenne and salt. The turtle meat, balls of forcemeat and some of the flavourful gelatinous fat were added to the soup before serving.[6] As the authors of the article 'The London Tavern' confessed as they mused over their dinner: 'Our first thoughts are of zoology; our second of soup.'[7]

Turtle soup was such a luxury that enterprising cooks, who were unwilling to prepare the live reptile, developed mock versions using calf's head and tongue. Authors on both sides of the Atlantic gave mock-turtle soup recipes. Eliza Acton devoted six pages to the soup's preparation for an 'Old Fashion' version and also provided an updated one.[8] Her recipes were similar to those given nearly two decades later by Mrs Beeton. To make mock-turtle soup, a veal stock fortified with either Madeira or sherry was prepared with vegetables and herbs. The stock was usually seasoned with lemon juice and cayenne to finish the illusion, and slices of tongue and forcemeat balls of lean veal were added. Mock-turtle soup was so entrenched in the culture, Beeton's work even provided an economical version, at a third of the cost, for those on limited budgets. For this, veal knuckle and cow-heel created an inexpensive stock which was then dosed with anchovy or Harvey's sauce to approximate the original.[9]

Catherine did not suggest mock-turtle soup often, but when she did, the rest of the menu contained delicacies such as cod's head and other revered dishes, which she reserved for small winter dinner parties. Although real turtle soup was not listed in her menus, she did serve it at home. Once when the soup was received as a present with venison, they invited Thomas Beard to dinner. Dickens proclaimed, 'the notice is short because the turtle *won't keep* and its not a thing to be trifled with.'[10] And so the question, 'What shall we have for dinner?' was answered at least for that evening.

On other occasions, as guests finished their sherry in the drawing-room, tureens of piping hot soup or garnished platters of seafood were being carefully assembled below stairs. When these traditional beginnings were in place, the host led the guest of honour and the others to the dining-room. 'Volumes might be written on soups,' declared the article 'Common Cookery' in *Household Words*.[11] In his magazine, Dickens promoted nourishing meals assembled from inexpensive ingredients.[12] Influenced by rising food prices, crop failures, and first-hand experience in France, he and his reporters argued for practical changes. It was a battle, however, since his readership could afford more elaborate meals and the lower classes lacked practical culinary training. As the Edinburgh cookery-book author 'Meg Dods' observed, the English were 'at the very bottom of the scale' in their love of flavourful broths and hearty, well-prepared soups. She ranked the Scots second, deferring only to the French, in their facility to make soups.[13]

Perhaps as a result of her Scottish upbringing, nearly 45 per cent of Catherine's menus start with soup. In later editions, she adds nine more varieties of soup to the menus and includes six soup (or soup-stew) recipes to the appendix. These hearty concoctions are mainstays for cold weather, and the more delicate soups brighten her spring-summer menus. As the *Household Words* articles had advocated, Catherine too makes the most of 'unpromising materials', that is, she uses less desirable cuts of meat combined with root vegetables and grains as the backbone of healthy economical cookery. The authors of 'Common Cookery' cite the rules for making soups and their culinary cousins, stews: start with cold water for root vegetables and boiling water for meats, before reducing to a simmer until the ingredients are tender.[14]

The Dickenses' cook would have left the stockpot on the range all day. As Jennifer Davies has explained, in large homes, one pot was reserved for white stock made from chicken or veal, which was usually thickened, and another pot for brown stock made from beef bones, usually to produce a *consommé*. A quart of the rich brown stock could be boiled down to create an inch or so of glaze. When cooled, the glaze hardened and could be stored in skins like sausages. Small pieces were cut off as needed to enrich gravies and soups. Venison glaze was especially prized.[15] Fat removed from the stock was not wasted. It was melted and cooled several times until the lard was absolutely pure, and then carefully stored for use in making pastry or for deep-frying.

From Catherine's recipes, it is clear that she regularly had available fish stock, rich brown stock, beef and veal stocks, and broth made from fowl for soup-making. In her menus, only oxtail soup rivals vegetable soup in popularity. A delicate asparagus soup, for early summer menus, is the next most popular and, even though it was widely known, she provides a recipe in the appendix. Pea soup, made from dried peas in the winter and fresh green peas when available, appears in all seasons, and colourful soups like carrot, probably puréed, are cheerful winter openers. There are three soups with similar names: Scotch mutton broth, mutton broth and Scotch broth. The first she later renames winter soup. It is served with a fried cutlet added to the broth at the last moment. The second and the third are lightly garnished soups, which both produce secondary dishes from the boiled meat and vegetables that could be served separately.

When Catherine suggests only one soup in the bills of fare, it is usually a hearty one with meat or giblets. Following the convention, if she serves two or more soups, one is cream-based and the other is a clear broth usually with diced vegetables and meat. White soup, according to recipes by Eliza Acton, 'Meg Dods' and Isabella Beeton, is usually based on a white stock and a purée of veal or poultry. It may be combined with unsweetened almond paste, and is often seasoned with lemon peel and ground mace, then finished with cream.[16] Oyster soup, again thickened with cream, overflows with dozens of barely poached whole oysters. If there is a white cream soup on the one hand, on the other will be something contrasting: oxtail, hare, vermicelli, mock-turtle, and asparagus are all examples. Very occasionally, in one extra-large menu in the 1851 and 1852 editions, Catherine goes as far as suggesting three soups (hare, oxtail and mock-turtle) on the table at once, although the family kitchen inventory only lists two tureens. This idea was dropped for the 1854 edition but her repertoire has by then expanded to include some new soups, such as julienne, lettuce, semolina, macaroni and vermicelli. In the 1854 appendix, Catherine chose four soup recipes, among them vermicelli and vegetable, potato, and soup maigre. Her fourth soup was Palestine, also known as Jerusalem artichoke.[17]

Just as today, soup soothes a stuffy head. Catherine includes instructions for the cook to leave some of the fat in the mutton broth recipe when intended as a remedy for a severe cold. One could bet that whenever the Dickens household suffered from ill health, such as during London's influenza epidemic in 1847–1848, or during other common maladies and childhood illnesses, soup was an important part of the meal. Dickens's letters certainly testify to this, 'I shall be at home all day and evening. I have a sitch

[sic] of a cold!…There is cold roast beef, I *know* – and some soup,' his note assured. 'We are quite alone, and Kate recovering.'[18]

Soups are so comforting, it is not surprising that Dickens makes them central to his grimly charming fairytale *The Magic Fishbone*. The tale is about Princess Alicia, whose family is in reduced circumstances, and the magic fishbone she received from her fairy godmother that would grant one wish. Before the right opportunity presented itself, the practical princess (as babysitter) decides to entertain her seventeen siblings by letting them make lunch after their cook had run off. 'You shall all be cooks,' she declared.

> They jumped for joy when they heard that, and began making themselves cooks' caps out of old newspapers. So to one she gave the salt-box, and to one she gave the barley, and to one she gave the herbs, and to one she gave the turnips, and to one she gave the carrots, and to one she gave the onions, and to one she gave the spice-box, till they were all cooks, and all running about at work, she sitting in the middle, smothered in the great coarse apron nursing the baby.
>
> By and by the broth was done; and the baby woke up, smiling like an angel, and was trusted to the sedatest princess to hold, while the other princes and princesses were squeezed into a far-off corner to look at the Princess Alicia turning out the saucepanful of broth, for fear (as they were always getting into trouble) they should get splashed and scalded. When the broth came tumbling out, steaming beautifully, and smelling like a nosegay good to eat, they clapped their hands. That made the baby clap his hands; and that, and his looking as if he had a comic tooth-ache, made all the princes and princesses laugh. So the Princess Alicia said, 'Laugh and be good; and after dinner we will make him a nest on the floor in a corner, and he shall sit in his nest and see a dance of eighteen cooks.' That delighted the young princes and princesses, and they ate up all the broth, and washed up all the plates and dishes, and cleared away, and pushed the table into a corner; and then they in their cooks' caps, and Princess Alicia in the smothering coarse apron that belonged to the cook that had run away with her own true love that was the very tall but very tipsy soldier, danced a dance of eighteen cooks.[19]

******

Whitstable oysters, succulent lobster, firm-fleshed turbot, and world-famous Dover soles served with shrimp sauce and prawns were regional specialities on the Kentish coast in the Dickenses' time.[20] However, in today's 'land of fish and chips', the ordinary mid-nineteenth-century Englishman apparently did not like fish that much.[21] Enterprising London street vendors around 1850 were just introducing the crisp finger-food for a penny and, instead of fried potatoes, a slice of bread accompanied the inexpensive plaice or sole that was deep fried.[22] (Baked potatoes were sold by other vendors.)

Despite the advent of this new street food, several articles in Dickens's magazine chided his countrymen's dislike of fish. 'A Popular Delusion', co-authored by Dickens and William Wills for the very first volume of *Household Words,* rebuked the persistent 'old Celtic prejudice against fish': [23]

> Few poor persons will eat fish when they can get meat; many prefer gruel, and some slow starvation…Is this aversion to fish unconquerable? If it be not, what an enormous augmentation of wholesome food might be procured to relieve the increasing wants of the humble and needy.[24]

An article by Henry Morley in *Household Words* the next year stated flatly, 'we live surrounded by these ocean-fields, here we live in an island, we absurd people, and we don't eat fish.'[25] Even Soyer chastised his readers, 'Of all aliments that have been given to the human race for nourishment, none are more abundant or more easy to procure than this antediluvian species, and yet of how few do we make use.'[26]

Steeped in the philosophy of entitlement typical of the Victorian era, Dickens and Wills cited fecundity studies from W. Yarrell's *A History of British Fishes* to back their arguments that fish was a reliable food source.[27] To extol the virtues of eating fish, the authors described a fine dinner for twenty gentlemen at Mr Simpson's 'Fish Hord'n'ry' where the four o'clock meal began with pints of stout and porter. 'Suddenly a fine salmon sparkled and twinkled like a silver harlequin,' while a 'goodly dish of soles was set lower down' on the table. Flounders, fried eels, stewed eels, codfish, melted butter, lobster sauce and potatoes appeared in quick succession. The diners quickly offered grace before the five or six flushed waiters scurried about in preparation for the next course of boiled beef, mutton, and a huge dish of steaks that appeared and disappeared, as did the glasses of brandy. 'Cheese melted away. Crusts dissolved in air,' at the meal's conclusion.[28] Although the dinner was prepared by a commercial establishment, the well-fed authors heartily encouraged readers to prepare fish at home, and to share the dinner in pleasant company.

They also acknowledged the vastly improved transport systems servicing the densely populated cities and towns inland.[29] In the 1850s, the London market was well supplied with live, fresh, and preserved fish and seafood in all price ranges. Although by the 1820s, Scotch salmon had been successfully shipped on ice by George Dempster, a London fishmonger who created a profitable market for himself, he only catered to the wealthy. With the advances in transport, ice became cheaper and more practical for conveying perishable goods. Likewise, more sophisticated deep-sea trawlers were being designed, and could make longer voyages to fish at deeper levels.[30] Large store-boats with enormous swim tanks held the salt-water catch closer inland but these boats had to remain as low as Gravesend to maintain the proper salinity.[31] Fish would then be transported to market by land carriage, or by well-boats with the night tide, up to Billingsgate.[32] By 1856, the East Counties' 'fish trains' speedily shipped the hampers packed with the latest catch taken off the Yarmouth coast.[33] With the general accessibility of fresh fish, the popularity of and reliance on salted and pickled fish, such as herring, showed a noticeable decline from around 1850.[34]

George Dodd recalled that in 1829, 'before the railway commenced, there were very few fishmongers in this town, and fish were scarce and dear.'[35] But by the 1850s, Henry Mayhew described the London fish markets in almost Dickensian prose. 'The tangled rigging of the oyster-boats and the red worsted caps of the sailors' could be seen through the opened end of the old fish market shed at Billingsgate. The busiest time for buying fish was seven o'clock on a Friday morning. Even costers (street vendors), who regularly sold vegetables, purchased a little fish on Fridays to sell to the Irish Catholics, who observed their meatless fast day, and to those whose budgets ran short by the end of the week.

'The morning air is filled with a kind of seaweedy odour,' Mayhew reported of the almost overwhelming smell as one entered the market. 'Everyone comes to Billingsgate in his worst cloths,' he confessed. Porters struggled with heavy, black oyster bags slung over their shoulders, men in coarse canvas jackets carted loaded hampers, and women, with 'long limp tails of cod-fish dangling from their aprons,' elbowed their way through the crowd. In the dim light of the market shed, the contrasting colours of the white bellies of turbot, scarlet red of cooked lobsters, and stacked piles of brown baskets, must have been second only to the cacophony of sounds.[36]

The old market was roughly divided by specialities. In one section were the auction tables with groups of men turning over piles of fish for inspection by the bidders. Another part was reserved for sacks full of yellow-shelled whelks. In another area, raggedly dressed boys eager for employment hung around the dried fish and herring barrels to help customers cart off their purchases. Oyster-street, the wharf named for the long row of moored oyster boats, was always lively. Each boat displayed a black signboard, as ambitious salesmen wearing white aprons shouted their prices as pedestrians climbed on the deck to make their purchases.[37]

In August of 1852, just in time for 'oyster day', part of the newly rebuilt Billingsgate was opened for business as the primary fish and seafood market for London. The former maze of sheds that Mayhew had so colourfully described, was replaced by a handsome two-storey, red brick, arched Italianate building with a central clock tower boasting a ventilation shaft cleverly concealed within. Thick glass panes provided natural light, and gas lighting brightened the dark early-morning chaos. To help keep the stalls clean, filtered water could be pumped from the Thames supplying both the upper storey (at street level) reserved for fish, and the lower level that catered to the shellfish trade. Not only had the Billingsgate market changed physically, but the zesty opportunists, who spoke their own market jargon, exploited the changes brought with the railways. Salesmen, fishmongers, bummers (speculative dealers), porters, street hawkers, and those who rerouted fish for retail operations in the country districts beyond London, all played a role in developing the new business mode for the fish market.

Whether a result of Catherine's Scottish background, Dickens's own humble upbringing, or the family's summers at the beach – the Dickenses loved having fish and seafood on their menus. Numerous references are found in Dickens's letters. When he found himself a 'graceless bachelor, for a day or two' while his family was at the seaside, he invited Forster and Maclise for dinner: 'a piece of Salmon and a Steak are cooking in the kitchen…a fire lighted – the Wine sparkles on a side table…plates are warming.'[38] But this love of eating fish was not matched by skill at fishing. They caught four herrings the previous night, Charles reported in 1850, 'in seventy five million, six hundred and eighty four thousand, nine hundred and fifty three, yards of net'.[39]

When Dickens wrote of Sir Jonas Clutterbuck in the introduction for *What Shall We Have For Dinner?* we are told Clutterbuck made visits to Richmond and less frequently to Blackwall and Greenwich where the fish dinners, particularly whitebait, were the great attraction. Hordes of

Londoners flocked to these towns on the Thames for recreation. Whitebait, the small, two- to six-inch, silvery-whitish fish appeared in greatest profusion during the month of July. In 1851, when Catherine's menu book was first printed, the scientific information about whitebait was still controversial. It was believed to be the young fry of a local fish, but authorities argued about whether the parent was a species of sprat, smelt, herring, anchovy, bleak or, the more likely, shad.[40] Today, authorities realize that the majority of the catch are young herrings and sprats, but may include the fry of as many as thirty-two different species.[41]

Londoners could have bought whitebait at market and kept them on ice until they were cooked, but the fish are best when freshly caught and fried. Mrs Beeton gave the availability as April to August and Eliza Acton from July to September. Both authors provided a recipe for the home cook.[42] *Household Words* reported that Chef Soyer recommended that the delicate fish be dried gently in a couple of cloths without touching them with one's hands. Providing a recipe in his *Gastronomic Regenerator,* Soyer combined an equal amount of breadcrumbs and flour for a light coating, before he deep fried the fish for just one minute in hot lard. He believed 'these lilliputian fish' could not be cooked at home with the same perfection as they were by the practised hands at Greenwich and Blackwall taverns.[43] Undoubtedly, the Dickenses felt the same way. The fish entries in Catherine's menus do not list whitebait once and, judging from her husband's letters, their entourage routinely set out at the end of March to enjoy the first whitebait dinner of the season in one of the taverns.

English taverns in Dickens's day were the equivalent of today's restaurants, and often fine restaurants at that, as the article 'London Taverns' in *Household Words* explained:

> The genuine tavern furnishes not beds. It affordeth not the casual chop to the stray
> wanderer. It issueth not the occasional bottle of wine to the solitary toper. It has no
> coffee-room partitioned off for mankind as Mr. Huxley fattens oxen, by stall-feeding;
> but, on the contrary, displays broad acres of snow-white pasturage teeming with the
> richest viands and sparkling with the brightest wines. It is not a place at which a man
> can say, indifferently, that he has 'had his dinner;' but where, he will tell you
> unctuously that he has 'dined' – a vast distinction: the first being a mere impulse of
> physical voracity; the second a Rite.[44]

Greenwich supported many well-known taverns and, until 1859, a popular fair was held at Easter and Whitsun, attracting tens of thousands of people from all income levels.[45] Families with limited resources enjoyed shrimp dinners and tea, or packed their own bulging baskets and picnicked in the park or on the sunny decks of riverboats. The wealthy, however, consumed huge tavern dinners of seafood, beginning with boiled flounder and seven or eight different preparations of salmon, sole, and fried eels, each enrobed in its own special sauce. Then the celebrated moment arrived and golden mountains of piping hot whitebait were placed on the table. The fish are so tender, they are eaten whole. Brown bread, butter, lemons, and cayenne pepper accompanied the treat.[46] To wash down the whitebait, there was iced champagne or cold punch, and sherry or claret often finish the meal.[47] The Dickenses enjoyed strolling in the park beforehand and then eating in the best taverns.[48] Invitations to the Crown and Sceptre, the Trafalgar, and the Ship abound in Charles's letters. From 1837, these visits often signalled festivities.[49]

The tradition was especially cherished after the Dickenses returned from their North American tour. Not only was a whitebait celebration planned to welcome home the Boz, but a 'Ladies Dinner' for Catherine was also proposed by Jane Reynolds Hood, Thomas Hood's wife. She wanted to go to Greenwich 'seeing how much good it has done me,' Hood told Dickens.[50] Later, when out-of-town guests visited, a whitebait dinner was often a part of the schedule. They took Cornelius Felton straight to the Trafalgar where he and Dickens also indulged their passion for oysters.[51] Dinners for the theatrical company of *Used Up*, among others, testified to their appetite for whitebait. 'It has been proposed, as a social reunion of our little company,' Dickens said, inviting the amateur actors to discuss the theatre schedule and arrangements over whitebait, 'at a cost not exceeding five and twenty shillings each.'[52]

Blackwall, which was also mentioned in Lady Clutterbuck's introduction, is across the river from Greenwich. Lovegrove's (the Brunswick) was one of the most popular taverns, and usually 'thronged to the very windows'. Perhaps this was the type of establishment where Alderman Clutterbuck would have socialized with politicians and wealthy merchants. Lovegrove's reputation was maintained by their cook's special preparation of whitebait, served in as little as twenty minutes after the fish were caught in the reach. Epicures preferred Lovegrove's.[53] Dickens certainly did. Letters show that

John Leech and Daniel Maclise would meet him mid-morning to take the train from Fenchurch Street to Brunswick Wharf and, despite not running on 'church-time', they would arrive at Blackwall in time for dinner.[54]

Richmond, the third place mentioned in the introduction, was an up-river excursion, but an equally popular retreat and much enjoyed by the Dickens family and their cronies. 'The second of April, is our wedding day and his [Forster's] birthday,' Dickens wrote to Felton, 'on which high festival, we always go down in great state to Richmond (an exquisite place upon the River Thames: some twelve miles off).' The purpose, he explained, was to 'hold a solemn dinner, whereat we empty our glasses, you may believe.'[55] Beside the regulars, John Forster, Daniel Maclise, Georgina Hogarth, other friends and family were among the annual party. The Dickenses were familiar faces in Richmond establishments. 'My good friend Mr. Ellis of the Star and Garter is used to me, and knows how to make us comfortable,' he confided to the visiting British Consul to Genoa about their impending excursion.[56]

Fish is by far the favourite first course in his wife's menus at home. Catherine chose fish nearly three times as often as soup for the first course when only a single dish is listed. The fish she selects is indicative of their station. She does not mention salt-water fish like inexpensive plaice, which was extremely abundant off the English coast and generally purchased by the poor. Nor did she list the largest of the flat fish, halibut, that was sold cheaply (in slices) between March and April. Both halibut and hake were thought to be a coarse, dry, flavourless fish by some.[57] Also absent from her menus are some salt-water fish that seasonally migrate to rivers to spawn, such as sprat, whitebait, and sturgeon. Likewise Catherine excludes freshwater fish like pike, perch, bream and carp. In fact, it is surprising how few freshwater fish she suggests in her menus.

Catherine does not offer scallops, mussels, cockles, periwinkles, or land snails (escargot) in her menus in any of the editions.[58] This probably reflects socio-cultural prejudices since periwinkles and whelks were eaten most often by the poorer classes. Mussels and other molluscs also had a reputation as being poisonous.[59] Thomas Webster's report notes that even the freshwater mussels were 'never eaten with us', and the esculent snails, so highly prized in Europe, 'are never brought to table'.[60] Exotics like frog legs were apparently too foreign for the Dickenses' kitchen, although an article, 'A Dish of Frogs', was published in Household Words.[61]

In the earliest editions, Catherine's favourite thirteen species of fish include sole, brill, flounder, plaice, cod, salmon, haddock, whiting, mackerel, herring, smelt, anchovy, and eels. By 1854, she adds John Dory, skate, salmon trout, and red mullet. Seafood such as prawns, crab, lobster, and oysters also play important culinary roles in all the editions of her bills of fare.

Sole and turbot were highly prized in the early 1850s. According to Alexis Soyer, the London market provided sole principally from the North Sea in great abundance. The fish were caught in trawl nets, sometimes as many as 1,000 fish per haul, and were held live in the swim-wells since the fish did not keep otherwise.[62] Sole were also kept alive in ponds. The finest fish, caught off Plymouth and in Torbay, were up to two feet long and weighed four to ten pounds a pair. Some varieties spawned at the end of February and were undesirable for a few weeks afterwards, but others were available all year, and were frequently found on the tables of London's wealthier classes.[63]

Sole is Catherine's most frequent choice among the nearly 140 fish dishes. Her roughly forty entries for sole are divided between fried or filleted preparations. She does not distinguish between Dover sole, lemon sole, or other varieties, but neither did authorities such as Thomas Webster's *Encyclopædia of Domestic Economy*, which was published that same year.[64]

Soyer considered turbot 'the finest of flat-fishes', but acknowledged its flavour was dependent on where it was caught and what it ate. A diet of young crabs and lobsters made lobster sauce a natural, if traditional, accompaniment. Soyer preferred a mid-size turbot that was bled and what he described as the red belly spots rubbed off with salt and lemon. He advised holding it for forty-eight hours after being killed so that the fine flavour (and digestibility) could develop before cooking.[65]

Catherine suggested turbot in only 6 per cent of the menus with fish, but nearly 88,000 turbot a year were brought into the London market as a result of the great demand. Turbot, sometimes weighing as much as thirty pounds, were caught off the south coast of England 'in great plenty'. However, preference was given to the species from Holland's coast since the Dutch supplied firm white-fleshed turbot that had a finer richer flavour. Since the adult fish do not spawn at the same time, turbot was available year-round, nevertheless, the price was dear.[66] Perhaps expense and social status influenced Catherine's menu choices. She usually reserves turbot as a special dish for larger dinner parties, sometimes accompanied by smelts, but most often served with shrimp sauce.

Brill, a salt-water fish closely related to turbot, was much cheaper and 'brought in abundance to the London market'.[67] Catherine only suggests brill in a few menus. Although she does not specify how it was prepared, most likely she poached the fillets to retain their delicate flavour. She always pairs brill with shrimp sauce.

Flounder was thought to be sweet, easy to digest, abundantly available and inexpensive, but it was also the least esteemed of the flat fish, with the exception of Thames flounder. Catherine recommended 'fried flounders' and shrimp sauce only once. She does not distinguish whether it was Thames flounder, but the late summer menu overlaps the species' availability. Soyer's advice was that flounder 'should never be eaten in London; they ought to be placed almost alive in the frying pan'. He conceded that a five-minute interval could elapse between the fish swimming in water and in fat in a frying-pan, with another five minutes to complete the cooking. At the time, epicures debated whether flounder caught in fresh or brackish water were the best. Soyer thought the latter, unless they were caught with whitebait.[68]

A variety of 'round' fish dominate Catherine's menus with cod and salmon competing as her favourite choices. The ubiquity of cod gave rise to an adage that Dickens was not above using: 'All work and no play makes Jack a dull boy. I [underlined twice] am as dull as a Codfish.'[69] Cod was a reliable market fish and when handsomely dressed for the table, it held its own.

Common cod, the cold-water ocean fish, was found as far north as Greenland and as far south-west as New England. The 1850s London market was supplied with fresh cod from fisheries between Dogger Bank, Well Bank, and Cromer on the east coast of England. The Dogger Bank variety has a sharp nose with a dark brown-coloured body and was the most esteemed.[70] Cod were favoured in the winter and especially in demand around Christmas, but caught all year. Unusually large cod could weigh as much as sixty pounds, although thirty-pound fish were not uncommon in the early 1850s. Ideally a six- to eight-pound cod was thought best for the table, but codling, fish that weighed a pound or less, were also popular.[71] Taking that advice, Catherine only serves cod and codling in a few menus, and salt fish (dried, salt-preserved cod) with egg sauce in one other. She provides a recipe for a made-dish of flaked fish and mashed potatoes called cod rechauffé to use the leftovers.

The cod's head, so highly prized by gastronomes, had to be prepared, it was said, within twenty-four hours of being caught or its delicate flavour was lost.[72] Catherine lists cod's head in five menus, two of which are elaborate many-coursed dinners. To prepare the dish, their cook would place the cod's head (including a portion of the shoulders several inches past the gills) in cold salted water, and gently simmer it for fifteen to twenty minutes. Many people garnished the head with horse-radish and walnut pickle, or the roe and liver.[73] Oyster sauce, Catherine's usual accompaniment for cod dishes, is also a traditional pairing.

Catherine proposes salmon on many occasions, but never the fry (less than a year old) which were provided by London fishmongers as salmon peel or grilse, until Parliament enacted a law forbidding salmon weighing under six pounds to be sold commercially.[74] Soyer lists the younger fish and their common names ('smelt' a year old, 'sprods' at two years, 'morts' at three, 'fork-tails' at four, and 'half-fish' in their fifth year), but he only recommends the six-year-old salmon for the kitchen.[75]

The chief salmon fisheries of Europe were in Britain and the Baltic. Before the 1850s, the finest were caught in the Thames, but pollution brought on a decline, and the prized first catch of the season in England was delivered from the Severn and the Wye. For the most part, the Tweed in Scotland supplied the London market.[76] The Scotch trade had a long history; before 1770, salmon was brought to London on horseback, and afterwards, by light carts and wheeled carriages, until steam ships changed the trade. Salmon caught in early spring were packed in straw and shipped in baskets, but during the warm weather the fish were boiled or pickled and arrived in small kegs (kits) called 'kitted salmon'.[77] Soyer preferred early salmon from Aberdeen caught in February or March, and those from the various rivers of Great Britain through the other months when the fish was in season.[78] By mid-century, fast sailing ships and steam ships from the Tweed, Spey, Tay, and Dee in Scotland, quickly dispatched salmon packed in ice. Storage in the ice houses, built in the 1840s along those rivers, brought the market price for salmon as low as sixpence per pound in the early 1850s, but Webster complained that the quality of the iced-down salmon, which often froze, generally suffered from being held. By the close of 1854, concerns for wild fish populations and over-fishing prompted experiments in fish-rearing and re-stocking.[79] Experimental salmon farming was successful, although commercial salmon were thought inferior since the flesh lacked the darker coral-colour and wild salmon's rich taste.[80]

With the availability of fresh salmon, salted salmon was becoming only a memory by the 1850s and preserved fish was being shunned. Catherine does serve Newcastle salmon (boiled pickled fish) in several warm-weather menus, and pickled salmon certainly appears in Dickens's fiction. In *Martin Chuzzlewit*, the friends of Mrs Gamp, who usually laid a handsome table considering her limited means, expected 'a bit of pickled salmon, with a nice little sprig of fennel, and a sprinkling of white pepper' with a 'cowcumber' (cucumber), 'new bread, a pat of fresh butter, and a mossel of cheese.'[81]

Six- to ten-pound salmon were thought ideal for serving whole. Some writers admonish cooks to boil it well, 'otherwise it is unwholesome', and to serve it unaccompanied since shrimp or lobster sauce further decreased its digestibility.[82] Boiled (actually poached) salmon is Catherine's favourite preparation for the first course of large dinner parties with fourteen to twenty guests. Undoubtedly, serving salmon reflects her Scottish culinary traditions. For family meals with two or three persons, she prefers broiled salmon steaks napped with shrimp sauce. She reserves salmon curried 'à la Soyer' for a couple's dinner or shared with only a few guests. Catherine does not include salmon trout in her repertoire until the 1854 edition, when she replaces one entry for salmon and lobster sauce.

Haddock, a salt-water fish resembling cod, inhabits the northern seas of Europe. Haddock were kept in salt-water ponds and became so tame they could be hand-fed.[83] Soyer highly recommended haddock, and thought that the fish between six and seven pounds were the best size. The larger twelve-pound fish, called 'Dublin Bay' in the London market, were generally caught off the Sussex and Hampshire coasts.[84] Catherine serves baked stuffed haddock for dinners with two to ten persons. She does not indicate the type of stuffing, but a common forcemeat in contemporary recipes was made from bacon, beef suet, sweet herbs finely chopped, breadcrumbs, and egg to bind the ingredients together. Chopped oysters and a teaspoon of anchovy catsup improved the flavour.[85] Soyer also suggests a veal forcemeat.[86]

The tender delicate whiting was thought to be the lightest flavoured of the salt-water fish. They gather in large shoals in spring and were caught on a line. Typically, whiting were ten to twelve inches and around one and a half pounds, but four- to eight-pound specimens were still found near the Dogger Bank in the 1850s. Laws protected small fish, six inches or under. Two other species closely resembled whiting: whiting pout (also called pouting or bib), which was commonly caught around the mouth of the

Thames and along the coast in November and December. Whiting pollack (also known as pollack) found along the coast, was also easily mistaken for whiting by inexperienced cooks.[87] Salted, dried Cornwall whiting were sold in the winter months as buckhorn. The best months for fresh whiting were January and February, but the fish could be bought at any time. Catherine took advantage of whiting's availability in her year-round menus. She fries whiting, and sometimes pairs it with sole in a first course for up to ten persons.

Atlantic mackerel was thought to be among 'the most elegant in its form among our fish', and certainly one of the most beautifully coloured with its shiny green and black markings. Mackerel is a sea fish that migrates from colder waters and it appeared in large schools on the English coast in the spring, first at Land's End in March, the Devonshire bays around April, moving towards Brighton through May, and caught the following month on the Suffolk coast. In the Orkneys, mackerel were not seen until late summer. When the schools were running, there was such glut of mackerel that on Sundays when the Billingsgate market was closed, authorities turned a blind eye to sales since the fish was so perishable. On those Sundays, fishmongers were allowed to announce its availability in London streets. In England, mackerel was seldom preserved with salt, as it was in France.[88] Young mackerel, called shiners, are four to six inches long and voracious feeders. As adults, they ordinarily reached lengths of fourteen to twenty inches and one and a half to two pounds in weight. Larger fish were not considered suitable for the table, and the debate raging among gourmands in the Dickenses' time centred on whether mackerel was better to eat when carrying roe, or after the fish recovered from spawning.[89] Catherine serves mackerel broiled for two or three persons. The fish would have been split down the back by the cook, brushed with a little oil, and placed skin side down on a hot gridiron. Mackerel was prized by the Romans, who seasoned it with *garum*, a fermented fish sauce (superseded by anchovy sauce in Britain).[90] Catherine lists mackerel à la maître d'hôtel in the menus, and gives the recipe for the butter-parsley sauce in the appendix. A well-known combination that Catherine does not appear to use was mackerel with gooseberry sauce. The sharp sauce made of the puréed berries appropriately highlighted the rich meatiness of the fish.[91]

Atlantic herring, an abundant salt-water fish caught in the northern seas, was sold to the poorer classes. 'I suppose you eat nothing but herrings and ship biscuit, and that you drink out of a small wooden keg,' Dickens jested about base eating habits. He had noticed *The Times'* report of shipwrecks near Yarmouth and, like a commodity trader, commented: 'They say that the "late gales" will do severe damage to the bloater trade.'[92] The principle British herring fisheries in the 1850s were on the east and west coasts of Scotland, the west coast of Ireland, and the Yarmouth, Lowestoft, Kent and Sussex coasts of England. Large quantities of herring also were caught at the mouth of the Thames by the fishing smacks (sloop-rigged boats) of London, Folkestone, and Dover. Their haul was usually sold in the London market.[93] 'Fishing For Herring', an article published in *Household Words*, provided statistical information from the Fishing Board Report for 1851. About 10,480 boats manned by 40,362 fishermen and boys were employed in the seas predominantly around Scotland and the Isle of Man. Another 68,939 persons were engaged inland to cure, salt, and otherwise process the 687,401 barrels of herrings caught yearly.[94]

Herring is an oily fish and was thought to be more difficult to digest. Even pickled or salted, herring was recommended only in small quantities by some authorities, who advised that it be served with 'plenty of potatoes or other vegetables' to make the preserved fish less objectionable. On the other hand, when it was in season and the roe was developing, Soyer claimed that 'the richness of the fish at this period is extraordinary, and renders it worthy the table of the greatest epicure,' even though he knew that the coastal fishermen would declare his statement foolish.[95] Catherine only uses fresh herring in a couple of menus for parties of seven. Usually fresh herring was poached by the cook and sent to table piping hot with a simple butter sauce. To eat the small fish, which were served whole, a savvy diner would cut off the tail, pinch the middle to release the bony skeleton, and draw the frame out when removing the head.[96]

Red herrings, also known as the unsalted smoked Yarmouth bloaters, 'excited thirst and tended to create fever' according to some.[97] Catherine held a higher opinion. She suggests bloaters, probably Yarmouth bloaters, as the savoury course following the dessert at small dinner parties of two to seven persons. Yarmouth bloaters were brought to the metropolis in prodigious numbers by 1856. Unsold fresh herring stored in Yarmouth sheds were converted, within twenty-four hours of being taken from the sea, into either dry herring to sell in Catholic countries, or the delicately salted bloaters. Bloaters had a particularly gamy flavour since they were salted and smoked without being gutted. They were served with the heads and tails removed, the back sliced open, flattened, and grilled on both sides. Bloaters could be served with fresh butter and a heated captain's biscuit as Queen Victoria's former head chef, Charles Francatelli, recommended. Another preparation opened two fish down the back and paired them so that the skin was on the outside. The fish were then wrapped in buttered paper and heated in the oven for about twenty minutes. A fancier method used by Soyer paired a bloater and a fresh herring before baking.[98]

Red mullet, another fish held in high esteem by the Romans, was added by Catherine to the 1854 menus to replace fried oysters, and it remained in subsequent editions. The fine white-fleshed fish, with its elegant rose-red and olive tint, was caught off the Cornish and Sussex coasts, but was rare in the more northern waters.[99] Catherine's inclusion of mullet was probably more directly a result of improved train transport since shipments were being brought from Cornwall by the Great Western Railway for the 'fastidious palates' of London's West End.[100]

The John Dory was also taken off the Cornish and Devonshire coasts, although it was a rare fish even by 1850. Probably named for the French term *dorée* meaning gilded, the stunningly coloured but rather ugly fish was easily recognizable. Since the flesh was tough when freshly caught, it was held for a day or two before cooking. This also made the fish convenient to send to the London market by land-carriage, until the trains became a more economical form of transport.[101] In the 1854 edition, Catherine replaces brill and mackerel with John Dory in her menus for small dinner parties, most likely because the fish was more readily available.

The true smelt is an elegantly tapered, thin-skinned fish with an almost transparent body and small silvery scales that are easily removed. Its peculiar odour was thought to resemble cucumbers or violets, but vanishes within about twelve hours of being caught. Once abundant, schools of smelt swarmed the Thames when they migrated upriver from August, returning to the sea around March after spawning. Smelt were rare on the south coast of England in the early 1850s, and the market was being supplied from Holland. Soyer consider the Dutch imports inferior to those from the Medway where once smelt had been so plentiful that the corporation of Rochester would present a dish of the fish to the Lord Mayor of London on his triennial visit. On the last two occasions, Soyer noted, there were hardly any smelts for the city to procure.[102] Sand-smelt on the other hand, were plentiful and could be bred successfully in ponds. They were sold in Southampton, along the Hampshire coast, and in local markets. Compared to the true smelt, the sand smelt was considered inferior eating unless dressed with liver and roe.[103] Catherine serves smelt in less than one in twenty of those menus that contain any fish at all, and then only in dinners for six to ten persons, sometimes pairing it with turbot. She does not distinguish the variety, but serves the little fish either fried or baked.

Skate, also called 'maid' or 'ray', was taken off the English coast in the 1850s and could weight up to 200 pounds, but were known to be much heavier when caught from deeper waters. The prolific females expel their young, one at a time, enclosed in a black horny purse that often washes up on shore when empty.[104] The thick, easily digestible flesh of the skate's wing was appreciated more by the French than the English. Since Catherine did not add skate to her menus until after living in France, she was more likely influenced by its use there. The thick flesh was usually crimped, that is, cut into fillets or slices when very fresh and boiled rapidly 'till crisp and curdy'.[105] Soyer, however, recommended that the piece be tied to keep its shape, and poached gently for about 20 minutes, before it was served with a butter sauce.[106]

True anchovy, also known as the European anchovy, is a salt-water fish about three to four inches long found in the Mediterranean, and in the northern and Atlantic seas where schools of anchovies approach the shores to spawn during the spring. The great anchovy fisheries in the 1850s were on Gorgona, a small Italian island between Leghorn and Corsica, where thousands of barrels were cured for export.

Anchovy catsup, anchovy sauce, and extract (essence) of anchovies were an important flavour component in British cooking. To make the preparation commercially, fresh anchovies were first processed in salt and then boiled to help dissolve the bones. Before pickling, the bitter-tasting head was removed. True anchovies, when freshly pickled, are white on the outside and red inside. Their backs are rounded, not flattened like sardines, which were used frequently as an inferior substitute. Unscrupulous merchants also doused the young fry of pilchards, and the closely related sprats, with anchovy liquor and coloured the mixture red with cochineal or poisonous red lead to imitate processed anchovies. Dependence on anchovies as a flavouring component was so great that domestic economists recommended purchasing them by the double barrel (thirty-eight to forty pounds weight) for thirty shillings since the fish would keep well if covered completely with brine.[107]

A bottled anchovy sauce could be made at home by combining one teacup each of walnut pickle and mushroom pickle, three pounds of anchovies, a pounded clove of garlic, and a half teaspoon of cayenne pepper.[108] Anchovy extract was another useful preparation which was made by the gallon: three pounds of anchovies were worked through a fine hair sieve; the bones were boiled in six pints of salted water, strained and the liquid was thickened with flour before passing the paste through the sieve again. Only bright lobster roe was recommended as colouring.[109] A simple anchovy sauce could be made with three teaspoons of extract added to half a pint of melted butter seasoned with mace and cayenne.[110] When Mrs Beeton was first published, extracts of anchovies and other commercial flavourings were so common that she did not need to include the recipe.[111] (Worcestershire sauce, in more common use today, contains anchovies.)

On occasion, Catherine serves anchovies on toast as the savoury finish to the meal. Perhaps her cook, like Mrs Beeton, pounded the hard roe from smoked herrings (bloaters) with anchovies in a mortar, and spread the relish on toast.[112] Or like Miss Acton, the Dickenses' cook may have simply removed the skin of a dozen 'fine mellow anchovies', pounded them, put the paste through the sieve, and then added half a pound of butter. The anchovy paste was well seasoned with cayenne, nutmeg, powdered mace, and salt. It could be coloured with rose-pink before putting into a prepared mould, and served cold in the shape of the fish.[113] Not only were anchovies prepared for dinner, but Dickens used them medicinally in combination with other home remedies. 'Before acting on the Wednesday night, I had a mustard poultice on my throat – being hoarse,' he told Thomas Mitton, 'and ate a bushel of anchovies, without bread or anything else, in the course of the evening, to keep my voice going! the oldest and best theatrical recipe.'[114]

European eels, a migratory fish with only a pectoral fin, look more like snakes. They could be jellied, fried, collared, boiled, or stewed (as Catherine preferred hers). The fish inhabits both fresh and salt water, but can stay alive for several days in just wet sand. Eels were so plentiful, Webster reported, that thousands could be caught in a single casting of the net. Fisheries, ponds and rivers supplied regional markets. In 1850, the silver freshwater eel with its brightly coloured belly was caught in the running waters of the Thames, and was thought to be the best eating. The Dutch eels, which lived in ponds, had a decidedly muddy taste; nevertheless, Dutch fishermen supplied the

London market. Eel scoots *(schuyts)* were vessels with capacious wells, which were filled with 15,000 to 20,000 pounds of eels from Holland and held live at Billingsgate for the market. The eel's flavour actually improved when they were held this way.[115] 'The consumption of eels in our large cities is considerable,' Webster noted.[116] Eels were not favoured by the lower classes, and particularly not by the costermongers. The vendors were aware of unscrupulous dealers, who mixed dead eels with live ones usually in equal portions and 'accounted [it] a fair deal'. Costermongers generally distrusted dead fish of any kind, but a special prejudice was held for eels.[117] The celebrated eel pie was made from the rich, nutritious meat baked in a flaky puff-pastry crust. One spring, Daniel Maclise, Dickens, and other friends made at least one excursion to the Eel Pie House on Twickenham Island, a popular resort on a seven-acre island in the Thames. One assumes they relished an eel pie or two, but Dickens only mentioned 'eating lamb chops, and drinking beer, and laughing like a coal-heaver'. While he may not have been describing the Eel Pie House in particular, his reminiscences provided the old-time atmosphere in these taverns:

Good God how well I know that room! Don't you remember a queer, cool, odd kind of smell it has, suggestive of porter and even pipes at an enormous distance? Don't you remember the tea-board, and the sand, and the press on the landing outside full of clean linen intensely white? Don't you recollect the little pile of clean spittoons in one nook near the fireplace, looking like a collection of petrified three-cornered hats once worn by the dead-and-gone old codgers who used to sit and smoke there? The very sound of the bell – flat like a sheep-bell as if it had caught its tones from listening to it in its idle, shady, drowsy time of rest – the jingling wire more noisy than the bell – I have it in my ears. And closing my eyes, I'm down stairs in the bar where the soda water comes out of the window seat on which the landlady sits o' fine evenings, where the lemons hang in a grove each in its own particular net, where 'the cheese' is kept, with great store of biscuits hard by in a wicker basket – where those wonderful bottles are, that hold cordials. You know 'em? great masses of grapes painted on 'em in green, blue, and yellow, and the semblance of an extraordinary knot of ribbon supporting the emblem of a label, whereon is the name of the compound? On one of these is 'Lovitch'. Great Heaven what is Lovitch? Has it any connection with peppermint, or is it another name for nectar? Tell me my heart, can *this* be Love-itch.[118]

One of the most distinctive patterns in Catherine's menus is her tight partnering of a specific variety of fish with a particular sauce. Shrimp sauce, her most adaptable accompaniment, is paired with fried or filleted sole, fried whiting, broiled salmon, turbot, brill, and flounder. She reserves lobster sauce for salmon, and oyster sauce for cod and codling. Salt fish is napped in its egg sauce, which was probably made with melted butter (not milk and flour) chopped hard-boiled eggs and a simple seasoning.[119] She usually pairs sole with shrimp sauce, but sometimes breaks free, and serves the fillets with a brown sauce or maître d'hôtel sauce. Her brown sauce was most likely a meat gravy or perhaps an espagnole-based sauce with mushroom, walnut or anchovy catsup fortified with port or Madeira and flavoured with spices. Catherine's cucumber, onion, mushroom, asparagus, and herb sauces are never paired with fish or seafood. She does provide the Anglo-Indian recipe for salmon curry, which was an adaptation from Soyer.

Aside from fish, seafood is prevalent in Catherine's menus. Celebrated historically by Roman poets and epicures, British oysters had long been prized. In Georgian times, the oysters from Colchester and Rochester were the best known and distinguished for their delicacy. The green hue on the lobes and mantle of the thin shell and its pearly interior made the 'natives' easy to identify. Their peculiar but sweet flavour was thought to come from the iron and alkaline iodides in the mollusc body. Demand for oysters was heaviest from September to April, and literally millions were sent to the London market alone.[120] Catherine's menus attest to the family's love of oysters, and T.W. Hill's overview of Dickens's writing in reference to the bivalves verifies this:

> The consumption of food is one of the principle pleasures of life, and Dickens as the apostle of happiness was fully alive to the possibilities of the oyster; there are very many allusions scattered through his writings using the succulent shellfish in its gustatory, figurative, social, sociological, and decorative aspects, to say nothing of its use as a medium for the expression of friendship and affection.[121]

Dickens's passion for oysters was shared by his American friend Cornelius C. Felton. Dickens playfully imagined Felton writing a 'first-rate facetious Novel, brim full of the richest humour,' entitled 'Oysters in Every Style or Openings of Life by Young Dando'.[122] The legendary oyster eater, John Dando, consumed 20 dozen at a sitting without paying for them, according to Dickens's letter. Dando became a caricature among the London literary circle, and Felton, needless to say, was billed as the American Dando.[123] Although Felton's letters to Dickens have not survived, Dickens's letters are zealous.

> Come to England! Come to England! Our Oysters are small I know; they are said by Americans to be coppery, but our hearts are of the largest size. We are thought to excel in shrimps, to be far from despicable in point of lobsters, and in periwinkles are considered to challenge the universe. Our oysters, small though they be, are not devoid of the refreshing influence which that species of fish is supposed to exercise in these latitudes. Try them and compare.[124]

Dickens was certainly aware of their aphrodisiac affect and used it with excellent effect in his fiction about the 'fat, red-faced, whiteheaded' main character in 'The Misplaced Attachment of Mr. John Dounce'. The middle-aged Dounce had lived for more than twenty years without change when his entire world turned topsy-turvy 'by the simple agency of an oyster'. One night after a birthday party fuelled by a 'brace of partridges for supper, and a brace of extra glasses afterwards,' new temptations presented themselves:

> his eyes rested on a newly-opened oyster-shop, on a magnificent scale, with natives laid, one deep, in circular marble basins in the windows, together with little round barrels of oysters…Behind the natives were barrels, and behind the barrels was a young lady of five-and-twenty, all in blue, and all alone – splendid creature, charming face and lovely figure!…He entered the shop. 'Can you open me an oyster, my dear?' said Mr. John Dounce.
>
> 'Dare say I can, sir,' replied the lady in blue, with playfulness. And Mr. John Dounce eat one oyster, and then looked at the young lady, and then eat another, and then squeezed the young lady's hand as she was opening the third, and so forth, until he had devoured a dozen of those at eightpence in less than no time.
>
> 'Can you open me half-a-dozen more, my dear?' inquired Mr. John Dounce.
>
> 'I'll see what I can do for you, sir,' replied the young lady in blue, even more bewitchingly than before…[125]

In his own commentary, Dickens confessed to Felton that, 'in the meantime total abstinence from oysters seems to be best thing for me' during Catherine's ninth month of pregnancy.[126]

Within the span of Dickens's career, oysters transcended their low status as cheap food for the poor at four pence a dozen in 1840, to a scarce luxury as a result of reckless dredging of the natural oyster beds.[127] In the early 1850s, new beds were found between Shoreham and Le Havre and the harvest was shipped by train to London, but the coarseness of the oysters' flavour was only compensated by their cheapness. Through the 1850s, the seafood market was erratic; public distrust decreased sales during the cholera epidemic in 1854–5, although thereafter demand rose again.[128] Even so, the Victorians were slow to respond to conservation and artificial cultivation. By 1876, Peter Simmonds stated flatly that 'those golden days' when oysters were moderately priced 'unfortunately have fled, and, unless active and practical steps be taken to replenish our oyster beds, they can never be expected to return.' His report on the French efforts was more positive, 'Ostreiculture, thanks to the care and wise regulations of the Government, is making rapid progress, both to the benefit of the fisherman and the public.'[129]

The life-cycle and breeding habits of the oyster were known. Edmund Dixon's article 'Oyster Seed', commissioned by Dickens for *Household Words*, declared that the nineteenth century no longer intended 'to leave the progeny of the sea to their own devices.' The modern science of pisciculture and mariculture would turn 'the sea to profitable account' with oyster culture (ostreiculture) as 'the scheme in vogue'.[130] The French had developed their oyster-fisheries over the past two decades.[131] The cultivated oysters were rebuked as having 'grayish and greenish complexions, which an English native would be ashamed to own for a relation,' Dixon declared, grateful though he was for the repopulation of dwindling oyster beds.[132] A mature oyster produced as many as one to two million offspring yearly. The muddy liquor found in the 'mother oysters' in spawning season contained the microscopic young, which is why oysters are of poor quality in spring and summer months without an 'r' in their name.[133] By 1858, research reported to the government of Napoleon III recommended that tree branches that were sunk into the oyster beds before the spawning season would provide enough refuge for the 'legions of living dust'. With the Emperor's financial support, oyster culture began on the north coast of Brittany and was adapted elsewhere in France.[134]

For the English who could afford them, native oysters were purchased by the barrel for home use. In 'moderate weather', some varieties would live for two or three days in salted water, changed twice a day (presumably to mimic the tide). However, to retain their flavour, authors advised storing them out of water and packed so tightly in the barrel that the shells remain closed. They could be kept this way for a week to ten days.[135] Eliza Acton refreshed the oysters before serving them by covering them with cold salt water (about 7 oz of salt to 1 gallon of water) so they would purge the sand and grit inside the shell.[136]

Like other frugal housewives, Catherine clearly makes the most of every succulent expensive morsel. Her recipes stretch the use of oysters to flavour forcemeat for mutton or add richness to steak and kidney pudding, and allows her to feed many more diners. She serves oyster patties, a far more elegant presentation than today's fried chopped 'cakes', also known as patties. Referred to as 'English Oyster Patties' by Miss Acton, the individual puff-pastry cases and lids were baked to a golden-brown. A hot minced seafood mixture, bound together with cream or a *béchamel* sauce, and seasoned with lemon juice, anchovy sauce, cayenne pepper, and an accent of pounded mace, filled the cases.[137]

Oyster curry, oyster soup and oyster sauce were other Victorian favourites. Although Catherine does not suggest oyster soup often, her preparation was probably similar to Acton's white oyster soup (also called 'Oyster Soup *à la Reine*'). The recipe called for eight to twelve dozen oysters, depending on their size – that is, two to three dozen for each pint of soup. Charles Francatelli, in *The Modern Cook*, calls for four dozen oysters for eight persons in his recipe for oyster soup *à la Plessy*.[138] And Beeton's recipe for ten diners called for six dozen oysters at a time, when oysters were more of a luxury than a 'poor man's dish'.[139]

The versatile oyster sauce required three dozen oysters to make a half pint (about six oysters per person).[140] Even Soyer's *Shilling Cookery for the People*, written for those on tight budgets, called for one dozen oysters to make a half-pint of sauce.[141] Oyster sauce is a standard accompaniment for fish in Catherine's original bills of fare, and appears in 12 per cent of her menus. In one menu, which serves up to eighteen diners, she lists oyster sauce twice in the first course (with cod's head, smelts, soles, and stewed eels) and in a later course to accompany fowl. Catherine does not have any compunction about serving oysters in soup, curried in the entrées, and as a sauce in the same menu (see page 58 of the transcript). Platters of individual cold (raw) oysters on a bed of ice, or fried oysters piled high in a napkin folded into the shape of a flower, were reserved for intimate dinners for two or at most three other guests. Nine oysters per person was demmed a generous first course when served in this style.[142]

By 1854, Catherine's use of oysters slims down. She replaces oyster sauce in five menus, and replaces dishes of fried oysters in two others. It is difficult to tell if this reflected the growing expense of the mollusc, or her awareness of the repetitiveness of the earlier menus. When she does serve fried oysters, they are accompanied with lemon and cayenne, which was probably the seasoning used in the earlier menus, but unstated.

Lobsters, that 'moving mass of spiteful claws and restless feelers', were for the most part being shipped from the Norwegian fiords to the London market. In 1856, Dodd noticed the availability of lobsters was strongly influenced by the extension of the railway system. Lobsters were sent to boiling houses in Duck Lane and Love Lane, near Billingsgate, and boiled in huge cauldrons for twenty minutes before being sent to the market for sale.[143] The 'worse Nancy' was an ancient marketing terminology for 40 small lobsters sold as a unit, and 'best Nancy' or 'best Double', 'Score', and a 'Ten' denoted the successively larger bodies. Lobster season was predominantly May through August, since few diners appreciated soft-shelled crustaceans (including soft-shelled crabs). By 1878, Peter Simmonds commented that the 'supply to London has fallen off very much these last few years'. Predictably, the price rose, and 'the scarcity is beginning to be felt'.[144]

Like oysters, Catherine also cleverly uses lobster meat and the shells by creating a number of different preparations – sometimes for the same meal (see page 60 of the transcript). She serves lobster sauce made from the shells (paired with salmon), the lobster tail meat as fillets and cutlets, and the remainder of the meat with the claws for curry, or diced for special salads or a seafood filling for the patty (puff-pastry) cases. In her menus, lobster is never served to less than four persons, and lobster salad, a popular concluding savoury, is reserved for parties of fourteen to twenty.

Dudley Costello's amusing article in an 1854 issue of *Household Words* indulged his sentiments as a cook who adored lobster. Halifax, Nova Scotia, set the scene for a cloudy summer's night at full tide when the lobsters were close to shore, and an experienced fisherman could catch forty to fifty per hour. The enthusiastic author offered several recipes for the haul. [145]

Shall we stew him after the Irish fashion, or curry him in the Anglo-Indian manner, or scallop him, or distribute him in patties, or prepare him as an omelet in the artful manner now practised in the kitchen of Trafalgar, at Greenwich?[146]

Costello's article almost summarized Dickens's attitude for well-prepared fish and seafood dishes as an integral part of a good English meal. In 'Fish Dinners' Henry Morley added the blessing: 'Let fish descend from the mahogany of the epicure to the labourer's board.'[147] Meanwhile, Catherine's menus illustrate how fish and seafood contribute variety to the meals in a middle-class household. The Dickenses believed that inexpensive fish and seafood would provide nutritious meals for those less well-off financially, particularly since the effects of the potato famine were still palpable.

CHAPTER VIII

MEATS, GAME, DAIRY GOODS AND CONDIMENTS

George Dodd gloated about the London markets, 'If a gourmand wished for a dish of peacocks' brains, or stewed humming birds, or doves' hearts, doubtless his taste might be gratified; it would simply be a question of price.'[1] While gourmets may have looked to exotics for a heartwarming dinner, the Englishman requested roast beef – or so the myth professed.

> The lyrists exalt the times when roast-beef was the staple food of Englishmen, ennobling their hearts, enriching their blood, and making their soldiers brave; that the effeminacy, the ragouts, and the dances of France, imported at a later date, had deteriorated the bold Britain; that in the good old days of Queen Bess, before coffee and tea and such slip-slops were known, and when roast-beef was in full vigour, our yeomen were robust and strong, our plump tenants rejoiced and sang, our soldiers had stomachs to eat and to fight, our enemies' fleets dared not to appear on the ocean, and the world was in terror if e'en the Queen did but frown – Such were the imputed virtues of roast-beef.[2]

Doubtless Catherine Dickens was well aware of the preoccupation with roast beef as an English birthright; her husband's writing helped entrench that view. But, if her menus spoke for the household dinner table, the Dickens family did not claim that privilege as often as one might expect. Other than that, the choice of meats in Catherine's larder offers no real surprises. Generally, she prepares mutton, lamb, beef, veal, pork, and domesticated fowl. Of the game meats, only venison, rabbit, and hare are represented along with a few game birds. Her use of offal includes calf's liver, sheep's heart, tongue (unspecified as to ox, calf or lamb), sweetbreads (either calf or lamb), tripe (either oxen or calf), and kidneys (probably mutton).[3] Fruit and meat combinations such as goose braised with plums, and wild duck paired with orange or cherries, which were particularly popular in the Kent region, are not specifically identified in her bills of fare. Other well-worn combinations like roast beef and Yorkshire pudding appear in only a couple of menus. Catherine does not use goat, horse, or any exotics like boar.[4]

To her credit, she does not suggest delicacies like ortolan, the small song birds imported from France and Italy. These highly-prized delicacies, fattened until they weighed about three ounces, were thought to be among the great luxuries of the table. Menus with ortolans would have screamed of social pretension, as they did in an incident relayed by the novelist William Makepeace Thackeray. He, Dickens, John Leech, and Mark Lemon were invited to dinner, but Dickens was unable (or unwilling) to attend and asked Thackeray to carry an apologetic note to the hostess. Upon reading the message, the fatuous woman was overheard telling her cook: 'Martin, don't roast the ortolans; Mr. Dickens isn't coming.' Thackeray said he never felt so small, 'There's a test of popularity for you! No ortolans for Pendennis!'[5]

Before considering the meat dishes in Catherine's bills of fare, a glance at the developing transit systems for conveying both livestock and freshly butchered meat to London's markets may be useful. As the railways continued rapidly to stretch their networks in the 1850s, the availability of products increased, as did the new-fashioned middlemen who completely transformed the trade. By 1856, livestock was brought into London by seven railways, by steamers landing at the many wharves on the Thames, and by all the major roads. Dodd estimated that two-thirds of the two million live oxen, calves, sheep, lambs, and pigs arrived 'by steam' (trains and ships) annually, and were in far better condition than hitherto.[6] The transport system also allowed fresh milk to be brought from twenty- or thirty-mile distances, and other perishable goods could be sent 'in a sweet and perfect state from most of the northern counties'.[7]

Newgate and Leadenhall markets generally handled 'dead meat' (butchery),[8] Smithfield the livestock. 'Great Day' at Smithfield, took place on the Monday before Christmas-week to reserve all types of livestock for the holidays. Herds of cattle overran the place. 'The cauldron of steaming animalism overflowed from [its] very fullness,' as 30,000 of the 'finest animals in the world' were corralled tightly into the four or five acres. Although the last chaotic 'Great Day' was held in 1854 at the old market, George Dodd thought that special event had been 'a sight worth seeing'. The original Smithfield meat market closed two days before the new one was ceremoniously opened by Prince Albert on January 13, 1855. The Great Northern railway was well sited to deliver both livestock and other produce.[9]

Although fruiterers, greengrocers, milkmen, fishmongers, and other vendors delivered goods daily to their customers' kitchens, housekeepers usually purchased meat at the butchers' and poulterers' shops themselves. One suspects that the Dickenses had a number of meat purveyors, although only a few letters mentioned them. Their own butcher, who lived near Devonshire Terrace, may have been as colourful a character as this description in *Martin Chuzzlewit*:

> To see the butcher slap the steak, before he laid it on the block, and give his knife a sharpening, was to forget breakfast instantly. It was agreeable, too – it really was – to see him cut it off, so smooth and juicy. There was nothing savage in the act, although the knife was large and keen; it was a piece of art, high art; there was delicacy of touch, clearness of tone, skilful handling of the subject, fine shading. It was the triumph of mind over matter, quite.
>
> Perhaps the greenest cabbage-leaf ever grown in a garden was wrapped about this steak, before it was delivered to Tom [Pinch]. But the butcher had a sentiment for his business, and knew how to refine upon it. When he saw Tom putting the cabbage-leaf into his pocket awkwardly, he begged to be allowed to do it for him; 'for meat,' he said with some emotion, 'must be humoured, not drove.'[10]

When looking at the menu books, the preferences for particular meats are evident. Nearly half of all the meat dishes, in all of the editions, are made from mutton or lamb, and even in menus with only three items, lamb usually makes up the main course. This should not be surprising considering that as children, both Catherine (in Scotland) and her husband (in Kent), were raised on regional cuisines featuring mutton.

The priority of early sheep farmers had been wool production, therefore meat was largely from older animals. This influenced long-term British taste, although production for meat rather than wool had taken root by the nineteenth century. Many, but not all, considered the hill sheep of Wales and Scotland to produce the best meat – a lean, close-grained flesh with fine flavour, particularly when raised on wild herbage.[11] Mutton was thought nutritious and easy to digest. Although five-year-old beasts were preferred, most London butchers tended to offer three-year-olds. Good cooks looked for dark meat and marbled fat to define a choice cut. When a haunch or hind quarter was intended for roasting, it was generally hung in the larder for several weeks in the winter, and in the summer for as long as possible before tainting. Hanging produces the rich colour and tenderizes the meat.[12] The Dickenses certainly followed this practice, as one of Dickens's dinner invitations reveals: 'there is a Leg of delicate Welsh Mutton in the Pantry (to be served up at half past five) which deserves attention.'[13]

In her bills of fare, Catherine suggests mutton and lamb roasts three times more often than beef and veal roasts. Except for a few pairings with onion sauce, special sauces rarely accompany her roasts, which suggests that she probably strained and served the roasting liquids from the pan (*au jus*). Her first preference is for Welsh mutton, especially the saddle cut that weighed about ten pounds. Alexis Soyer had developed a new cut where butchers trimmed the saddle-back from the two loins (still joined by the central bone) into a double-saddle shape. For smaller pieces, Soyer cut half-inch-thick butterfly-shaped chops from the saddle.[14] Catherine adopts the saddle readily for larger dinner party menus. Authors like Eliza Acton noted that the cut was 'served usually at good tables, or for company-dinners instead of the smaller joints.'[15]

Catherine's second preferences are for the leg and the loin of lamb and mutton. She sometimes stuffs a fillet or a leg of mutton with a veal forcemeat, but more often uses oysters to prepare it according to the recipe in her appendix, which suggests the roast be accompanied with a pungent brown sauce. She usually roasts the haunch and shoulder cuts and would have used the remaining joint to serve cold, or prepared as a *rechauffé à la Soyer* (a made-dish using the leftovers combined with mashed potatoes).

Catherine lists mutton cutlets and chops in about 4 per cent of the original (1851) publication, and reduces this to 3 per cent by the last edition. Since she probably pan-fried the cuts, the meat may not have been accompanied by a special sauce. In the updated 1854 menus and the later editions of her book, she replaces some of the mutton chops with other dishes, such as veal cutlets and tomato sauce, broiled Cambridge sausages on mashed potatoes, and boiled beef with suet dumplings. Although she only mentions boiled mutton (as such) in two menus throughout the editions, there must have been plenty of it, since many of her soups depend on mutton stock. She may have used the nicer pieces for dishes such as the mutton curry, mutton hashed with vegetables, or minced mutton with bacon. Boiled mutton would have also been used for the family's lunches and for the servants' meals.

There are several types of mutton stews in Catherine's menus, which altogether fill out nearly 8 per cent of the original menus. Irish stew, and another called haricot of mutton, predominate. Haricot appears to have evolved from an ancient recipe called 'alicot' in the Middle Ages.[16] The stews use either meat from a bony portion (like the scrag of the neck), or a loin cut into chops or smaller pieces, which are floured and pan-fried until just browned. After removing the fat, diced root vegetables such as turnips, onions, and carrots are sautéed briefly. In Kent, two dozen chestnuts and 'two or three lettuces cut small' would have added a regional touch, while a bundle of herbs, several blades of mace, salt, pepper, and sometimes cloves seasoned the dish. Like all stews, they are better when made a day ahead and could also be served as a cold dish.[17] Catherine adds recipes for both 'marooned mutton' (a made-dish of thin slices of mutton swimming in a rich gravy) and her native Scottish stew, hotch potch, to the 1854 recipe appendix.

Although mutton was preferred, Catherine does make use of lamb. Six- to eight-month-old lamb may have been more tender than mutton, but most thought it 'less exciting' or flavourful. The best choice was 'house lamb' born in the spring, suckled for six months, and then fattened indoors for two months after being weaned. Technically in season from December through February, lamb was actually available all year long, especially with the Dorset breed supplying the London market.[18] Catherine's cooking methods for lamb mirror those for mutton, as roasts, cutlets, minced lamb, and lamb's fry. She roasts lamb's ribs, and makes a lamb stew with peas, which may have been a regional dish. For small family dinners, Catherine serves lambs' hearts or lamb's head with minced liver and provides a brief recipe for her readers. For larger parties, she sometimes pairs sweetbreads with mushroom sauce. Like the character Mrs Sparsit, the elderly housekeeper in *Hard Times* who ate delicate sweetbreads in a savoury brown sauce as a favourite supper, Catherine may have served sweetbreads this way herself. Catherine introduces kidneys *à la brochette* in 1854 and includes the recipe, but she does not mention a popular dish of lamb's tail, which was made from the thicker end of about two dozen tails, flayed and jointed for an 'ordinary size pie'. The bones cook down to a much-relished gelatinous texture.[19]

Since beef reigned in the kitchen – at least in English sentiments – holiday traditions were (and still are) associated with large roasts. Ernest A. Hart's article in *Household Words* declared that if there was anything Britain was known for, it was her roast beef.[20] Christmas beef, the most sacred of all preparations, warmed the childish hearts of the coldest Englishmen. 'Even the churl who would shut a house-door in the face of his brother,' Henry

Morley wrote, 'upon a Christmas Day opens it gladly to his beef.'[21]

A dramatic shift in livestock practice had occurred during the Dickenses' time. Oxen (five-year-old male cattle) had formerly been grazed on pasture, but the Victorian trend was for raising animals in stalls for greater efficiency. Pastured beef was supplied from August to November, when cattle were fed 'after-grass' or hay until they were slaughtered.[22] The quality had always depended on the breed, sex, age, and diet. With the new diet of turnips, carrots, and other root vegetables as winter feed, the flavour of the meat changed. Although oil cakes were sometimes used, and Booth's distillery in Brentford even fattened six-hundred cattle on grains and mashes of barley meal and clover chaff, this did not produce meat of the same calibre as pastured animals.[23]

Aside from these changes in raising cattle, the conditions in the butchering industry were notoriously unsanitary and Dickens, for one, was revolted by them. He used *Household Words* to make the public aware of the wretched operations and gruesomely corrupt practices found in London. 'The Cattle-Road To Ruin' by Richard Horne was a chilling article about once-wholesome oxen so mistreated they were covered with sores and injuries by the time they reached the slaughterhouse. If inspected, the animals would have been condemned; however, underhanded dealers removed the 'more sound parts' of the diseased bullocks for sale or to incorporate with horsemeat in choppers that ultimately spat out sausages. The 'dead market' was worse still, since carcasses were butchered from animals that died before they even reached the slaughterhouse. The cause of their deaths was unquestioned.[24]

The yearly Christmas cattle show held at Baker Street, London, showed off the best of the four most important breeds: the tawny-coloured Devons, the white-faced Herefords, the remarkably variable new breed of shorthorns, and the dark Scots mountain cattle that were deemed 'the aristocracy of beef'. These, also called Highlands or Galloways, were brought down to Falkirk for stall-feeding, and spent several comfortable months in Norfolk before arriving at Smithfield for slaughter. West End butchers sold the best Scots beef at 'a penny or twopence' more per pound. Shorthorn cattle provided the greatest proportion of beef for Christmas dinners, though stall-fed oxen continued to be bred for market since they grew more quickly, although their fat was oilier and the texture of the meat coarser.[25] Everyone, it seemed, held non-negotiable views about how they liked their beef prepared, as George Sala expressed pungently in *Household Words*:

Give me my beef, hot or cold, roast, boiled, or broiled; but away with your beef-kickshaws, your beef-stews, your beef-haricoes, your corned beef, your hung beef, and your spiced beef. I don't think there is anything so contemptible, fraudulent, adulterine [sic] in the whole world (of cookery) as a beef sausage.[26]

Overwhelmingly, Catherine prefers beef be roasted rather than boiled. In fact, she only lists boiled beef twice in the nearly seventy entries for the meat in her original bills of fare. Her popular beef-steak puddings were probably made with two kidneys, a dozen oysters, and perhaps a few mushrooms, like the one Dickens described in 'Doctor Marigold' in *Christmas Stories*, 'a pudding to put a man in good humour with everything, except the two bottom buttons of his waistcoat.'[27] Beside the puddings, Catherine includes beef pies and beef stews made from rump roasts. Some of the stews must have been particularly rich with vegetables judging from their titles. One wonders if she prepared stews like Elizabeth David's description of the old English dish of stewed steak (original to Sussex) which used mushroom ketchup, ale or stout, and port to make the rich gravy.[28] Catherine was reported serving stewed steak to Henry Wadsworth Longfellow when he visited.[29]

Catherine does create other made-dishes of minced beef (with bacon) from the tougher cuts, and collops, also called Scotch minced collops in her recipe appendix, which uses finely chopped fillet. Bubble and squeak was made in mid-Victorian times from slices of boiled beef warmed in a pan and covered with fried cabbage and onions.[30] Since that time, it has evolved into a fried, mashed potato and chopped cabbage side-dish to accompany meat. For small dinner parties of six or seven people, her bills of fare include more elaborate dishes such as a rolled ribs or rolled stuffed rump steaks where the stuffing is flavoured in one way or another, then bound with butcher's knots to ensure a nice presentation, and roasted. Catherine provides the recipe for rump steak à la Soyer in the original appendix, and instructions for breaded rump steak (or cutlets) are given in the 1854 recipes. She serves the steaks with a horse-radish sauce, which she also includes in the recipes. In the 1854 edition, Catherine adds a new item, boiled beef with suet dumplings, to replace mutton chops. In addition, the recipe for beef sandars, a made-dish of cooked minced beef, provides more variety.

Calf's liver and bacon are found in only two of her menus, but most of the offal (including other liver dishes) is not identified, so it is impossible to know if the menu entries for sweetbreads and tongue, for example, were from calf or sheep. She often boils tongue with chicken and serves them together in the dish. Her 1854 bills of fare offer stewed tripe (either from oxen or calves) for the first time in the revised menus. Catherine's 1854 edition exhibits other changes. 'Broiled bones' are substituted for mutton chops, and marrowbones replace a pound pudding, both served in the last course. She may have had the ribs prepared by rubbing them with mustard, pepper, and salt, and then grilled over an open flame, as does Soyer.[31] A paste of flour and water protected the tips of the bones and was removed before serving.

While Victorians appreciated their beef, some authorities thought veal was less tender, nourishing, and digestible.[32] Others renounced it for moral reasons. The article 'Nice White Veal', in the first volume of *Household Words*, objected to the cruelty of bleeding calves to blanch the meat, and argued for the more humane method that was used to kill cattle.[33] Despite this, the Dickenses were fond of veal. Perhaps the time they spent in Italy with Jane, their adept cook, allowed them to appreciate the texture and flavour of well-prepared veal dishes. In fact, the only time Catherine lists tomato sauce, she pairs it with veal cutlet, perhaps as veal parmesan. Her other veal entries include roasted fillet, stewed breast, cutlets, and a forcemeat that she uses to stuff a roasted leg of mutton. Two made-dishes, minced veal and veal and ham patties, are included in the bills of fare. The minced filling for the puff-pastry shells (patties) may have used grated lemon peel, mace, sweet herbs, and onions for seasoning, as Soyer suggests, and then have been bound with béchamel sauce or cream.[34] The minced veal would have been garnished with toasted or fried sippets of bread.

Veal olives, another made-dish of thin slices of roasted veal layered with a sheet of bacon and well-seasoned forcemeat, are not in Catherine's original edition, but she introduces the dish in the 1852 menus. Like 'Meg Dods', she would have rolled the meat (like stuffed olives) to hold the forcemeat, and covered them with egg and bread crumbs, before baking or stewing in a rich gravy.[35] In 1854, she replaces veal olives in some of the menus with a new dish, tendrons of veal, both as a recipe and menu item, which most likely reflects changing food trends. Two braised French dishes, veal fricandeau and grenadine of veal, which Catherine includes, are particularly intriguing. Veal fricandeau was not originally listed in 1851, but she adds the preparation a year later, and then includes it in a few more menus in the 1854 publication onwards. These bills of fare are all fancy dinner party menus. Whether or not she was influenced by Soyer's advice is unknown, but he declared veal fricandeau 'a favourite'. He argues that the dish shows resourcefulness since 'it is generally considered an expensive one, but the way in which I do it is not so.' Aside from the hype, Soyer did note that it 'gives a nice piece of veal at table' and is good 'when a fillet would be too large'. Veal fricandeau is made from the topside of the leg (referred to as *sous-noix*) cut into slices about 3.5cm thick and studded with bacon fat or larded.[36] If served cold, the fricandeau is coated with the strained braising liquor and served with a garnish of chopped meat jelly. Indeed, clear jelly (aspic) is included in her menus with this dish.

'Grenadines of veal' (*grenadins de veau*), which Catherine suggests in two large 1851 dinner party menus – and in 1854 she adds to a smaller family menu – is similar, but uses smaller, thicker escalopes. The loin is cut into triangular or rectangular slices, and interlarded with bacon fat or salt pork before being braised with sautéed onions and carrots in white wine. The braising liquid is defatted, reduced, and served as a sauce. This dish, offered either hot or cold, appears in Catherine's entrées for large dinner parties of up to twenty persons.[37]

Sausages of all kinds were made from veal, beef, pork, or a combination of meats, and were produced on a much larger scale by the mid-1850s. Steam engines were developed for commercial use to chop ingredients and fill casings, while hand-cranked equipment was patented for home use. Regional sausages, such as those made in Kent of lean pork, were seasoned with sage, cloves, nutmeg, mace, pepper, salt, and a hint of lime zest. The meat was formed into cakes, floured, and roasted in a Dutch oven.[38] Link sausages, known since the seventeenth century, and other skinless round sausage cakes, were also popular, either fried or roasted.[39] Such sausages were reminiscent of those Captain Cuttle cooked for his god-daughter Florence in *Dombey and Son*, 'hissing and bubbling in a most musical manner' in small frying-pans for family dinners.[40] Although sausage was a prime target for the use of unsavoury meats, one expects that the Dickenses shopped at reputable butchers. Catherine suggests Brunswick sausage as a closing course in several of the 1852 menus for large dinner parties. In the updated 1854 edition, she adds broiled Cambridge sausage served on mashed potatoes as a starter course, and her entries for thin slices of German sausage are combined with a small undressed salad to conclude the meal. She does not list blood sausage or black puddings.

There is more 'variety in pig-meat' than for other animals, declared one authority who considered not only the pickling or curing methods, but also the variety of pigs that was being raised. Crossbreeding of indigenous stock with Chinese, African, Spanish, and Portuguese breeds, or with wild boar, produced a fatter pig with more delicate flesh. Porkers, five or six months old, were slaughtered for meat, and full-grown males at eighteen to twenty-four months were converted to the most flavourful hams and bacon.[41] Bacon-pigs were usually fattened in the autumn so that they would be ready in time for Christmas. The high-quality, roughly salted large flat 'sides' of Irish bacon were sent to English bacon-curers to complete the processing before selling them in the London market. In addition, bacon from Cincinnati and hams sent in bulk from New Orleans flooded the British market to supply predominantly the poorer classes.[42] Pork was generally considered inferior to other meats and only a few prized cuts were served on the tables of the middle and upper classes.

Beside breed, a pig's diet was important in the development of meat quality. The worst fat-to-lean ratio and flavour came from pigs raised on beans, potatoes or oil cakes. The best pork resulted from a diet of skimmed milk, peas or oats, and barley meal.[43] After being well fed, the slaughtered pigs needed to be carefully processed.[44] According to George Dodd, traditional London butchers generally salted and pickled meat by time-honoured methods but a patented salting machine, invented in the early 1850s, was coming into use. The syringe-like apparatus forced the salting solution into the hams to reduce the brining time.[45] For those who preferred to cure their own hams, authors like Eliza Acton gave directions. For processing 'hams superior to Westphalia', Acton recommended a vinegar-brine, and for the 'Kentish mode of cutting and curing a pig', she pickled the hams and cheeks in a strong brine of bay-salt, saltpetre, common salt, and coarse sugar. The hams were 'fit for table and delicate' in about three or four months.[46]

Catherine included a 'hand of pickled pork' starting with the 1852 menus. Judging from Charles's letters, she stopped at nothing to make sure they had quality hams. 'Kate begs *me* to beg *you* to tell Tish with her love that she wished to encumber you with a Ham,' he implored his brother-in-law, '(which you shall afterwards eat, for your trouble) and that our butterman has orders to send the same to your house.' They apparently could not find a good ham in Winterbourne, Bonchurch where the Dickens family had taken a place for the summer.[47] The ham toted from London would have appeared as a boiled knuckle of ham for the first night's dinner, served cold in thin slices at the next meal, and then minced with veal as a filling for puff-pastry (patty) shells to make its last appearance.

With frequent entries for ham in Catherine's menus, it is not surprising that another of Dickens's notes asked their local English grocery to procure a proper British ham when they lived in Genoa. He wrote, 'Catherine says she will take it as a great favour, if you will buy her, at your leisure and in the course of your own marketings, three pounds of black tea, and a Ham.' Whether or not he was truly embarrassed, we will never know, but the letter continued, 'If blushes could be forwarded in a note, this paper would be red with consciousness of the trouble it gives you, by the time it comes to hand.'[48] And blush he should, if they did not appreciate the Italian hams available.

Well over fifty pork dishes in Catherine's menus call for cutlets, sausage, ham, and bacon. Pork cutlets are both the most popular cut of pork served as well as the most popular cutlet she chose. That is, she suggests pork cutlets three times more often than mutton or veal cutlets. On occasion, she serves them with savoury sauce, a bacon-flavoured butter sauce made with stock from sweet root vegetables (onion, carrot, and turnip), parsley, and thyme.[49] Although bacon and 'boiled bacon' appear as separate dishes in many menus, in others, bacon flavours some of the made-dishes or other meats like calf's liver. The larding of lean meats with strips of bacon fat or salt pork is implied especially for beef fillets and game, although sometimes she does identify the process in the name of the dish, such as larded capon.

In 1854, after their stay in France, Catherine adds pigs feet with truffles to her menus. Trotters stuffed with truffles was a well-known dish served at the Parisian restaurant Véry's that the Dickenses frequented. In fact, it was so well-known that César Gardeton wrote in 1828 that 'as soon as a foreign gourmet sets foot in Paris, he makes straight for *Véry*'s and, having made its acquaintance, he returns many times.'[50]

Catherine replaces the term 'pig's jaw' used in the original menus with 'pig's face' in the next edition. Both dishes are made from the mandible and garnished with beans, so it is likely that the change only reflects a more polite terminology. While most of the pork that Catherine lists in the bills of fare are relatively small cuts, she adds a whole roast suckling pig to an 1852 dinner party menu, and retains it in the drastically overhauled bills of fare of the later editions.

The Dickenses may have relied on farmed animals, but game, like deer, held a place of honour on their table. 'I have been thinking about a breast of

Venison next Sunday,' Dickens wrote to Thomas Beard soon after they returned from their North American tour.[51] In anticipation, Dickens wrote three days later saying,

> I have consulted Mr. Groves of Charing Cross. His suggestive mind gave birth to this remarkable expression – 'then why not consider this here breast o' wenson, off – and let me git another prime 'un in good eatin' order for you, for Sunday week? What' – continued Mr. Groves – 'is the hodds to a day?'
>
> Mr. Groves slapped a piece of venison as he spoke, with the palm of his hand; and plainly signified, by his manner no less than by his word, that this was wisdom. What do you say to it? – And what your sister?[52]

Typically, Dickens's whimsical invitations for game provided an air of celebration. 'A haunch of Wen'son will be roasted here, next Sunday' was the usual Wellerian cry.[53]

On the other hand, when looking at Catherine's menus, she only suggests a haunch of venison or hashed venison once in the 1851 and 1852 editions. The latter figures in an overly large bill of fare for three people, which includes pea soup, pickled salmon, mutton chops, cold Bath chaps (pig's cheek), peas, potatoes, cold lemon pudding for dessert, with toasted cheese and watercress salad to conclude. By 1854, she replaces hash with veal fricandeau. Yet hashed venison is of particular interest when looking specifically at their own family dinners. Not only did Catherine have a special serving platter for hash among her 'common green dishes' that suggests they may have eaten it more often than the menus imply – but among Dickens's correspondence is this outlandish invitation:

> Victoria By The Grace of God Queen Defender of The Faith, to her trusty subjects John Forster and Charles Dickens, Greeting.
>
> This is to will and require you, the said John Forster and Charles Dickens to have in your safekeeping, at No 1 Devonshire Terrace on this present Thirtieth day of January at half past five exactly, the body of Clarkson Stanfield, Royal Academician, and him in safe Custody to keep and hold, until the said Clarkson had taken his fill of certain Meat, to wit hashed Venison from America, and has washed down the same with certain liquors, to wit fermented liquors, provided at the said Charles Dickens' proper cost and charge.

Herein fail not at your peril.

   Victoria.

Countersigned

   Charles Dickens

   John Forster[54]

While it is possible that venison was being shipped from America, it is far more likely that Catherine was merely trying out an American recipe. The most likely source is *Domestic Cookery Book* written by Eliza Leslie. Miss Leslie (1787–1858) was born in Philadelphia and lived in England as a child before her family returned to her birthplace. Catherine and Charles met the Leslies at a party while touring Philadelphia the previous year. As Dickens described the evening, 'I had to dress in a hurry, and follow Kate to Cary's [sic] the bookseller's, where there was a party. He married a sister of Leslie's,' he explained. 'There are three Miss Leslies here, very accomplished.'[55] One was actually their aunt, Mrs Henry C. [Martha] Carey, whose husband was an owner of Carey and Lea, the Philadelphia publishing firm. The sisters were Anne, a talented painter like her father Charles R. Leslie, and Eliza, the author.[56]

The party entertained Catherine while they waited for her husband to arrive. Surely they talked about home-making, cooking, and the children. Eliza Leslie had written successful books on domestic economy and children's stories, which were published by the Carey family firm. In 1828, she wrote the popular American cookbook *Seventy-five Receipts for Pastry, Cakes, and Sweetmeats,* and in 1832 issued *Domestic French Cookery,* which she stated was chiefly translated from Sulpice Barué's *La cuisinière de la ville et de la campagne* of 1829. Five years later, she published *Directions for Cookery.* When Catherine met the author, who was twenty-eight years her senior, Leslie's successful first book was already in its twentieth edition; her other books sold equally well. (By the time Catherine completed her menu book in 1851, forty-one editions of Miss Leslie's popular book had already been published.)[57] It is very likely that she gave the young Catherine Dickens copies of her books or sent them on to her later.

If 'hashed venison from America' referred to the preparation, then Miss Leslie's recipe 'To Hash Cold Venison' is a probable choice. To make the dish, meat is cut 'in nice small slices' while a broth of the trimmings and bones is made and thickened with a *beurre manié* and added to leftover gravy, and some currant jelly. The slices are merely warmed in the sauce before serving.[58]

In the early years of their marriage, they purchased venison through their butcher but, later, the Watsons sent annual gifts during the hunting season at Rockingham Castle. 'Since then I have had the kindest notes from you. Since then, the finest of venison,' Dickens wrote to thank Lavinia Watson.[59] In October 1847, the meat was delivered ready for the table, having been hung for the usual two weeks to tenderize it. Dickens invited the actor Samuel Phelps 'to dine with us on Sunday at Six o'Clock' with two other guests, 'to dispose of a Haunch of Venison that has arrived today.' Later, two other letters suggest that the Dickenses may have taken over the hanging and butchering process themselves. The game arrived in late July. 'There's a haunch of Venison in the larder,' he wrote to invite a friend for Sunday dinner. To Beard, whom he invited for an extended visit, Dickens outlined, 'On Sunday next, ribs of venison. On Sunday week, a haunch of ditto, just sent up from Northamptonshire.'[60]

Generally, a steady supply of meat of all kinds would hang in the larder. If Mrs Beeton is any indication, a good housekeeper would always have a joint hanging, and it would be replaced immediately with another when taken down to be cooked: the only way to ensure that the meat would be in prime condition for roasting.[61]

Venison was not the only game the Dickenses enjoyed. At home or in restaurants, they dined on rabbit (which had never been protected by the game laws) and hare (which had) in the winter. 'You may hear of us at Simpson's – where we go for a Rabbit,' Charles wrote referring to the Albion Tavern.[62] His taste for the creature is reflected in the description by Charley Bates, one of the gang of thieves in *Oliver Twist*: 'Such a rabbit pie, Bill [Sikes]...disclosing to view a huge pasty, "sitch delicate creeturs, with sitch tender limbs, Bill, that the wery bones melt in your mouth, and there's no occasion to pick'em".'[63] Rabbits were plentiful and those raised in Holland were beginning to dominate the mid-1850s market since they could be skinned, shipped by steamer, and sold fresh at a reasonable price.[64] Catherine was fond of rabbit curries and served rabbit pie and boiled rabbit but, judging by the number of entries, she actually preferred roast hare and leveret (a young hare). She would have served the dish in the traditional manner with the hare sitting in a life-like position on a garnished platter. Jugged hare, a method of placing seasoned meat in a container (jug) cooked slowly in a pan of water, also appears in Catherine's dinners, as do hare hash and hare soup.

In 1856, poultry was more expensive than butcher's meat in the London market.[65] An article, 'Our Back Garden', contributed by James Payn to *Household Words*, recited a humorous backyard tale of raising chickens for those who had the space and the patience.[66] Agriculturists, particularly in Sussex, had experimented with 'fattening mixtures' in the early 1850s and, according to Webster, full-grown birds could weigh seven pounds.[67] In 'Poultry Abroad' by Edmund Dixon, English breeds were favourably compared to French. For breeders and hobbyists, the Great Exhibition of 1851 created a magnificent display of the wide range of poultry being raised in England.[68] 'Poultry mania', a mid-century phenomenon, resulted in amateurs paying extravagant prices for showy varieties of breeding stock. As a result, the first poultry society was formed in 1852 to hold shows but, more importantly, the group encouraged research and publication. As a result, artificial hatching in incubators turned 'a penny egg into a shilling chicken'. Incubation increased both poultry production and relieved laying hens to produce larger quantities of eggs.[69]

The London market supplied a variety of richly flavoured eggs from hens, turkey, duck, goose, and the smaller eggs laid by guinea-fowl and other land birds such as plover, lapwing, and ruff.[70] In his short-lived series, 'Illustrations on Cheapness', in *Household Words*, Charles Knight stated that in 1850, 'good [hen's] eggs' could be bought at sixteen for a shilling (about the same price as two pounds of beef).[71] Reviewing the history of the egg market, he showed how the price went down and the availability went up over the centuries, allowing the poorer classes to buy eggs more regularly. Improved transport, imports from France and Ireland (and to a lesser extent Wales and Scotland), supplied about one hundred and fifty million eggs annually for the late 1840s London market alone. English farm eggs still fetched higher prices from the dairymen or poulterers in fashionable districts. Snow-white and 'warranted new-laid' eggs could sometimes reach prices three times the general market rate, that is, a shilling for four to six eggs, and for 'purposes of polite cookery', eight eggs were sold for a shilling.[72] By 1856, the price of eggs was reduced to a halfpenny a piece, but British consumption still did not rival the French who reportedly consumed 100 eggs per person annually.[73]

Six domesticated breeds of chickens dominated the market. The most popular was the white 'Barndoor', also known as the Dunghill, since they thrived on table scraps. At maturity, the medium-sized birds were the most delicate and flavourful of all the breeds. The five-toed Dorking fowl from

Surrey were larger and had a yellowish flesh. Capons were generally taken from this breed, and the pullets produced large eggs. The plump black Poland, with its white top feathers, also produced an abundance of large eggs. The small Bantam, having feather-covered feet, were considered 'convenient' since they laid well and would also nurse the eggs of partridge and pheasant. The Chittagong, also called the Malay, was an Indian breed and the largest of all. The coarse, dark flesh made delicious stock.[74] The flavourful small game-fowls were prized along with their delicate eggs, but were aggressive fighters and difficult to raise. The eggs of the guinea-fowl were abundant and appreciated, as was its slightly gamy flesh (particularly as wild game went out of season).[75] Catherine's entries contain both domestic and wild fowl. She lards the drier meat of older poultry. Large birds such as chicken, capon, and turkey are often 'boiled', that is, simmered to poach the meat and to create stocks for sauces and soups. Boiling poultry is particularly evident in the earlier editions but, after living in France, she substantially reduces the entries of boiled fowl for the 1854 issue. When she includes boiled fowl, particularly in larger menus, she accompanies the meat with a variety of sauces.

In 1856, geese that were sold in the London market were still being reared on the commons and heaths of Surrey and Lincolnshire, although they needed daily extra rations of oats and barley. 'Fatteners', as a commercial speciality, took care of these young geese from March onwards and paid 'unremitting attention' to them. They crammed the young, pampered birds, known as 'green goose', with oats, peas, and skim or buttermilk, and made sure they were clean, exercised, and well kept. They were brought to market early and in large numbers. The ten-pound birds commanded high prices.[76] Catherine includes goose in only one 1851 and 1852 dinner menu, but she creates a new menu for the next edition (1854) that includes the specially fattened youngster. The dinner for up to five people offers green goose, curried skate, rice, French beans, mashed potatoes, and finishes with grated Parmesan probably served with fruit.[77] Her April–February menus take in the Michaelmas celebration (on September 29) when Victorians served a fat fragrant goose as part of the traditional meal.

Of all the fowl represented in Catherine's menus, the blue-dove house pigeon, also known as the ring dove or when young as a squab, is the most versatile bird for kitchen use. She makes stews and roasts with it, but pigeon pie appears to have been especially beloved in the Dickens household. There are several references to it in Charles's letters. In one, he invites his amateur theatrical company 'to a gipsey [sic] sort of cool dinner' after rehearsal, of 'viands, pickled salmon and cold pigeon pie'.[78]

Turkey was also popular in the Dickens home and was a common holiday gift. In 1839, Charles invited the lawyer Thomas Mitton to 'come and partake of Smithson's [who happened to be Mitton's partner] turkey'.[79] But his most humorous note was to Miss Burdett Coutts: 'A thousand thanks for the notable turkey,' Dickens wrote about the Christmas present she sent to Catherine. 'I thought it was an infant sent her by mistake, when it was brought in. It looked so like a fine baby.'[80]

A native of the New World, turkey had been domesticated in England since the reign of Henry VIII. Turkeys were raised on small farms in areas with dry, poor soils, since the pesky free-ranging birds were mischievous and had to be kept from field crops. Several breeds were available on the London market. 'The Black' turkey, which most closely resembled the wild bird, was larger and more hardy. 'Blacks' were raised in Norfolk and, when bred with the 'Virginian', they could reach weights of fifteen pounds. This was probably the highly prized bird that the Dickenses received as a gift. The white variety of turkey was rare in England, but common in France.[81] These turkeys were perfumed with truffles and so appreciated, Dixon claimed, that in the 1830s nearly thirty-six thousand were sold in Paris alone from November through February.[82] There, the truffled turkey had been well cherished in the eighteenth century and possibly earlier.[83]

According to the titles of the dishes, Catherine roasts and broils turkey (probably the younger birds) and boils the older ones. In fact, turkey is the fourth most popular bird in her menus. In 1851 and 1852, she suggests broiled turkey legs, but drops this dish in 1854. Although Catherine includes turkey legs for family meals of two or three persons, surely she realized how awkward they were to eat. If nothing else, her husband's humorous description of drumsticks in *Bleak House* would have been enough for her to eliminate them from the menus:

> Every kind of finer tendon and ligament that is in the nature of poultry to possess, is developed in these specimens in the singular form of guitar-strings. Their limbs appear to have struck roots into their breasts and bodies, as aged trees strike roots into the earth. Their legs are so hard, as to encourage the idea that they must have devoted the greater part of their long and arduous lives to pedestrian exercises, and the walking of matches.[84]

Just as American and Canadian cooks today struggle with turkey leftovers after Thanksgiving, Victorian housewives often faced the same problem after Christmas. In a testament to recycling leftovers, Dickens's note to their publishers began: 'I determined not to thank you for the Turkey until it was *quite gone,* in order that you might have a becoming idea of its astonishing capabilities.' He recounted: 'The last remnant of that blessed bird made its appearance at breakfast yesterday – I repeat it, yesterday – the other portions having furnished forty seven grills, one boil, and a cold lunch or two.'[85] Although his note was facetious, it does suggest that turkey was not always cooked whole, but butchered at home, and the parts were used individually to make dishes like the turkey legs in Catherine's earliest menus. The cooked meat was then worked into 'made-dishes' for other meals.

By the time of Catherine's first edition, frozen food could be transported from North America. Dickens thanked Russell Sturgis, a shipping merchant, for sending a brace of canvas-back ducks as a Christmas gift. 'They arrived in admirable condition and flourished exceedingly at Yesterday's dinner.'[86] Duck was one of Catherine's favourite menu items, including ducklings in the spring menus and wild duck in the winter months.

Their love of game, particularly pheasant, must have been well known. While Dickens was convalescing from an operation, gift baskets arrived from well-wishers, and he assures them that they would 'enjoy it heartily'.[87] They also ordered the birds from their dealer saying, 'I shall be happy to receive the Pheasant and eat them with the appetite of a Hunter.'[88] In Catherine's autumn and winter meals, pairs of pheasant and other fowl are succulently roasted. In her later editions, she occasionally replaces pheasant with partridge, which may have been more readily available. Partridge appear to be a personal favourite. Although she only lists them in three menus, she requested the birds as a special treat to celebrate her arrival at Broadstairs after her confinement. 'I have spoken to Georgy about the partridges, and hope we may find them,' her husband wrote in a note confirming her travel plans.[89]

Woodcock, partridge, grouse, and snipe are also autumn-winter delicacies found in her bills of fare. Game as a legal commodity was relatively new, as a result of the Game Act of 1831. Before, it had been illegal for non-land-owners to kill or sell game. However, plenty of game reached Leadenhall market surreptitiously, but no one dared ask whether it had been poached or genuinely hunted.[90] If Dodd's 1856 figures were accurate, the yearly averages for the sale of game are impressive, if mot shocking: 313,000 larks, 107,000 snipes, 57,000 grouse, 46,000 plovers, 44,000 woodcocks, and 60,000 wild ducks.[91] Depending on the size of the menu, Catherine serves meats, game, and birds as entrées, removes, second, and third courses, and on occasion as a savoury finish to the meal. To distinguish when the various dishes were served, a look at her menus in the transcript will provide the sequence.

******

Dairy goods and a wide variety of other items were supplied to Victorian kitchens by home deliveries and shops. Healthy cows and unadulterated milk were tremendous concerns for London consumers particularly in the poorer districts. In fact the second volume of *Household Words* published Richard Horne's article that appealed for improved sanitary conditions.[92] When the Dickenses were first married, and before itinerant milk-dealers advertised 'railway milk', the market for dairy products was restricted by distance. Farmers could send large tin cans of milk on spring vans, and fresh butter and cheese by heavy broad-wheeled wagons, to retailers in town but milking by cowkeepers occurred mostly within six to eight miles of the city centre, while the suckling of calves and lambs formed the next ring of market-centred husbandry about ten to thirty miles from the heart of London.[93]

During the summer months, street vendors sold milk (which was often diluted) from cans at Smithfield, Billingsgate, and other markets on the weekdays. On Sundays, milk sellers could be found in Battersea Fields, Clapham Common, Camberwell Green, Hampstead Heath, and similar places. Dressed in their characteristic smocks, the sellers cried 'Half-penny half-pint! Milk!'[94] while milkmen and their cows walked through the markets at 7:30 a.m. shouting, 'New milk from the kee-ow! Milk it in your own jugs – milk it in your own jugs, all hot, piping hot, new milk from the kee-ow!'[95]

Londoners with limited incomes may have purchased from street-sellers but the more affluent found more reliable sources. Mark Lemon, the Dickenses' friend, kept cows at Westbourne Grove to provide milk for his family.[96] With a larger number of growing children, the Dickens family may also have kept cows, but this cannot be substantiated. Dickens referred to their 'butterman' in a letter, and it is more likely that they had arranged for regular home deliveries of dairy products.[97] Referred to as a 'milk-walk', these were verbal contracts made between a dairyman and perhaps a dozen or so customers who purchased their daily supply of milk. The estimated retail price per quart in 1855–6 was about threepence and each household kept an account book to record deliveries.[98] Given the household (with five small children ranging in age from eleven to three years old) when Catherine first compiled her menus, and all the dairy products used in the kitchen, a milk-walk to the Dickens residence must have been lucrative.

For households needing a little credit, a supplier might make chalk-marks on the door-post or railing as a reminder.[99] The character of less charitable milkmen, at least, had resonated with Dickens. His description in *David Copperfield* not only portrayed the vendor, but the milk-walk. Since labour was cheap, milk was delivered several times a day and the purchaser's container was filled from the milkman's pint and half-pint ladles rather than being delivered in bottles.

As to his dealing in the mild article of milk, by-the-bye, there never was a greater anomaly. His deportment would have been fierce in a butcher or a brandy-merchant.

The voice of the youthful servant became faint, but she seemed to me, from the action of her lips, again to murmur that it [the bill] would be attended to immediately.

'I tell you what,' said the milkman, looking hard at her for the first time, and taking her chin, 'are you fond of milk?'

'Yes, I likes it,' she replied.

'Good,' said the milkman. 'Then you won't have none to-morrow. D'ye hear? Not a fragment of milk you won't have to-morrow.'

I thought she seemed, upon the whole, relieved by the prospect of having any to-day. The milkman, after shaking his head at her darkly, released her chin, and with anything rather than good-will opened his can, and deposited the usual quantity in the family jug. This done, he went away, muttering, and uttered the cry of his trade next door, in a vindictive shriek.[100]

English production of butter was supplemented in 1852 with high-quality butter imported from Holland called 'Osten butter'. Salted butter was also being imported from Ireland in an economic shift as the potato crops began failing and, by 1856, this held its own in a competitive market with the more expensive and flavourful butter freshly made in Cambridge and Epping. The Irish butter, known as 'firkin-butter' for the 80- to 85-pound barrels it was shipped in, was made with a ratio of seven pounds of salt to fifty pounds of butter. Because of the condition of the Irish dairies, the butter had a peaty or smoky taste and smell. However, shopkeepers preferred salted butter, since it could sit on the counter at room temperature for weeks before spoiling.[101]

Twenty years earlier there had been few of the middlemen that George Dodd identified as a new breed of tradesmen in his 1856 report. These 'butter jobbers' contracted with dairies for their output and were beginning to monopolize the market. Consumption of butter was high. Dodd estimated that each person used ten to sixteen pounds annually but, in reality, more butter was eaten by the upper than the lower classes.[102] Cooks had other culinary fats available. Suet, the hard leafy tissue from around the kidneys, added richness to desserts boiled in pudding cloths, and provided a light flakiness to pastry crusts. Beef suet was considered best, but veal suet and the fat from the loin or neck of mutton could make delicious savoury crusts. Lard from rendered pork fat and clarified beef drippings were generally used in cooking, but had only a small role in dessert pastries. If fresh and used sparingly, drippings could make excellent short crusts and were even incorporated into cake batters.

Commercially processed foods were becoming available as well. After the 1851 fiasco, when the Admiralty was supplied with canisters of spoiled meat, government pressure demanded improvements in the canning industry. By 1856, Dodd reported that the manufacturers had 'devised the means of potting or "canistering" an almost countless variety': nearly twenty kinds of soup, broth, and meat essences; twelve or fifteen kinds of fish, poultry, game, butcher's meat (tongue, ham, bacon, kidney, tripe, marrow), and 'nearly all the fruits and vegetables ordinarily eaten'. Milk and cream were also 'now preserved in canisters for lengthened keeping'. The expensive canned goods offered convenience, but the use of preserved meat was usually limited to military meals or expeditions.[103] Given the type of recipes Catherine chose for the menu book, it seems unlikely that canned goods filled her pantry, particularly since adulteration and suspicion still plagued the industry. However, 'mushroom ketchup, harvey, cayenne, and such like condiments' stood ready on the sideboard in the Dickenses' dining room.[104] Mushroom ketchup was a Victorian favourite, and anchovy, walnut, tomato, and fruit ketchups were also popular accompaniments for meat, game and fowl or added to sauces. These humble condiments were usually made at home, but could be easily purchased from provisioners.[105] Commercially bottled sauces had been available from the end of the eighteenth century. Among the first were Mrs Elizabeth Lazenby's anchovy essence and her brother Peter Harvey's sauce, both retailed by her husband at his London grocery store.[106] Alexis Soyer had produced a relish, sauce, and mustard as well, but even he used Harvey's sauce in his recipes. Harvey's sauce was so ubiquitous in British cooking that magazines like Beeton's *Englishwoman's Domestic Magazine* provided recipes to make reasonable copies.[107] Horse-radish, a perennial plant growing naturally in marshy places and by the sides of ditches in some parts of England, was another important condiment for meat.[108] The recipe Catherine gives for a hot horse-radish sauce is unusual since it first calls for onion stewed in a little fish stock until soft, and then flavoured with anchovy essence and lemon pickle. She provides substitutes for lemon pickle for those whose taste or cupboard was spare. For the most part, the sauces she chooses are tried-and-true combinations that have survived to our own times and are still served occasionally at our own tables. Steak with horse-radish sauce, mutton with onion sauce, pork cutlets with savoury sauce, lamb cutlets with cucumber sauce, sweetbreads with mushroom sauce are among her favourites. In the larger menus, where a guest was presented with numerous options for the main course and removes, Catherine includes oyster sauce, asparagus sauce, and sometimes lobster sauce to enhance boiled fowl.

CHAPTER IX

VEGETABLES, FUNGI AND FRUIT

E very mother in every era has probably uttered the immortal words, 'Eat Your Vegetables!' to her unwilling children. However, discovering whether they did so, either as children or as adults, has posed problems for economic historians. Peter Atkins, in research concerning the British diet 1850–1950, noted that there is a lack of reliable data pairing the various economic groups and the consumption of fruits and vegetables during the early part of the twentieth century.[1]

By the middle years of the nineteenth century, the urban British were already enthusiastic for their gardens. Edmund S. Dixon's 'My Garden Walks' in *Household Words* addressed that burgeoning interest. He compared European and English markets 'to discover in part whence all this horticultural abundance comes' before admitting that 'a passion for gardening seizes us before we know what horticulture means'.[2] Families enjoyed even their small plots for food, herbs, flowers and recreation; and gardening books allowed home owners and tenants alike to make the most of their limited opportunities. Suburban sites became 'gardens of pleasure', often landscaped with a central grassy area bordered by vegetables, fruiting shrubs, and small fruit trees with the objective a succession of flowers and culinary delicacies through the seasons. For those who could afford it, jobbing gardeners kept the plots neatly trimmed.[3]

Having a garden was always important to the Dickens family. Even when finding a home for his parents, Charles commented on the outside amenities: 'There is a good garden at the side well stocked with cabbages, beans, onions, celery, and some flowers.'[4] Charles and Catherine were attracted to the spacious garden enclosed by a high brick wall in their Devonshire Terrace home. Before the family moved in, their gardener was already at work.[5] The plot faced Marylebone Road and had a coach house and stable, with loft above as groom's quarters. Shaded by a large pear tree, this was where Grip, their notorious raven, and his successors, carried out their mischief.[6] Through the years, the garden became a refuge. 'I am walking round and round the garden this exquisite morning,' Dickens wrote one frosty February day, 'to think of the subjects for next No., and indulging in visions of the country.'[7] During the warm months, he sat reading 'luxuriously, in the garden.'[8]

When the weather cooperated, they and their very small white dog Snittle Timberg (later called Timber) entertained visitors outside.[9] Mary Cowden-Clarke remembered 'one of these more quiet occasions, when Mr. and Mrs. Dickens, their children, and their few guests were sitting out of doors in the small garden in front of their Devonshire Terrace house, enjoying the fine warm evening.'[10] On other occasions, battledore, shuttlecock, or a 'riotous game of trap-bats and ball' were played.[11]

They employed a gardener who put the flower beds 'into perfect order' every spring. Afterwards he attended 'once a week as usual' to keep the area looking its best, which included adding new gravel on the walks when needed.[12] One assumes colourful flower beds and lush green shrubs outlined the perimeters, and surely pots of scarlet red geraniums, Dickens's favourite, accented the architecture.[13] A kitchen garden most likely was tucked into a sunny corner.

When the Dickenses leased their next home, Tavistock Place, at the end of 1851, they redesigned the garden as well as the house. Dickens sent the details and a ground-plan to William Wills, his business manager, who made the arrangements while they were away.[14] Richard Wood, the nurseryman from Haverstock Hill, looked over the grounds at Tavistock House with an eye to 'whether the greater part of the shrubs &c in the garden, can be transplanted' from Devonshire Terrace. 'I put them there,' Dickens declared to Wills, 'and I don't want to leave them there.'[15] When Dickens wrote to Wood for an estimate for the proposed garden plan, he was uncertain about keeping the poplar trees. Ultimately, Dickens negotiated an agreement with his neighbours to extend the three gardens and common walls in order to maximize all three.[16] When the project was completed, large handsome lilacs greeted spring visitors to the front court, and a 'Bower of Roses' presided over the back where Dickens sat 'during the whole of this delicious day'.[17]

Besides the sheer relaxation of sitting in a fragrant garden, flowers and greenery were prominent in Victorian home décor and found a special place at the Dickenses' table. From Boulogne, Charles wrote:

> the flowers are beautiful...Mary is improving in her powers of floral arrangement every day. In two parts of the garden, we have sweet peas nearly seven feet high, and

their blossoms rustle in the sun, like Peacocks' tails. We have a honey-suckle that would be the finest in the world – if that were not at Gad's Hill. The house is invisible at a few yards' distance, hidden in roses and geraniums.[18]

Their daughter Mary (Mamie), now eighteen years old, was following her parents' lead: flower arrangements and small bouquets had decorated their dinner-party tables for decades, and her mother had recommended garnishing dishes with colourful blossoms to bring the splendour of the outdoor garden inside.

Even at Gad's Hill Place, the grounds were carefully redesigned. By 1857 when their tenant served out his lease, the Dickenses were able to renovate the house and gardens. By this time, they had prominent acquaintances like Sir Joseph Paxton, who had designed the Crystal Palace for the 1851 exhibition, to ask for recommendations. 'Mrs. Dickens or Miss Hogarth will have full powers from the source of all domestic authority to conclude treaties,' Dickens wrote when making arrangements with a gardener in case he was not available himself. When Charles Barber took on the post of gardener in early August,[19] Dickens appealed to Paxton:

(at the urgent solicitation of the Gardener) that if you can send me any 'cuttings', of any kind, out of your great wealth in such things, 'here's an empty house and empty grounds' – I quote the gardener – 'and nothing from Sir Joseph could possibly come amiss'. – That's *his* opinion.[20]

Needless to say, the grounds at Gad's Hill Place flourished. The selection of plants provided seasonal colour in a variety of forms and textures, if we can judge from the sale catalogue after Dickens's death.[21] The amount of produce supplied by the Dickenses' own garden is unknown, but undoubtedly most fruits and vegetables were purchased. By the 1850s, when Catherine began compiling her menus, London's fresh produce and market operations were noticeably changing. Peter Atkins notes the extraordinary impact London had on food production in the surrounding areas. Over the next two decades, the enlargement of the railway network, combined with urban pressures, pushed small-scale producers farther from the city centre. The appearance of middlemen increased the emphasis on wholesale operations, often linked to the railway infrastructure, while industrial-scale jam-making and canning factories created a larger demand for fruit and produce.[22] George Dodd predicted that 'We have to look forward to the railway depôts becoming food markets.' He noted that many buildings at King's Cross were potato warehouses for the market.[23]

In 1851, about 80 per cent of London's supply of fresh-picked fruits and vegetables came from only a short distance away (by river or road) and were often sold directly by the grower.[24] Land-use patterns show that sections to the north and north-west of the city were predominantly dairying pastures, but within two miles north and south of the Thames was an elongated swath of market gardens and nurseries on the 'warmer' and better-drained soils. Access to the river was fundamental for shipping produce to market and, on their return, shippers hauled fertilizer (as manure) from the town stables and cowsheds. Altogether, an estimated 12,000 acres had been devoted to vegetables and another 5,000 acres for fruit cultivation in what was known as the 'charmed circle', with easy access to market. Since labour was also relatively abundant, the owner-operators could 'indulge in the speculative production of delicate luxuries like asparagus'.[25] Even the Dickenses' friend and solicitor, Thomas Mitton, had taken up market-gardening in Middlesex where he lived.[26]

By roughly 1860, when Catherine's last-known edition was printed, London's fruit and vegetable production had begun a transformation. Although an inner circle of 'spade cultivation' was retained for the higher-priced vegetables such as asparagus, seakale, French beans, celery, radishes, lettuces, mustard, and cress, there were two outer zones defined by less valued produce. The middle area produced bulky, less perishable crops such as peas, beans, onions, Brussels sprouts, broccoli, and cauliflower. The outermost zone rotated cabbage, potatoes, turnips, and carrots.[27] Staggered sowings in old cucumber or melon beds and February plantings 'on gentle hot beds of dung or leaves' forced additional harvests of these crops.[28] Soft fruits were also cultivated in the outer zones, but since tree fruits required years to mature, orchards were pushed farther beyond the city. Microclimates and soil types divided the areas so that specialization often occurred. Mortlake was renowned for asparagus, Battersea for cabbage and cauliflower, Deptford for onions, Mitcham for herbs, and Charlton for pears.[29]

A German journalist declared: 'English gardeners produce beautiful vegetables; especially cauliflowers, of such enormous size and exquisite flavour, that I have never seen nor heard of the like in any other country.'[30] The market gardens boasted 'regiments of rhubarb with waving plumes, bristling squares of onions, orderly battalions of cabbages, wild rabbles of radishes and onions.'[31] The various markets were complementary in their function, but served different areas and populations.[32] The heavy, cheaper vegetables were sold to the poorer classes at the Borough, which accommodated south London, while Spitalfields served the East End. Other smaller markets, like Farringdon and Portman, had a limited range of fruits, vegetables, and nuts.[33] Other attempts to establish non-specialist retail markets, such as Miss Burdett Coutts's Columbia Market in the East End, were not particularly successful.[34]

Not surprisingly, Covent Garden, which catered to inner west London, was among the most impressive and tended to monopolize the more expensive produce. 'Few of our market-places link the present with the memory of the past so fully as Convent Garden.' Originally the Westminster Abbey garden, it had evolved over six and a half centuries to serve the wider community.[35] Chartered in 1670, Covent Garden had from the first been a successful horticultural market, but gradually diversified. If a fruit or vegetable was in season locally, could travel by railway, or could be imported, Catherine and her cook could purchase it at Covent Garden among the colourful 'costermongers with baskets, porters in knee-breeches, "hagglers", fruiterers, greengrocers, eating-house keepers, salesmen, and carters [who] swell the restless multitude.'[36] Even off-season hothouse items like slender French beans were offered, although at the exorbitant price of three shillings a hundred. Likewise a quart of early peas sold at £2, and a pound-weight of new potatoes at four shillings and sixpence in 1853.[37] During the Dickenses' time, Covent Garden was opened as a wholesale market on Tuesday, Thursday, and Saturday, and on the other days vendors sold retail.[38] With the advent of the 'electro-telegraphic message', tradesmen could transmit information quickly when clipper ships arrived, and swiftly arrange the movement of produce into London, or send a glut of comestibles outward into the surrounding markets.[39]

Seasonality played an important role in the availability of produce at the markets and in the planning of menus. At the height of the asparagus season for example, it was typical for Catherine and her contemporaries to serve the spears as a soup, sauce, and a vegetable during the same meal. In the lean months, bills of fare may not list any fresh fruits or vegetables. To add flexibility to her menus, Catherine sometimes just wrote 'greens' or 'vegetables', but usually the dish titles specify the item and often the preparation (mashed, boiled, stewed or broiled). With the exception of fresh watercress salad, which was served often as a last course, her most popular greens and vegetables are French beans, cauliflower, broccoli, peas, and spinach. These crops have long growing seasons that both extended their availability and moderated their price for more economical meals. The cabbage group (broccoli, cauliflower, and Brussels sprouts) alone make up a quarter of all the vegetables she mentions. For variety, Catherine serves broccoli and cauliflower as gratin dishes, which she attributes to Soyer. She usually reserves the more pedestrian vegetables, like summer cabbage, for small family dinners.

Legumes, particularly beans and peas, fill her menus. Her overwhelming single favourite is French beans which make up 17 per cent of all the vegetable dishes. These dwarf species of kidney beans are picked as young pods, boiled, and probably served with butter from May to February. Dried beans (haricot blanc or those from scarlet runner beans) were combined in casseroles with meat. Numerous varieties of peas were available as early and late producers with the Prussian Blue, Rouncival, Marotto, Marrowfats, and Egg the most important varieties in England at that time. During the height of the season, shopkeepers employed scores of women solely to shell the peapods. [40] Peas are well represented in Catherine's menus. She often suggests fresh spring peas, possibly the sweet young peas from her own garden. She would have stewed mature peas in green pea soup early in the summer, and used dried white or yellow varieties, known as 'boilers' to accompany a lamb dish, or as a purée for pea-based soups (pease pudding) in late-season menus.

From May through September, Catherine prepares fresh young spears of asparagus and saves the larger stalks for purées. Green asparagus (or 'spruegrass' as Soyer called it) was preferred in England to the thick, whitish, stronger flavoured spears touted by Europeans. John C. Loudon, the garden writer, believed asparagus was cultivated in the London neighbourhoods 'to a greater extent than anywhere else in the world' and often occupied the largest portion (about an eighth) of a gentleman's garden. [41] Unfortunately there are no records as to the Dickenses' cultivation of asparagus in their various gardens over the years, but it would not be surprising if they followed suit.

Celery's origin as a wild plant called 'smallage', a rank-smelling, acrid green found in wet areas and ditches, meant that to produce a more subtle, acceptable flavour, the garden plant needed blanching by covering with a bank of earth so that only the dark upper leaves were exposed.[42] Celery was so esteemed by the Victorians that speciality glassware and silver were designed to serve the raw stems, usually with a cheese course at the end of the meal.[43] According to their inventory, the Dickenses owned a celery glass.[44] In only a single bill of fare does Catherine suggest celery as a stewed vegetable. In none does she propose celeriac, the root which, according to Thomas Webster, was rarely used by anyone else in England.[45] Parsnips, seakale, spinach and turnip tops are other vegetables that she incorporated into her dinners, as are stewed Spanish onions and mashed turnips. Whether or not she preferred 'bashed neeps' made from the yellow turnip or swede she would have known as a child in Scotland, we do not know.[46]

Globe artichokes found their way into a few of Catherine's menus but, judging from an 1841 letter from Daniel Maclise, the Dickenses learned about them rather late. Maclise described the meal he enjoyed with another guest, John Forster, where artichokes were served as the 'remove' dish:

> one a-piece – quite enough – I understand you don't know this creation. It is a soft sort of Fir tree fruit shaped production – made thus [sketch of an artichoke on a plate] served up with melted butter – and to be peppered. You detach with your fingers each layer, dip the rim in butter and eat the tip and lining – dreadful nonsense. I class it with the much ado things of the Sparrow grass kind. [Edward Lytton] Bulwer doats upon it – After this we had cheese and a pat of Butter.[47]

Artichokes were typically boiled plain, but the heart also could have been stewed in milk. Artichokes have an odd property of heightening the sweetness of things eaten afterwards; perhaps knowing this, Catherine once accompanied artichokes with batter pudding, but for the most part she reserves them as a vegetable for larger dinners of up to ten people.

Some vegetables like carrots are silent workhorses flavouring soups and stews, or adding colour to other dishes like her kalecannon. Although Catherine includes carrot soup in the menus, she rarely mentions carrots as an individual vegetable, but they do accompany potatoes and boiled beef – perhaps for a boiled dinner. Catherine suggests cucumber as a vegetable only a few times, but of course they were constantly in use as garnish to fish platters or as a sauce for lamb cutlets.

Salads were very popular in the Dickens household. 'You do not know in England the importance of the salad question,' began 'The Roving

Englishman', a series in *Household Words*. With a facetious tone, the authors Eustace (Grenville) Murray and Henry Morley professed that salad-making belonged to the fine arts and could no more be acquired by rule than poetry, sculpture or painting. The proportions of the four key elements, 'the herbs' (salad greens), oil, vinegar, and salt are critical. In fact, to properly dress a salad, it required 'the united efforts of four different men: a spend thrift for the oil, a miser for the vinegar, a sage for the salt, and a maniac for the mixing.'[48] But as every expert salad-maker knows, 'lettuce requires little oil and endive very much.' Morley praises other leafy candidates such as chicory (wild endive) in another article on the subject.[49] Delicious salads composed of vegetables such as cauliflower in Italy were also chronicled by the authors. In a comparable spirit, Catherine provided several types of salads and gives instructions for Spanish salad dressing in the appendix. Her 'small salads', as they are written in the menus, do not refer to the portion size, but rather to the type of greens. 'Small salading' was understood by gardeners and cooks alike as the juvenile leaves (often called 'seed leaves') or the very young plants of watercress, mustard, radish, rape, lamb's lettuce, and pot herbs (known as 'salad herbs') such as sorrel. Delicately flavoured leaves could also be picked from lettuce, white cabbage, and endive before their strong flavours developed. Small salading demanded less sunlight and was grown commercially on the floors of the hothouses where peaches and other trees were forced into fruiting.[50] T.W. Hill postulated that Dickens must have loved salads since his favourite adjective for them was 'nice cool' and his other descriptor, 'crisp', often labelled lettuce leaves and celery stalks to connote crunchy freshness.[51] One of Dickens's most endearing descriptions of a salad is when Mrs Gamp's friend, Betsey Prig, visits her in *Martin Chuzzlewit*. Mrs Gamp could not produce a 'cowcumber' for their meal of pickled salmon:

Mrs. Prig, looking steadfastly at her friend, put her hand in her pocket, and with an air of surly triumph drew forth either the oldest of lettuces or youngest of cabbages, but at any rate, a green vegetable of an expansive nature, and of such magnificent proportions that she was obliged to shut it up like an umbrella before she could pull it out. She also produced a handful of mustard and cress, a trifle of the herb called dandelion, three bunches of radishes, an onion rather larger than an average turnip, three substantial slices of beetroot, and a short prong or antler of celery, the whole of this garden-stuff having been publicly exhibited, but a short time before, as a twopenny salad, and purchased by Mrs. Prig on condition that the vendor could get it all into her pocket. Which had been happily accomplished, in High Holborn, to the breathless interest of a hackney-coach stand. And she laid so little stress on this surprising forethought, that she did not even smile, but returning her pocket into its accustomed sphere, merely recommended that these productions of nature should be sliced up, for immediate consumption, in plenty of vinegar.[52]

In keeping with her husband's sentiments, more than half of Catherine's menus, over the decade of her editions, include some type of salad. She serves salads either as one of the vegetables, or as the last savoury course; it depends on the size of the bill of fare. She suggests beetroot, sometimes combined with celery, as both a salad and a vegetable dish throughout the year, implying the use of pickled beets when fresh ones were no longer available. The yellow variety was more prized because of its sweetness, but red and white beets were also available. Although beet tops were widely served, Catherine never specifically lists the greens as a separate dish as she does turnip tops. Mayonnaise of fowl, that is chicken served over a quartered head of lettuce with a mayonnaise sauce, is a recipe she gave in the appendix and is suggested as one of the removes in menus for six or more diners. By the 1854 edition, Catherine adds chicken salad as a last course, just as lobster salad had been served as the concluding savoury. Excluding kalecannon, a moulded mixture of a variety of cooked vegetables, Catherine never proposes potato salad, cabbage salad (coleslaw) or salads made from combinations of other dressed cooked vegetables that were popular with her contemporaries.

Other vegetables which are entirely absent from Catherine's various editions include endive, bulb fennel, gherkins, pumpkin, rhubarb, salsify, or vegetable marrow. All of these would have been available at market or cultivated in a small garden plot. The absence of tomatoes, other than one entry for tomato sauce, is less difficult to understand. Tomatoes, still sometimes referred to as 'love apples', were connected to their infamous nightshade cousins. Tomatoes were not generally eaten raw in Britain and, according to some authorities, they were not openly accepted until the end of the nineteenth century.[53] They may have figured, of course, in the Dickens kitchen in their more normal Victorian guise as additions to soups and sauces, or as juice preserved for winter use as a ketchup for meat and fish.[54]

Rice does not figure prominently in Catherine's dinners. Perhaps her husband knew how typical their family was: he published John Capper's article in *Household Words* on the varieties of rice and the history of its use in other cultures.[55] Capper admonished readers who only prepared rice 'in no other shape than puddings, [who] may with truth be said to know nothing of it as an article of food.'[56] But the English use in sweets was not singular: even the French, who gave rice a 'place of honour from the start of the nineteenth century', and served rice in the 'meals of the highest excellence' followed this same sweet fashion. Jean-Paul Aron found, in looking at Baron Brisse's 1867 menus, that rice was used 67 times more often than potatoes, but that it was usually 'presented in the form of a sweet; the custom of treating it as a vegetable became widespread only rather late in the culinary-day.'[57] Using rice in sweet dishes seems certainly true of the Dickens household. Catherine deploys it as a savoury starch almost exclusively with curried dishes, often serving it in the same course with potatoes. Even so, about two-thirds of the curried dishes are not paired with rice in the early editions (ignoring her own note 'serve as usual with rice separate' in her recipe for salmon curry). By the 1854 edition, she amends those menus so that both curry and rice appear in the same course. Yet, like her countrywomen, she continues to suggest sweet dishes using rice far more frequently (in fact, three times more often) than in savoury form. For these desserts, she relies on ground rice as a thickening agent or uses the cooked grains in combination with baked fruit, rice pudding custards, and as fried croquettes.

Throughout, potatoes predominate as the meal's starch component. Webster reported: 'London is well supplied with potatoes from various parts of the country; and the varieties are so numerous, that every town has some sort peculiar to its vicinity.'[58] In nearly 95 per cent of Catherine's bills of fare she lists potatoes – and in several large 1852 and 1854 menus she includes them in two courses. Yet, their ubiquity is almost staggering given the catastrophic failure of the Irish crop not many years before, which continued even into the early 1850s. Henry Morley observed in *Household Words*, 'With equal generosity [potatoes] are prompt to place a luxury upon the rich man's gravy, or a heap of food beside the poor man's salt.'[59]

Unlike the large smooth, oval tubers on our tables, the Dickens family and their contemporaries ate more colourful, oddly shaped, deep-eyed, and flavourful varieties. Among them were the 'Irish Apple', introduced around 1770, with good keeping qualities available early in the season. These red and white tubers were renowned for their dry, mealy consistency when boiled, but unfortunately the variety succumbed to the blight of 1846. The 'White

Kidney', another favourite, was an exceptional early kidney-shaped potato introduced around 1815 which supplied fresh tubers in July and August. [60] Soyer was particularly fond of the 'ash-leaf kidney' for fried potatoes.[61] The best-known variety was the 'Manly', an early and heavy cropper introduced in 1776 that survived until at least 1859. 'Lumper' produced the enormous harvest on which the poorer classes depended. Although it played the most devastating role in the famine years of 1845–6, the variety continued to be grown. 'Cups', a very popular red-skinned type cultivated since 1808, was thought to be more nutritious, but less digestible. It was regarded as 'the luxury potato' and a great favourite in both England and Ireland until the famine.[62]

The 1845 potato crop had occupied roughly two million acres, and the anticipated harvest was well over thirteen million tons for the year, half of which would feed the poor. The 'lazybed' system of cultivation where tubers were kept in raised beds and covered with manure, seaweed, and soil to protect them from moisture, created the perfect reproductive environment for the potato rot fungi. Additionally, 40 per cent of the crop was already infected, and those tubers were allowed to rot in the fields which further encouraged spore incubation.[63] Although regional failures occurred every few years, disastrous harvests in 1846 and 1847 'literally shook Ireland to the very roots of her economic, social, and political being.'[64] Since then a wealth of scholarly research has been published on the famine and its consequences, which need not be discussed here, except to note that it took time for the English to understand the significance of the blight.[65] There was empathy for the poor tenant farmers', but little support was given to the government's action described in a letter from Dickens on 24 March 1847: 'This is the day which our wise legislators have appointed for a general fast…I despise them for such rot.'[66] The Privy Council had ordered the day be appointed 'for public fast and humiliation before Almighty God' to obtain a pardon for sins and His heavy judgments. The order strongly suggested that shops be closed and encouraged church attendance. According to the *Examiner* and *The Times*, many Londoners treated it as a public holiday.[67]

Ultimately there was concern about the failure of the impending potato crop, but the English growers suffered less at harvest time than the Scottish and the Irish. The blight brought about the 1846 repeal of import duties on cereal grains regulated by the Corn Laws, but essentially the famine years in Ireland made all food dear throughout England.[68] Dr William P. Alison sent his pamphlet, *Observations on the Famine of 1846–7 in Scotland and Ireland, as Illustrating the Connection of the Principle of Population with the Management of the Poor* (1847), to Dickens.[69] At the time, publications, including *Household Words,* discussed potato crops without fully realizing the havoc created in the lives of the poor. Henry Morley's light-hearted article 'A Dish of Vegetables' merely lamented:

> The Potato family has been for many years one of the noblest benefactors to the human colony, and when it was prevented lately by ill-health from the fulfillment of its good intentions, great was the anxiety of men, and many were the bulletins of health sought for and issued. Its constitution still appears to be a little shaken, and we all still hope for the complete recovery of so sincere and influential a friend.[70]

Six years later, Eliza Linton's article 'The Growth of Our Gardens' recognized in hindsight 'one of the most heart-rending famines on record'.[71]

Experiments stimulated by interest in breeding resistant potato varieties had already begun. The long kidney-shaped 'Lapstone Kidney', an early variety, held its own during the second half of the nineteenth century. The 'Prince Regent', also known as the 'Regent', was introduced in 1841 and was popular with breeders and cooks. Soyer declared the Regent the favourite baked potato served in London clubs and homes.[72] The 'Fluke', a long, flat oval-shaped late variety, dominated the market until its rival, 'Paterson's Victoria', overshadowed it. In Ireland, the 'Rock' was a favourite and replaced 'Lumper' and the 'Cup', but it was eclipsed by 'Champion' around 1863.[73] From the early twentieth century, the public almost universally expected their potatoes to be oval or kidney-shaped with a white skin and a smooth surface, but these unfortunately often resulted in less favourable 'cookers' than those that would have been consumed by the Dickens household.[74]

Statistically, each Londoner ate a pound of potatoes a day,[75] and correspondence mentioning potatoes is not difficult to find. In 1842 the Dickenses' friend Jane Welsh Carlyle, for example, mentioned that they had so many potatoes, the barrel she sent to a family member was returned, 'being amply supplied'. From the early years of the poor harvests through the 1850s, the only impact on the middle and upper classes, other than price, were the varieties available – and the best way to prepare them. 'We boil them now with the skins on and find them *all* [italics hers] eatable and *some* of them excellent,' Mrs Carlyle explained. 'I think they need very long and slow boiling – our man's are *prettier* to look at but have not such a "genuine real unadulterated" potato-taste.' [76]

The proper method of boiling potatoes was much debated. Should the skins be removed or just scrubbed? Was it best to start them in a pot of cold or boiling water? Even Eliza Acton devoted three pages just to boiling potatoes.[77] Of course, the method depended on the waxy or mealy qualities of the variety, but the reputation of an English cook was largely based on the outcome. According to Wills' article, 'A Plain Cook', when candidates for the cook's position at the Pall Mall Club were interviewed, the first question they were asked was, 'Can you boil a potato?'[78]

'New potatoes', and those Catherine lists simply as 'potatoes', are most likely boiled, and served whole or sliced, glistening with a few tablespoons of *maître d'hôtel* butter. Boiling was often just the first step; potatoes 'mashed and brown[ed]' are her overwhelming favourite, carrying nearly 80 per cent of the entries in the early editions. The mashed potatoes were probably heavily enriched with egg yolks and cream or hot milk and butter, before the fluffy mixture was browned with a hot salamander (a flat iron) to achieve a golden crust. The crisp crust apparently fell out of favour in the Dickens household: by 1854 Catherine replaces a third of those entries with plain mashed potatoes. And if there were leftovers, they were not wasted. Catherine added fish or chopped meat to mashed potatoes for made-dishes such as cod rechauffé served with oyster sauce, and even provided a recipe. For variety, she suggested forming the mashed potatoes into balls, and baking or frying them. Fried potatoes, apparently not yet referred to as 'chips', demand more attention in the kitchen, and she only includes them in two of her early menus, but adds a few more entries by 1854. Baked potatoes, as such, are never mentioned, and the whimsical turned shapes, such as 'olives' or 'crulles' made from a continuous spiralling curl, were not yet in fashion.[79]

Although fungi add a rich meaty flavour to preparations, they were typically classified as vegetables in cookery books of the period. Garden or cultivated button mushrooms were the most common, but in season, wild species were prized finds. Numerous identification books were published in Britain for amateur mycologists interested in collecting edible fungi in fields and open pastures. Morels, which popped up after the May and June rains, satisfied a particular passion, and they were carefully dried or powdered to extend their use through the off-season. There is contemporary evidence that we British were not as suspicious of wild fungi as we often think ourselves to be. In his *Household Words* article, 'What Mushrooms Cost', Edmund S. Dixon contrasted French and British attitudes toward wild and cultivated fungi. 'The fool-hardiness of those insular experimentalists in *l'eccentrique Angleterre*,' he stated, 'who feast themselves on inky toad-stools, cotton-woolly puff-balls, and leathery morels, is to them sufficient proof that, droll as we are, we are by no means deficient in courage.'[80] The large-scale culti-vation of mushrooms in Lezennes, France demanded twelve-hour days by labourers in unventilated cellar-caves. Mushroom-growing in England was more informal, 'any dark outhouse or convenient cellar' in the heart of town or country produced a crop, which could also be purchased readily from market gardens. Victorians happily supplemented these commercial varieties with field-gathered fungi. 'A wild agaric grilled ever so deliciously, bathed in butter and powdered with blended pepper and salt,' Dixon insisted, would not be served in France. 'Unless mushrooms can be warranted as garden produce, it is in vain to set them before a Gallic epicure.'[81] Mushrooms are among Catherine's culinary delights. She lists them in many menus as a separate dish simply prepared (either broiled or stewed) or paired with broiled meats. Or she wraps them in pastry as mushroom patties.

In addition, the Dickenses' pantry certainly would have contained bottles of home-made mushroom ketchup, which Dixon acknowledged as 'a British sauce that many a Frenchman would label Poison.' He confessed, 'we are not over-nice about the ingredients which enter it,' but this was certainly an exaggeration.[82] Contemporary cookbooks insisted that only the finest ingre-dients be used since so much time was invested in the preparation. Freshly gathered mushrooms, picked on a dry day, were well cleaned, then spread between layers of salt in a warmed earthenware jar to release their essence over twenty-four to seventy-two hours. The strained mash was squeezed, seasoned with whole black pepper, and boiled for a half an hour before stronger spices, like whole allspice, cloves, blades of mace, slices of ginger, cayenne and nutmeg, were added. The aromatic liquid was then boiled down. The cook may have fortified the sauce with brandy to extend the shelf-life, and then carefully preserved the reduction in small bottles sealed with rosin-dipped corks.[83] Judging by her recipes, Catherine added ketchup to enhance the flavour of scotch minced collops, rump steak à la Soyer, and scotch mutton broth, among other recipes. Although she does not specify the type of ketchup, mushroom would have undoubtedly been her first choice.

Mushroom sauces which accompanied entrées and roasts varied in their composition depending on whether the sauce was served with white or dark meat. Often mushroom ketchup and sliced or chopped fresh mushrooms were the essential ingredients, but in the off-season, mushroom powder, made from the dried mushrooms, could be substituted. Catherine particularly liked the pairing of mushroom sauce with sweetbreads.

'Cook's truffles', the greyish black truffles with whitish interiors, were actually common on the downs of Hampshire, Wiltshire, and Kent, and especially abundant in the light dry soils of the oak and chestnut forests with which the fungi have a relationship.[84] British truffles were collected in the summer and used in the same ways as morels for their 'delicious flavour'. Webster believed that 'many of the virtues attributed to them are imaginary,' although he did not elaborate on truffles as an aphrodisiac.[85] British mushroom hunters thought of their inelegant truffles as just one more wild mushroom, rather than according them the unique status of the more esteemed truffles of France and Italy.[86] Edmund S. Dixon acknowledged that appreciation for those fungi required 'an education to understand them properly'. Imported truffles were rarely used in England when Dixon's 1855 article was written. He suggested that 'to the evils of ignorance was joined the national obstinacy,' that black truffles do not marry well with 'cayenne pepper, Durham mustard, and high-spiced sauces.' He believed British flavourings deprived the fungus of whatever fragrant properties it retained after its long journey from France.[87] Dixon may have been correct; in *The Modern Housewife*, Soyer did not list truffles or even discuss them briefly. Acton provided four recipes from 'the best French authority', but stated 'we cannot, from our own experience, give receipts for dressing it'. She dutifully provided a footnote on bottled truffles.[88]

In the early 1850s, Catherine, too, may have lacked appreciation for the black truffle but, after her extended stay in France, she adds truffles to decorate pig's feet (trotters) in a fancy bill of fare for up to seven diners in her revised 1854 edition. Of course, previous gifts of pâté acknowledged in the correspondence suggest that the Dickenses occasionally counted the luxury upon their family's table.[89] But truffles did not generally seduce the Victorian middle-class as they did on the Continent; even by 1865, Mrs Beeton stated flatly that truffles were still 'not often bought in this country'.[90]

******

'Nowhere, perhaps, are the essential conditions better proportioned than on the Kentish rag, the weald of Sussex, on the lava beds of South Devon, in Shropshire, in the Lothians of Scotland, and North of Ireland, [and] in the dales and vales of the Midlands,' stated John Wright in *The Fruit Grower's Guide*. Both the climate and soil of Britain were ideal for raising temperate fruits and home cultivation was encouraged.[91] 'My Garden Library', an article in *Household Words*, provided general references for the home enthusiast.[92] Meanwhile, writers and growers reduced the staggering list of about 1400 apple types that were given in 1831 by the Horticultural Society of London, to a manageable 150 best varieties for small-scale cultivation.[93] Home orchardists faced an abundance of choices ranging from dwarf to full-size trees and the time of harvest as early, succession, or late bearers. The varieties of apples ranged in flavour from honey-sweet to lemony-tart with white to orange-coloured pulp and skins from yellow to russet. There were juicy eating apples or those most suited to baking, saucing, drying, or pressing, and they could be found in all shapes and sizes.

Thomas Webster had exclaimed that 'no fruit in Britain is so abundant, and so generally useful, as the apple,' to which the Dickens household could certainly testify.[94] For small dessert apples, Wright listed twenty-five 'first quality varieties', their harvests so tightly overlapping (or with convenient keeping properties) that only the month of June was without fresh apples.[95] Although the Dickens kitchen inventory does not list speciality equipment, like a tin apple-corer or apple-roaster, apples fill the dessert courses of Catherine's menus. Where specific fruits are mentioned, 36 per cent of the desserts contain apples. Of these, four favourite types emerge: apples steamed in suet puddings, boiled with rice, baked in tarts, and fried as fritters. Unlike today, many of the varieties of baking apples were usually stewed first in wine or water to soften the flesh and curtail tartness as part of the preparation. This can be seen in Catherine's recipe for Swiss pudding.[96]

Although steamed puddings are enjoying a revival today, so too might recipes that combine boiled rice and apples. These were fairly common desserts on both sides of the Atlantic. It is difficult to know the 'apples and rice' preparation to which Catherine refers in her menus, since cookery books offer several recipes with the same name. In one, apples are poached in a sugar syrup, thickly covered with rice (previously boiled in milk and spices) and baked. For variety, currants or raisins could be added.[97] Rice and apple snowballs are another intriguing possibility.[98] In Eliza Acton's version, rice is parboiled and heavily coats a cored, peeled baking apple that was stuffed with butter, sugar, and spices. Each ball is tied in a well-floured pudding cloth and boiled until the apple is tender.[99] This delicious and showy dessert is worth reviving especially with today's more convenient use of cling film to hold the rice in place.

Catherine includes a variety of other fruits in her dessert courses, particularly raspberries, currants, gooseberries, strawberries, plums, cherries, and citrus. Of these, she uses raspberries and currants most often – combining them, for example in rasberry and currant tarts. Two native varieties of raspberries, the red and the sweeter white fruits, were cultivated in Isleworth and Brentford for sale in the London market.[100] Since raspberries deteriorate rapidly, the majority of the crop was preserved as jam, wine, vinegar or brandy. Raspberries, like other fruits, could also be cooked down into a thick fruit cheese or paste, rolled in sugar, and stored. Over 7 per cent of Catherine's desserts feature raspberries, and about half of these use the fruit in popular formats such as puffs, raspberry jam puddings and raspberry jam sandwiches (made of pastry). Raspberry tarts and tartlets in the off-season imply the use of a jam filling, but the late summer menus would have featured fresh berries.

Red and white currants were sold in Covent Garden in fifteen- and twenty-pound baskets. Catherine does not specify which sort she employs in her menus, although the whites were occasionally preferred by Victorian cookery book writers for desserts and wine-making, while red currants made the best jellies. Sometimes, a combination raspberry and currant jam was made, just as those raspberry and currant tarts referred to above.[101] The most common cultivated varieties of black currants were Black Naples (later called Baldwin) and Black Grape.[102] Catherine only once specifically mentioned black currants (for a dessert), but they may have held a special sentiment; early in their courtship, Dickens sent his young fiancée a jar of black currant jam when she was recovering from scarlet fever.[103]

Gooseberries were naturalized in Britain and touted as the most useful of the berries, particularly since their flavour improved with a colder climate. Webster reckoned the name to come from their use both as a stuffing for goose and the sauce served with it,[104] i.e. they were defined by their culinary employment, much as they were in France where the sauce to accompany mackerel led them to be called *groseille à maquereau*. It is more likely, however, that the English is a straight derivation from *groseille*. Catherine does not propose the French combination in any menu. [105] Indeed, she only suggests gooseberry tarts twice, in summer menus. Appearing by late April, gooseberries were the earliest garden fruit and the season generally ran until August, although late-maturing varieties set fruit for a September harvest and others could survive mild winters. About seventy types of gooseberries were highlighted by the Royal Horticultural Society, yet the growers themselves recognized upwards of seven hundred. [106] Gooseberries were not only believed to be the most wholesome of fruits, they had other desirable properties. When made into wine, they created a sparkling drink often passing for champagne. Like currants, gooseberries were easy to clean and contained pectin which produced exceptional preserves. [107]

Named for the straw laid under the plants before they set fruit, strawberries came into season in late June, but by 1851 there were many varieties available from early June to September. [108] Light spring-vans brought the delicate fruit to market, and the 'porteresses', also known as the 'strawberry women', sold them on the street. [109] Doubtless strawberries fresh or preserved were used liberally in the Dickens household in season. Catherine proposed a refreshing strawberry cream in an April through July menu and uses jam fillings out of season. Perhaps the family had strawberry plants neatly tucked into the back garden. Edmund Saul Dixon's article on strawberry varieties discussed home cultivation. Among those he grew and recommended were Nicholson's Ajax, Captain Cook, Fill Basket, Ruby, Swainston's Seedling, Hooper's Seedling, Pelvilain's Comte de Paris, Haquin's Liegeoise, Myatt's Globe, Prolific Hautbois, and Trollop's Victoria the Magnificent. For fine flavour he suggested Downton, Myatt's Elisa, and the Old Caroline, but for fruit size he liked Kiley's Goliath and Wilmot's Superb. Dixon's favourite early varieties were Black Prince, Princess Royal, British Queen, Elton Pine, and the variety named Sir Harry, which was becoming an astonishingly productive novelty. 'You will find the succession of flavours much more entertaining than a succession of names,' Dixon predicted, arguing that a schedule of luscious fruits could be grown in the garden 'throughout all the heats of haysill and harvest, through the London season, the bathing season, and the shooting season.' Covent Garden 'will supply specimens, early and late, numerous and true.' Among the varieties Roseberry, Bath Scarlet, and Keen's Seedling were regularly available. [110] Hothouse cultivation extended the season, and pottles of British Queens or Black Princess could be purchased in 1853 for a pricey shilling an ounce.[111] The mystique surrounding strawberries continued even in the Dickenses' time. Physicians recommended strawberries for patients with fevers and gouty or rheumatic conditions who were restrained from eating other fruits.[112] Fresh strawberries not devoured with a sprinkling of sugar and thick cream were made into preserves, liqueurs and vinegars. Catherine relied on strawberry jam for garnishing desserts, and spread the preserve liberally in a rolled jam pudding. She also added an unusual recipe for a strawberry preserve to the 1854 appendix.

Plums, specifically greengages and damsons, were used by Catherine in puddings, tarts, and tartlets, including the only 'open faced tartlet' noted in the dessert courses. According to Webster, plums were believed to be a less wholesome fruit and should only be eaten in moderation. The best dried plums (prunes) were imported from France, such as the sweet reddish-yellow Brignolle plum from Provence, or the Damascene (damson) plum and the 'common medicinal prune' from Bordeaux.[113]

The wild cherry of Britain was common in England as well as in Catherine's native Scotland, where she may have often eaten the 'geans' of Aberdeenshire as a girl.[114] In 1851, about 200 commercial varieties of cherries were in cultivation. London vendors sold the Kentish and May-Duke varieties that lead the autumn season, and these were followed by the yellow Spanish cherry and dark-skinned sour Morellos that appeared in late winter.[115] Hannah Glasse, in her eighteenth-century book *The Complete Confectioner*, included a recipe for 'Red cherry wine as made in Kent'.[116] Acton's recipes for a compote of Kentish or Flemish cherries and compote of morella (morello), each called for a little over a pound of ripe cherries, sweetened and simmered in a half pint of water for about five minutes to soften for 'a delicious compote', which she recommended heartily.[117] The tart Morello cherries are best for pies, tarts, and jams, and they preserved well as whole fruits, bottled in sugar and brandy, or candied and dried. Cherries do not figure too often in Catherine's book. She offers a cherry tart once in season that most likely used fresh fruit rather than jam and, in the recipes, she recommends a cherry liqueur, crème au marasquin, to flavour the cream filling for charlotte russe.

By contrast, oranges and lemons, as well as other citrus fruit, were well employed in the Dickenses' kitchen. Catherine includes flavourings, fresh zest, and candied peels of citron, lemon, and orange in her dessert recipes.

Orange jelly and lemon jelly, sparkling clear gelatins flavoured with citrus juice and oils, most likely contained fruit sections carefully arranged in fruit-juice moulds. Orange-flower water, infused from the fragrant spicy blossoms, and orange or lemon oils, produced from the small glands in the rind, are found in the recipes Catherine chose. London was well supplied with oranges from October through December. Webster reported that about twenty-seven million sweet oranges were imported annually into England by the early 1850s. Oranges were picked before they were ripe (as they are today). The best sweet oranges came from St Michael's in the Azores, but quality fruit was also grown in Portugal, Spain, and Malta. Bitter or Seville oranges imported from Andulusia were prized for their sublime essential oils and made the best marmalade.[118] Lemons were imported from Sicily but, according to Webster, lemon trees were trained on walls in some parts of Devonshire and required no more than a straw covering to keep them over the winter.[119] Citron, which was closely related to lemons and the first citrus fruit introduced to Europe, was even more hardy, and several varieties were in cultivation in England. Citron juice was used to make lemonade, punch, and negus, and also had medicinal value. Like other citrus fruits, citron peel was candied. The fragrant Etrog citron, the Jewish ceremonial fruit, was available in season. Limes were more costly, but most citric acid was produced from them.[120]

Exotics, such as mango, could not yet be transported unless they were pickled, candied or made into chutney. Likewise, bananas and plantains were rare for the 1851 table, but experimental cultivation was under way. Banana trees had fruited in the high-ceilinged hothouses of the Royal Caledonian Horticultural Society in Edinburgh, and were sent to the Lord Mayor of London for a banquet given in honour of Queen Victoria, but it would take years to solve the shipping problems in order to provide bananas commercially.[121] Not surprisingly, bananas did not make an appearance in Catherine's last-known edition of 1860.

Perhaps of more interest are the fruits that were commercially available to Catherine in the 1850s but not mentioned by her. Fruits such as grapes, melons, and pineapples were brought to table as fresh fruit or candied sweet-meats and although she does not list them in the menus, they were undoubtedly served with the dessert course. Dickens's letters attest to their presence in the household: 'Many thanks for the grapes…they were a prodigy of excellence.'[122] Grapes figure too as domestic and imported raisins and dried currants, which were actually smaller varieties of grapes, important ingredients of Christmas pies and other puddings. The largest and most prized raisins were dried muscatel grapes which sold for double the usual price.[123]

Throughout Britain, pineapples were produced in special hothouses called pineries which allowed the ripe fruit to be brought to the London market daily. By 1851, Webster noted that the price of pineapples had already dropped through the extension of supply. Competitions for the largest fruit produced giants weighing nearly fifteen pounds and brought fame to their owners. The English developed their own style for serving the fruit, that is by cutting it into horizontal slices, which was quite different from that current in its place of origin, the West Indies.[124]

One would expect to see stone-fruits such as peaches, nectarines and apricots represented in Catherine's bills of fare as a filling for tarts or as preserves, but they are not mentioned. Other fruits she did not include are medlars, barberries, mulberries, blackberries, and quince, which were all popular for jams and jellies. Sloes and elderberries were often made into wine, cordials, and refreshing summer drinks, but are likewise absent. Rhubarb was a well-established garden cultivar, but is not found as a sauce or sweet in Catherine menus.[125] Perhaps the absence of the flavourful native fruits such as the English cranberry, service, barberry and whortleberry is more understandable, they had already fallen out of favour and were rarely used in the 1850s.[126] One would not expect the fashionable Mrs Dickens to suggest such antique varieties.

Yet the most surprising omission is that of pears. This conspicuous absence is especially difficult to explain, since a pear tree grew in the Devonshire Terrace garden when she first compiled the menus.[127] Pears were a popular fruit and about 150 varieties were listed in the 1850s horticultural catalogues, with most suggested as hardy trees that would grow in any soil.[128] The lack of pears in Catherine's menus exemplifies the limits of the written record, and to our understanding of how her book reflects the meals served in the Dickens household. All culinary history should be savoured with an undocumented 'grain of salt'.

CHAPTER X
SWEET AND SAVOURY CONCLUSIONS

I
f well-trained young men learned to carve roasts, their sisters were sweetly directed towards the arts of the dessert. As Hannah Glasse professed: 'every young lady ought to know both how to make all kind of confectionery and dress out a dessert; in former days it was look'd on as a great perfection in a young lady to understand all these things.'[1] One suspects Catherine was raised with this philosophy. Scots tablet, a type of sugar fudge, was commonly sold on the streets of Edinburgh, along with other boiled sugar candies. As a young girl, Catherine would have known the 'sweetie-shops' found in the back streets of many Scots towns and cities. Even in the eighteenth century, Scotland's sweet tooth was 'a source of amazement to foreign visitors'.[2] These items were so well known in the Dickens household that when Dickens was in Edinburgh on his 1858 reading tour he spent £6 to £8 at Littlejohns the confectioner to buy sweeties, cairngorms, shortbread, and other regional treats as presents for his daughters.[3]

Sugar processed from sugar cane was sold in conical loaves in weights of three to fourteen pounds. In the Dickenses' day, muscovado (raw sugar) was obtained from the sugar-bakers in Britain who made the loaf or refined lump sugar. Muscovado was also sold by grocers as 'brown or moist sugar'. To refine muscovado, the British sugar-bakers added lime-water and the serum of bullock's blood or beaten egg whites to the raw sugar in a clarification process which was much like that used for stocks in making consommé. After standing overnight to dissolve, the liquid was boiled to coagulate the blood or egg whites and bring the impurities to the top where they were skimmed off. Continuous heating saturated the sugar solution, and violent agitation with wooden oars encouraged the sugar to crystallize. The concentrated liquid was poured into conical-shaped wooden moulds that were pointed downward. When the sugar loaves cooled, a plug at the smaller end of the cone was opened to drain the molasses (treacle), and an inch of wet pipe-clay was placed over the larger opening at the top of the mould. The water from the wet clay, which was kept moist, percolated through the sugar crystals, and carried off more of the impurities as it dripped out of the opening.[4] 'Lisbon sugar', also known as 'clayed sugar', was imported from Portugal, Spain and France. The refining process was similar, but the raw sugar in solution went directly into conical clay pots. A wet layer of clay flushed out more of the molasses and impurities leaving a whiter sugar loaf after it dried in the cone.[5]

In the late 1840s, manufacturers began experimenting with different processes using vacuum pans heated by steam. The granulation process took less time (1 work-day) and produced a higher grade of molasses, but the overall yield was less. 'Vacuum sugar', more commonly known as demerara sugar, was admitted at the same duty as 'ordinary raw sugar'.[6] By 1850, the improved process reduced the atmospheric pressure above the evaporation pans by using an air pump that allowed the sugar to boil and the water to evaporate *in vacuo* at a lower temperature. After granulation was completed in the pans, the crystallized solution was put into curing boxes with metallic screen bottoms. When the air was drawn away, it forced the runny molasses through the screens leaving behind the sugar crystals that were nearly pure and much easier to dry before packing. The process increased the yield from 63 lb to 78 lb of refined sugar per batch and, once the patent had expired, the process began being used widely.[7] Workers transformed moist brown sugar into white loaves so efficiently that the price of sugar plummeted. If Dodd's annual consumption rates are to be believed, the use in the United Kingdom escalated from 16 lb of sugar per person in the 1840s, to 36 lb by 1854 as a result.[8]

To use loaf sugar, the cook or kitchen maid broke off chunks with a mallet and then clipped those into smaller pieces using special snippers. For powdered (icing) sugar, she pounded the pieces in a mortar until they had the right texture. Molasses or treacle, the uncrystallized saccharine juice and a by-product of refining cane sugar, was used in spicy recipes or common rock-candies.[9] Although sugar had been processed from sugar beet in France since 1812, the cost was a third higher than cane-sugar and only a small amount was imported into England.[10] Palm sugar, called jaggery, was available from India, and honey also continued to be used as a sweetener.

These facts about sugar are pertinent: Catherine's menus provide well over two hundred dessert entries ranging from large boiled puddings to individually baked tartlets in each of the editions. Eighty-eight per cent of her menus include at least one dessert. Likewise, nearly a third of the recipes she records in her appendix are for sweet dishes.

Fashionable desserts came and went just as they do today. In *Household*

Words, Eliza Linton reported that 'exquisite *sufflés* [sic], and delicious *méringues*, ice puddings, and *vol-au-vents*' were 'all the latest refinements of the Café de Paris' that were being adopted in London circles.[11] In truth, these desserts were included in cookery books far earlier than the publication of that 1858 article, so it is not possible to claim that Catherine's repertoire anticipates the trend. Although Catherine never includes meringues, ice pudding and *soufflé* (pudding) are among her 1851 bills of fare, and *vol-au-vents* are added by 1854 after the family returned from their extended stay in France. More to the point, her menus show that humble desserts mixed routinely with showy sweets, even for smaller, presumably family meals.

Catherine's kitchen held a very respectable array of baking equipment especially when compared to Soyer's list of *batterie de cuisine*.[12] Beside the basics, such as a flour jar, dredger, rolling-pin and 'paste board' for rolling dough, a 'paste brush' for glazing pie crusts, two wooden mixing bowls used to beat batters, and a variety of basins, she possessed a respectable number of speciality items. The 1844 inventory lists numerous patty and tartlet pans, in addition to the individual pie dishes from her blue china service. For steamed, baked, frozen, or jellied preparations, a variety of neatly stacked moulds lined the pantry shelves, including tin, copper, and earthenware pieces.[13] Although the kitchen inventory does not record a spice-box, the pantry would have held extracts and infusions of vanilla, almond, lemon, and orange-flower water, which are used as flavourings in her recipes. Catherine frequently relies on cinnamon, nutmeg, and zest from various citrus fruits or candied peels. Sweet wines, brandy, and liqueurs added depth to the recipes she chose. They were among her husband's favourite toppings:

> The strong water distilled from the cherry of the Black Forest, is, I am astounded to discover, *all gone*. But I send in its stead, a bottle of sweet wine of rare perfection, made from the Muscatelle Grape. Drunk with ice, or ice pudding, you will find it most delicious – with a generous and fragrant smack of the bright sun in it, that I have very seldom tasted, It was presented to me some years ago by a Merchant (this sounds, I find as I write it, like the Arabian Nights), and is really an uncommon – shall I say, Article.[14]

Ice pudding was a rather generic term for rich ice-creams. The Dickenses' cook may have made the frozen concoctions at home, but no suitable equipment was listed in the inventory. Ice could be ordered from the fishmonger or other suppliers as needed. Blocks were wrapped in clean sacking and placed in the metal-lined cavity of an ice-box refrigerator. Ice, chipped off the old block, was crushed to a more uniform size for table or beverage use. Ice-cream, better known as ice pudding in the Dickenses' household, had to be made early in the day in order to freeze properly, especially in warm weather. For an ice-cream bomb, clever cooks first froze a thin layer of fruit water in the metal form, so that when the bomb was turned out, a thin protective film of ice surrounded it.[15] Iced desserts would have been available locally from a pastry-cook or confectioner. Although Catherine offers ice pudding in only three menus, they owned twelve frosted cut-glass 'iceplates', which suggests that ice-creams, fruit water ices, sorbets, and other frozen desserts may have been served more often in the Dickens household than her bills of fare imply.[16]

Catherine shuns fanciful British names such as fools, flummeries, or syllabubs for the dairy-based desserts. Cooked puréed fruit creams, such as strawberry cream and strawberry jam cream, are represented, as is an old Tudor and Stuart dessert called marble cream, formerly known as marble rose cream to acknowledge the rose-water flavouring. The dessert was originally made from equal amounts of flavoured whipped cream and sweetened puréed raspberries swirled together but, as fashions and tastes changed, cherry liqueurs replaced the rose-water and the name was shortened.[17]

Devonshire cream is Catherine's voluptuous accompaniment for fruit tarts. She serves cream cheese, technically a cream drained sufficiently to be cut with a knife, both as a savoury and sweet. Italian cream, given in her recipes, is more like a soft cheese, which she usually reserves for larger dinner parties as one among a multiplicity of sweets. Judging by the frequency, cheesecake is not a popular dessert, but custards, custard puddings, custard tarts, and cream tarts are beloved. She mentions other dairy preparations indirectly, such as rice blancmange and the Bavarian cream filling for charlotte russe. Unfortunately, the sumptuous dessert, Atholl brose, a Scottish concoction (now usually made of whipped cream) with whisky, honey and toasted oatmeal, is not included even in the 1854 edition when she reclaimed her Scottish heritage. (The entry 'Charlotte Brosse' most likely stands for charlotte russe but, given Catherine's tortured handwriting, there exists a slim possibility that the compositor misinterpreted Atholl brose when he set the type.) The home-processing of basic ingredients is not always evident. In Catherine's scant recipe for rice blancmange for example she merely says: 'Boil rice in milk, put into a mould, and let stand until cold.'[18] Even an inexperienced cook would know that beforehand, a quantity of sugar had to be processed from the conical loaf and that the rice, which needed to be washed and dried, was ground into a powder with a pestle and mortar. To prepare the blancmange, the rice flour was mixed into a smooth paste with some milk before being added to flavoured, sweetened hot milk (at the ratio of about a quarter pound of rice to a quart of milk).[19] The swollen starch grains thickened into a sticky white pudding after the mixture boiled for about ten minutes. The gelatinous mass would then be poured into a well-oiled mould to cool before being turned out and decorated. Although this is a handsome, delicious dessert that should be revived, Catherine may have included the recipe as a reminder of an elegant moulded dessert that did not rely on gelatine or the skills required to make fancier jellies.

Shimmering moulded desserts, from the opaque whiteness of blancmange to the transparent sparkling jellies, added culinary architecture to the Dickenses' dessert table. While it is possible that they purchased the fancy jellies, the moulds listed in the Devonshire Terrace inventory suggest that the magnificent desserts would have been made at home, provided that their various cooks possessed the requisite skill and patience. With today's commercial products, one forgets what a labour of love jellied dishes were. As Peter Brears aptly points out: 'To convert a gang of grubby calves feet, or the shavings of hartshorn, ivory dust, or isinglass into a crystal-clear jelly was no easy business, and so the resulting products were greatly appreciated, receiving the respect which they truly deserved.'[20]

Isinglass, a commercial gelatine made from the air bladder of the sturgeon, was recommended for blancmange because of its whiteness and purity.[21] (Powdered gelatine was not available until the 1860s.) Isinglass, known from Roman times, was imported from Russia. To use the semi-translucent sheets, the cook soaked them in cold water until they swelled and became flexible. Boiling water was then poured over them to dissolve all but the smallest impurities.[22] High-quality isinglass remained odourless and tasteless after use. Another gelling substance available to the Victorians was carrageen, made from red seaweed known as Irish moss, although it could also be extracted from other species. 'The Purple Shore', in *Household Words,* reported on the contemporary use of dulse, Irish moss, and various other seaweeds by coastal cooks.[23]

Jellies, having centuries-old traditions, had been brought to the 'highest standards of aesthetic and technical excellence'. Eighteenth-century wooden moulds were replaced by salt-glazed pottery and, later, with creamware manufactured by Spode, Wedgwood, and other firms. By capitalizing on the transparent and opaque properties of jellies, a skilled maker could create fantasy pieces varied in flavour, shape, texture, and contents. Triumphant, the majestic architecture would have sparkled on any candle-lit mahogany dessert board.[24] The Dickenses were obviously seduced by the dazzling performance of moulded jellies and creams and Catherine's enthusiasm for gelatine desserts changes fairly dramatically through her various editions. In 1851 she only suggests eight jellies, and the majority of these are for very large dinner parties, but by the 1852 edition she increases the number to thirteen. The total remains the same in the 1854 revision, but there are fewer menus and the types of jellies she suggests show a greater diversity. Her 'clear jelly' may have been transparent or it could have displayed arrangements of fruit (previously poached in sugar syrup). Other gelatine preparations, such as orange, lemon, or maraschino jellies, are defined by both the flavouring and the layers of fruit decorations carefully assembled as the gelatine cooled in the moulds. For a smaller dinner party of only four or five diners, the bitter-almond-flavoured noyau jelly is suggested. The punch jelly that Catherine lists may have been made from her husband's own concoction. In her larger menus, jellies added diversity to the cream-based sweets and heavy boiled puddings that often accompany them.

Not everyone appreciated British desserts; even a German humorist in Dickens's magazine described English pastries as an 'awkwardness and stagnation of ideas' compared to the sweet poetry of French *pâtisserie*. His solution was straightforward: 'Let Parliament decree that a Vienna Mehlspeis Köchin, or a female cook of puddings' be brought to England and given a salary 'equal the sum which was paid to Jenny Lind, for the purpose of enabling so meritorious a female to devote all her energies to the good of the nation.'[25]

But if the ornate jellies exemplified elegance, then those lovable boiled puddings upheld tradition. Perhaps Catherine and her cook produced lighter and more delicate versions of these stodgy desserts by using equal amounts of flour and bread crumbs, rather than just flour. And if her cook was really particular, she would have passed the day-old bread through a sieve, and the suet would have been grated, rather than chopped, so that the pieces were a uniform size. Certainly every good cook knew the trick of wetting the pastry cloth in boiling water, wringing it out, and flouring it so the suet pudding did not stick when it was unwrapped after boiling.[26] Rinsing the cloth would not have made the pudding lighter, but a handsome presentation was always valued by diners. Catherine suggests boiled classics, like batter pudding, for smaller family meals, while the more elaborate cabinet pudding makes its appearance at a dessert for twenty guests. She includes plum pudding, which was served outside of the holidays, for only a few dinners. Plum pudding, which tends to hold an honoured place on our holiday table, was actually a commonplace dessert.[27] In fact, it was sold as a relatively inexpensive street food. Mayhew described the street sellers of plum 'duff' or plum dough, which the women sold as rounded plum puddings or rolled as a roly poly. By Mayhew's 1861 edition, the hot pudding was already in decline, both in the quality of the dough and in the number of vendors.[28]

As Catherine Dickens's menus show, plum pudding was not reserved for Christmas nor was it always steamed (or boiled). She included a fried plum pudding in her 1851 menus, but abandoned it the following year. She offered plum pudding as dessert in dinners from April to September. The elevation of plum pudding to holiday fare is more closely related to the rising popularity of her husband's *A Christmas Carol*. As his readers would have understood, but we may need to be reminded, the relatively inexpensive pudding revealed the Cratchit family's dire circumstances. Yet Dickens's description, including the distinct aromas, as 'the pudding was out of the copper', have a universal appeal. 'A smell like a washing-day! That was the cloth. A smell like an eating-house and a pastry cook's next door to each other…That was the pudding' were familiar, even for those who could afford more expensive desserts. Yet whose heart is not warmed even today when reading: 'In half a minute Mrs. Cratchit entered: flushed, but smiling proudly: with the pudding, like a speckled cannon-ball, so hard and firm, blazing in half of half-a-quartern of ignited brandy, and bedight with Christmas holly stuck into the top,' as her appreciative husband exclaimed, 'Oh, a wonderful pudding!' believing it 'the greatest success achieved by Mrs. Cratchit since their marriage'?[29]

Mince pies (mincemeat tarts) are a popular sweet for Catherine's smaller parties of up to ten persons.[30] She provides the recipe for Eve's pudding as a variation on a popular apple dessert made on both sides of the Atlantic. Bread-and-butter pudding and a variety of other baked or boiled desserts, such as rice pudding and tapioca pudding represented survivals from the nursery, comfort-foods if you will, that she restricts to family-sized meals.

Excluding Twelfth Night cake, one wonders if the Dickens family even liked cake. 'We hear little of pies, pastries, cooked or preserved fruits, custards, and almost nothing of home-made cakes,' T.W. Hill observed of Dickens's fiction.[31] Presumably Catherine served cake at tea time (which was becoming fashionable), although cookbook writers like Alexis Soyer listed 'iced cake with fruits' in his examples of a bill of fare for an aristocratic dinner party.[32] After all, two cake tins were listed in the Dickenses' inventory, and cake was implied by some menu entries such as pound-cake pudding and cabinet pudding, even though she never lists cake directly as part of the dessert. Cake baking has always been a tricky art, but in Catherine's day there were far more preparatory tasks we no longer undertake. Recipes gave directions such as 'have sugar sifted' (and that's after it was clipped from the cone and pounded), or 'flour of good quality dry and sifted', and even dried fruits such as raisins had to be 'stoned or picked, washed, and dry, or rubbed in a towel'.[33] All cake batters were beaten by hand, usually in wooden bowls since the Archimedian egg whisk (known as the rotary whisk or Dover egg-beater) was not available until 1861.[34] For leavening agents, a baker could use yeast, or add carbonate of soda (baking soda) which required an acid (like sour milk or buttermilk) to activate it. Commercial baking powder was not introduced until around 1856.[35] Besides leavening, cakes could also be lightened by incorporating air into the sugar-butter mixtures (called 'pastes' in most cookery books), or by beating eggs in the batters as for Genoese sponges. More often, however, British recipes seem to offer dense dry-fruit or spice cakes from doughs that could be rolled out and cut into small rounds with a wine glass.

Creating a light batter was only half the challenge, the other was proper baking. To judge the temperature of the oven, flour was thrown inside and if it turned brown, the temperature was just right. Likewise a sheet of paper could be used for the test. If it burst into flame, the oven was too hot, but if it only turned dark brown, it was ready for puff-pastry (about 400–450°F; gas mark 6–8) which requires high heat to encourage the layers of flaky dough to separate and crisp. A light-brown paper indicated that pies could be baked, a dark yellow colour was good for cake baking, and light yellow meant it was just right for puddings, biscuits, cookies, and small pastries. Fancy cakes were generally baked in the afternoon when the oven cooled. A cautious cook would have placed the filled cake tin on a tray holding several inches of sand to act as a buffer in the oven and keep the bottom of the cake from burning.[36]

Pies with or without a top crust, tarts, tartlets, puff-pastry, roll jam pudding, and raspberry jam sandwiches made from pastry, altogether constitute about 20 per cent of Catherine's dessert entries. These pastries are a cosmopolitan category which she made and served the year round. Catherine suggests pancakes only once, most likely served as a stacked torte with jam between each layer. She only recommends sweet omelettes, probably with a tuck-in of jam, for small groups since they are made individually and have to be well timed for the last course. When Catherine lists 'savoury omelets', they are usually paired with sweet desserts. The more precarious preparation required for a soufflé, which she calls both a soufflé pudding and a fondue (actually a cheese soufflé) she considers only for special company meals of up to ten diners. As anyone who has made a soufflé knows, timing is everything, since the finished dish waits for no one.

Judging from the 1851 edition, one would assume Catherine did not care for fried sweets, since only a few are listed, but in the 1854 revisions she adds two versions of a recipe for orange fritters and suggests apple or orange fritters for up to ten diners. For apple fritters, perhaps their cook used Eliza Acton's recipe for crisp 'Kentish fritters'. Acton's yeast batter of eggs, milk, and flour was made a day ahead to ferment in a warm jug by the fire. By dessert time, chopped apples were added to the risen batter and pieces of the dough were fried golden brown before they emerged from the kitchen piled high on a cloth-lined serving dish.[37] College pudding was another fried dessert, made of bread crumbs, suet and egg flavoured with citrus peel. The fried plum pudding in Catherine's 1851 edition was a passing fad omitted the following year.

Catherine includes other sweets that have such common titles they are difficult to identify. For example, lemon pudding could be either a baked dessert made in a tin that is lined with a pie crust or puff-pastry and filled with lemon curd, or it could be a boiled jam roll. Other desserts like Saxe Gotha pudding remain a mystery, although one might guess that it was a steamed pudding mixture using brown (wholewheat) bread.

Catherine never includes Malvern pudding, a speciality of the spa where she was treated in 1851 (although her stay did precede that year's berry harvest). The dessert may have held a certain stigma associated with 'health' food, since at the time it was becoming known as 'hydropathic pudding', after the water-treatment. Practitioners believed that the bread used to encase the fruit and juices was easier to digest than pastry crust.[38] Referred to today as summer pudding, the Malvern sweet is a seasonal favourite when red currants and raspberries are plentiful.[39]

There is a more conspicuous absence: Catherine never mentions chocolate in any form, in any of the five editions. True, in the early 1850s home consumption of chocolate was mostly as a hot drink. In fact, consumption statistics during that period only compare chocolate with coffee and tea. As a beverage, chocolate was thought to be so nutritious that 'homœopathic cocoa' was sold as one of the four commercial forms, which also included 'plain cocoa', 'soluble chocolate', and 'vanilla chocolate'.[40] Soluble chocolate refers to Van Houten's 'dutched' powdered cocoa developed in 1828, and 'vanilla chocolate' characterized the chocolate developed by the Bristol manufacturers J.S. Fry & Sons. Fry produced the first true bars of non-brittle 'eating chocolate' by blending cacao powder, sugar, and cacao butter. Other chocolate and cocoa products were available from the Cadbury family, purveyors to Queen Victoria by 1853, or from the Rowntree family, among other companies that were founded a bit later.[41] To use a block of unsweetened chocolate, cooks had to first grate it uniformly, but cocoa nibs (the processed and roughly chopped seeds) were also available.[42] The plethora of chocolate desserts, including chocolate cakes, with which we are now familiar, had a relatively slow start especially given the length of time that chocolate was available. Cookery books contemporary with Catherine's bills of fare reveal a definite lack of imagination for the flavouring potential of chocolate, particularly when viewed through the subjective lens of our own chocoholic times. 'Meg Dods', for example, only gave a recipe for hot chocolate drink. Eliza Acton offered chocolate-covered almonds, chocolate drops, and a custard, in addition to the hot drink. Alexis Soyer's 1850 *Modern Housewife* used chocolate for ice-cream and an icing, beside his preparations for the hot beverage. Even Mrs Beeton's 1865 compilation only used chocolate in a moulded chocolate cream, a soufflé, a box of chocolate for dessert, and the drink. It seems to have taken some time for chocolate cake to make its appearance on the tea table, let alone as a fashionable dessert served after dinner.

Conversely, savoury preparations that are no longer fashionable today dominated the end of a Victorian meal. Among Dickens's personal favourites were toasted cheese (briefly discussed later) and versatile preparations of macaroni, both sweet and savoury. The adaptation of foreign foods like pasta is particularly interesting, since in England it was not served at the beginning of the meal as the Dickenses and their contemporaries would have enjoyed in Italy. They were often brought with the desserts, or in large dinner menus were sometimes considered a separate course. Macaroni was adopted first by the continental-travelling upper classes, and the authors of the 1856 article entitled 'Common Cookery' propose the pasta as a solution to inexpensive meals:

> Many other materials of food are cast aside altogether, or comparatively but very little used. Thus macaroni, of which a pound at fivepence gives four pounds of food when boiled, is almost unknown among our poor. Yet, seasoned with pepper and salt, and flavoured with grated cheese (which the poor can buy very cheap) or sweetened with sugar and butter, it makes a dish not to be despised, even by epicures.[43]

Before the Dickens family left for residence in Genoa, a colleague humorously jibed, 'I hear that you are going to learn on the spot to eat Italian macaroni.'[44] Although the Dickenses learned to enjoy Italian wines, judging from Catherine's menus they appear to have retained their English preferences in regard to pasta. Nor, except for a rare entry of tomato sauce which accompanied meat, does Catherine incorporate other Italian sauces. And it is doubtful that her listings of macaroni with bacon resembled a carbonara sauce. However, the topic of 'Macaroni-Making' was not so esoteric as to escape Dickens's attention. Henry Wreford wrote an article for *Household Words*, giving a lively first-person account of his visit to an Almalfi manufacturer. His article described the process of washing the hard wheat in the mountain streams of Puglia, milling the grain, and creating the macaroni shapes by hand or with extruders. Aware that 'in England, it is boiled to a pulp', he supplied directions for 'a good tomata sauce, or a rich meat gravy' with a sprinkling of cheese. Ridiculing his countrymen and their restriction of macaroni to 'that long sort which we English use as a dolce or au gratin. All the others are used to thicken soup, like barley,' Wreford encouraged them to look beyond these uses.[45]

The Dickens family reflect Wreford's profile, and one suspects the magazine's subscribers and Catherine's potential readers did as well. She uses vermicelli as a filler in the winter soup, and adds two recipes for the 1854 edition for vermicelli and vegetable soup, and macaroni soup. Besides soup, her use of macaroni follows English conventions: over a third of her 1851 and

1852 menus end with a macaroni dish, although by 1854 she trims these numbers a bit, yet never adopts other uses for pasta. Catherine's bills of fare that end with macaroni are for dinners served to up to ten persons, which suggests that the dish was too commonplace to be appropriate for larger, more festive, dinner parties. Typically, Catherine suggests macaroni with dessert (before a last savoury course), or after dessert in which case it is more likely a savoury macaroni and cheese dish. In the few cases where dessert is excluded and macaroni is the last course, the preparation could have been sweet or savoury. These baked-custard macaroni dishes or those made as unmoulded decorated timbales were popular with middle-class Victorians judging from the numerous recipes in British (and American) cookery books. Elizabeth David suggested, after studying William Verral's *The Cook's Paradise* (1759), that macaroni cheese may have been an adaptation from French, rather than Italian kitchens. The derivation of the name, she believed, was from *macarons* or macaroons, and not *macaroni*.[46] Jean-Paul Aron believed the pasta entered the French culinary tradition after the wars of the Directoire and of the Empire, where it became the rage between 1820 and 1840. Even Balzac was 'very fond of it, in the form of little pasties, which he devoured in the pâtisseries on the Boulevard.'[47]

It seems odd to discuss salads after desserts, but that is often where they appeared in mid-Victorian meals and this was true of the Dickenses' table as well. In about a quarter of the menus, Catherine pairs salad greens with toasted cheese. The favourite salad is the slightly spicy watercress, also known as English garden cress or 'pepper-grass'. Watercress had been cultivated in England from about 1808 at Northfleet Spring near Gravesend and quickly became popular as an excellent spring salad. With experimentation, growers soon learned that the beds could be replanted twice a year, and that by planting different varieties in succession, watercress was available nearly all the year round. The green-leaf variety was the easiest to cultivate, the small brown-leaf was more flavourful, but the most difficult to grow, and the large copper-coloured leaf did well in deep water. These varieties of English cress differed in Victorian times from the small green lyre-shaped leaf that is cultivated in North America and more common today. (The leaf known as Indian cress, also a peppery salad green, is related to nasturtium.)[48]

By 1856, Dodd reported that the Great Western Railway brought 'a ton [of watercress] a week from the neighbourhood of Cookham and Shrivenham', but the best was still from the original beds near Gravesend. If fifteen million bunches of watercress were sold in a week at the London markets, one wonders how many of those had the Dickenses' name on them.[49] Catherine pairs watercress with macaroni, omelettes, Brunswick sausages, or seafood such as crab, prawns, the red herring (bloaters), and anchovies or anchovy toast. She serves watercress in a quarter of the 1851 and 1852 bills of fare. She replaces the greens in about 10 per cent of those entries revised for the 1854 menus onward with radishes, spring onions, endive salads, and cucumbers. These dishes held more cachet after the Dickenses returned from France where they experienced new culinary fashions.

Lobster salad was another favourite Victorian finish to a meal. In his article, Dudley Costello chronicled the use of lobsters and was emphatic on two points: he preferred lobster salad to any other preparation of the crustacean, and there were no salad greens in the salad. 'Nothing,' in his opinion, 'ought to interfere between a man and lobster' except perhaps a few glasses of East India Madeira. To make the salad, Costello recommended finely dicing cooked lobster tail and combining the meat 'gently' with the liver and coral, using only a finger and thumb. 'Strew a little salt, two drops of vinegar, a light shower of cayenne,' and two or three large tablespoons of first quality olive oil, which were mixed for five minutes. He insisted that no cucumber was added, as many contemporary recipes suggested.[50]

Beside salads, another savoury conclusion to the Dickenses' dinners was cheese. As one author opined: 'Poor men eat cheese for hunger, rich for digestion.'[51] Nearly a third of Catherine's bills of fare list some sort of cheese, but very rarely by specific variety (Stilton the exception). In the main, her cheese is cooked. Stilton, Cheshire, Gloucester (single and double) Cottenham, Sage, Chedder, Brickbat, and Dunlop cheeses were all common to the London market, as were imported cheeses such as Parmesan, Gouda, Swiss, Scottish, and Irish varieties.[52] By 1856, 'American cheese', most likely Cheddar, was slowly gaining in popularity.[53] Plain cheese was probably accompanied by rusks, savoury biscuits, fruit or celery, and port. Catherine serves cream cheese, possibly mixed with Parmesan as a spread, and cauliflower or broccoli *au gratin* as other cheese-based dishes that usually appeared after or with the dessert.

However, toasted cheese, the culinary cousin to rarebit or fondue, seems to be the favourite last course in the Dickens household. The cheese toaster listed in their 1844 inventory was a variation on the chafing dish that had a covered glass or metal container for the velvety cheese spread and a reservoir for hot water underneath to hold the temperature. [54] The simple preparation required grating any type of cheese, which was melted with seasonings, often mustard and pepper with a little port or porter, to loosen the mixture. Butter could be added for enrichment if the cheese was too dry.[55] The top of the creamy mixture was browned with a hot salamander, before the cheese toaster was sent to table with buttered slices of bread or toast. One can imagine Dickens and his cronies enjoying the molten mass with a glass of his prized old ruby port. Toasted cheese is so strongly associated with Dickens that even his son Charley purportedly commented on 'how many dinners begun with a glass of Chichester milk-punch; how many were finished with a dish of toasted cheese.'[56] In the menus, Catherine serves toasted cheese throughout the year after dessert, or in place of it. The dish appears in a third of her 1851 bills of fare, but never for menus serving over seven diners, which suggests gatherings of family or close friends. She usually accompanies the dish with a lightly dressed salad of watercress. By the 1854 revision, Catherine drops the listings to less than a fifth of the menus. In a few, she replaces toasted cheese with fondue or stewed cheese (which were very similar and more likely just reflect a change of names), or with more fashionable offerings such as sardines or anchovies, served with chili vinegar; dressed crab; or hung beef grated onto buttered bread.

EPILOGUE

Perhaps it is not surprising that Ellen Ternan, the young actress with whom Dickens fell in love, and ultimately for whom he abandoned his wife, played the part of sweet young Mary in an 1858 performance of *Used Up* at Haymarket Theatre.[1] More to the point, Ellen was willing to endure the limitations of being 'the other woman'. Dickens hid her successfully from the public's eye, even when he openly fuelled the scandal of separation from his wife. Dickens, the author who most personified home and hearth in his work, took extraordinary measures to explain his side. Influential friends questioned his judgement; nevertheless, he wrote a personal statement in *Household Words*, but it only compounded the problems.[2]

In a somewhat biased account by Harriet Martineau, who contributed articles for Dickens's magazine, one begins to appreciate the humiliation and gossip that Catherine faced even from her defence (the italics are Martineau's):

About the Dickens case, – I will just say that my rejoicing in the domestic happiness I formerly heard so much of from their intimates was deepened by some surprise; – so that I am not so wholly confounded at this manifestation as many people are. I mean that I always, from the observation of a long life, distrust such an amount of *sentimentality*, combined with selflove in the husband, as has always existed in the D household. Moreover, amidst it all, he openly & thoroughly regarded his wife as 'his woman'; provided another to take care of the children & walk with him, when Mrs D. was unable, – which she usually was; – chose her to dress in black velvet, & sit at her embroidery, at leisure *for him*, & so on. After this sort of life, – now, when she has borne him above a dozen children (9 living) & the time for collapse has come, – exhaustion, indifference, indolence &c, is she to be turned adrift, because she is (*if she is*) subject to that *fretfulness & jealousy* which are the *specific results* of such a life as he has chosen that her's sh^d be? – And not a daughter has she with her! – only that weak son. No, – she does not drink (though that is the first thing that strikes every body: but if she does not now take to the bottle, or to suicide, she will show that she has *some* strength.) – I have been told (long ago) on authority which I believe good that *the one thing* that a man never gets over among men is – dismissing his wife at such a time of life, & under such circumstances as in this case; & truly I hope it is so, – though I know no more of the present case than what I send you. (The letter is from an old friend of mine & of the D's to my niece, who wrote for me, to inquire the truth.) [3]

After their separation, Dickens's position as a literary lion remained strong. Meanwhile, Catherine lived her life privately, yet remained active.[4] She continued to be invited to performances, outings, and dinner parties by friends such as Thackeray and the Lemon family who remained loyal to her.[5] The separation from her children, particularly the youngest boys (at six and nine), no doubt was exceedingly painful. As Lillian Nayder points out about any large family, some of the children were closer to their mother and later cherished her as the grandmother of their own children.[6] While the older three boys boarded at school or lived away, only Katey Dickens, the spitfire, defied her father, and visited her mother with any frequency. Mamie Dickens, the oldest daughter who remained unmarried, only began seeing her mother after her father's death in 1870.

The irony that Dickens had a stroke at the dining-room table, and died the next day having never left that room, has not escaped notice. But the death of her husband, a man whom Catherine still loved, changed her social status from the estranged incompetent wife about whom people whispered, to the grieving widow to whom Queen Victoria sent condolences. Yet the legal claws of Dickens's cruelty reached from beyond his grave. His last will and testament greatly reduced Catherine's annuity. The money was to be managed by her two sons. This may not be so surprising when one considers that if Catherine had remarried, any property or money Dickens left to her would have been legally at the disposal of her second husband and thus lost as an inheritance for the Dickens children. More difficult to understand, however, is that Dickens appointed Catherine's sister, Georgina Hogarth, as guardian to her under-age children. Dickens also added a note in his will reminding the children how much they owed to their aunt, and how generous he had been to their mother.[7]

Catherine Thomson Hogarth Dickens died nine years after her husband on 22 November 1879 at the age of sixty-four. She lies buried with her infant daughter, Dora Annie, in Highgate cemetery. Before Catherine's failing health became alarming, she reconciled with Georgy and gave a cherished bundle of Dickens's letters to her daughter. Catherine's last request was that the letters from Charles, written from the time of their courtship, be given to the British Museum – so 'that the world may know that he loved me once.'[8] Catherine Dickens's accomplishment in undertaking the menu project and seeing it through a series of five (known) publications, as well as her life with the author and her social contributions, are finally being more fairly assessed by historians. One suspects we will find a personable, intelligent woman holding her own in a diverse social milieu.

APPENDIXES

APPENDIX I

When the Dickenses rented their home to Mrs Sophia Onslow in May 1844, they listed the furnishings and books. The silver service, silver tableware, or expensive table linens were not included. The inventory begins from the front door looking into the entrance hall and moves through the rooms systematically: the library, dining-room, dressing-room, carpet and covers of the stairs, first landing including the framed prints and chairs, best bedroom, drawing-room, second bedroom, second landing, day nursery, night nursery, women's bedroom, and attic. The kitchen and pantry equipment were probably listed according to the arrangement on the shelves. Here, I have extracted those items relating to kitchen and dining-room affairs. Historians interested in the proximity of the equipment, should consult the original listings in the inventory, printed in Kathleen Tillotson (ed.), *The Letters of Charles Dickens* vol. 4 (Oxford: Clarendon Press, 1977) 704–726. The list below has been reorganized by use.

Store Room
Dresser – Deal Table – two chairs – Screen with four flaps

Butler's Pantry
Bath – Board & trestles – Sandwich tray & fittings complete
Butler's tray & trestles – bottle rack – Green curtain – roller Blind – Press for Glass and China – Two chairs – Fender – Pair of Steps – Clothes Horse

Kitchen
dressers, shelves etc. etc.
deal table & four chairs
Dutch clock

Kitchen Utensils & Equipment

2 wine baskets	1 iron footman [stand for kettle placed
2 corkscrews	before fire]
2 ice pails	Bottle Jack. Wheel. Chain etc.
2 tea urns	
2 coffee pots	8 dinner mats
2 metal teapots	knives & forks
3 tea kettles (1 each of iron, tin, copper)	knives & forks, small
1 grog kettle [possibly the Scottish 'hot toddy kettle']	2 knife trays
	1 mahogany bed tray
meat screen	1 kitchen tray

2 plate baskets
7 block tin dish covers
6 common dish covers

1 bread grater
6 iron spoons
4 kitchen teaspoons
1 toasting fork
hair sieves
pestle & mortar
1 flour dredger
bread pan
Flour jar & rolling pin
paste board
1 paste brush
scales & weights
1 funnel
2 copper moulds
3 tin moulds [probably different sizes]
2 tin moulds
9 earthenware moulds
2 white basins
6 pudding basins
2 small glazed blue basins
2 wooden bowls [for mixing]
24 patty pans
2 cake tins
4 tartlet pans
2 large iron pots & covers
1 Dutch oven
1 fish kettle
4 large iron saucepans & covers
6 small saucepans & covers
3 iron stewpans
1 copper stewpan
2 tin saucepans
1 warming pan
1 dripping pan
1 gridiron
2 fryingpans
1 steamer & cover
1 salamander
1 cheese toaster
cheese pan & cover

2 chopping boards
2 choppers
1 saw
1 egg slicer
5 vegetable cutters
1 cullender [sic]
2 cannisters [sic]
1 spice box
1 pepper box
1 salt cellar
1 mustard pot
1 lemon squeezer

1 copper preserving pan
47 preserving pots
16 large preserving pots
22 preserving bottles
14 stone jars
1 white stone jar with cover
2 stone jugs with plated covers
2 smaller jugs with plated covers
1 black beetle trap

2 copper coal scuttles
1 coal scuttle
1 fireguard
1 fire basket
1 coal shovel, fender, poker, & tongs
2 pails
1 water cann [sic]
2 flat irons & stand

2 common lamps, 1 for bracket at the foot
of the stairs

1 footwarmer
1 footbath
2 brooms
2 turks' heads [round-headed broom]
2 housemaids' boxes, broom, & dustpan
1 shaving pot
1 pewter inkstand
5 small tea plates
7 kitchen cups & saucers

3 rope mats
6 brass candlesticks
Japan Writing candlestick for 2 candles,
   with sliding shade

2 candle boxes
4 rush light shades

China

A Blue Dinner Set containing
10 dishes
1 soup tureen, stand, & cover
4 vegetable dishes & covers
4 sauce tureens, dishes, & covers
1 salad bowl with wooden spoon & fork
2 common blue dishes
27 large plates
12 small plates
16 pie dishes
11 soup plates

Another Dessert Service
[possibly for the blue set of dishes]
1 centre
7 dishes
12 plates

Blue Tea-Set, containing
10 cups & saucers
6 coffee cups & saucers
1 slop basin
1 cream jug
2 dishes

A common green dinner-set, containing
5 dishes
1 soup tureen, stand, & cover
1 hash dish
4 butter tureens
1 vegetable dish
24 large plates
6 water plates
3 blue jugs
2 stone jugs
1 brown jug
3 blue ¹/₂ pint jugs

Another Dessert Service (common green)
1 centre dish
4 other dishes
11 plates

Best Dinner Set containing
1 large dish
1 'less' [large dish]
1 'less'
2 'less'
2 'less'
2 'less'
4 'less'
1 large well dish [a meat dish with a well at
the end for gravy]
20 other dishes
2 soup tureens and stands [probably with
  covers, but not mentioned]
4 sauce tureens, 4 stands, 3 covers
1 salad bowl
1 fish drain
1 pie dish
2 smaller pie dishes
4 dishes and covers
1 cheese stand
54 dinner plates
20 soup plates
40 small plates

Best Dessert Service, containing
18 plates
8 dishes
1 centre dish

Best Tea Set, containing
12 cups & saucers
12 coffee cups & saucers
1 slop basin

1 cream jug
2 bread & butter plates
12 small plates

Breakfast Service, containing
6 cups & saucers
1 slop basin

Glassware
2 cut jugs
1 claret jug
4 quart decanters & stoppers
5 pint decanters & stoppers
2 large ornamental water goblets
4 water bottles
2 large ornamental water goblets
1 tumbler for water
12 tumblers
12 wine glasses
12 sherry glasses
11 engraved cabinet drinking glasses
1 very large glass – same pattern
14 champagne glasses, oval shape
14 champagne glasses, long shape
12 ale glasses

1 cream jug
6 egg cups
4 dishes
6 plates
1 muffin dish & cover

12 hock glasses
11 liqueur glasses
14 engraved claret glasses
6 salts, cut glass
1 celery glass
12 glass dishes
2 butter dishes, stands & covers with silver cows
12 iceplates, cut & frosted
14 finger glasses, cut & frosted
2 small glass dishes
6 custard cups
glass dish for Epergne
1 glass basin
1 green glass basin

APPENDIX II

FOOD CATEGORIES IN THE 1852 MENUS

SEAFOOD (total 194)

Type of Seafood	Frequency	Comments
sole	42	
oysters	28	excluding oyster sauce

(oyster sauce 20 entries; fried oysters 8; oyster curry or curried oysters 5; steak, oysters & kidney pudding 4; leg of mutton stuffed with oysters 4; oyster patties 4; oyster soup 2; cold oysters 1)

Type of Seafood	Frequency	Comments
cod	23	including codling & cod's head
salmon	22	
lobster	13	excluding lobster sauce

(lobster sauce 10 entries; lobster cutlets 4; lobster curry 3; lobster patties 3; lobster salad 2; filleted lobster 1)

Type of Seafood	Frequency	Comments
whiting	12	
turbot	9	
mackerel	8	
bloaters	7	unsalted smoked herring
smelts	7	
haddock	6	
brill	5	
anchovy	3	
prawns	3	
fresh herring	2	
eels	2	
flounder	1	
dressed crab	1	

SOUPS (total 77)

Type	Frequency	Comments
vegetable	17	including 3 spring vegetable soups
ox-tail	11	
asparagus	9	
mutton broth based	8	including barley soup & Scotch broth
pea and green pea	8	
carrot	7	
giblet	3	
mock-turtle	3	
vermicelli	3	
white	3	ground almond base
oyster	2	
hare	2	

MEATS (total 391)

Type of Meat and Cuts	Frequency
mutton (includes Irish Stew & kidneys)	99
fowl	76
beef	68
(steak 17 entries)	
(collops according to Mrs Dickens's recipe 7 entries)	
veal	16
pork	55
(bacon 21 entries)	
(ham 12 entries)	
(sausage 5 entries)	
lamb (not including tongue, sweetbreads)	41
unspecified	
(tongue 9 entries, sweetbreads 5 entries, patties, cutlets etc.)	26
hare (including soup)	16
rabbit	8
venison	2

FOWL AS A SEPARATE CATEGORY (total 78)

Type	Frequency	Comments
'fowl'	21	
pigeon	10	
chicken & larded capon	9	
turkey	8	
pheasant	7	often as pairs
duck	7	including ducklings and wild duck
grouse	3	
partridges	3	often as a brace
woodcock	3	often as pairs or more
guinea-fowl	2	
lark	2	
snipe	14	
black-cock	1	
goose	1	

SAUCES ACCOMPANYING MEATS AND SEAFOOD

Type	Frequency	Comments
shrimp sauce	53	served with fish, occasionally boiled fowl
oyster sauce	20	usually served with cod and codling
lobster sauce	10	served mostly with salmon
maître d'hôtel sauce & butter	8	including 'parsley and butter sauce'
onion sauce	4	mainly with mutton roast, also boiled rabbit
brown gravy	2	served as sole in brown gravy

horse-radish sauce	2	served with beef
mushroom sauce	2	served with sweetbreads
asparagus	1	served with boiled chickens
cucumber sauce	1	served with lamb cutlet
egg sauce	1	served with salt cod
savoury sauce	1	served with pork cutlets
tomato sauce	1	served with veal
white sauce	1	served with rabbit curry

VEGETABLES, NOT INCLUDING SOUPS OR SAUCES (total 145)

Type	Frequency	Comments
watercress	41	as salad ending the meal
French beans	23	'beans' also used once to garnish platter
cauliflower	17	once as an *au gratin* dish
broccoli	16	twice as an *au gratin* dish
peas (excluding soup)	15	
spinach	15	
beetroot	10	often as a salad combined with celery
asparagus (excluding soup & sauce)	9	
mushrooms	8	patties, broiled, and stewed
celery	6	stewed or as salad with beets
turnips	53	prepared as mashed roots; 2 as 'greens'
cucumber (excluding sauce)	5	
onion (excluding sauce)	5	Spanish onions, often stewed;
summer cabbage	4	
artichokes	3	
Brussels sprouts	3	
kalecannon	3	mixed vegetables in mould
greens	2	
sea kale	2	
'vegetables'	2	
parsnips	1	
carrots	1	

DESSERTS (total 220)

General Categories	Frequency	Comments
'puddings'	81	used in the title
pies, tarts & tartlets	42	
cream desserts	26	
rice desserts	22	
jellies	13	
other	36	

'PUDDING' USED IN TITLE AS A SEPARATE CATEGORY

custard pudding	11	also as 'custard' and 'cold custard pudding'
cabinet pudding	10	
rice pudding	9	including 'ground rice pudding' = blancmange
batter pudding	8	
roll jam pudding	8	
lemon pudding	6	including 3 cold lemon puddings
apple pudding	5	
bread and butter pudding	5	
pound pudding	4	
Eve's pudding	4	she included the recipe in the appendix
plum pudding	4	
ice pudding	3	(an almond-milk ice cream)
tapioca pudding	2	
currant pudding	2	1 as black currant pudding
college pudding	1	
damson pudding	1	
fruit pudding	1	
marrow pudding	1	
Prince Albert's pudding	1	she included the recipe in the appendix
raspberry jam pudding	1	
Saxe Gotha pudding	1	
soufflet [sic] pudding	1	
Spanish pudding	1	yeast cake-bread; her recipe is in the appendix
Swiss pudding	1	she included the recipe in the appendix

PIES, TARTS AND TARTLETS AS A SEPARATE CATEGORY

apple tart	8	
currant & raspberry tart	7	also given as 'raspberry & currant'
greengage tart	7	also as tartlets
marmalade tartlets	5	
mince pies	3	also 'cold minced pies'
unspecified tart and tartlets	3	
plum tart	2	
gooseberry tart	2	
damson tart	2	also an 'open damson tartlets'
raspberry jam tart	2	also as tartlets
cherry tart	1	
cream tartlets	1	
currant tart	1	

CREAM-BASED DESSERTS AS A SEPARATE CATEGORY

custard	9	also as 'cold custard puddings'
(cold, ground)rice blancmange	9	
cream & Devonshire cream	9	usually accompanied other desserts
Italian cream	7	(recipe in the appendix)
charlotte russe	5	
ice pudding	3	(ice-cream)
strawberry cream	2	also strawberry jam cream
cream tartlets	1	
marble cream	1	
cream cheeses	1	

JAM- OR MARMALADE-BASED DESSERTS AS A SEPARATE CATEGORY

roll-jam pudding	8	fruit not specified
tart, tartlets, and creams	7	most with marmalade
jam sandwiches	5	all used raspberry jam
raspberry jam pudding	1	
strawberry jam cream	1	
raspberry puffs	1	probably used jam

RICE-BASED DESSERTS AS A SEPARATE CATEGORY

ground rice pudding	9	'cold ground rice pudding'; 'rice blancmange'
apples and rice	6	'boiled apples & rice' also 'rice & apples'
rice pudding	5	'baked rice pudding'
croquits [sic] of rice	1	
rice	1	served with roll jam pudding

JELLIES AS A SEPARATE CATEGORY

clear jelly	5
noyau jelly	2
punch jelly	2
lemon jelly	1
orange jelly	1
unspecified	2

OTHER DESSERTS AS A SEPARATE CATEGORY

sweet omelette	4	also 6 not specified as sweet or savoury
fritters	3	made with apples or oranges
pancakes	1	possibly stacked like cake layers
macaroni		
(when served with other desserts)	22	this is also served as a savoury dish after the desserts, but is not included here.

NOTES AND REFERENCES

ABBREVIATIONS

Throughout these notes, the magnificent collected Pilgrim edition of the letters of Charles Dickens is referred to by the abbreviated title *Letters* followed by the volume number in parentheses and the page reference, e.g. Graham Storey, Kathleen Tillotson, and Angus Easson, eds., *The Letters of Charles Dickens*, vol. 7 (Oxford: Clarendon Press, 1993) 243 is abbreviated as *Letters* (7) 243.

The full bibliographic references of these volumes are as follows:

Madeline House and Graham Storey, eds., *The Letters of Charles Dickens*, vol. 1 (Oxford: Clarendon Press, 1965).

Madeline House and Graham Storey, eds., *The Letters of Charles Dickens,* vol. 2 (Oxford: Clarendon Press, 1969).

Madeline House, Graham Storey, and Kathleen Tillotson, eds., *The Letters of Charles Dickens*, vol. 3 (Oxford: Clarendon Press, 1974).

Kathleen Tillotson, ed., *The Letters of Charles Dickens*, vol. 4 (Oxford: Clarendon Press, 1977).

Graham Storey and K. J. Fielding, eds., *The Letters of Charles Dickens*, vol. 5 (Oxford: Clarendon Press, 1981).

Graham Storey, Kathleen Tillotson, and Nina Burgis, eds., *The Letters of Charles Dickens*, vol. 6 (Oxford: Clarendon Press, 1988).

Graham Storey, Kathleen Tillotson, and Angus Easson, eds., *The Letters of Charles Dickens*, vol. 7 (Oxford: Clarendon Press, 1993).

Graham Storey and Kathleen Tillotson, eds., *The Letters of Charles Dickens,* vol. 8 (Oxford: Clarendon Press, 1995).

Graham Storey, ed., *The Letters of Charles Dickens*, vol. 9 (Oxford: Clarendon Press, 1997).

Notes to Chapter I, pages 77–111.

1   The 1851 (2nd) edition is catalogued in the National Library of Ireland and on microform at the New York Public Research Library; the British Library owns a copy of the 1852 'New Edition' and the Charles Dickens Museum (London) archive has a photocopy of that edition. The Schlesinger Library at Harvard University houses an 1854 'New Edition' by 'Lady Clutterbuck'. The Beinecke Rare Book and Manuscript Library at Yale University recently purchased the 1856 edition. This may be the same one Slater cited from Jarndyce's catalogue no. 83 (Winter 1991–2). See Michael Slater, *Dickens' Journalism: The Uncommercial Traveller and Other Papers 1859–70* (Columbus: Ohio State Univ. Press, 2002) 420, 421. The New York Academy of Medicine owns an 1860 edition.

2   Ian Watt, 'Oral Dickens', *Dickens Studies Annual* 3 (1974) 165–181, 240.

3   See also the following publications: Chris R. Vanden Bossche, 'Cookery, not Rookery: Family and Class in David Copperfield', *Dickens Studies Annual* 15 (1986) 89–109; William Ross Clark, 'The Hungry Mr. Dickens', *Dalhousie Review* 3 (1956) 250–257; Simon Edwards, 'Anorexia Nervosa versus the Fleshpots of London: Rose and Nancy in Oliver Twist', *Dickens Studies Annual* 19 (1990) 49–64; Sarah Gilead, 'Barmecide Feasts: Ritual, Narrative, and the Victorian Novel' *Dickens Studies Annual* 17 (1988) 225–247; Barbara Hardy, 'Food and Ceremony in Great Expectations', *Essays in Criticism* 13 (1963) 351–363; Margaret Lane, 'Dickens on the Hearth', in *Dickens 1970*, ed. Michael Slater (London: Chapman & Hall, 1979) 154–171. For an analysis of food in Dickens's magazines see James E. Marlow, 'Social Harmony and Dickens' Revolutionary Cookery', *Dickens Studies Annual* 17 (1988) 145–177; for Dickens's portrayal of cooks see Leicester Romayne, 'Cooks à la Boz', *Dickensian* 2 (1906) 173–175.

4   16 Dec. 1851 letter to F. Evans, *Letters* (6) 554.

5   Robert Patten, *Charles Dickens and His Publishers* (Oxford: Clarendon Press, 1970) 223.

6   Mamie Dickens, *My Father As I Recall Him* (London: Roxburghe Press, 1897) 19.

7   Dena Attar, *A Bibliography of Household Books in Britain 1800–1914* (London: Prospect Books, 1987) 12, 13.

8   [mid-April 1836] letter to J. Macrone, *Letters* (1) 147. The book was written by C.W. Day under a pseudonym.

9   *Anecdotes* was written by J.P. Malcolm in two volumes, 1808 and 1811. Dickens purchased the work in March of 1841 from the estate sale of Tom Hall. Dickens also borrowed Catlen's *Letters and Notes on the Manners, Customs, and Condition of the North American Indians* (1841) before they went on their North American tour, *Letters* (2) 229n; 2 Dec. 1841 letter to Mrs Hall, *Letters* (2) 437, 438.

10 Attar 13.

11 Richard D. Altick, *The English Common Reader: A Social History of the Mass Reading Public, 1800–1900* (Chicago: University of Chicago Press, 1957) 1, 138–140.

12 Altick 129–140.

13 4 Feb. 1850 letter to B. Coutts, *Letters* (6) 28. *Household Words* was published for only nine years. The 19 volumes, 479 issues, and roughly 11,780 pages succumbed in the aftermath of the Dickenses' separation. Dickens's last article, entitled 'A Last Household Word', in the May 28, 1859 issue stated in part: 'The first page of the first of these Nineteen Volumes, was devoted to a Preliminary Word from the writer by whom they were projected, under whose constant supervision they have been produced, and whose name has been (as his pen and himself have been), inseparable from the Publication ever since', *Household Words* 19 (1859) 620. By the end of its publication, some 40,000 copies a week were sold before the magazine was auctioned on 16 May 1859, and secretly purchased for Dickens. It was folded into his next venture *All The Year Round* premiering later that year: Anne Lohrli,

Household Words: *A Weekly Journal 1850–1859* (Toronto: University of Toronto Press, 1973) 23, 24. For details see the 15 May 1859 letter to Miss G. Hogarth, *Letters* (9) 65. Dickens's interest in culinary topics continued, but has not been explored for this history.

14   Charles Dickens, 'A Preliminary Word', *Household Words* 1 (1850) 1.

15   Altick 347.

16   Anne Lohrli, '*Household Words* Anthologies for American Readers', *Dickens Studies Annual* 14 (1985) 205–240.

17   Lohrli (1973) 5.

18   William H. Wills, 'Constitutional Trials', *Household Words* 5 (1852) 423.

19   Richard Horne, 'Death in the Bread-Basket', *Household Words* 2 (1850) 323; William Wills, 'The Troubled Water Question', *Household Words* 1 (1850) 49–53; Charles Strange and William Wills, 'Death in the Teapot', *Household Words* 2 (1850) 277; James Hannay, 'The Great Coffee Question', *Household Words* 3 (1851) 49–53; Henry Morley, 'Our House', *Household Words* 5 (1852) 41–42; Henry Morley, 'Starvation of an Alderman', *Household Words* 11 (1855) 213–216; Henry Morley, 'Poison', *Household Words* 13 (1856) 220–224.

20   Lohrli (1973) 25, 26.

21   Lohrli (1973) 333–335, 357–361, 421–426.

22   Lohrli (1973) 211, 320, 321, 341.

23   *Letters* (6) ix; Slater (2002) 420, 421.

24   Attar 52, 54.

25   Attar 54.

26   See note 1, above.

27   18 Dec. 1835 letter to Miss C. Hogarth, *Letters* (1) 109. George Sala noted that Dickens 'rather leaned towards the old-fashioned English hotel, with its old port, its old sherry, its old landlord and landlady, its old bill of fare, its sirloin of beef, leg of mutton, boiled fowl and broiled veal cutlet, and its old scale charges', George Augustus Sala, *Things I Have Seen and People I Have Known,* vol. 1 (London: Cassell and Co. Ltd., 1894) 126.

28   Popular articles seasonally give modernized recipes for general Dickensian Christmas foods, for example Anne Mendelson's 'The Meal As Mirror' (*Gourmet,* Dec. 2000). One cookbook by Helen Cox entitled *Mr. and Mrs. Charles Dickens Entertain at Home* was based on Mrs Dickens's publication. M.F.K. Fisher reviewed Cox's work and declared it 'the worst tradition of mass-produced mediocrity-at-table' for her use of canned goods and gelatin rather than staying true to Mrs Dickens's intentions and Victorian traditions, *Dickens Studies Newsletter* 3 (1952) 50–53. There is also *The Charles Dickens Cookbook* by Brenda Marshall (Toronto: Personal Library, Pubs., 1981).

29   9 Oct. 1848 letters to J. Leech and F. Stone, *Letters* (5) 422.

30   Alexis Soyer, *The Modern Housewife or Ménagère* (London: Simpkin, Marshall & Co., 1850) 81.

31   The etymology of 'pie' might have come from shortening *pied à pied* referring to the protruding feet when the practice originated before pie dishes were used and loaves retained the feet for handles, Jennifer Davies, *The Victorian Kitchen,* large print ed. (Oxford: Clio Press, 1991) 207. Mrs Beeton, *Mrs. Beeton's Every Day Cookery and Housekeeping Book* (1865, facsimile ed. NY: Gallery Books, 1984), Plate III.

32   5 May 1856 letter to Mrs Dickens, *Letters* (8) 108.

33   9 May 1856 letter to Miss G. Hogarth, *Letters* (8) 115.

34   13 Nov. 1840 letter to Mrs Macready, *Letters* (2) 149, 150.

35   7 Nov. 1847 letter to G. Lewis, *Letters* (5) 190.

36   William Blanchard Jerrold, *The Epicure's Year Book and Table Companion* (London: Bradbury, Evans & Co., 1868) 14. Included in the text are several recipes attributed to distinguished authors. 'Iced Biscuits, à la Charles Dickens' (pp. 197, 198) combined small blocks of peach and chocolate ice-cream and biscuits as a frozen dessert. W.B. Jerrold was

the eldest son of their friend Douglas Jerrold and was a regular contributor to *Household Words*. A copy (not attributed to Jerrold, but clearly the same publication) was listed in J.H. Stonehouse, *Catalogue of the Library of Charles Dickens from Gadshill* [sic] reprinted from Sotheran's *Price Current of Literature* (London: Piccadilly Fountain Press, 1935) 43. Blanchard Jerrold also published *The Dinner Bell: A Gastronomic Manual Teaching the Mistress How to Rule A Dainty and Thrifty Cuisine, and the Cook How to Prepare a Great Variety of Dishes with Economy* (London: W. Mullan, 1878).

37   Jerrold 14, 15.

38   Jerrold 17, 19

39   Jerrold 21, 23.

40   Jerrold 24, 25.

41   Jerrold 27, 29.

42   Jerrold 30, 31.

43   Jerrold 32, 33.

44   All the other menus provided the specific months rather than an 'All the Summer' or 'All the Winter' appellation. Even when the menu could be served year round, 'Jan. to Dec.' was given as the seasonal frame. The placement of these menus in the original text is noteworthy as well. Nine 'All the Summer' menus in the section for 2 to 3 diners are inserted between the 'May-September' menus beginning on page 32 of the transcript above. In the other sections, they are generally added at the end, except for page 57 where the last 'All the Summer' menu was shifted to fill a larger space in the original. The 'Nov. to March' menu is dropped in before 4 more 'All the ...' menus. The second 'Nov. to March' menu should have followed its companion on page 57, but instead appears as the last menu on page 61. This menu is too small to accommodate 18 to 20 persons where it was mistakenly placed. The two 'Nov. to March' menus (that are out of sequence) would have nicely filled the bottom of page 39 in the original (p. 57 in the transcript) which is where they belong and should have been placed by the compositor. Likewise, this set of 'All the Summer' and 'All the Winter' menus (on pages 57–59) should have been placed with those under the 18 to 20 persons category. The menus are excessively large for 8 to 10 diners where they were placed. If the shortest menu on page 61 were put in its proper space, that is, on the bottom of page 57, the new section (for 14 to 20 persons) would have started on page 58 rather than on page 60. And the menus on pages 58 and 59, very likely written for the new edition, would have correctly been given for the largest dinner parties of 18 and 20 persons.

45   Anne Willan, *French Regional Cooking* (New York: William Morrow & Co., Inc.: 1981) 164–165.

46   One assumes that oatcakes, although not mentioned in the menus, had long been served in the Dickens and Hogarth households. The exclusion of haggis (a dish prepared from oatmeal and pluck cooked in the sheep's own paunch) from Catherine's menus, while it was traditional and surprisingly delicious, may not be so remarkable. Haggis rarely excited non-Scottish cooks, and Catherine apparently was not an evangelist. The Edinburgh cookery book that she used by Margaret Dods (Christian I. Johnstone), *The Cook and Housewife's Manual, a Practical System of Modern Domestic Cookery and Family Management,* provided many variations for lamb's and calf's haggis, including ultra-rich preparations such as Royal Haggis, but English colleagues generally ignored the Scottish dish altogether. Other well-known Scottish treats, such as shortbread, biscuits, and Scotch whisky-flavoured teacakes would have been made for tea-time, but not for the dessert course of a dinner.

47   [5 July 1841] to J. Forster, *Letters* (2) 323; 11 July 1841 to J. Forster, *Letters* (2) 328.

48   Since auction catalogues only contain the most valuable items or the easiest to sell, copies of Catherine's work would not be expected to be included nor was it found in the listings

for Dickens, Thackery, or Sala. Thackeray owned a volume of 'German Cookery Book: *Supp', Gemüs' und Fleisch: ein Kochbuch für bürgerliche Haushaltungen*, clever etching by Neureuther, fcap. 8 vo. 3x. Darmstadt, 1856' as described by J.H. Stonehouse, *Catalogue of the Library of W. M. Thackeray* reprinted from Sotheran's *Price Current of Literature* (London: Piccadilly Fountain Press, 1935) 169. Sala's library contained at least fourteen volumes on the culinary arts in French, Italian, and English including a prized first edition of Hannah Glasse's *The Art of Cookery Made Plain and Easy*. Sala is distinguished by having written his own cookbook just before he died in 1895, *The Thorough Good Cook: A Series of Chats on the Culinary Art and Nine Hundred Recipes*. Sotheby, Wilken and Hodge, *Catalogue of the Library of George A. Sala* (London: Dryden Press, 1895).

49 [13] Jan. 1854 letter to M. Lemon, *Letters* (7) 243.

50 Edward Hewett and W. F. Axton, *Convivial Dickens: The Drinks of Dickens & His Times* (Athens, OH: Ohio University Press, 1983) i.

51 Keith Turner and Jean Turner, *The Pudding Club Book* (London: Headline Book Publishing, 1977) 83.

52 Eliza Acton, *Modern Cookery In All its Branches* (London: Longman, Brown, Green, & Longmans, 1845) 376.

53 A Lady (Hannah Glasse), *The Art of Cookery Made Plain and Easy*, (1747, facsimile ed., London: Prospect Books, 1983) 106.

54 Topics like recipe plagiarism and 'the sense of individual creativity and personal property in culinary ideas' are certainly not new topics to culinary history, but they serve little purpose here. See Stephen Mennell, 'Plagiarism and Originality – Diffusionism in the Study of the History of Cookery', *Petits Propos Culinaires* 68 (2001) 29.

55 See Helen Morris, *Portrait of a Chef: The Life of Alexis Soyer* (Oxford: Oxford University Press, 1980).

56 Alexis Soyer *Gastronomic Regenerator* (London: Simpkin, Marshall, & Co., 1847) 21, 33, 581. Soyer slightly revised these recipes for *The Modern Housewife or Ménagère* (London: Simpkin, Marshall, & Co., 1850) 73.

57 Soyer (1850) 73.

58 Soyer (1850) 202.

59 Soyer (1850) 64.

60 Soyer (1850) 63–65.

61 Annie Hood, 'Kentish Food, or Food of Kent', *Petits Propos Culinaires* 45 (1993) 13.

62 11 July 1845 letter to Miss Acton, *Letters* (4) 330

63 This quote is from chapter 39 in *Martin Chuzzlewit* (Maryland: Penguin Books, 1968) 672, 673. The next excerpt, which describes their visit to the butcher's, has been included in the chapter on meats, below.

64 Chapter 45 page 766.

65 To make 'Ruth Pinch's celebrated pudding (known also as Beef-Steak Pudding à la Dickens), substitute six ounces of butter for the suet in this receipt, and moisten the paste with the well-beaten yolks of four eggs, or with three whole ones, mixed with a little water; butter the basin very thickly before the crust is laid in, as the pudding is to be turned out of it for table.' In all else proceed exactly as Small Beef-Steak Pudding given below.
'Small Beef-Steak Pudding
'Make into a very firm, smooth paste, one pound of flour, six ounces of beef-suet, finely minced, half a teaspoonful of salt, and half a pint of cold water. Line with this a basin which holds a pint and a half. Season a pound of tender steak, free from bone and skin, with half an ounce of salt and half a teaspoonful of pepper well mixed together; lay it in the crust, pour in a quart-pint of water, roll out the cover, close the pudding carefully, tie a floured cloth over, and boil it three hours and a half. We give this receipt…as an exact

guide for the proportions of meat puddings in general.'
[for the pastry crust] 'Flour, 1 lb.; suet, 6oz.; salt, $^1/_2$ teaspoonful; water, $^1/_2$ pint;'
[for the filling] 'rumpsteak, 1 lb.; salt, $^1/_2$ oz.; pepper $^1/_2$ teaspoonful; water, $^1/_2$ pint;'
[Bake in a moderate oven about 350°F] '3 $^1/_2$ hours.' Eliza Acton, *Modern Cookery in All Its Branches* (London: Longman, Brown, Green, Longmans, 1845) 369.

66   Acton 323. She gives the mayonnaise sauce on page 134.

67   Acton 18–20.

68   Acton 304, 305, 380, 233.

69   Mrs Hale wrote several editions of *The Good Housekeeper or The Way to Live Well and Be Well While We Live* [1839], *Keeping House and House Keeping* [1845], *Lady's New Book of Cookery: A Practical System* [1852], *The New Household Receipt-Book* [1853], *Mrs. Hale's Receipts for the Million* [1857], and *Manners: or Happy Homes and Good Society All the Year Around* [1867]. Biography provided in Isabelle Webb Entrikin's *Sarah Josepha Hale and Godey's Lady's Book: A Dissertation* (Philadelphia: Lancaster Press, Inc., 1946) 137–155. In addition, Mrs Hale represents a culinary overlap by being the editor of *Juvenile Miscellany*, a Boston magazine founded by Lydia Marie Child. She later hired Eliza Leslie as her assistant editor at *Godey's Lady's Book* after assuming the editorship in Philadelphia. Patricia Okker, *Our Sister Editors: Sarah Josepha Hale and the Nineteenth Century American Women Editors* (Athens: University of Georgia Press, 1995) 180, 190, 197.

70   11 March 1842 letter to Mrs Hale, *Letters* (3) 114, 115. Mrs Hale's other publications include the *Women's Record or Sketches of Distinguished Women* in 1853. She also influenced Matthew Vassar who founded the women's college.

71   Sarah Josepha Hale, *The Ladies' New Book of Cookery*, 5th edition (New York: H. Long & Brother, 1852) 26, 120, 317. The Charlotte Russe recipe was later reproduced in *Mrs. Hale's New Cook Book* (Philadelphia: T.B. Peterson and Brothers, 1857) 362–363.

72   Sarah Freeman, *Mutton and Oysters: the Victorians and Their Food* (London: Victor Gollancz Ltd., 1989) 194.

73   Wilson 313. George Sala, for one, reintroduced Oyster Sausages which called for a half-pound of lean beef or mutton, half-pound of beef suet, two score of scaled oysters (about 40) chopped together and bound with bread-crumbs and egg yolks. The mince, seasoned with salt and white pepper, could be enhanced with either mace and nutmeg or 'a very savoury' mixture with cayenne, minced shallot, and a spoonful of garlic vinegar: *The Thorough Good Cook* (New York: Brentano's, 1896) 184.

74   If Catherine's mother owned a cookbook, it most likely would have been Glasse's work which continued to be a best-seller for the next one hundred years. The last edition of *The Art of Cookery* was printed in 1843. Glasse was only supplanted when Mrs Beeton's more comprehensive household manual was published in the 1860s: Virginia Maclean, *A Short-Title Catalogue of Household and Cookery Books Published in the English Tongue 1701–1800* (London: Prospect Books, 1981) 60. One recipe called for buttons of mutton suet seasoned with salt, pepper, nutmeg, and mixed with hard-boiled egg yolk. The leg was studded with cloves and when partially cooked, a slice was removed from the underside so the meat would take up the liquor and water added from a pint of oysters. As the liquid reduced while the mutton was roasting, a sauce was made with the pan juices thickened with a beurre manié (butter-flour paste) which was stirred in: Glasse 24, 25.

75   Charles Carter, *The Complete Practical Cook: Or, A New System of the Whole Art and Mystery of Cookery* (1730, facsimile ed. London: Prospect Books, 1984) 51: 'First take your Oysters, and set them, and beard them; then take some Parsley, Thyme, Pepper, Salt, and some crumb'd Bread; mix all these well together; then take the Yolks of four Eggs; mix up your Oysters in all this; then raise a few Holes, and stuff your Mutton with three Oysters in a Hole; then cover with a Mutton Caul, and so roast it gently: Garnish with Mutton Cutlets.' *Mrs. McLintock's Receipts for Cookery and Pastry-Work* (1736, facsimile ed.

Aberdeen: Aberdeen University Press, 1986) 58.

76   20 Nov. 1840 letter to D. Maclise, *Letters* (2) 152. Dickens was noted for his long walks to observe people and to develop plots for his fiction, and often implored his friends to join him.

77   Charles Dickens, *Little Dorrit* (New York: Penguin Books, 1978) 346, 348. T. W. Hill, 'The Oyster; A Close-Up', *Dickensian* 36 (1940) 143, 144. Serialization of the monthly parts for *Little Dorrit* began in December 1855 and continued through June 1857. Norman Page, *A Dickens Companion* (New York: Schocken Books, 1984) 194.

78   Mistress Margaret Dods (Christian Isobel Johnstone), *The Cook and Housewife's Manual* (Edinburgh: Oliver & Boyd, 1833) 140.

79   Catherine Brown, *Broths and Bannocks: Cooking in Scotland 1690 to the Present Day* (London: John Murray, 1990) 37–38. See also Rose Arnold, 'Meg Dods: a character and a cookery book', *Petits Propos Culinaires* 44 (1993) 7–10.

80   George Sala asked the question: 'Is a steak a convertible term for a chop?' when he noticed that Hannah Glasse preferred the term chop for recipe titles, but instructed cutting meat into steaks in the directions. For his readers' edification, Sala offered Douglas Jerrold's quip explaining the two terms. Jerrold had remarked about the execution of Mary, Queen of Scots 'that the poor lady had for supper her last steak, prior to her final "chop" the next morning.' Sala (1896) 53.

81   Dods 305.

82   Alan Davidson, *Oxford Companion to Food* (Oxford: Oxford University Press, 1999) 197.

83   Dods 304.

84   Henry Dickens, *The Recollections of Sir Henry Dickens, K.C.* (London: William Heinemann Ltd., 1934) 19.

85   To make the dish, the cook usually had the butcher saw the head in half. The brain was removed and soaked in cold water and vinegar to blanch it, while the rest of the head was soaked in warm water and salt. The nostrils were scraped and the head thoroughly cleaned before blanching. The lamb's head was then started in the soup pot. 'Powsowdie', sheep's-head broth, was a by-product. Ena Baxter, *Ena Baxter's Scottish Cookbook* (Stirling: Johnston & Bacon Books, Ltd., 1974) 11. In Catherine's recipe, she browns the meat and serves it with the cooked liver. Maisie Steven, *The Good Scots Diet: What Happened to It?* (Aberdeen: Aberdeen University Press, 1985) 57.

86   Harriet Martineau, 'A New Plea for a New Food', *Household Words* 3 (1851) 138. The British term cornflour is American corn starch.

87   J.H. Clapham, 'Work and Wages', *Early Victorian England 1830–1865*, vol. 2 (London: Oxford University Press, 1963) 69.

88   Thomas Webster, *An Encyclopædia of Domestic Economy* (London: Longman, Brown, Green, & Longmans, 1847, 1852) 741.

89   The article has Martineau's and Dickens's characteristic political and moral overtones: that maize was grown by freemen compared to cotton which was cultivated by slave labour.

90   Harriet Martineau, 'A New Plea for a New Food', *Household Words* 3 (1851) 139.

91   5 July 1856 letter to W. Irving, *Letters* (8) 150–1.

92   Eliza Lynn and William Wills, 'Common Cookery', *Household Words* 13 (1856) 43.

93   George Dodd, 'Pot and Kettle Philosophy', *Household Words* 8 (1854) 334. A few notable coffee pots were available: both Count Rumford and Beart offered percolators and there were Parker's patent steam fountain coffee maker, Brain's vacuum or pneumatic filter, and Evan's apparatus on the market. Thomas Webster, *An Encyclopædia of Domestic Economy* (London: Longman, Brown, Green, & Longmans, 1852) 711, 712.

94   The loan was made to Thomas J. Thompson, Christiana Weller's husband: 19 April 1851 letter to T. Mitton, *Letters* (6) 359.

95   Robert Patten, *Charles Dickens and His Publishers* (Oxford: Clarendon Press, 1978) 216–218.

96   Patten 224–227.
97   *Letters* (6) ix.
98   Gladys Storey, *Dickens and Daughter* (London: Frederick Muller, Ltd., 1939) 22.
99   Cedric Dickens, *Dining with Dickens* (Oxford: Alden Press, 1984) 12.
100   Laura Peek, 'Cookbook reveals Dickens nakedly as a chef', *The Times* 22 Dec. 2001 p. 15. www.thetimes.co.uk/article/0,2-2001592049,00.html. I would like to thank Lillian Nayder for providing a copy of this article.
101   G. Storey 22, 23; Henry Dickens, *The Recollections of Sir Henry Dickens, K.C.* (London: William Heinemann, Ltd., 1934) 19.
102   Dickens was not above using culinary allusions, like calling their friend's twins 'prematurely ripe little Stiltons': 18 October 1950 letter to T. Beard, *Letters* (6) 193.
103   Eustace (Grenville) Murray, 'The Roving Englishman: His Philosophy of Dining', *Household Words* 6 (1852) 232.
104   Michael Slater, *Dickens and Women* (London, The Chaucer Press, 1983) 120–122.
105   2 Dec. 1844 letter to Mrs Dickens, *Letters* (4) 234.
106   Slater 113.

Notes to Chapter II, pages 112–138.

1   For example, Dickens conveyed his wife's regrets at not being able to attend the Weller-Thompson wedding, saying that she 'made her last public appearance for some time', dated about a week before giving birth to Alfred on the 28th, *Letters* (4) 406n. See also letters to E. Bulwer-Lytton on 4 Aug. and R. Horne on 10 Aug. 1848, *Letters* (5) 383, 388, 389 where Dickens describes his wife as 'being in an uninteresting condition, has besought me to bring her out of that stagnant air of London for two months.'
2   28 June 1850 letter to C. Dickens, *Letters* (6) 121.
3   22 July 1850 letter to Burdett Coutts, *Letters* (6) 134. Angela Georgina Burdett Coutts (1814–1906), later Baroness Burdett-Coutts, from the wealthy banking family, became friends with the Dickenses and acted as patroness to Charley at Eton. She depended on Dickens's help to organize her philanthropic projects including her 'Home for Homeless Women' at Urania Cottage, *Letters* (6) 4n.
4   Her sister Mary's premature death delayed the christening of Charley, the first born, and Catherine asked her cousin, Mary Scott Hogarth, to act as godmother: 30 May 1837 letter to Miss Mary Scott Hogarth, *Dickensian* 63 (1967) 79. Ultimately the event occurred on 9 December 1837 and Charles Culliford Boz Dickens or 'the living wonder', as Dickens referred to his heir, was scheduled for a noon ceremony at St Pancras New Church in Woburn Place. Thomas Beard, his sisters, and other friends including Samuel Lover, William Jerdan, T.J. Culliford, and John Forster joined the extended Dickens and Hogarth families for the evening celebration at their Doughty Street home: [6 Dec. 1837] letter to T. Beard, *Letters* (1) 338, 339. Catherine was already six months pregnant with their next child, Mary (Mamie) Dickens, the first of two daughters, who was christened in the same church on 7 January 1839. She was born on 6 March 1838: 28 December 1838 letter to S. Blanchard, *Letters* (1) 478. The Dickenses invited Dr Frederic H.F. Quin, their doctor and the first homeopathic physician in England, who established a fashionable practice despite opposition from the conventional medical community, and who founded the London Homeopathic Hospital in 1850. Dickens's invitation to him explained, 'We christen a "babby" here next Monday, and hold sundry festivities in the evening, whereof quadrilles and supper do form a part': [3 January 1839] letter to Dr Quin, *Letters* (1) 489, 490.

5   17 August 1840 letter to J. Harley, *Letters* (2) 117; biographical information, *Letters* (1) 167.

6   'The Failed Middle Class Marriage' and 'Dependants and Family', in Michael Hollington, ed., *Charles Dickens Critical Assessments*, vol. 4 (E. Sussex, England: Helm Information, 1995) 15, 16.

7   16 March 1852 letter to Miss Burdett Coutts, *Letters* (6) 627. Edward Bulwer Lytton Dickens was born on the 13th of March, and was the last of ten children. In announcing the birth to W. Howitt on March 19th, Dickens wrote, 'I am not quite clear that I particularly wanted the latter, but I have no doubt that he is good for me in some point of view or other': *Letters* (6) 629. Six months later, Richard Horne's wife Catherine described the baby, now nicknamed 'Plorn' by Dickens, as 'a dear little thing and even Dickens takes notice of it and calls it the J.B. in W. which being interpreted means the Jolliest Boy in the World': *Letters* (6) 769n.

8   5 May 1852 letter to E. Lytton, *Letters* (6) 662n.

9   Although physical complications could have occurred with Catherine's last birth, it seems likely that the Dickenses practised birth control. Patricia Branca's work acknowledges that Victorian women in Catherine's day expected more from their marriage than their grandmothers had fifty years earlier. Besides having a love-relationship within the marriage bed, women took an active role in their reproductive health. Early in the nineteenth century, statistics for England began showing fewer births and a dramatic drop around the 1870s. The French urban middle class had previously cut their population growth. Given the Dickenses' residences abroad and their social circle (particularly with career-women in the arts who were far more likely to control pregnancies), if Catherine did not know about birth-control when she first married, she surely could have learned methods in her candid conversations with other women. Besides abstinence, *coitus interruptus* or the use of condoms, Catherine alone could have controlled pregnancy by using douching solutions afterwards, or planning beforehand by using the sponge, which was available in England by 1825. In 1843, the relatively new vaginal diaphragm (cervical cap) made of a softer, more flexible, vulcanized rubber was being used: Patricia Branca, *Silent Sisters: Middle Class Women in the Victorian Home* (London: Croom Helm, 1975) 117, 131–134.

10   The account was published in Gladys Storey's work *Dickens and Daughter*. The authenticity of her interviews with Mrs Kate Perugini, Dickens's second daughter, was investigated by David Parker and Michael Slater and published as 'The Gladys Storey Papers' and 'The Gladys Storey Papers A Footnote' by David Parker, *Dickensian* 76 (1980) 3–16, 158, 159.

11   G. Storey 97. Catherine's father and sister, Mrs Helen Roney, lived nearby at 10 Gloucester Crescent until about 1873. F. R. Dean, 'George Hogarth', *Dickensian* 43 (1947) 24.

12   *Letters* (8) 578n. In his 12 May 1869 will, Dickens provided his wife with the interest from £8,000, invested by their son Henry: Norman Page, *A Dickens Chronology* (London: MacMillan Press, Ltd., 1988) 346.

13   William Wills, 'A Legal Fiction', *Household Words* 11 (1855) 589–599. Provoked by Lord Chancellor Cranworth's Marriage and Divorce Bill, the article discussed the inequality of the laws pertaining to women. As early as 1842, Dickens relayed a fairly sympathetic account of women whose children were taken from them by their husbands. This happened to Mrs Norton, but she had successfully persuaded her husband to let their three children live with her for half the year: *Letters* (3) 438n. For a fuller discussion, see Lillian Nayder, *Wilkie Collins* (New York: Twayne Pub., 1997) 71–99.

14   Elisabeth G. Gitter, 'The Rhetoric of Reticence in John Forster's Life of Charles Dickens', *Dickens Studies Annual* 25 (1996) 127–130.

15   Gitter 132.

16   Margaret Lane, 'Mrs. Beeton and Catherine', in *Purely for Pleasure* (London: Hamish Hamilton, Ltd., 1966) 185.

17 27 October 1841 letter to Miss Burdett Coutts, *Letters* (2) 411.

18 *Letters* (4) 710.

19 For example, 'I write to you (very hurriedly), because you have seen the different packets in my hands, and can no doubt make out the Newgate one, pretty readily....' 29 July 1857 letter to Miss G. Hogarth, *Letters* (8) 391.

20 14 March 1856 letter to Miss G. Hogarth, *Letters* (8) 70, 71.

21 29 May 1857 letter to Mrs Horne, *Letters* (8) 334; 30 July 1857 letter to T. Fairbairn, *Letters* (8) 393. She also entertained Hans Christian Andersen during his long visit from 11 June to 15 July, 1857, *Letters* (8) 372–3n.

22 [31 Dec. 1856] letter to Miss Burdett Coutts, *Letters* (8) 248.

23 In the 1963 portrait entitled *Unwanted Wife: A Defence of Mrs. Charles Dickens*, Hebe Elsna offers a hagiography which lacks citations, but does acknowledge the complications of a relatively undistinguished woman caught in a high-profile literary clique (London: Jarrolds Publ. Ltd.).

24 Michael Slater, *Dickens and Women* (London: J.M. Dent & Son, Ltd., 1983) 108, 109, 119, 120.

25 Lillian Nayder, 'The Widowhood of Catherine Dickens', *Dickens Studies Annual* 32 (2002) 277–298; 'The Other Dickens And America: Catherine in 1842', *Dickens Quarterly* 19 (2002) 141–149; 'Constructing Catherine Dickens', *Hiroshima Studies in English Language and Literature* 47 (2003) 1–19. The details of the Dickenses' life are sometimes difficult to untangle. Charles often used the first person singular in letters, which obscures others, including Catherine, who shared the experience.

26 The secret was Forster's intended marriage: 11 March 1856 letter to Miss G. Hogarth, *Letters* (8) 70.

27 28 June 1850 letter to Catherine, *Letters* (6) 119, 120.

28 21 Dec. 1855 letter to Catherine, *Letters* (7) 769–70. Dickens was invited to dinner with Forster, Evans, Mark Lemon, Peter Cunningham.

29 1 Feb. 1838 letter to Catherine, *Letters* (1) 366.

30 *Letters* (1) 299n. The street has been renumbered today and the house has not been identified. Little is known about her maternal grandmother who died in 1841, but her grandfather, George Thomson (1757–1851), a 'clean-brushed commonplace old gentleman in Scratchwig', held the position of Clerk to the Board of Trustees for Encouragement of Art and Manufactures in Scotland from 1780 to 1839. As an enthusiastic amateur musician, he published collections of Scottish, Welsh, and Irish songs with scores written for him by Haydn, Beethoven, Weber, and his son-in-law (Catherine's father). George Thomson was a friend of the poet Robert Burns, and commissioned about 120 songs from him alone: *Letters* (1) 134n. From 1840 to 1843, Catherine's grandparents lived in London: [25 Oct. 1841] letter to J. Forster, *Letters* (2) 410.

31 Michael Slater, *Dickens and Women* (London: J.M. Dent & Sons, Ltd., 1983) 104.

32 *Letters* (1) xlii, xliii, 54n, 55n.

33 George Hogarth's publishers included Richard Bentley and Bradbury & Evans, two London companies who became important to his son-in-law. Catherine's work was also published by Bradbury & Evans.

34 *Letters* (1) 54n, 55n.

35 Hogarth became a music critic for the *Daily News* eleven years later, but this time under Dickens's editorship. Hogarth held the position for twenty years, long after Dickens left: Norman Page, *A Dickens Companion* (New York: Scocken Books, 1984) 34, 35.

36 Michael Slater, *Dickens' Journalism: Sketches By Boz and Other Early Papers 1833–39* (Columbus: Ohio State University Press, 1994) xxiii, xxiv.

37 The Hogarth home was on the south side of Fulham Road, about 150 yards east of the Queen's Elm turnpike: *Letters* (1) 67n.

38　From Eleanor E. Christian's description in 'Recollections of Charles Dickens', *Temple Bar*, LXXXII [1888], 481, reprinted in *Letters* (1) 60n.

39　Although Miss Waller's 'ladies school' and Dr Frampton's 'academy' were next door to the Hogarths' home, Catherine had probably finished her education before the family moved to Chelsea. She may have been a pupil of William Dove, of Huddersfield, when the Hogarths lived in Halifax from 1832 to 1834. Dove later wrote *A Treatise on Penmanship* (1836) but, judging from Catherine's difficult hand, she profited little from this instruction: *Letters* (1) 67n, 68n.

40　Page (1984) 34, 35; C.G.L. DuCann, *The Love-Lives of Charles Dickens* (London: Frederick Muller, 1961) 64–67. I am grateful to Lillian Nayder for the names and birth order of the other Hogarth children, Robert (the second child), George, William, James, and the infant twins, Edward and Helen Isabella.

41　For an upwardly-mobile Dickens, Catherine Hogarth and her family's social graces may have polished his own informal approach. His letter, three and a half years into their marriage, reveals the difference in their styles. 'I inclose [sic] to Mrs. Blanchard an Invitation from my worser half to a gentle "flare" with which we are going to celebrate that stirring event, – a christening. We are very homely and unceremonious people, and Mrs. Dickens labours under some apprehension that there should have been previous callings and interchanges of formality. I have undertaken, however, to dispense with any such preliminaries, trusting that as we (i.e. you and I) understand each other moderately well, Mrs. B. and Mrs. D. may arrive at a similar interchange of friendliness without first playing at company': 28 Dec. 1838 letter to S.L. Blanchard, *Letters* (1) 478.

42　11 Feb. 1835 letter from Miss Hogarth to Miss Mary Scott Hogarth, 'New Letters of Mary Hogarth and Her Sister Catherine', *Dickensian* 63 (1967) 76.

43　*Letters* (1) 69n.

44　[May 1835] letter to Miss C. Hogarth, *Letters* (1) 60; 4 July 1835 letter to Miss Mary Scott Hogarth, *Letters* (1) 68.

45　*Letters* (1) 62n.

46　4 July 1835 letter to Miss Mary Scott Hogarth, *Letters* (1) 68.

47　[? June 1835] letter to Miss C. Hogarth, *Letters* (1) 64.

48　[? June 1835] letter to Miss C. Hogarth, *Letters* (1) 64–66.

49　Frederick Dickens (1820–1868), his younger brother, often acted as messenger. He escorted Catherine and Mary Hogarth when Dickens worked late: *Letters* (1) 47n.

50　[30 October 1835] letter to Miss C. Hogarth, *Letters* (1) 86.

51　*Letters* (1) 64n.

52　*Letters* (1) 131n.

53　[?8 March 36] letter to Miss C. Hogarth, *Letters* (1)) 138.

54　27 Feb. 1836 letter to W. Thomson, *Letters* (1) 135.

55　[10 March 1836] letter to Miss C. Hogarth, *Letters* (1) 138, 139.

56　Reverend Charles Kingsley, whose son wrote *Westward Ho!*, did not officiate, as so often repeated: *Letters* (1) 144.

57　Thomas Beard (1807–1891), has often been referred to as Dickens's oldest friend, although Dickens met Thomas Mitton (1812–1878) first, who acted as his solicitor. Beard later became Charley Dickens's godfather. Beard was a frequent dinner guest and often took his vacations at Broadstairs with the family. The Dickenses' letters to Beard provide insight and details about household activities: *Letters* (1) 3n, 35n.

58　*Letters* (1) 3n.

59　*Letters* (1) 8in.

60　[?25 March 1836] letter to J. Macrone, *Letters* (1) 142.

61　The set remained with Dickens after he and his wife separated: *Letters* (1) 8in

62　*Letters* (1) 144n; J. W. T. Ley ed., *The Life of Charles Dickens* by John Forster (London:

Whitefriars Press, Ltd., 1928) 78, 79; Alex J. Philip, *Dickens' Honeymoon and Where He Spent It* (London, Chapman & Hall, Ltd., 1912) 1–3. There are no records of the meal, but tradition suggests that it would have included beautifully garnished salads of game and oysters; collared and potted meats; jellied venison; and platters of ham, tongue and turkey placed with formal symmetry around the table. Compotes of fresh and preserved fruits, such as pineapples, melons, or cucumbers would have mingled with mountains of delicate meringues, pastry sandwiches oozing marmalade and caramel baskets that overflowed with fancy confectionery and perfumed biscuits. The magnificent bride's cake held the place of honour in the centre of the decorated table. 'Those useful vulgar commodities' like rashers of bacon, eggs, muffins, rolls and buttered toast were usually placed on the sideboard. Urns of coffee, tea, hot chocolate and cut-glass pitchers filled with cold water were typically available, but glasses of champagne were generously offered in celebration of the young couple's nuptials. Mistress Margaret Dods (Christian I. Johnstone), *The Cook and Housewife's Manual*, 5th edition (Edinburgh: Oliver & Boyd, 1833) 71.

63   *Letters* (1) 144n.

64   Gladys Storey, *Dickens and Daughter* (London, Frederick Muller Ltd., 1939) 22, 23. Embroidered covers on two high-backed praying chairs, a pedestal screen, and cover are listed in the 1845 (1844) household inventory and were probably Catherine's work as well: *Letters* (4) 707.

65   The cottage on the road between Gravesend and Rochester was identified in 1905, but reevaluated and commemorated on June 14, 1911. Mrs Kate (Dickens) Perugini and Georgina Hogarth were in attendance. The bronze plaque was executed by Percy Fitzgerald, a fellow author and friend. The plaque's partial inscription reads: 'In this house Charles Dickens spent his honeymoon in 1836.' Their acknowledgement of Catherine as his wife was apparently still too difficult for the Dickens Fellowship four decades after Dickens's death: Alex J. Philip, *Dickens' Honeymoon and Where He Spent It* (London: Chapman & Hall, Ltd., 1912) 37–46; 'Dickens and Chalk: Unveiling of Tablet', *Dickensian* 7 (1911) 186. Thanks to David Parker for providing the current status of the honeymoon cottage in our correspondence.

66   15 May [1836] letter from Mary Hogarth to Mary Scott Hogarth, *Letters* (1) 689.

67   [? April 1836] letter to T. Macrone, *Letters* (1) 148.

68   30 July 1836 letter to G. Thompson, *Letters* (1) 159.

69   F.R. Dean, 'George Hogarth', *Dickensian* 43 (1947) 19, 20.

70   Dean 22.

71   According to Altick, with the introduction of Sam Weller in the fourth number (July 1936), success was evident. By February 1837, sales had reached 14,000 copies for the month, and increased to 40,000 by the end of the fifteen-part serial in September: Richard Altick, *The English Common Reader: A Social History of the Mass Reading Public, 1800–1900* (Chicago & London: University of Chicago Press, 1957) 65–81, 279–281.

72   *Letters* (1) xliii.

73   *Letters* (1) xliv.

74   The Charles Dickens Museum, formerly the Dickens House Museum, was established in 1923 by members of the Dickens Fellowship who restored the residence with a wealth of furnishings, personal memorabilia, and archives. The museum opened two years later.

75   Anonymous, *The Dickens House Museum Guidebook* (Banbury: Cheney & Sons, n.d.) 16, 20.

76   John Greaves, *Dickens at Doughty Street* (London: Trinity Press, 1975) 55. Even the book reviewer took issue with this point, stating that 'Greaves undercuts the imagination here.' Angus Eassen, 'John Greaves. *Dickens at Doughty Street*', *Dickens Studies Newsletter* 7 (1976) 92.

77   Letters serving as examples include [mid-Dec. 1837] to J. Forster, [Aug. 1838] to J. Forster,

Letters (1) 426, 427; 26 July 1842 to D. Maclise, and so forth: *Letters* (3) 287.

78   26 June 41 letter to J. Forster, *Letters* (2) 317. Dickens once even wrote to his sister saying he would visit 'if you would ask me to accept of a mutton chop', while Mrs Dickens was in confinement after giving birth: 1 Feb. 1849 letter to Mrs Austin, *Letters* (5) 484.

79   [12 April 1837] letter to T. Beard, *Letters* (1) 248.

80   [28 April 1837] letter to R. Bentley, *Letters* (1) 253; Dean 23. For culinary historians, Richard Bentley and later his son published a number of cookbooks – most notably the editions of Charles Elmé Francatelli's *The Modern Cook* and Mrs Harriet Toogood's *The Treasury of French Cookery: a Collection of the Best French Recipes Arranged and Adapted for English Households*.

81   From a manuscript in the Berg Collection, *Letters* (1) 253n.

82   [8 May 1837] letter to W.H. Ainsworth, *Letters* (1) 257.

83   8 May 1837 letter to G. Thomson, *Letters* (1) 256, 257.

84   8 May 1837 letter to R. Bentley, *Letters* (1) 257, 258.

85   17 May 1837 letter to T. Beard, *Letters* (1) 259, 260.

86   30 May [1837] letter to Miss Mary Scott Hogarth, 'New Letters of Mary Hogarth and her Sister Catherine', *Dickensian* 63 (1967) 80.

87   *Letters* (1) 261n.

88   C.G.L. DuCann, *The Love-Lives of Charles Dickens* (London: Frederick Muller, 1961) 74–77.

89   Lillian Nayder, 'The Widowhood of Catherine Dickens', *Dickens Studies Annual* 32 (2002) 291.

90   *Letters* (1) 598n.

91   The literary and drama critic was Paul E.D. Forgues, *Letters* (3) 502n.

92   *Letters* (4) 72n.

93   J. Shaw, 'Dickens in Devonshire Terrace', *Dickensian* 7 (1911) 235. Dickens wrote to Amédée Pichot, the French editor of *Revue Britannique*, saying 'I shall hope to have an early opportunity of presenting you to Mrs. Dickens and my six live volumes now in private collection': 30 Dec. 1846 letter to A. Pichot, *Letters* (4) 687.

94   *Letters* (4) 72n; Shaw 235.

95   [25 Nov.] 1839 letter to J. Forster, *Letters* (1) 605; 30 Nov. 1839 letter to W. Snoxell, *Letters* (1) 608, 609.

96   *Letters* (1) 645, 646.

97   *Letters* (4) 705.

98   The manufacturer was probably John Wilson at 253 Strand who painted floor cloths: *Letters* (3) 306.

99   20 May 1845 letter to T. Mitton, *Letters* (4) 312.

100   20 May 1845 letter to T. Mitton, *Letters* (4) 312.

101   14 April 1845 letter to T. Mitton, *Letters* (4) 297, 298.

102   *Letters* (4) 707.

103   *Letters* (4) 707.

104   *Letters* (3) 306n.

105   7 Aug. 1842 letter to F. Dickens, *Letters* (3) 306.

106   1 Sept. 1842 letter to C. Felton, *Letters* (3) 316.

107   7 Aug. 1842 letter to F. Dickens *Letters* (3) 305, 306.

108   8 Sept. 1847 letter to T. Mitton, *Letters* (5) 162.

109   10 Sept. 1847 letter to J. Barnes, *Letters* (5) 163.

110   *Letters* (8) 254n.

111   28 Jan. 1851 letter to Burdett Coutts, *Letters* (6) 269.

112   18 April 1851 letter to F. Stone, *Letters* (6) 357.

113   14 July 1851 letter to H. Austin, *Letters* (6) 431.

114   *Letters* (6) 440n. By September 8, 1852, the negotiations were completed for the purchase

price of £1,542, but in the meantime the renovations had begun.

115   9 July 1856 letter to N. Powell, *Letters* (8) 157.

116   7 Sept. 1851 letter to H. Austin, *Letters* (6) 478, 479.

117   11 Sept. 1851 letter to Mrs C. Dickens, *Letters* (6) 481.

118   24 Sept. 1851 letter to H. Austin, *Letters* (6) 490, 481n.

119   Appendix C 'List of Imitation Book-Backs Sent to T. R. Eeles on 22 October 1851', *Letters* (6) 851.

120   5 Oct. 1851 letter to H. Austin, *Letters* (6) 505.

121   14 Oct. 1851 letter to H. Austin, *Letters* (6) 519–521.

122   14 Oct. 1851 letter to H. Austin, *Letters* (6) 520.

123   25 Oct. 1851 letter to H. Austin, *Letters* (6) 526.

124   *Letters* (6) 469n, 470n. Marcus Stone created eight wood-engravings for the Illustrated Library Edition of *Great Expectations* and forty wood-engravings, including the wrapper, for *Our Mutual Friend*.

125   1 Oct. 1851 letter to H. Austin, *Letters* (6) 501, 502.

126   14 Oct. 1851 letter to H. Austin, *Letters* (6) 521.

127   28 Sept. 1851 letter to H. Austin, *Letters* (6) 498.

128   17 Oct. 1851 letter to H. Austin, *Letters* (6) 523.

129   31 Oct. 1851 letter to Mrs Watson, *Letters* (6) 533.

130   13 Nov. 1851 letter to Mrs C. Dickens, *Letters* (6) 537.

131   6 Oct. 1851 letter to R. Wood, *Letters* (6) 507, 508.

132   1 May 1855 letter to C. Ellis, *Letters* (7) 602.

133   6 Feb. 57 letter to Miss Burdett Coutts *Letters* (8) 276.

134   25 Nov. 1851 letter to Mrs Gaskell, *Letters* (6) 545.

135   21 Dec. 1851 letter to Mrs Gaskell, *Letters* (6) 558.

136   [?] & 30 Dec. 1851 letter to Emily [Tagart] from Mrs Gaskell, Chapple 175.

137   Henry Morley, 'Pottery and Porcelain', *Household Words* 4 (1851) 32; auction catalogue for August 10–13, 1970 (Charles Dickens Museum archives) 33, 34.

138   Henry S. Solly, *The Life of Henry Morley, LLD* (London: Edward Arnold, 1898) 200, 301.

139   14 Mar. 1856 letter to Miss G. Hogarth, *Letters* (8) 70, 71.

140   15 March 1857 letter to W. Macready, *Letters* (8) 302.

141   15 Feb. and 6 March 1857 letters to H. Austin, *Letters* (8) 283, 296.

142   13 May 1857 letter to Lord Stanhope, *Letters* (8) 325.

143   17 May 1857 letters to T. Beard and W. Collins, *Letters* (8) 326, 327.

144   14 May 1857 letter to B. Webster, *Letters* (8) 326.

145   12 May 1857 letter to H.C. Andersen, *Letters* (8) 323.

146   3 April 1857 letter to H.C. Andersen, *Letters* (8) 307.

147   Elias Bredsdorff, *Hans Andersen and Charles Dickens: A Friendship and its Dissolution* (Copenhagen: Rosenkilde and Bagger, 1956) 109, 110.

148   Bredsdorff 109, 110.

149   Quoted from William Bloch's diary for 12 April 1872. Bloch travelled with Andersen and he recorded their conversation about Andersen's last visit fourteen years earlier and his subsequent relationship with Dickens: Bredsdorff 127, 128.

150   10 Jan. and 3 Oct. 1856 letters to Miss Burdett Coutts, *Letters* (8) 16, 198.

151   20 July 1857 letter to Miss Burdett Coutts, *Letters* (8) 380–1.

152   20 June 1857 letter to Miss Burdett Coutts, *Letters* (8) 356–7.

153   17 Aug. 1857 letter to F. Stone, *Letters* (8) 412.

154   14 Feb. 1857 letter to W. Collins, *Letters* (8) 282.

155   13 August 1857 letters to W. Wills and T. Fairbairn, *Letters* (8) 410, 409.

156   It should be noted that this letter is no longer extant and is thought to have been destroyed by Forster after the biography was written. [?3 Sept. 1857] letter to J Forster,

Letters (8) 430.

157   11 Oct. 1857 letter to Mrs Cornelius, *Letters* (8) 465.

158   13 Oct. 1857 letter to J. Buckstone, *Letters* (8) 465, 467.

159   11 Feb. 1858 letter to F. Régnier, *Letters* (8) 519.

160   14 April 1858 letter to Mrs Hogge, *Letters* (8) 545, 546.

161   12 May 1858 letter to S. Fraser, 10 May 1858 letter to Miss G. Hogarth, *Letters* (8) 563, 561.

162   Lillian Nayder, 'The Widowhood of Catherine Dickens', *Dickens Studies Annual* 32 (2002) 277–298.

Notes to Chapter III, pages 139–157.

1   J.W.T. Ley, ed., *The Life of Charles Dickens* by John Forster (London: Whitefriars Press, Ltd., 1928) 853, 854.

2   Despite the love of the ocean and Broadstairs beaches, Dickens may not have been able to swim or at least swim well. When his eldest son Charley needed to pass a swimming test before using the boats at Eton, Dickens wrote to Beard, who was 'amphibious', and asked him to teach his son 'the noble art': 22 May 1850 letter to T. Beard, *Letters* (6) 71.

3   Charles Dickens, 'Our Water Place', *Household Words* 3 (1851) 433.

4   1 Sept. 1843 letter to C. Felton, *Letters* (3) 548.

5   See also Lillian Nayder, 'The Other Dickens and America: Catherine in 1842', *Dickens Quarterly* 19 (2002) 141–150.

6   26 Sept. 1841 letter to F. Dickens, *Letters* (2) 391, 392.

7   21 Sept. 1841 letter to W. Macready, *Letters* (2) 387, 388.

8   26 September 1841 letter to F. Dickens, *Letters* (2) 391, 392.

9   Her brother died on 24 October 1841 and Dickens regretted giving up the grave next to Mary's for his brother-in-law's burial: 24 Oct. 1841 letter to Mrs Hogarth, *Letters* (2) 408.

10   The Dickenses' tour of North America took them from Boston (22 January–5 February 1842), west to Worcester and Springfield, Massachusetts, and south to Hartford and New Haven, Connecticut and Yale College (5–12 February); New York City (12 February–5 March); Philadelphia, Pennsylvania (5–9 March); Washington, DC, and then to Richmond and Fredericksburg, Virginia; on to Baltimore, Maryland, and by canal to Pittsburgh, Pennsylvania (9 March–1 April). They travelled south-west again to Cincinnati, Ohio, and then to the westernmost points by steam boat from Cairo to St. Louis and the Looking Glass Prairie in Missouri, then returned eastward by stopping in Columbus and Sandusky, Ohio and Buffalo, New York; then visited both the American and Canadian sides of Niagara Falls (26 April–4 May). In May, they travelled through Canada visiting Queenstown, Toronto, Cobourg, Kingston, Montreal, Three Rivers and Quebec. (See Goldie Morgentaler, 'Dickens in Canada', *Dickens Quarterly* 19 (2002) 151–159.) During the last leg of the expedition, they travelled down the North River to Whitehall, Albany, and West Point in New York State (1–7 June, 1842) and sailed home from New York City on the *George Washington* to Liverpool, England. After nearly six months on tour, they finally returned to London on June 29th: *Letters* (3) xxiii, xxiv, and map on xxviii.

11   13 Dec. 1841 letter to A. D'Orsay, *Letters* (2) 497.

12   14 March 1842 letter to C. Felton, *Letters* (3) 130. The Dickenses rented out their home, after Fred, the four children including the baby, and several servants moved to No. 25 Osnaburgh Street near their friends, the Macready family: *Letters* (2) 392n.

13   3 Jan. 1842 letter to D. Maclise, *Letters* (3) 8, 9.

14   If Catherine took the 'womanish' advice that Harriet Martineau offered her through their mutual friend Mrs William Macready (née Catherine Frances Atkins), she dressed for the

voyage in a close-fitting quilted black silk cap and wore a wadded, quilted petticoat hidden under her dress for warmth. Her hands, covered by horsehair gloves, would have clutched a flat-sided earthenware bottle filled with hot water for the frigid January crossing of the Atlantic: 29 Dec. 1841 letter from Miss Martineau to Mrs Macready, Valerie Sanders, *Harriet Martineau: Selected Letters* (Oxford: Clarendon Press, 1990) 62, 63. [See Pierre Morand's sketch of Catherine well wrapped in her shawl, plate 4. Noel C. Peyrouton, 'Re: Memoir of an *American Notes* Original', *Dickens Studies* 4 (1968) 24, 25, plate 1.]

15 Noel C. Peyrouton, 'Reminiscence of Charles Dickens' First Visit to America By a Fellow Passenger', *Dickens Studies* 4 (1968) 27.

16 30 Jan. 1842 letter from Mrs Dickens to Mrs H. Bernett, *Letters* (3) 629.

17 E.L. Pierce, *Memoir and Letters of Charles Sumner*, vol. 2 (Boston: Robert Brothers, 1893) 201. Sumner, who became Dickens's principal Boston escort, shared an office with George Hillard. Other faculty members who shared anti-slavery views, such as Henry Wadsworth Longfellow and Cornelius C. Felton, accompanied Dickens and made introductions: *Letters* (3) 21n.

18 Allan Nevins, ed., *The Diary of Philip Hone (1828–1851)*, vol. 2 (New York: Dodd, Mead & Co., 1927) 583, 584.

19 Nevins 584–8; *Letters* (3) 71n, 72n.

20 Nevins 586, 587.

21 Mrs Sarah Hale, *The Good Housekeeper or the Way to Live Well and to be Well While We Live Containing Directions for Choosing and Preparing Food* (Boston: Weeks, Jordan & Co., 1839) 86.

22 *Letters* (3) 94n.

23 Nevins 589, 590; Julia Ward Howe, *Reminiscences 1819–1899* (Boston: Houghton, Mifflin & Co., 1899) 25, 26. In England, the female guests were also relegated to an upper floor gallery that overlooked the banquet hall. The June 5, 1844 benefit for the Sanatorium was among the first events to change women's seating; Dickens earnestly advocated, 'The dinner is to comprize [sic] the new feature of Ladies at the tables with the Gentlemen', to Clarkson Stanfield whom he hoped would act as Steward. (The ladies' tickets at 12 shillings and the gentlemen's for a guinea were sold for the London Tavern dinner): 30 April 1844 letter, *Letters* (4) 116.

24 *Letters* (3) 20n.

25 30 Jan. 1842 letter to Stephen Longfellow, Edward L. Tucker, 'References in Longfellow's *Journals* (1856–1882) to Charles Dickens', *Dickens Studies Annual* 24 (1996) 198.

26 Nevins 588.

27 Robert Lucid, ed., *The Journal of Richard Henry Dana, Jr.*, vol. 1 (Cambridge, MA: Belnap Press, 1968) 61. I thank Joseph M. Carlin for pointing out that Dana's work, *Two Years Before the Mast* (1840) was an early and significant American 'food book'.

28 Anonymous, *The Boz Ball: Account of the Ball Given in Honor of Charles Dickens* (Cedar Rapids, Iowa: privately printed, 1908) 40. *The Aurora-Extra* newspaper wrote the parody about the New York City event on Valentine's Day 1842 given in Dickens's honour at the Park Theater. The facetious account exemplifies the public's relentless fascination with the Dickenses. The piece continues: 'She was, of course, the star of the evening, second in brightness. Great interest was felt on seeing her, the world being aware that she had loved the leading star of the night without knowing his "place in the heavens", and wedded him before his rising. And besides this, there was the interest felt always in the wife of a man of genius – priestess as she is to the bright fire – nearest and dearest to the wondrous heart which supplies to his imaginations all their reality – model as she must be for the subtlest delineations of pure love, the truest and fairest features of his pictures of women. She has risen with him, she and her children, a cluster of stars around him, and the world is

perhaps not overstepping the limit of delicacy in bending, on the whole constellation, the telescope of affectionate curiosity' (p. 63).

29   J.F. Jameson, ed., 'Correspondence of John C. Calhoun', *Annual Report of the American Historical Association* 2 (1899) 506, in *Letters* (3) 132n, 133n.

30   Elizabeth Tyler Coleman, *Priscilla Cooper-Tyler and the American Scene 1816–1889* (University of Alabama Press, 1955) 96, 97.

31   15, 16 & [17] April 1842 letter to J. Forster, *Letters* (3) 196.

32   12 May 1842 letter to J. Forster, *Letters* (3) 236.

33   10–11 Aug. 1844 letter to J. Forster, *Letters* (4) 175.

34   Slater (1983) 116.

35   15 March 1842 letter to J. Forster, *Letters* (3) 132.

36   24 & 26 April 1842 letters to J. Forster, *Letters* (3) 204, 205.

37   *Letters* (3) 205n.

38   On the six-hour passage from New Haven to New York City, the Dickenses socialized with their new Harvard friend Cornelius Conway Felton. They 'ate all the cold pork and cheese' (probably as sandwiches) and 'drank all the porter on board': 17 Feb. 1842 letter to J. Forster, *Letters* (3) 69, 70n.

39   28 March 1842 letter J. Forster, *Letters* (3) 169, 170.

40   16 April 1842 letter to J. Forster, *Letters* (3) 201.

41   Nearly a century and a half later, his great-grandson was introduced to the Mint Julep in New Orleans at the oldest American Pickwick Club (founded in 1857) and enjoyed the drink as much. Cedric Dickens, *Drinking With Dickens* (New York: New Amsterdam Books, 1980) 62, 83.

42   23 March 1842 letter to William [Guy], *Letters* (3) 166. Dickens wrote: 'I am truly obliged to you for the beautiful and delicious mint julep you have so kindly sent me. It's quite a mercy that I knew what it was. I have tasted it, but reserve further proceedings until the arrival of Washington Irving whom I expect to dine with me, tete a tete [sic]; and who will help to drink your health, with many thanks to you.'

43   Toynbee 267.

44   A special thanks to David Parker for providing background details concerning mint juleps being served in the Dickens household; Cedric Dickens 11, 83.

45   See the chapter 'American Sensations' in Edward Hewett and W. F. Axton, *Convivial Dickens: The Drinks of Dickens & His Times* (Athens, OH: Ohio University Press, 1983) 156–175. The authors also note that the dog given to them by American friends was named for the drink Timber Doodle and later appears as Mr. Snittle Timberry in *Martin Chuzzlewit*.

46   Other drinks included the Sherry Cobbler, Egg-nog, and Brandy Smash: Sarah Freeman, *Mutton and Oysters: The Victorians and Their Food* (London: Victor Gollancz, Ltd., 1989) 106, 107.

47   Catherine was seven months pregnant with their fifth child, and just as the question had been posed for their trip to North America, they debated about taking the new-born (due by mid-January) or leaving the baby in the care of Catherine's mother (1 & [2] Nov. 1843 letters to J. Forster, *Letters* (3) 587, 591). Catherine had suffered with the extreme heat that summer and through her ninth month (17 Sept. 1843 letter to T. Mitton and 26 Dec. 1843 letter to W. Behnes, *Letters* (3) 566, 612). By the new year Dickens wrote, 'We have not yet achieved that family performance I told you of; which I expect will come off in the course of next week, Kate is not quite as well as usual: being nervous and dull. But her health is perfectly good, and I am sure she might rally, if she would. I shall be much relieved when it is well over' (2 Jan. 1844 letter to C. Felton, *Letters* (4) 3). Finally, on the 15 January 1844, Francis Jeffrey Dickens was born. 'Nurses, wet and dry; apothecaries; mothers-in-law; babbies, with all the sweet (and chaste) delights of private life; these, my countrymen, are

hard to leave', but in the next breath, he accepted a dinner invitation for an outing in Richmond: 17 Jan. 1844 letter to J. Forster, *Letters* (4) 21.

48   24 March 1844 letter to A. Fletcher, *Letters* (4) 81.

49   [20 July 1844] letter to J. Forster, *Letters* (4) 156, 159.

50   22 July 1844 letter to D. Maclise, *Letters* (4) 161. The Genoa variety turns a light green when ripe.

51   [22 July 1844] letter to J. Forster, *Letters* (4) 157.

52   [12] Aug. 1844 letter to Mitton, *Letters* (4) 176; 24 Aug. 1844 letter to J. Forster, *Letters* (4) 182.

53   My thanks to David Parker for pointing out that the Hogarth family was familiar with the Italian language, perhaps as an accompanying interest in music. A book in Italian, with an inscription from her father, was given to Georgina when she was in her teens, and was recently acquired by the Charles Dickens Museum.

54   [20 July] 1844 letter to J. Forster, *Letters* (4) 157.

55   [10, 11 Aug. 1844] letter to J. Forster and [12] Aug. 1844 letter to T. Mitton, *Letters* (4) 175, 176.

56   [31 Aug. 1844] letter to J. Forster, *Letters* (4) 188.

57   [30 Sept. 1844] letter to J. Forster, *Letters* (4) 195.

58   16 Nov. 1844 letter to D. Jerrold, *Letters* (4) 219.

59   [17–18 Nov. 1844] letter to J. Forster, *Letters* (4) 222, 223.

60   Cochineal is a brilliant red dye made from pulverizing the bodies of female scale insects (*Dactylopius coccus*); indigo creates a dark blue to greyish-purple dye from plants in the genus *Indigofera*; carmine is a crimson to purplish-red pigment derived from cochineal, and gamboges is a resin from trees in the genus *Garcinia* which produces a strong golden yellow pigment.

61   W.A. Jarrin, *The Italian Confectioner: or Complete Economy of Desserts According to the Most Modern and Approved Practice* (London: E.S. Ebers & Co., 1844) 339, 340.

62   [17–18 Nov. 1844] letter to J. Forster, *Letters* (4) 223.

63   28 Nov. 1844 letter to Mrs Dickens, *Letters* (4) 231.

64   17 & 22 Feb. 1845 letter to T. Mitton, *Letters* (4) 269.

65   17 & 22 Feb. 1845 letter to T. Mitton, *Letters* (4) 269.

66   17 & 22 Feb. 1845 letter to T. Mitton, *Letters* (4) 270, 271.

67   The first extant letter where Dickens acknowledged his wife's pregnancy said: 'a coming event which I hadn't reckoned on, is casting its shadow before Mrs. Dickens in a very disconcerting manner' was on 28 April 1845 to Lord Robertson; Alfred D'Orsay Tennyson was born on 28 October 1845: *Letters* (4) 301.

68   9 May 1845 letter to D. Maclise. The children's nurse, Charlotte, also had 'found a lover', but since he was an English servant, there were no legal complications when they returned home with the family and married: *Letters* (4) 306, 307. As an aside, Dickens's jottings dating from January 1855, known as 'the Berg Notebook' in the New York Public Library collections, recorded plot lines including 'The man who marries his cook at last, after being so desperately knowing about the sex': Norman Page, *A Dickens Companion* (New York: Schocken Books, 1984) 350.

69   12 May 1845 letter to J. Forster, *Letters* (4) 309.

70   Jane and her husband evidently returned to England before 1851. Dickens's 25 April 1851 letter to Mr de la Rue informed him that their former cook was happily married and living with her sister. Ultimately the couple married in both the Protestant and Roman Catholic churches: *Letters* (6) 364.

71   After arriving at the Hotel Gibbon in Lausanne on June 11th, Dickens began looking for a house. At first, he shunned the small villas usually sought by the English, but ultimately rented Rosemont, 'the doll's house', he first viewed before the grander places. Rosemont

was within a ten-minute walk of the hotel and had 'two pretty little salons, a dining-room, hall, and kitchen, on the ground floor.' Upstairs, a spare room accommodated frequent guests, and the study had French windows that opened onto a balcony for a breathtaking view of the lake and the surrounding mountains. A profusion of roses covered the bowers and a two-room pavilion that stood in their garden. Dickens observed, 'There are all manner of walks, vineyards, green lanes, cornfields, and pastures full of hay' commenting that it was as remarkably neat as in England' and the town had many bookshops: [13 or 14] June 1846 letter to J. Forster, *Letters* (4) 560, 561.

72   [28} June 1846 letter to J. Forster, *Letters* (4) 575.

73   9 and 10 Aug. 1846 letter to J. Forster, *Letters* (4) 601.

74   Slater 109.

75   Mamie Dickens, *Charles Dickens by His Eldest Daughter* (1889 2nd ed., reprinted Brooklyn, NY: Haskell House Pub., Ltd., 1977) 76.

76   *Letters* (4) 574n.

77   Diary entry for 29 June 1846, MS Commander Michael Saunders Watson in *Letters* (4) 574n.

78   *Letters* (4) 574n. Richard Watson kept a diary referring to the group's activities, as did Christiana Weller Thompson, the pianist whom Catherine Dickens helped. The Thompsons made an extended visit to Lausanne from Aug. 1846 and Christina noted social engagements with the Dickens family.

79   22–23 Nov. 1846 letter to J. Forster, *Letters* (4) 659.

80   27 Nov. 1846 letter to R. Watson, *Letters* (4) 666.

81   2 Dec. 1846 letter to T. Thompson, *Letters* (4) 672.

82   29 December 1846 letter to Charles Sheridan, *Letters* (4) 686.

83   11 June 1853 letter to E.M. Ward, *Letters* (7) 95, 96.

84   20 Aug. 1854 letter to H. Austin, *Letters* (7) 401.

85   18 June 1853 letter to W. Wills, *Letters* (7) 99.

86   26 June [1853] letter to John Forster, *Letters* (7) 103.

87   26 June [1853] letter to J. Forster, *Letters* (7) 103.

88   24 June 1853 letter to P. Cunningham, *Letters* (7) 102.

89   22 June 1854 letter to Miss Burdett Coutts, *Letters* (7) 359, 360.

90   16 Oct. 1855 letter to Mrs Dickens, *Letters* (7) 719, 720.

91   21 Oct. 1855 letter to W Wills, *Letters* (7) 723–5.

92   George Augustus Sala, *Things I Have Seen and People I Have Known,* vol. 1 (London: Cassell and Co., Ltd., 1894) 112.

93   19 Jan. 1856 letter to W. Collins, *Letters* (8) 30.

94   The 'epicurians' were thought to be the Régniers: 8 April 1856 letter to Miss Power, *Letters* (8) 84, 85.

95   According to George Sala, Dickens 'exhibited a strong partiality for feasting at the Palais Royal restaurants, which at that period had not completely lost the prestige which at present seems wholly to have departed them. The Boulevards restaurants he thought too noisy, and their cuisine he deemed slightly too greasy,' but under the arcades of the Palais Royal there was Véry's, Trois Frères Provençaux, the Café Corazza or the Restaurant d'Ouix. After dinner they 'would sometimes go for an hour to one of the great Boulevard cafés; but more frequently we would repair to the theatre' where Dickens preferred the light operatic burlesques at Bouffes Parisiens: Sala (1894) 129–131. Trois Frères Provençaux was originally run by three brothers-in-law, Maneille, Barthélemy, and Simon who came from the Durance valley in upper Provence, and developed it from a mediocre establishment located on the undistinguished rue Helvétius in 1786. Under Maneille's management, they moved to a more elegant address at the galerie de Beaujolais with a view of the Palais-Royal gardens, and revamped the menu to offer their regional classics

'uprooted from peasant origins' like bouillabaisse and brandade of salt cod, which established an appreciative clientele, like the Dickens family. Unfortunately, the large English clientele the restaurant attracted, according to Balzac and other French writers, was also to blame for its decline: Jean-Paul Aron, *The Art of Eating in France: Manners and Menus in the Nineteenth Century*, trans. Nina Rootes (London: Peter Owen Ltd., 1975) 19, 26, 27, 45.

96   22 April 1856 letter to W. Collins, *Letters* (8) 95.

97   7 Jan. 1856 letter to Madame Viardot, *Letters* (8) 13; [20 Jan. 1856] letter to J. Forster, ibid. 33, 34.

98   [20 Jan. 1856] letter to J. Forster, *Letters* (7) 33. Girardin (1806–1881) was the illegitimate son of Count Alexandre de Girardin and with the publication of his first, autobiographical novel *Émile* in 1827, he took his father's name. Girardin founded *Le Voleur* (1828) as a monthly review of the arts and sciences, began establishing himself in Parisian society and in 1831 married the writer Delphine Gay. He had numerous other successes as a publisher, particularly with *La Presse*, which he founded in 1836 and priced so competitively that the circulation soared and it became enormously profitable (2002 Enyclopædia Britannica http://search.eb.com/eb/article?eu=37635 accessed December 16, 2002).

99   22 April 1856 letter to W. Collins, *Letters* (8) 95; [17?–22 April 1856 letter to [Rev. J. White], ibid. 97.

Notes to Chapter IV, pages 158–174.

1   Theresa M. McBride, *The Domestic Revolution: The Modernization of Household Service in England and France 1820–1920* (New York: Holmes & Meier Pub., Inc., 1976) 12–15.

2   McBride 12.

3   Lillian Nayder, *Wilkie Collins* (New York: Twayne Pub., 1997) 72, 73. In 1850, liberal MPs began debates on women's property rights and, seven years later, the Divorce and Matrimonial Causes Act was passed allowing husbands to divorce their wives for adultery, and wives to divorce their adulterous spouse if there was cruelty, bigamy, incest, or bestiality involved.

4   'His Eldest Daughter' [Mamie Dickens], *Charles Dickens* (1889 second ed., reprinted Brooklyn, NY: Haskell House Pub. Ltd., 1977) 102, 103.

5   20 May 1845 letter to T. Mitton, *Letters* (4) 313, 314.

6   5 July 1845 letter to D'Orsay, *Letters* (4) 325.

7   [8 July 1845] letter to J. Forster, *Letters* (4) 329.

8   McBride 12.

9   Isabella Beeton, *Mrs. Beeton's Every Day Cookery and Housekeeping Book* (1865, facsimile ed., NY: Gallery Books, 1984) xi–xiv.

10   McBride 14.

11   1 Jan. 1842 letter to Messrs Chapman & Hall, *Letters* (3) 2.

12   'Charley had previously confided to a confidential friend of his (a washerwoman) …': 31 July 1842 letter to W.H. Prescott, *Letters* (3) 295. Apparently the identity of the woman was of some interest, Dickens had two notes asking if she was Mr Mantalini's wife, which apparently she was not. Dickens's inquiry highlights the distant relationship between the employer, the household servants, and low-level employees: *Letters* (2) 435n.

13   23 Dec. 1856 letter to T. Beard, *Letters* (8) 243.

14   28 Sept. 1842 letter to H. Austin, *Letters* (3) 333.

15   5 July 1845 letter to D'Orsay, *Letters* (4) 325.

16   21 March 1850 letter to F. Evans, *Letters* (6) 70.

17   *Letters* (2) 217n.

18   19 Nov. 1838 letter to J. Forster, *Letters* (1) 457.

19   [22 Feb. 1839] letter to J. Forster, *Letters* (1) 511, 320n.

20   *Letters* (1) 521n.

21   1 Sep. 1842 letter to C. Felton, *Letters* (3) 316, 317.

22   21 Oct. 1856 letter to W. Wills, *Letters* (8) 212.

23   *Letters* (8) 283n.

24   20 April 1854 letter to W. Wills, *Letters* (7) 319; *Letters* (8) 540n.

25   17 Jan. 44 letter to J. Forster after Francis's birth on the 15th, *Letters* (4) 21.

26   Judging from the cheque book entries, the expenses during confinement ranged between
      £33 and £40. The entry for Dec. 6th [1839], 'House (including all bills during Kate's
      confinement)' £45. House expenses generally ranged from £4 or 3s, but were as high as
      £12. Dr Pickthorn's 'fee on Kate's confinement £4' was listed separately, as was payment to
      CD's 'Mother – attending Kate in her confinement' £5, and to the nurses: *Letters* (1) 644–
      646.

27   *Letters* (1) 644–646.

28   26 Jan. 1837 letter from Miss M. Hogarth to Miss Mary Scott Hogarth, 'New Letters of
      Mary Hogarth and her Sister Catherine', *Dickensian* 63 (1967) 77.

29   *Letters* (1) 644–646.

30   14 March 1842 letter to C. Felton, *Letters* (3) 130.

31   9 May 1845 letter to D. Maclise, *Letters* (4) 306.

32   11 Aug. 1845 letter to Messrs Bradbury & Evans, *Letters* (4) 352.

33   25 June 1846 letter to Miss Burdett Coutts, *Letters* (4) 570.

34   10 Aug. 1852 letter from C. Knight to his daughter Mary, Alice A. Clowes, *Charles Knight
      A Sketch* (London: Richard Bentley & Son, 1892) 124, 125.

35   22 April 1856 letter to W. Collins, *Letters* (8) 97.

36   Dickens's letter of 23 August 1855, accompanying their wedding gift, congratulated Miss
      Brown on her marriage, *Letters* (7) 693, 694.

37   16 Dec. 55 letter to Mrs Dickens, *Letters* (7) 764; 5 Feb. 1856 letter to Mrs Dickens, *Letters*
      (8) 42.

38   26 Sept. 1841 letter to F. Dickens, *Letters* (2) 392.

39   Anon., *The Dickens House Museum* (Banbury: Cheney & Sons, *ca.* 1980) 16.

40   22 April 1856 letter to W. Collins, *Letters* (8) 97.

41   21 June 1856 letter to T. Beard, *Letters* (8) 138.

42   29 July 1856 letter to W. Collins, *Letters* (8) 168.

43   8 Nov. 1856 letter to Mrs Dickens, *Letters* (8) 220.

44   Catherine Dickens hired Sarah Hatfield as her cook and Matilda Albright as her
      housemaid. The servants later married and were replaced by Marie Bywaters and Emily
      Brooks. Thanks to Lillian Nayder for this information.

45   Common remedies, or those prescribed by the attending physician, such as mustard
      poultices to relieve pain, mustard baths for scrapes and bread-poultices to treat the bites of
      leeches used during medical treatment were all made at home. Others were simple
      concoctions like Dickens's well-known drink for maintaining stamina, 'a tumbler-glass,
      containing the yolk of a newly laid egg, discreetly mixed with Golden Sherry'. This is the
      basic recipe for cold flip, so the addition of nutmeg and powdered sugar may have been
      understood: 1 April 1842 letter to W. Macready, *Letters* (3) 174. Chichester punch and
      orange brandy assuaged a cough and cold: 10 Dec. 1847 letter to Lyttelton, *Letters* (5) 207.

46   25 Sept. 1849 letter to F. Evans concerning John Leech's accident when he was knocked
      around by a large wave and hit his head badly while vacationing with the Dickenses at
      Bonchurch during the summer, *Letters* (5) 614, 615.

47   26 Sept. 1849 letter to M. Lemon, *Letters* (5) 615.

48 13 Feb. 1841 letter to G. Cattermole, *Letters* (2) 211.

49 Dickens had insisted on calling in a specialist to give Catherine chloroform, a rather controversial aid, to ease the labour pain during Henry's birth: 2 Feb. 1849 letter to W. Macready, *Letters* (5) 486, 487.

50 George Newlin, *Every Thing in Dickens: Ideas and Subjects Discussed by Charles Dickens in His Complete Works* (Westport, CT: Greenwood Press, 1996) 159.

51 Alexis Soyer, *The Modern Housewife or Ménagère* (London: Simpkin, Marshall, & Co., 1850) 405.

52 *Letters* (4) 706–711.

53 *Letters* (4) 710, 711.

54 *Letters* (4) 710, 711.

55 *Letters* (4) 709.

56 Other common equipment which was not listed in the 1844 inventory, but implied in the recipes or letters, included larding needles, soup ladles, wire baskets, meat hooks, scoops for dry pantry items, or wooden equipment like potato or turnip mashers, spoons, ladles, egg beaters, and a spaddle (round short stick flattened at one end and used to cream butter and sugar). A wooden kneading-trough for yeast doughs, cake or bread boxes for storage, basketry (for market and laundry) or demijohns (large basket-covered bottles for vinegar, treacle, etc.) were all absent from the list. Likewise pantry items, such as barrels of anchovies, flour, sugar and so on were excluded so there is no record of common provisions.

57 For routine kitchen tasks, the cook would have had a supply of coarse linen for use as tablecloths, and very thick linen (called Russian sheeting) cut into squares for pudding-cloths and for making dumplings. Yard-long linen kitchen towels and dish cloths, often recycled from old bath towels or bed sheets, would have been used to wash and wipe glassware and china. The used cloths ended life as a pot scrubbers.

58 George Dodd, 'Pot and Kettle Philosophy', *Household Words* 8 (1853) 333–336.

59 Caroline Cookson, 'The Technology of Cooking in the British Isles, 1600 to 1950; Part II: Gas and Electricity', *Petits Propos Culinaires* 3 (1979) 47.

60 Caroline Cookson, 'The Technology of Cooking in the British Isles, 1600 to 1950; Part I: Before the Use of Gas', *Petits Propos Culinaires* 1 (1979) 33–35.

61 Jennifer Davies, *The Victorian Kitchen*, large print ed. (Oxford: Clio Press, 1991) 57

62 Cookson 33, 34.

63 *Letters* (4) 711.

64 *Letters* (4) 709, 711.

65 Davies 56–58.

66 *Letters* (6) 523n. Ice from the United States was shipped routinely from June 1843. In a Feb. 26, 1844, Dickens commented in a letter to his wife that a block of Boston ice weighing fifty pounds was set on the ship's table in the HMS *Britannia's* saloon: *Letters* (4) 51. See Elizabeth David, *Harvest of the Cold Months: The Social History of Ice & Ices* (London: Michael Joseph, Ltd. 1994) 173, 337, 338.

67 Henry Morley and William H. Wills, 'Ice', *Household Words* 3 (1851) 482.

68 George Newlin, *Every Thing in Dickens: Ideas and Subjects Discussed by Charles Dickens in His Complete Works* (Westport, CT: Greenwood Press, 1996) 139, 140. Dickens issued *Our Mutual Friend* in nineteen monthly parts beginning in May 1864 to November 1865. Bella, and Dickens's later heroines, have been attributed to his involvement with Ellen Ternan. The character's name Bella was considered a word play on her name, as was the surname Wilfer for wilful: Norman Page, *A Dickens Companion* (New York: Schocken Books, 1984) 225–238.

69 See *The Dinner Question* by 'Tabitha Tickletooth' (1860, facsimile ed. Totnes: Prospect Books, 1999). See also Jean-Paul Aron, 'The Art of Using Leftovers: Paris, 1850–1900', in *Food and Drink in History,* Robert Forster and Orest Ranum, eds. (Baltimore: Johns

Hopkins University Press, 1979) 98–108.

70   Alexis Soyer, *The Modern Housewife or Ménagère* (London: Simpkin, Marshall & Co., 1850) 202–288.

71   28 January 1850 letter to Miss Burdett Coutts, *Letters* (6) 17.

72   Henry Morley and William H. Wills, 'Not Very Common Things', *Household Words* 14 (1856) 39–41.

73   Morley and Wills, 40. See also the 1856 Dickens-Coutts correspondence in *Letters* (8) and Appendix C 'Miss Coutts's Prizes For Common Things' on pages 731–735.

74   William H. Wills, 'A Good Plain Cook', *Household Words* 1 (1850) 139–141.

75   Harriet Martineau, 'The New School for Wives', *Household Words* 5 (1852) 84.

76   The School of Cookery and Restaurant was located near the Christ Church schools on Albany Street, Regent's Park, in a small shop. The names of the founders were not disclosed: William H. Wills, 'A School For Cooks', *Household Words* 16 (1857) 138.

77   Wills 138.

78   Wills 138.

79   Eliza Lynn (Linton) and William H. Wills, 'Common Cookery', *Household Words* 13 (1856) 40–46.

80   Lynn and Wills 46.

81   Eliza (Lynn) Linton, 'Uncommon Good Eating', *Household Words*, 19 (1859) 289–293.

82   Eliza Lynn (Linton), 'Obsolete Cookery', *Household Words* 11 (1855) 24.

83   William Hardman, 'The Roll of Cookery', *Household Words* 15 (1857) 550.

Notes to Chapter V, pages 175–201.

1   This includes a chapter in his great-grandson Cedric Dickens's book *Dining with Dickens* (Goring-on-Thames, England: Elvendon Press, 1984). See also David Parker's 'Dickens and the American Christmas', *Dickens Quarterly* 19 (2002) 160–169.

2   Mary Dickens, *My Father as I Recall Him* (Westminster: Roxburghe Press, 1897) 25, 26.

3   [Mary Dickens], *Charles Dickens by His Eldest Daughter*, (1889 2nd ed., reprinted Brooklyn, NY: Haskell House Pub. Ltd., 1977) 110.

4   2 Jan. 1844 letter to C. Felton, *Letters* (4) 2, 3.

5   M. Dickens (1977) 110.

6   M. Dickens (1897) 26.

7   Dickens was so concerned about forgetting the steps, Forster relayed a story about him jumping out of bed to practice in the cold night air. J.W.T. Ley ed., *The Life of Charles Dickens* by John Forster (London: Whitefriars Press, Ltd., 1928) 528, 529.

8   16 Jan. 1852 letter to H. Austin, *Letters* (6) 577.

9   Diary entry for Saturday, 6 Jan. 1838, *Letters* (1) 630.

10   28 Dec., 1842 letter to F. Stone, *Letters* (3) 406, 407.

11   [22 Dec. 1844] letter to J. Forster, *Letters* (4) 242.

12   See Bridget Ann Henisch, *Cakes and Characters: An English Christmas Tradition* (London: Prospect Books, 1984).

13   18 March 1845 letter to Miss Burdett-Coutts, *Letters* (4) 279.

14   [22 Dec. 1844] letter to J. Forster, *Letters* (4) 242.

15   M. Dickens (1977) 93.

16   3 Jan. 1843 letter from Mrs Dickens to Mrs Blanchard, *Letters* (3) 419n.

17   M. Dickens (1977) 92, 93.

18   Dickens developed another food trick called 'The Loaf of Bread Wonder' where he conjured a lady's watch from a metal box 'into the heart of an ordinary half-quartern loaf':

Letters (5) 706, 707. In a 20 Jan. 1844 letter to Jeannie Welsh, Mrs Jane Carlyle gave her sardonic description of another guest who asked Dickens's daughter if she would like a plum pudding in every house in London after Dickens conjured up the pudding: Leonard Huxley, *Jane Welsh Carlyle: Letters to Her Family, 1839–1863* (New York, Doubleday, Page & Co., 1924) 179.

19   28 Nov. 1850 letter to C. Knight, *Letters* (6) 220; Charles Knight, 'A Christmas Pudding', *Household Words* 2(1851) 300–304. Ostensibly, the article expressed their views on free trade and the recipe, provided by the main character's wife, allowed Knight to reproach human exploitation in the countries from which the main ingredients came. The recipe for 'A Pound Christmas Pudding' makes several puddings: 'One pound raisins; one pound currants; one pound suet; one pound bread-crumbs; quarter pound orange-peel; two ounces citron-peel; two ounces lemon-peel; one nutmeg; one teaspoonful powdered ginger; one teaspoonful powdered cinnamon; one wine-glassful brandy; seven eggs; one teaspoonful salt; quarter pound raw sugar; milk enough to liquefy the mass, if the eggs and brandy be not sufficient for this purpose.'

20   24 Dec. 1853 letter to M. Lemon, *Letters* (7) 232.

21   13 October 1840 letter to G. Cattermole, *Letters* (2) 134, 135.

22   13 Oct. 1840 letter to C. Gray, *Letters* (2) 135.

23   20 October 1840 letter to W. Macready, *Letters* (2) 138.

24   [14, 15 Oct. 1840] letter from E. Franklin to G. Franklin: David Parker, Anno Wilson, and Roger Wilson, 'Letters of a Guest at Devonshire Terrace', *Dickensian* 95 (1999) 57.

25   [26 Oct. 1840] letter from E. Franklin to G. Franklin: Parker 59.

26   For example she invited guests to her sister's concert, 'I expect a few friends to supper tomorrow evening and I [would] be very happy to see you and Mr. [illegible] about 9 o'clock. 19 April [no year] 70 Gloucester Crescent': Charles Dickens Museum archive accession #B44. Other notes acknowledge her invitations, such as 'I shall be with you on Wednesday at the James home as appointed', written in 1862: Charles Dickens Museum archive accession Suz C2 B43.

27   Monday (no date) letter from Mrs Dickens to T. Beard: Charles Dickens Museum archive accession #B15. When a ribbing was in order, Dickens, always ripe for a good joke, fell into character, thus the 16 April 1844 note he sent to Thomas Powell, a writer who ingratiated himself by sending elegant gifts of food (until 1846, before embezzlement and forgery charges brought down the wrath of the literary circle he tried to befriend), *Letters* (3) 577n, 578n. Powell had misunderstood the original message delivered by Dickens's younger brother Augustus ('Shrimp'), but as Dickens acknowledges the gift of 'potted chair' (referring to the trout-like fish called char) in his facetious note, he also illustrates the care he and Catherine took in choosing congenial dinner guests: 'Lord bless you! Thursday or Friday!!! Why, I composed (though I say it, as shouldn't) the best little party you can imagine; comprehending everybody I had room for, whom I thought Mr. [Thomas] Chapman would like to know. Let me see. [Samuel] Rogers for Poetry, Sydney Smith for Orthodoxy, Charles Kemble and [Charles M.] Young for Theatricality, Lord Denman for Benchity, Lord Dudley Stuart for Polarity, Mr. and Mrs. Milner Gibson for Anti Corn Law Leaguality, Mrs. Norton [Caroline E.S. Sheridan] for beauty, and divers others for variety. Lord love you! Why, at this time of the year it couldn't be done again under three weeks. Not to mention the Dwarf – General Tom Thumb – whom on the word of a Spiritiwal creetur, I had summoned, and have summoned, for the Evening in question. No. We won't come down with the run. We'll have a long notice, and see what can be done with the second wentur. When we doos go in, we plays to win Sir.
    'Says Shrimp to me (I allude to the humble individual who has the honour to be my brother) "Mr. Powell is coming up one evening". – "Shrimp", said I. "Why evening? We dine at half past 5." "Cannot" said Powell, "with a day's notice (to ensure my not being

out) come up to dinner?" I saw that I had touched him; and had a modest confidence in my Message reaching you safely. Whether Shrimp broke down, or Prawn (otherwise Powell) I don't know. But until this point is cleared up, I decline to acknowledge the receipt of potted chair. If indeed that *be* chair in a black bag; which I don't believe': *Letters* (4) 106, 107.

28   George Dodd, *The Food of London: A Sketch of the Chief Varieties, Sources of Supply, Probable Quantities Modes of Arrival, Processes of Manufacture, Suspected Adulteration, and Machinery of Distribution* (London: Longman, Brown, Green, and Longmans, 1856) 99.

29   12 Nov. 1840 letter to J. Forster, *Letters* (2) 149. Even in America in the early 1840s, dinner at 5:00 or 5:30 p.m., depending on the region, was thought to be the fashionable hour while the old guard in Washington, DC still had dinner at 2:30 p.m. and in Boston at 2:00 p.m.: A. Nevins, ed., *The Diary of Philip Hone (1828–1851)* (New York: Dodd, Mead & Co., 1927) 590; *Letters* (3) 19n.

30   27 Feb. 1843 letter to C. Stanfield, *Letters* (3) 446.

31   17 Jan. 1843 letter to R. M'Ian, *Letters* (3) 425.

32   27 Jan. 1854 letter to J. Leech, *Letters* (7) 260; *Letters* (5) 411n.

33   12 May 1841 letter to T. Mitton, *Letters* (2) 282.

34   Courtney Boyle, ed., *Mary Boyle Her Book* (London: John Murray, 1902) 236.

35   30 June 1852 letter to Miss Burdett-Coutts, *Letters* (6) 702.

36   22 April 1856 letter to W. Collins, *Letters* (8) 95.

37   *Letters* (8) 254n.

38   14 Oct. 1842 letter to H. Austin, *Letters* (3) 343.

39   Edward Tucker, 'References in Longfellow's Journals (1856–1882) to Charles Dickens', *Dickens Studies Annual* 24 (1996) 199; *Letters* (3) 335n.

40   25 May 1843 letter to T. Watson, *Letters* (3) 497.

41   *Letters* (3) 497n; Laura Richards and Maud Howe Elliott, *Julia Ward Howe, 1819–1910*, vol.1 (Boston: Houghton Mifflin, 1916) 84. The dinner description is all the more interesting considering Dickens's feelings about her husband: 'He is a cold-blooded fellow, that Howe – a regular American – and I wouldn't have taken the trouble' to make arrangements for an expedition to the 'thieves quarter' (prison) if it were not for A. Tracy's request: 9 June 1843 letter, *Letters* (3) 504.

42   Julia Ward Howe, *Reminiscences 1819–1899* (Boston: Houghton, Mifflin & Co., 1899) 110.

43   17 June 1848 letter to C. Evans, *Letters* (5) 343.

44   30 June 1848 letter to M. Lemon, *Letters* (5) 354.

45   1 July 1848 letter to Mrs Cowden-Clarke, *Letters* (5) 356.

46   Charles and Mary Cowden-Clarke, *Recollections of Writers* (New York: Charles Scribner's Sons, 1878) 310.

47   Cowden-Clarke 316. The dinners were in June of 1848.

48   Boyle 235.

49   Pliny Earle, *Memoirs of Pliny Earle, MD* (Boston: Damrell & Upham, 1898) 289, 290.

50   *Letters* (1) 602n.

51   *Letters* (4) 612n.

52   *Letters* (5) 497n.

53   *Letters* (5) 526n; Forster 526, 257.

54   L. Huxley, ed., *Jane Welsh Carlyle: Letters to Her Family, 1839–1863* (New York: Doubleday, Page & Co., 1924) 326.

55   When Dickens wanted critical feedback, he read his work to trusted friends. In 1844 when they resided in Italy, Dickens planned a short visit asking Forster to invite guests for dinner and a reading of 'Chimes' his next Christmas number. 'Carlyle, indispensable,' Dickens stated, 'and I should like his wife of all things: her judgment would be invaluable': 3 & [4] Nov. 1844 letter, *Letters* (4) 210. Although Mrs Carlyle's letters

commented on Dickens's activities, she rarely mentioned Catherine Dickens, but they maintained a friendship. After the birth of their fifth child, for example, Dickens reported to Mrs Carlyle that 'Your countrywoman is going on very favourably – though with Northern caution and slowness. She sends her love, and hopes to come and see you as soon as she is well': 27 Jan. 1844 letter to Mrs Carlyle, *Letters* (4) 33.

56 24 April 1843 letter from T. Carlyle to Mrs Dickens, *Letters* (3) 473n.

57 13 May 1849 letter to Annie Green from Mrs Gaskell, J.A.V. Chapple and Arthur Pollard, eds., *The Letters of Mrs. Gaskell* (Manchester: Manchester University Press, 1997) 828, 829.

58 Miss Beecher's 1841 publication, *Treatise on Domestic Economy*, led to the development of domestic science and the text was adopted by the public schools. See Sarah Stage and Virginia B. Vincenti, *Rethinking Home Economics* (Ithaca, NY: Cornell University Press, 1997) 321. She and her sister Harriet Beecher Stowe wrote *The American Women's Home: Or Principles of Domestic Science* (New York: J.B. Ford & Co., 1869).

59 The event was held on 26 November 1852. According to *The Times*, the address was signed by over a half million women and formed twenty-six volumes that were sent with a covering letter from Lord Carlisle to Mrs Stowe: *Letters* (6) 808n.

60 Harriet Beecher Stowe, *Sunny Memories of Foreign Lands* (Boston: Phillips, Sampson, and Co., 1854) 260, 264.

61 3 May 1853 from Mrs Dickens to Mrs Stowe, #14, Beinecke Rare Book and Manuscript Library, Yale University.

62 4 May 1853 letter to C. Felton, *Letters* (7) 77.

63 4 Aug. 1854 letter to Mrs Colden (an American), *Letters* (7) 387. Dickens was even less enchanted with Mrs Stowe after she published 'The True Story of Lady Byron's Life' in 1869, particularly since the break-up of Byron's and Dickens's marriages bore uncomfortable similarities: Harry Stone, 'Charles Dickens and Harriet Beecher Stowe', *Nineteenth-Century Fiction* 12 (1957) 188–202.

64 2 Dec. 1841 letter to J. Anderson, *Letters* (2) 437.

65 W.A. Fraser, 'Dickens and Thackeray at the Dinner-Table', *Dickensian* 3 (1907) 245, 246.

66 1 Sept. 1853 letter to Mrs Collins from her son: William Baker and William M. Clarke, eds., *The Letters of Wilkie Collins*, vol. 1 (New York: St. Martin's Press, Inc., 1999) 96. Unfortunately, the bill of fare is not believed to be extant. I am grateful for Paul Lewis's help in looking for the document.

67 27 March 1856 letter to W. Macready, *Letters* (8) 77. Collins's unconventional life-style added a liberating influence to Dickens. See Lillian Nayder, *Wilkie Collins* (New York: Twayne Press, 1997) and *Unequal Partners. Charles Dickens, Wilkie Collins, and Victorian Authorship* (Ithaca, NY: Cornell University Press, 2002).

68 23 Dec. 1843 letter to Jeannie Welsh from Mrs Carlyle: Leonard Huxley, ed., *Jane Welsh Carlyle: Letters to Her Family, 1839–1863* (New York: Doubleday, Page, Co., 1924) 168; 20 Jan. 1844 letter to Jeannie Welsh, Huxley 181, 182

69 Holy Thursday [5 April] 1849 letter to Jeannie Welsh from Mrs Carlyle: Huxley, (1924) 326.

70 Hans Ottomeyer, '*Service à la française* and *service à la russe*: or the evolution of the table between the Eighteenth and Nineteenth Centuries', in Martin R. Schärer and Alexander Fenton, eds., *Food and Material Culture* (Edinburgh: Tuckwell Press, 1998) 107, 108.

71 Ottomeyer 107–110.

72 Ottomeyer 108–110.

73 Ottomeyer 107–110.

74 For comparison see 'Diner à la Russe, 1868' as reported by Eugene Schuyler who travelled in Russia, reprinted in *Petits Propos Culinaires* 28 (1988) 22–27.

75 Ottomeyer 110

76 Percy Fitzgerald, 'The Real Cook's Oracle', *Household Words* 19 (1859) 384.

77 20 October 1840 letter to W. Macready, *Letters* (2) 138. [26 Oct. 1840] letter from E. Franklin to G. Franklin: Parker 59.

78 Jennifer Davies, *The Victorian Kitchen,* large print ed. (Oxford: Clio Press, 1991) 195.

79 Ottomeyer 112, 113.

80 Davies 195, 196. The Dickenses' 1844 kitchen inventory lists an egg slicer and vegetable cutters for making garnishes: *Letters* (4) 710, 711.

81 Ottomeyer 107, 111–113

82 Ottomeyer 113.

83 The 'English style', known as *à l'anglaise* serving style, later developed as a modification of the *à la russe* protocol, and worked well for smaller dinners and in homes with few upstairs servants. In fact, it is the family style most of us use today.

84 Dena Attar, *A Bibliography of Household Books Published in Britain 1800–1914* (London: Prospect Books, 1987) 54.

85 8 Aug. 1856 letter to Mrs Brown, *Letters* (8) 170.

86 Alexis Soyer, *The Modern Housewife or Ménagère* (London: Simpkin, Marshall, & Co., 1850) 389, 391.

87 Soyer (1850) 391, 392.

88 Alaric Alfred Watts, 'The Carver's College', *Household Words* 12 (1855) 107.

89 Attar 52, 53.

90 George Newlin, *Every Thing in Dickens: Ideas and Subjects Discussed by Charles Dickens in His Complete Works* (Westport, CT: Greenwood Press, 1996) 133.

91 Attar 52, 53.

92 Dickens held a life-long superstition about knives, yet valued precision cutlery. When Maclise sent him a carving knife and fork, Dickens acknowledged the old tale, 'Nothing in it, I dare say – but I send you a halfpenny in payment': 4 Oct. 1845 letter to D. Maclise, *Letters* (4) 397. Again, years later, John Brooks and his son sent him a case of fine cutlery for mentioning their Sheffield manufacturing firm in *David Copperfield*. In his note, he explained that in order not to sever 'friendship with knives', he needed to offer something in exchange and sent them his own copy of the novel.

93 Watts 108.

94 Soyer (1850) 391.

95 22 April 1856 letter to W. Collins, *Letters* (8) 96.

96 Soyer (1850) 390.

97 *Letters* (4) 710; Soyer (1850) 392.

98 Davies 194–196.

99 Huxley 326.

100 *Letters* (7) 250n.

101 *Letters* (4) 709, 710. Dickens and Wills wrote a piece on Staffordshire pottery and porcelain entitled 'A Plated Article' in *Household Words* 5 (1852) 117–121.

102 Fitzgerald 384.

103 *Letters* (4) 709, 710.

104 *Letters* (4) 709, 710.

105 *Letters* (4) 710.

106 Harriet Martineau, 'Birmingham Glass Works', *Household Words* 5 (1852) 32–38. The window panes for the Crystal Palace were manufactured at Birmingham. She describes the process of making sheet glass and briefly mentions the making of decorative objects.

107 *Letters* (4) 710.

108 28 Dec. 1842 letter to Mrs Child, *Letters* (3) 403, 404.

109 However, Emerson thought Dickens's prodigious consumption of alcohol was a reflection of his 'light' moral character. Dickens, he said, 'was sentimental over the prisons and orphanages he visited during the American tour' until 'dinner time': W. H. Gilman and J.

E. Parsons, eds., *Journals of Ralph Waldo Emerson,* vol. 8 (Cambridge, MA: Belnap Press, 1970) 222, 223.

110 *Dombey and Son* was published in nineteen monthly parts from October 1846 until April 1848. The early part of the book was written while the Dickens family lived in Lausanne.

111 George A. Sala and Charles Dickens, 'First Fruits', *Household Words* 5 (1852) 192.

112 'Margaret Dods' (Christian I. Johnstone), *The Cook and Housewife's Manual, a Practical System of Modern Domestic Cookery and Family Management,* 5th ed. (Edinburgh: Oliver and Boyd, 1833) 379–93

113 Charles Dickens, *Martin Chuzzlewit,* Chapter 5 (Maryland: Penguin Books, 1968) 137.

114 I thank David Parker for a personal communication which made this case. Gladstone's policy on the wine trade that passed in 1860 allowed shop-keepers to sell wine and further increased British consumption. Lord Askworth, *British Taverns: Their History and Laws* (London: George Routledge & Sons, Ltd., 1928) 62, 63.

115 Jean-Paul Aron, *The Art of Eating in France: Manners and Menus in the Nineteenth Century,* trans. Nina Rootes (London: Peter Owen Ltd., 1975) 102. For an overview of the wine being paired with food, see Francatelli's 'Instructions for the Service of Wines: Denoting the Order in which they should be drunk at the Dinner-Table': Charles Elmé Francatelli, *Francatelli's The Modern Cook* (1846, facsimile ed. New York: Dover Publishing, Inc. 1973) 506C–506 F.

116 *Letters* (4) 710.

117 [6 Nov. 1840] letter to W. Macready, *Letters* (2) 108.

118 [26 July 1840] letter to W. Macready, *Letters* (2) 148.

119 11 July 1842 letter to J. Ellis & Sons, *Letters* (3) 265.

120 Edward Hewett and W.F. Axton, *Convivial Dickens: The Drinks of Dickens & His Times* (Athens, OH: Ohio University Press, 1983) 177.

121 Thanks to David Parker for this information.

122 24 April 1846 letter to Ct. D'Orsay, *Letters* (4) 541.

123 *Letters* (4) 541n.

124 *Letters* (4) 550n.

125 17 August 1846 letter to J. Valckenburg, *Letters* (4) 612. There is no extant correspondence in the next decade with the Valckenburg family.

126 [24 & 25 Aug. 1846] letter to J. Forster, *Letters* (4) 610.

127 *Alfred Lord Tennyson: A Memoir By His Son,* vol. 1 (New York: MacMillan Co., 1898) 234. Tennyson's letter was written to Edward Fitzgerald.

128 16 Oct. 1846 letter to T. Thompson, *Letters* (4) 637.

129 17–18 Nov. 1844 letter to J. Forster, *Letters* (4) 222.

130 According to the 1870s auction list, Dickens's cellar held 18 bottles of Sauterne (unidentified), 30 bottles of 'Haut Sauterne' and 60 bottles of the celebrated Château 'yQuen' (Château Yquem): Hewett 177.

131 Edmund Saul Dixon, 'A Bottle of Champagne', *Household Words* 11 (1855) 55.

132 [5 or 6 Jan.] 1857 instructions to his servant John Thompson, *Letters* (8) 254n.

133 1 April 1842 letter to W. Macready, *Letters* (3) 174.

134 10 May 1848 letter to T. Beard, *Letters* (5) 302.

135 [24 April 1840] letter to T. Beard, *Letters* (2) 61.

136 13 July 1850 letter to Rev. J. White, *Letters* (6) 131; 19 July 1842 letter to Beard, *Letters* (3) 273. To this day, specific rituals accompany the passing of the port in British institutions. The opened decanter follows the sun. That is, the host begins by pouring a glass for the guest on his right, and then passes the decanter to the guest on his left. The ritual continues around the table with the port pausing in front of the host. The host may continue the rounds, but when he places the stopper in the decanter, it signals the end of the evening.

137 N. C. Peyrouton's article 'When the Wine Merchant Wrote to Dickens' provided the Ellis family's background. Both father and son were named Joseph. Dickens ordered alcohol from the two sons, Joseph, when in the Brighton area, and Charles in London: *Dickensian* 57 (1961) 105–111.

138 *Letters* (8) 254n.

139 Hewett 176.

140 16 Feb. 1849 letter to Countess Lovelace, *Letters* (5) 495.

141 11 July 1842 letter to J. Ellis and Son, *Letters* (3) 265.

142 Edmund Saul Dixon, 'A Bottle of Champagne', *Household Words* 11 (1855) 57.

143 5–6 Jan. [1857] note to J. Thompson, *Letters* (8) 254n.

144 Soyer (1850) 392.

145 17 Oct. 1851 letter to H. Austin, *Letters* (6) 523.

146 25 Oct. 1853 letter to Miss Hogarth, *Letters* (7) 175.

147 13 Oct. 1853 letter to Mrs Dickens, 23 Sep 1853 letter to T Beard, *Letters* (7) 164, 418; and 7 Jan. and 2 July 1856 letters to M. Lemon, *Letters* (8) 13, 142.

148 Dudley Costello, 'Our Wine Merchant', *Household Words* 8 (1853) 405.

149 [31 Aug. 1844] letter to J. Forster, *Letters* (4) 188.

150 Edmund S. Dixon, 'The Hill of Gold', *Household Words* 11 (1855) 28–36.

151 Edmund S. Dixon, 'A Dash Through the Vines', *Household Words* 12 (1855) 240–247.

152 Edmund S. Dixon, 'Claret', *Household Words* 12 (1856) 539–543; 'A Bottle of Champagne', *Household Words* 11 (1855) 51–57; 'Cognac', *Household Words* 11 (1855) 361–367; and George W. Thornbury, 'Sherry', *Household Words* 18 (1858) 508–514.

153 Edmund S. Dixon, 'The Hall of Wines', *Household Words* 13 (1856) 66–70.

154 John Capper, 'Strictly Financial', *Household Words* 11 (1855) 440.

155 John Capper, 'Really a Temperance Question', *Household Words* 6 (1852) 296–300; 'Strictly Financial', *Household Words* 11 (1855) 439–442.

156 Capper (1855) 441. The fungal diseases foreshadowed the devastation caused with the invasion of the root-eating insects *Phylloxera vastatrix* from North America which were seen in the 1860s.

157 Capper (1852) 299.

158 Percival Leigh, 'The Chemistry of a Pint of Beer', *Household Words* 2 (1851) 498–502.

159 Leigh 498–502.

160 William H. Wills, 'Constitutional Trials', *Household Words* 5 (1852) 422.

161 *Letters* (2) 462.

162 4 April 1842 letter to F. Dickens, *Letters* (3) 189; 26 Sept. 1841 letter to F. Dickens, *Letters* (2) 391, 392.

163 25 April 1840 letter to T. Beard, *Letters* (2) 62.

164 5 Feb. 1841 letter to W. Ainsworth, *Letters* (2) 204.

165 29 June 1852 letter to T. Beard, *Letters* (6) 699, 670.

166 25 June 1851 letter to T. Beard, *Letters* (6) 416, 417.

167 11 July 1851 letter to Mrs Watson, *Letters* (6) 428.

168 17 May 1847 and 12 Feb.1849 letters to J. Ellis, *Letters* (5) 68, 494; 16 and 18 Dec. 1851 letters to C. Ellis, *Letters* (6) 554, 556.

169 28 March 1842 letter to J. Forster, *Letters* (3) 172.

170 *Letters* (8) 254.

171 13 Nov. 1846 letter to L. Watson, *Letters* (4) 664n.

172 The recipe was also sent to Mrs Fillonneau (Henry Austin's sister) in January 18, 1847 letter: *Letters* (5) 10; K. F. Yapp, 'Dickens' Recipe for Brewing a Punch', *Dickensian* 1 (1905) 205, 206. The author interpreted the word 'silk' as 'milk' in the article.

173 Anonymous, 'To Make Moonbeams For Summer Drinking', *Dickensian* 2 (1906) 188.

174 Hewett 42.

175   9 July 1841 letter to J. Forster, *Letters* (2) 323–326.
176   To make these and other drinks, Cedric Dickens's book *Drinking with Dickens* (New York: Amsterdam Books, 1980) provides one of the better collections of recipes.

Notes to Chapter VI, pages 202–216.

1   Lillian Nayder, 'Constructing Catherine Dickens', *Hiroshima Studies in English Language and Literature* 47 (2003) 14.
2   The name of Dickens's theatrical company changed frequently during the 1848 season. For the June 3, 1848 performance, the public notices referred to the event as an 'Amateur Performance by Chas. Dickens, Esq. and Friends'. On July 17th, they were 'The Gentlemen from London connected with Literature and Art', and the following day the 'London Amateur Company of Gentlemen connected with Literature and Art'. When the play *Used Up* was revived at Rockingham Castle in 1851, the performers were known as 'The Amateur Company of the Guild of Literature and Art' which recognized the founding of the Guild through funds raised from previous performances: Walter Dexter, 'For One Night Only: Dickens' Appearances as an Amateur Actor', *Dickensian* 36 (1940) 21–30, 90–102.
3   26 May 1842 letter to J. Forster, *Letters* (3) 245, 247.
4   Mary's husband, Charles Cowden-Clarke, modernized Chaucer's work and gave public lecture tours believed to have influenced Dickens in doing the same: Richard D. Altick, *The English Common Reader: A Social History of the Mass Reading Public, 1800–1900* (Chicago: University of Chicago Press, 1957) 204. The couple first saw Dickens in 1839, at a large dinner celebration for William Charles Macready where she described him as 'superlatively handsome, with his rich, wavy locks of hair, and his magnificent eyes. No spoonful of soup seemed to reach his lips unaccompanied by a gathered oddity or whimsicality, no morsel to be raised on his fork unseasoned by a droll gesture or trick he had remarked in some one near.' They later met the Dickenses through the author Leigh Hunt and Mrs Cowden-Clarke offered to join the company as Dame Quickley in the *Merry Wives of Windsor*. Her credentials were well matched having published *The Complete Concordance to Shakespeare* three years earlier. Dickens's reply called her to rehearsal and briefly explained the fund-raising objectives. Following her actor-brother's advice, she performed in full voice and quickly gained recognition by both the members of the company and *The Times* reviewer: 14 April 1848 letter to Mrs Cowden-Clarke, *Letters* (5) 277–279; Charles Cowden-Clarke and Mary Cowden-Clarke, *Recollection of Writers* (New York: Charles Schribner's Sons, 1878) 295–300.
5   Dexter 25–27.
6   Spouses, siblings, and various friends met or travelled with the company. Since Mrs Clarke's husband was on a lecture tour, her unmarried sister, Emma Aloysia Novello, accompanied her in the railway carriage with the Dickenses and Mark Lemon. Emma had attended Henry Sass's drawing academy in Bloomsbury; her sketchbooks are in the Novello-Cowden-Clarke Collection, Brotherton Library, Leeds. See *Letters* (5) 374n.
7   Dexter 25.
8   Cowden-Clarke 300.
9   Cowden-Clarke 304; Dexter 28, 30.
10   Cowden-Clarke 322.
11   Cowden-Clarke 313, 315, 320. Mrs Cowden-Clarke embroidered the blotting case with forget-me-nots in the centre, and gold-lettered signatures of Dickens's various roles including 'YG' for 'Young Gas', a playful name he gave himself. She also dedicated *Meg*

and Alice, the Merry Maids of Windsor one of a series in *The Girlhood of Shakespeare Heroines* to him. Dickens invited her to the dress rehearsals and the performance of *The Lighthouse* and *Mr. Nightingale's Diary* at Tavistock House. She commissioned a white porcelain paperweight with two green leaves enamelled around Dickens's initials from Mr Osler in Birmingham Glass Works. The green leaves alluded to a poem-story published in the 1852 Christmas number of *Household Words*: Cowden-Clark 327, 328, 331.

12   Cowden-Clarke 322, 323.

13   Cowden-Clarke 321.

14   Cowden-Clarke 318, 319.

15   Charles Mathews, trans., *Used Up: A Petit Comedy in Two Acts* (New York: William Taylor & Co., 1845) 3. Since 'wurzel' is a country term for common species of beets and turnips, the farmer's name is particularly ripe for wordplay associations with the hardy, if unsophisticated, root crops. Thanks to David Parker for sharing his insight on this.

16   Mathews 10.

17   Mathews 12.

18   Mathews 18.

19   Mathews 34.

20   Mathews 38.

21   C.G.L. Du Cann, *The Love-Lives of Charles Dickens* (London: Frederick Muller Ltd., 1961) 204, 205.

22   Rockingham Castle became the country getaway for the Dickenses on other occasions until the untimely death of Richard Watson on 24 July 1852 at the age of 51. The castle inspired the description of Chesney Wold in Dickens's 1852 serial *Bleak House*, published in book form the following year: S. Ward, 'Topography of *Bleak House*', *Dickensian* 1 (1901) 200–203; 27 Aug. 1853 letter to Mrs Watson, *Letters* (7) 134–6.

23   30 Nov. 1849 letter J. Forster, *Letters* (5) 661. Henry Coleman's 1849 work had been reviewed by Dickens in the *Examiner* (21 July 1849) as 'An American in Europe'. Dickens and Forster probably agreed with *The Times* article calling Coleman 'the most inveterate twaddler ever produced on either side of the Atlantic': *Letters* (5) 661n.

24   Henry F. Dickens, *The Recollections of Sir Henry Dickens, K.C.* (London: William Heinemann Ltd., 1928) 28.

25   Courtney Boyle, ed., *Mary Boyle Her Book* (London: John Murray, 1902) ix.

26   H. Dickens 28.

27   Boyle xii–xvi.

28   *Letters* (5) 662n.

29   They arranged costumed performances of 'a hastily-concocted scene' from *Nicholas Nickleby* where the mad neighbour passionately declared his love to Mrs Kate Nickleby. Mary recalled, 'My shabby-genteel costume, with the widow's cap of the period, attracted universal admiration from its appropriate fitness, while the amorous outbursts of my adorer were given in a manner worthy of the actor-author.' Just as their relationship, 'this short and impromptu entertainment was only the prelude to theatrical performances on a larger and grander scale': Boyle 231, 232. According to his letter, they also acted scenes from *School for Scandal*, and he performed as a conjurer. The festivities ended with country dances 'of which we had two admirably good ones, quite new to me, though really old' before the party retired at 3 a.m. 'It was an excellent entertainment, and we were all uncommonly merry': 30 Nov. 1849 letter to J. Forster, *Letters* (5) 662. After the visit he wrote about Mary to her cousin, saying: 'Plunged in the deepest gloom, I write these few words to let you know that, just now, when the bell was striking ten, I drank to H.E.R.! [heart with the initials 'CD' and an arrow through it] and to all the rest of Rockingham; as the wine went down my throat, I felt distinctly that it was "changing those thoughts to madness." On the way here I was a terror to my companions, and I am

at present a blight and mildew on my home. P.S. – I am in such an incapable state, that after executing the foregoing usual flourish [on his signature] I swooned, and remained for some time insensible. Ha, ha, ha! Why was I ever restored to consciousness!!!

'P.P.S. – "Changing" those thoughts ought to be "driving." But my recollection is incoherent and my mind wanders': 30 Nov. 1849 letter to Mrs Watson, *Letters* (5) 663.

30 Novelist, dramatist, and politician, Sir Edward Bulwer-Lytton, the first Baron Lytton (1803–1873) was Dickens's close friend and among the founders of the Guild of Literature and Art: Norman Page, *A Dickens Companion* (New York: Schocken Books, 1984) 41. Without consulting her, Dickens wrote, 'Do you know Mary Boyle – the Hon. Mary – daughter of the old admiral? Because she is the very best actress I ever saw, off the stage – and immeasurably better than a great many I have seen on it,' adding the postscript, 'If we could get Mary Boyle, we would do *Used Up* – which is a delightful piece – as the farce': 3 Sept. 1850 letter to E. Lytton, *Letters* (6) 162, 163; Boyle 233. *Used Up* was not performed at the Lytton estate Knebworth Park in Hertfordshire, but he wrote her 'to say that I am *perfectly delighted* to know that we are going to act together, in that merry party' and described her juicy role as Lisette, the waiting maid in the farce *Animal Magnetism*: 'I have seen people laugh at the piece, until they hung over the front of the [theatre] boxes, like ripe fruit': 16 Sept. 1850 letter to Miss Boyle, *Letters* (6) 169. Unfortunately, a friend's death (and mourning period) necessitated Mary's replacement by the actress Anne Romer who had played the part in the 1848 performance: 30 Oct. 1850 letter to Miss Boyle, *Letters* (6) 200. Dickens's witty correspondence with Mary continued, at times replete with innuendo, for example the 15 Jan. 1851 letter to Miss Boyle, *Letters* (6) 262. 'I was in the seventh heaven,' she recalled, 'theatrical business was the only business I liked, theatrical properties the only property I possessed' and Charles 'the only despot [she] ever tolerated,' grateful to be in her 'real element': Boyle 234, 235.

Catherine Dickens rehearsed two parts as Tib in *Every Man in his Humour* and Mrs Humphries in *Turning the Tables*, but severely sprained her foot in a fall through the stage's trapdoor at rehearsal and was replaced by Mark Lemon's wife Nelly Romer who had been an actress before marriage. The 29 Nov. 1850 edition of the *Hertford Mercury* reported that Georgy Hogarth and Mrs Lemon played 'such charming *naivete*', they should have had larger roles: Dexter 93; *Letters* (6) 202n. See 24 Sept. 1850 letter to Mrs Watson for the rest of the cast, *Letters* (6) 179.

31 The costume and the character's simple warm-hearted nature were described in the 4 July 1848 letter to Miss Romer, *Letters* (5) 362.

32 Boyle 230. The small-scale scenery scrolls and the mechanical equipment to roll the painted cloth backdrops were specially designed by Lewis Nathan, the costume-maker from Titchbourne Street in Haymarket who had experience creating the 'little boudoir stage': 1 Oct. 1850 letter to Mrs Watson, *Letters* (6) 186.

33 A week before the performance, Dickens visited to discuss the stage fixtures. The scenery door needed to line up exactly with the door of the room or it 'might as well be in Africa,' he patiently explained to the neophytes. The thirteen-and-a-half-foot stage, reduced somewhat by the set fittings, cleverly used the adjacent room and staircase: 14 Dec. 1850 letter to Mrs Watson, *Letters* (6) 234, 235.

34 The *Northampton Herald* favourably reviewed the Wednesday evening production. *Used Up* opened the entertainment, a twenty-minute break for tea refreshed the audience and actors alike, and after the seventy families returned to their seats for *A Day after the Wedding* followed by *Animal Magnetism*. Dancing the Sir Roger de Coverly, among other reels, concluded the festive evening: *Letters* (6) 261n.

35 See 15 Jan. 1851 letter to Miss Boyle, *Letters* (6) 262.

36 24 Jan. 1851 letter to Mrs Watson, *Letters* (6) 266.

37 Arthur A. Adrian, *Georgina Hogarth and the Dickens Circle* (London: Oxford University

Press, 1957) 30.

38 He would learn both that Catherine continued a correspondence with Mrs Watson over the years – so their friendship had been maintained, and that some of Dickens's extant letters to Mary Boyle were pretty titillating.

39 Michael Slater, *Dickens and Women* (London: J.M. Dent & Son, Ltd., 1983) 122, 123, 404 note 74.

40 Du Cann 203.

41 Dickens believed that the solution was hydropathic treatment ('the water cure') adapted from methods used in Gräfenberg, Bavaria by Drs James M. Gully and James Wilson who developed Malvern as a spa-resort in 1842 where the two centres flourished for nearly thirty years: *Letters* (4) 28n.

42 8 March 1851 letter to Dr J. Wilson, *Letters* (6) 309, 310. Dickens responded that Anne Brown, Catherine's maid, would leave the following day to make suitable arrangements: 'I am so anxious that Mrs. Dickens should begin with a favourable impression of Malvern, and I am so certain of the impossibility of engendering that impression if she be on any visit, or in any house but our own, (from what I have lately observed when we have been staying in the country houses even of intimate friends) that I am obliged, however reluctantly, to decline your hospitable proposal in relation to ourselves.' Arrangements were made at Knotsford Lodge, a guest-house with a private apartment, 11 March 1851 letter to Dr J. Wilson, *Letters* (6) 313, 315n. Dickens was probably referring to Rockingham Castle as the country house. Perhaps he declined the physician's invitation for his wife's sake, but awkwardness may have remained after the wedding of Frederick Dickens and Anna Weller, of whom Charles did not approve. The wedding breakfast was given at Dr Wilson's home on Dec. 30, 1848 with only John Dickens, their father, representing the family and Mr Baker standing in for Charles as best man: *Letters* (5) 424n. The situation was very different when Alfred Dickens and Helen Dobson married two years earlier (May 16) and Catherine hosted their breakfast, *Letters* (4) 563n.

43 9 March 1851 letter to Mrs Watson, *Letters* (6) 311.

44 11 March 1851 letter from Mrs Dickens to Fanny Kelly. Miss Kelly owned a little theatre on Dean Street in Soho that she rented to Dickens for rehearsals, *Letters* (6) 195n, 309n.

45 *Letters* (6) viii, ix.

46 Dickens's captured the ritual. 'O Heaven, to meet the Cold Waterers (as I did this morning when I went out for a shower-bath) dashing down the hills, with severe expression on their countenances, like men doing matches [races] and not exactly winning!' [15 March 1851] letter to J. Forster, *Letters* (6) 316.

47 Harriet Martineau, 'Malvern Water', *Household Words* 4 (1852) 67–70. That February, Dickens grumbled, 'London is a vile place, I sincerely believe. I have never taken kindly to it since I lived abroad.' He continued, 'whenever I come back from the Country, now, and see that great heavy canopy lowering over the housetops, I wonder what on earth I do there, except on obligation': 10 Feb. 1851 letter to E. Bulwer Lytton, *Letters* (6) 287.

48 Others devalued the treatments; Miss Burdett Coutts's father died seven years earlier. 'They are very careful with the cold water here, and don't commit excesses,' Dickens assured her as she raised concerns for Catherine. 'I have faith in Hydropathy myself,' confided Dickens, 'drink cold water night and morning – and pour it down my back besides': 21 March 1851 letter to B. Coutts, *Letters* (6) 324. Dickens's appreciation of the water cure may have been well known, especially by the mid-1840s. Richard J. Lane, the lithographer to the Queen, published *Life at the Water Cure or a Month at Malvern* in 1846; in the preface he used a quotation from Dickens and referred to him in the text. The third edition (1855) was dedicated to Dickens and in that same year Lane published *Spirits and Water*: 18 March 1847 letter to R. Lane, *Letters* (6) 38.

49 23 Jan. 1844 letter to D. Jerrold, *Letters* (4) 28. Jerrold was treated at the centre twice and

wrote an article for *Punch* entitled 'Life at the Cold Brandy-and-Water Cure' for the Dec. 19, 1846 issue: *Letters* (4) 28n.

50 Bruce Haley, *The Healthy Body and Victorian Culture* (Cambridge, MA: Harvard University Press, 1978) 16. When Catherine was in residence, Charles Darwin brought his eldest daughter, nine-year-old Annie, on the 24 March 1851, stayed until the 31st, and returned again on 16th April when Annie's condition worsened before she died on the 23rd: John Bowlby, *Charles Darwin: A New Life* (New York: W.W. Norton & Co., 1990) 284 292, 293. He had been a patient himself, and in a 19 March 1849 letter to his sister Susan Darwin, he detailed his month's regime for gastro-intestinal problems. Although Catherine's symptoms and physician were different, his account of a patient's day is of interest. 'As you say you want my hydropathical diary, I will give it you – though tomorrow it is to change to a certain extent. – $^1/_2$ before 7. get up, & am scrubbed with rough towel in cold water for 2 or 3 minutes, which after the few first days made & makes me very like a lobster – I have a washerman, a very nice person, & he scrubs behind, whilst I scrub in front. – drink a tumbler of water & get my clothes on as quick as possible & walk for 20 minutes – I cd. walk further, but I find it tires me afterwards – I like all this very much. – At the same time I put on a compress, which is a broad wet folded linen covered by mackintosh & which is 'refreshed' – ie dipt in cold water every 2 hours & I wear it all day, except for about 2 hours after midday dinner; I don't perceive much effect from this of any kind. – After my walk, shave & wash & get my breakfast, which was to have been exclusively toast with meat or egg, but he has allowed me a little milk to sop the *stale* toast in. At no time must I take any sugar, butter, spices[,] tea[,] bacon or anything good. – At 12 oclock I put my feet for 10 minutes in cold water with a little mustard & they are violently rubbed by my man; the coldness makes my feet ache much, but upon the whole my feet are certainly less cold than formerly – Walk for 20 minutes & dine at one. – He has relaxed a little about my dinner & says I may try plain pudding, if I am sure it lessens sickness. – After dinner lie down & try to go to sleep for one hour. – At 5 oclock feet in cold water – drink cold water & walk as before. – Supper same as breakfast at 6 oclock....Tomorrow I am to be packed at 6 oclock A.M. for 1 & $^1/_2$ hour in Blanket, with hot bottle to my feet & then rubbed with cold dripping sheet...': Frederick H. Burkhardt and Sydney Smith, eds., *The Correspondence of Charles Darwin*, vol. 4 (Cambridge: Cambridge University Press, 1988) 224, 225.

51 Janet Browne, 'I Could Have Retched All Night: Charles Darwin and his Body', in Christopher Lawrence and Steven Shapin, eds., *Science Incarnate: Historical Embodiments of Natural Knowledge* (Chicago, University of Chicago Press, 1998) 251.

52 *Letters* (6) 309n. Joseph Howe was the former Speaker of the Nova Scotia House of Assembly. He had attended baby Dora's christening a month earlier: *Letters* (6) 280n, 309n.

53 John Dickens secretly suffered from a bladder condition that required the 'most terrible operation known in surgery' performed without chloroform. 'He bore it with astonishing fortitude, and I saw him directly afterwards – his room, a slaughter house of blood,' Charles wrote to his wife: 25 March 1851 letter to Mrs Dickens, *Letters* (6) 333. His father survived for six days. Afterwards Dickens wrote to Forster, 'I think I must go down to Malvern again, at night, to know what it is to be done about the children's mourning': 31 March 1851 letter to J. Forster, *Letters* (6) 343. Catherine apparently was unable to attend her father-in-law's funeral on April 5th. They were fairly close, he had often written to her, particularly if he needed money: [?30 Sept. 1844] letter to J. Forster, *Letters* (4) 197.

54 3 Feb. 1851 letter to Mrs Leech, *Letters* (6) 280.

55 [early Feb.] 1851 letter to J. Forster, *Letters* (6) 284.

56 26 March 1851 letter to Mrs Dickens, *Letters* (6) 334.

57 17 April 1851 letter from J. Forster to Dr Wilson, *Letters* (6) 353n.

58   17 April 1851 letter to F. Evans, *Letters* (6) 355.

59   18 April 1851 letter to B. Lytton, *Letters* (6) 356.

60   19 April 1851 letter to Mrs Austin, *Letters* (6) 357. As a source of comfort, Charles and Catherine read David Macbeth Moir's *Domestic Verses*. Among the poems were verses on the death of his own four children. Dickens had ranked the Scottish writer highly nearly a decade earlier at a public dinner in Edinburgh. 'Mrs. Dickens begs me to send you her kindest regards,' Dickens wrote to thank him for the book, 'We have had reason lately, to revert to your child-poems, and it has been comfortable to have your letter near the book': 25 April 1851 letter to D. Moir, *Letters* (6) 365, 366; *Letters* (2) 440n.

61   *What Shall We Have For Dinner?* above, p. 24.

62   Mathews 15.

63   Mathews 15.

64   22 July 1848 letter to Mrs Cowden-Clarke, *Letters* (5) 374. Dickens signed the letter 'Y.G. The (darkened) G.L.B.' meaning 'Young Gas' and 'Gas-Light Boy' noting the bright gas footlights of the stage and in a later letter referred to Catherine as 'Mrs. G.'

65   5 Aug. 1848 letter to Mrs Cowden-Clarke, *Letters* (5) 386.

66   29 July 1848 letter to Miss Coutts, *Letters* (5) 381.

67   13 Jan. 1849 letter to Mrs Cowden-Clarke, *Letters* (5) 476. Romer refers to Anne Romer who played Mary the farmer's niece.

68   Above, p. 23.

69   6 March 1844 letter to Rev. R. Barham, *Letters* (4) 63, 64.

70   Above, pp. 23–4.

71   Dena Attar, *A Bibliography of Household Books Published in Britain 1800–1914* (London: Prospect Books, 1987) 12, 57. Ruskin's publication of 1865 (and later editions) was often given to girls as a school prize. The book became 'a fixture in middle-class homes': Deborah Epstein Nord, editor's introduction, John Ruskin, *Sesame and Lilies* (New Haven: Yale University Press, 2002) xiv.

72   16 Aug. 1850 letter to W. Wills, *Letters* (6) 149. Dora Annie Dickens was born on 16 August 1850.

73   'I will not attempt to tell you my love, how delighted I have been to receive such good tidings of you, and what relief and happiness we [CD and Georgy] felt last night in coming down to think that it was all over, and that we left you so well,' he wrote adding, 'I think of you all day…God bless you my darling': 17 Aug. 1850 letter to Mrs Dickens, *Letters* (6) 150, 151. Writing again on August 20th he reported, 'I am quite delighted, and can stick to my work bravely, hearing such excellent accounts of you': 20 Aug. 1850 letter to Mrs Dickens, *Letters* (6) 152.

74   21 Aug. 1850 letter to Mrs Dickens, *Letters* (6) 153.

75   21 Aug. 1850 letter to W. Wills, *Letters* (6) 154.

76   *Letters* (6) 154n.

77   8 Sept. 1850 letter to W. Wills, *Letters* (6) 166.

78   George Augustus Sala, *Things I Have Seen and the People I Have Known*, vol. 1 (London: Cassell & Co., Ltd., 1894) 84, 85.

79   *Letters* (7) 449n; 3 May 1854 letter to M. Lemon, *Letters* (7) 327.

80   Sala 90–93.

81   Above, p. 24.

82   23 Aug. 1850 letter to F. Stone, *Letters* (6) 155.

83   *Letters* (7) 516n.

84   1 Nov. 1854 Mrs Watson, *Letters* (7) 453.

85   10 Feb. 1855 letter to Mrs Winter, *Letters* (7) 533.

86   'No one but myself has the slightest knowledge of my correspondence, I may add in this place.' He suggested she could even come to Tavistock House on a Sunday, ostensibly

'asking first for Catherine and then for me.' Since 'it is a positive certainty that there will be no one here but I, between 3 and 4,' (with Catherine undoubtedly visiting friends for afternoon tea, which was growing in popularity, she could visit Dickens without the risk of being identified if they were in a public place. Now a victim of his own popularity, he was 'a dangerous man to be seen with, for so many people know me'): 22 Feb. 1855 letter to Mrs Winter, *Letters* (7) 545.

87   Their older niece also attended the dinner on Tuesday 27 February 1854: 24 Feb. 1854 letter to Mrs Winter, *Letters* (7) 548, 533n.

88   Scholars generally agree the charming but frivolous Dora in *David Copperfield* portrayed his youthful passion, and plump Flora Finching in *Little Dorrit* the mature Mrs Winter.

89   While the younger Dickens children enjoyed their vacation, Charley, who had just completed his studies in Leipzig, Germany, began looking for a business apprenticeship in London, which Dickens believed would arm his son 'against the Demon Idleness'. After the holidays, their second son, Walter, 'departed from the parental roof, with a plum cake, a box of marmalade, a ditto of jam, twelve oranges, five shillings, and a gross of tears' as he headed back to Wimbledon for school: 31 Jan. 1855 letter to L. Hunt, *Letters* (7) 518. His younger brothers, Frank and Alfred, carried similar goodies and 'a large cake [which] they took back with them' to school in Boulogne: *Letters* (7) 665n; 17 Jan. 1856 letter to E. Pigott, *Letters* (8) 26, 27. For their youngest sons, Catherine evaluated a progressive new concept in schooling imported from Germany, called the 'Child-Garden' (kindergarten), which had just opened in Tavistock Square, and was recommended by Mrs Gaskell: 1 Feb. 1855 letter to Mrs Gaskell, *Letters* (7) 520. Dickens published several articles in *Household Words* about the schools.

90   Dickens explained, 'the wooden house at the back of the schoolroom', was built to expand the area to a 30 feet long space: 9 Dec. 1856 letter to Miss Burdett Coutts, *Letters* (8) 234.

91   1 Jan. 1857 letter to C. Stanfield, *Letters* (8) 249.

92   12 Jan. 1857 letter to B. Webster, *Letters* (8) 258.

93   9 Jan. 1857 letter to Dean of St. Paul's; 11 Jan. 1857 letter to C. Stanfield, *Letters* (8) 255, 258.

94   [20 Jan. 1857] letter to J. Forster, *Letters* (8) 267.

Notes to Chapter VII, pages 219–245.

1   Francis Crew, 'A Dickens Dinner Party, 1843', *Bulletin of John Rylands Library* 36 (1953–4) 9–14 reproduced in *Letters* (3) 544n.

2   Alexis Soyer, *The Modern Housewife or Ménagère* (London: Simpkin, Marshall, & Co., 1850) 127.

3   James Hannay and William H. Wills, 'The London Tavern', *Household Words* 4 (1852) 74.

4   Webster (1852) 437.

5   Soyer (1850) 127.

6   Webster (1852) 437, 899.

7   Hannay (1852) 74.

8   Eliza Acton, *Modern Cookery In All its Branches* (London: Longman, Brown, Green, & Longmans, 1845) 28–33.

9   Webster (1852) 892; Mrs Beeton, *Mrs. Beeton's Every Day Cookery and Housekeeping Book* (1865, facsimile ed. New York: Gallery Books, 1984) 199, 200.

10   2 March 1844 letter to T. Beard, *Letters* (4) 59.

11   Eliza Lynn (Linton) and William H. Wills, 'Common Cookery', *Household Words* 13 (1856) 43.

12   James Marlow, 'Social Harmony and Dickens' Revolutionary Cookery', *Dickens Studies*

Annual 17 (1988) 145–177; Chris R.V. Bossche, 'Cookery, not Rookery: Family and Class in *David Copperfield*', *Dickens Studies Annual* 15 (1986) 89–110.

13   'Margaret Dods' (Christian I. Johnstone), *The Cook and Housewife's Manual, a Practical System of Modern Domestic Cookery and Family Management*, 5th ed. (Edinburgh: Oliver and Boyd, 1833) 116.

14   Linton 46.

15   Jennifer Davies, *The Victorian Kitchen,* large print ed. (Oxford: Clio Press, 1991) 97, 98.

16   Acton 21–23; Dods 123, 124; Beeton 326–327.

17   The name Jerusalem artichoke was thought to be a corruption of the Italian, *girasole articiocco*, which acknowledged the flower's movement in following the sun. However, other scholars believe that the name is a corruption of Ter Neusen, a place in Holland whence the tubers were imported to England: Kenneth F. Kiple and Kriemhild Coneè Ornelas, eds., 'A Historical Dictionary of the World's Plant Foods', *The Cambridge World History of Food* (Cambridge, Cambridge University Press, 2000) 1792, 1793.

18   10 Jan. 1848 letter to M. Lemon, *Letters* (5) 229.

19   Charles Dickens, *The Magic Fishbone* (London: Frederick Warne & Co., Ltd., 1868) 13, 14.

20   Elizabeth Ayrton, *English Provincial Cooking* (NY: Harper & Row, 1980) 146–152.

21   Marlow 168, 169.

22   John Burnett, *Plenty and Want: A Social History of Diet in England from 1815 to the Present Day* (London: Thomas Nelson, 1966) 147.

23   Charles Dickens and William H. Wills, 'A Popular Delusion', *Household Words* 1 (1850) 217–221

24   Dickens and Wills (1850) 219, 220.

25   Henry Morley, 'Fish Dinners', *Household Words* 3 (1851) 421.

26   Soyer also pointed out 'how slight is our knowledge of their habits, for it is only within the last few years that the idea was exploded that the herrings made an annual migration from the Arctic seas to deposit their spawn on the shores of these islands': Soyer 110.

27   Victorians did not find the popular notion, that everything in nature was created to serve human needs, to be presumptuous. Publications, such as Robert Mudie's *A Popular Guide to the Observation of Nature* (1832) presented nature as a factory to serve man: W. Yarrell, *A History of British Fishes,* 2nd ed. (London: J. Van Noorst, 1841).

28   Dickens and Wills (1850) 221.

29   Dickens and Wills (1850) 220.

30   J.C. Drummond, *The Englishman's Food: A History of Five Centuries of English Diet* (London: Jonathan Cape Ltd., 1939) 366.

31   Gravesend was a shipbuilding town on the right bank of the Thames in the county of Kent and in the vicinity of the market-gardens.

32   Thomas Webster, *Encyclopædia of Domestic Economy* (London: Longman, Brown, Green, Longmans, 1852) 415.

33   George Dodd, *The Food of London: A Sketch of the Chief Varieties, Sources of Supply, Probable Quantities Modes of Arrival, Processes of Manufacture, Suspected Adulteration, and Machinery of Distribution* (London: Longman, Brown, Green, and Longmans, 1856) 344.

34   Drummond 366.

35   Dodd (1856) 119.

36   Peter Quennell, ed., *Mayhew's London* (London: Pilot Press, 1949) 97–101. Quennell selected from Henry Mayhew's 1851 study entitled *London Labour and the London Poor*, which documented the social, cultural, and financial activities of street vendors.

37   Quennell 100, 101.

38   1 Sept. 1842 letter to C. Felton, *Letters* (3) 316.

39   18 Oct. 1950 letter T. Beard, *Letters* (6) 193.

40   As an adult, shad is a sea-dweller entering rivers in May to spawn before returning near

the end of July. Mature shad rarely swim as far up river as the fry and were not caught in association with them: Webster 420.

41   Alan Davidson, *North Atlantic Seafood* (Totnes, Prospect Books, 2000) 30.

42   Beeton 376; Acton 69.

43   George Dodd, 'Exploring Expedition to the Isle of Dogs', *Household Words* 7 (1853) 275, 276.

44   James Hannay and William H. Wills, 'The London Tavern', *Household Words* 4 (1852) 73.

45   Whitsun is on the seventh Sunday after Easter.

46   Arthur L. Hayward, *The Days of Dickens: A Glance at Some Aspects of Early Victorian Life in London* (London: George Routledge & Sons, Ltd., nd) 53, 45

47   Edward Hewett and W.F. Axton, *Convivial Dickens: The Drinks of Dickens and His Times* (Athens, OH: Ohio University Press, 1983) 11–13.

48   22 March 1848 letter to M. Lemon, *Letters* (5) 314.

49   G. W. Younger, 'Greenwich Taverns', *Dickensian* 39 (1943) 193–196.

50   *Letters* (3) 264n.

51   This was during Felton's May 1853 visit: Younger 193–196.

52   18 May 1848 letter to G. Cruikshank, *Letters* (5) 307, 308. The dinner was held on 22 May 1848.

53   Hayward 53.

54   30 March 1850 letters, *Letters* (6)75.

55   2 March 1843 letter to C. Felton, *Letters* (3) 452.

56   14 Aug. 1850 letter to T. Brown, *Letters* (6)147.

57   Webster 413, 414.

58   What Americans call shrimp are prawns to the British.

59   Morley 421, 422.

60   Webster 436.

61   Dudley Costello, 'A Dish of Frogs', *Household Words* 14 (1856) 25–30.

62   Soyer (1850) 130.

63   Webster 413. This is possibly Tor Bay in the English Channel on the coast of Devonshire, but Torbay is also the name of a fishing village on the east coast of Newfoundland and a bay on the south-east coast of Nova Scotia: Angelo Heilprin and Louis Heilprin, *The Complete Pronouncing Gazetteer* (London: J.B. Lippincott Co., 1922) 1846.

64   Webster 413.

65   Soyer (1850) 128.

66   Webster 413.

67   Webster 415, 891.

68   Soyer (1850) 132, 133.

69   11 Jan. 1838 letter to J. Forster, *Letters* (1) 353. Richard Baker argued in his article 'Was Edwin Drood Murdered?' that we shall never know to what extent Catherine made her husband cognizant of Scottish terms, but Dickens's choice of the Scottish term, 'droud' (meaning 'a codfish; a dull lumpish fellow') for the character's family name in his last novel is similar enough to suggest that he was familiar with many words: *Nineteenth-Century Fiction* 4 (2000) 221.

70   Webster 415. Dogger Bank, a sandbank near water ranging from 50 to 120 feet in depth, is located between the shores of England and Denmark and acted as the seat of the extensive fisheries: Heilprin 538.

71   Webster 414, 415.

72   Webster 414.

73   Webster 891.

74   Webster 424, 425.

75   Soyer (1850) 111.

76   Webster 425.

77   Dodd 120.

78   Soyer (1850) 112.

79   Dodd 335.

80   Webster 424, 425.

81   Charles Dickens, *Martin Chuzzlewit*, Chapter 25 (Maryland: Penguin Books, 1968) 480, 829.

82   Webster 425.

83   Webster 415.

84   Soyer (1850) 115.

85   Webster 891.

86   Soyer (1850) 116.

87   Soyer (1850) 120, 121; Webster 415.

88   Webster 416; Dodd (1856) 359.

89   Webster 416; Dodd (1856) 359.

90   Webster 416.

91   Elizabeth David, *English Cooking Ancient and Modern 1: Spices, Salt, and Aromatics in the English Kitchen* (Harmondsworth: Penguin, 1970) 279. For Eliza Acton's preparation of gooseberry sauce, boil 1 pint of cleaned young gooseberries with a little water until tender, mash and strain out seeds. Pour the purée into a saucepan, add 1 tsp of sugar, about a tablespoons of butter, and some ginger if liked. Heat and serve over mackerel: Acton 115.

92   10 Dec. 1847 letter to S. Lyttelton, *Letters* (5) 207.

93   Webster 418, 419.

94   James Knox, 'Fishing for Herring', *Household Words* 3 (1851) 595–599.

95   Soyer (1850) 124.

96   Webster 892.

97   Beeton 157; Webster 418, 419. Bloaters are similar to kippers, but milder in flavour and more perishable since the small fish are not soaked first in brine: Prue Leith, *The Cooks Handbook* (New York: A & W Publishers, Inc., 1981) 59.

98   David 113.

99   Webster 412.

100   Dodd (1856) 360.

101   Webster 421.

102   Soyer (1850) 125

103   Webster 417.

104   Webster 417.

105   The definition was given for cod, salmon, skate, and turbot in 'Mistress Dods' section of the cookbook entitled 'Glossary of the More Unfrequent [sic] Culinary Terms, French and English': Dods 7.

106   Soyer (1850) 133, 134.

107   Webster 419, 420.

108   A Lady, 'A Fine Fish Sauce', *The Jewish manual or Practical Information in Jewish and Modern Cookery with a Collection of Valuable Recipes and Hints Related to the Toilette* (1846, facsimile ed. New York: Nightingale Books, 1983) 22.

109   Webster 421.

110   Acton 105

111   Beeton 2.

112   Beeton 157.

113   Acton 152.

114   8 Aug. 1847 letter T. Mitton, *Letters* (5) 145.

115   Soyer (1850) 140; Webster 430, 431.

116   Webster 430, 431.

117 Quennell 97.

118 12 May 1840 letter to L. Hunt, *Letters* (2) 66, 67.

119 David 79.

120 Peter L. Simmonds, *The Commercial Products of the Sea* (New York: D. Appleton & Co., 1879) 131–133.

121 T. W. Hill, 'The Oyster; A Close-Up', *Dickensian* 36 (1940) 139.

122 1 Sept. 1842 letter to C. Felton, *Letters* (3) 315.

123 31 July 1842 letter to C. Felton, *Letters* (3) 291.

124 14 March 1842 letter to C. Felton, *Letters* (3) 131. Dickens's musings in his 21 May 42 letter to Felton fantasize about the off-season: 'A terrible idea occurred to me…The oyster cellars what do they do, when oysters are not in season? Is pickled salmon vended there – do they sell crabs, shrimp, winkles, herrings? – The oyster openers, what do *they* do? Do they commit suicide in despair, or wrench open tight drawers and cupboards and hermetically-sealed bottles – for practice? Perhaps they are dentists out of the oyster season. Who knows!' *Letters* (3) 244.

125 Charles Dickens, 'Misplaced Attachment of Mr. John Dounce', in *Sketches by Boz* (London: J. M. Dent & Ltd., 1968) 216. The story was first entitled 'Love and Oysters': *Letters* (3) 131n.

126 2 Jan. 1844 letter to C. Felton, *Letters* (4) 3.

127 Drummond 367.

128 Dodd (1856) 361, 362.

129 Simmonds 133, 136.

130 Edmund Saul Dixon, 'Oyster Seed', *Household Words* 19 (1856) 498.

131 Drummond 367.

132 Dixon 498.

133 John Robertson, 'Seaside Eggs', *Household Words* 14 (1856) 128.

134 Dixon 498, 499.

135 [A Physician], *The Cooks Oracle: Containing Receipts for Plain Cookery* (Boston: Munroe & Francis, 1822) 197

136 Acton 92. Directions in Mrs Beeton's manual suggested letting the oysters 'stand' out of the tub with the flat shell up for twelve hours before serving, Beeton 232.

137 Beeton 230, 231; Acton 420.

138 Recipe # 336 in Charles Elmé Francatelli, *Francatelli's The Modern Cook* (1846, facsimile ed. New York: Dover Publishing, Inc. 1973) 116, 117.

139 Beeton 231; Acton 36; Soyer's oyster soup recipe on page 147 in *The Modern Housewife* suggested four dozen oysters for about two quarts stock which is reduced.

140 Beeton 231; Soyer (1850) 147.

141 Alexis Soyer, *A Shilling Cookery for the People* (1854, facsimile ed., New York: David McKay Co., Inc., 1959) 151.

142 Beeton 231, 232.

143 Dodd (1856) 360, 361.

144 Simmonds 92–94.

145 Dudley Costello, 'Lobsters', *Household Words* 9 (1854) 567–569.

146 Costello 568.

147 Henry Morley, 'Fish Dinners', *Household Words* 3 (1851) 424.

Notes to Chapter VIII, pages 246–267.

1 George Dodd, *The Food of London: A Sketch of the Chief Varieties, Sources of Supply, Probable Quantities Modes of Arrival, Processes of Manufacture, Suspected Adulteration, and*

Machinery of Distribution (London: Longman, Brown, Green, and Longmans, 1856) 2, 3.

2   Dodd (1856) 98.

3   Offal is a term derived from 'off falls' that is, the organs and parts which are removed to butcher the carcass: Elizabeth Pomeroy, *The Cookery Year* (London: Reader's Digest Assoc. Ltd., 1973) 44.

4   'Horse-eating', an article written by Edmund Saul Dixon, discussed the practice in history: *Household Words* 13 (1856) 313–318.

5   *Letters* (6) 642n. Thackeray wrote and illustrated the novel, *History of Pendennis: his fortunes and misfortunes, his friends, and his greatest enemy*, which was published by Bradbury and Evans and issued in 24 monthly instalments from November 1848 to December 1850.

6   According to Dodd, there were roughly 8,000 miles of railroad and 2,800 miles of canals in the United Kingdom, with 24,000 miles of turnpike roads and 104,000 miles of minor roads, just in England and Wales, to get the products to and from the stations: Dodd (1856) 104, 105.

7   Dodd (1856) 102, 103.

8   Dodd (1856) 29, 30.

9   Dodd (1876) 243–246, 263, 264.

10 The butcher provided the meat for Ruth Pinch's beef-steak pudding in section 15, chapter 39. (Maryland: Penguin Books, 1968) 674.

11 Thomas Webster, *An Encyclopædia of Domestic Economy* (London: Longman, Brown, Green, & Longmans, 1852) 374. See also William Youatt, *Sheep: Their Breeds, Management and Diseases with an Index* (London: Baldwin & Cradock, 1839).

12 Webster 374.

13 5 Nov. [1842] letter to T. Beard, *Letters* (3) 359, 360.

14 Recipe #452 'Soyer's New Mutton Chop', Alexis Soyer, *The Modern Housewife or Ménagère* (London: Simpkin, Marshall, & Co., 1850) 229–230.

15 Eliza Acton, *Modern Cookery In All its Branches* (London: Longman, Brown, Green, & Longmans, 1845) 266.

16 Barbara Wheaton, personal communication.

17 Annie Hood, 'Kentish Food, or Food of Kent', *Petits Propos Culinaires* 45 (1993) 21, 22; Isabella Beeton, *Mrs. Beeton's Every Day Cookery and Housekeeping Book* (1865, facsimile ed. NY: Gallery Books, 1984) 208, 209.

18 Webster 374.

19 May Byron, *May Byron's Pot-Luck or the British Home Cooking Book*, 6th ed. (London: Hodder & Stoughton, Ltd., 1923) 17.

20 Ernest A. Hart, 'The Boiled Beef of Old England', *Household Words* 17 (1858) 522.

21 Henry Morley, 'Beef', *Household Words* 8 (1853) 385.

22 Morley 385–388.

23 Webster 372, 373.

24 Richard Horne, 'The Cattle-Road To Ruin', *Household Words* 14 (1850) 325–330.

25 Morley 387, 388. See also William Youatt, *Cattle: Their Breeds, Management, Diseases with an Index* (London: Baldwin & Cradock, 1834).

26 George Sala, 'Beef', *Household Words* 13 (1856) 49.

27 George Newlin, *Every Thing in Dickens: Ideas and Subjects Discussed by Charles Dickens in His Complete Works* (Westport, CT: Greenwood Press, 1996) 131.

28 Elizabeth David, *English Cooking Ancient and Modern 1: Spices, Salt, and Aromatics in the English Kitchen* (Harmondsworth: Penguin, 1970) 144.

29 14 Oct. 1842 letter to H. Austin, *Letters* (6) 120.

30 Soyer 209; Beeton 50, 51.

31 Soyer 205.

32   Webster 373.

33   William H. Wills and John D. Perry, 'Nice White Veal', *Household Words* 1 (1850) 467, 468.

34   Soyer (1850) 308, 309.

35   Mistress Margaret Dods (Christian Isobel Johnstone), *The Cook and Housewife's Manual* (Edinburgh: Oliver & Boyd, 1833) 242; Beeton 359.

36   Soyer (1850) 217, 218.

37   Prosper Montagné, *The New Larousse Gastronomique* (NY: Crown Pub., Inc., 1977) 960, 961. See also Dods 285.

38   Acton 302.

39   Hood 13.

40   Newlin (1996) 143.

41   Webster 375, 376; see also William Youatt, *The Pig* (London: Routledge, Warne, Routledge, 1860).

42   Dodd (1856) 279, 282.

43   Webster 375, 376.

44   George Dodd, 'All About Pigs', *Household Words* 5 (1852) 473. Saltpetre is nitrate of potassium which is used in small quantities to cure hams, bacon etc. to retain an attractive red colour.

45   Dodd 277, 278.

46   Acton 293–295.

47   26 Aug. 1849 letter to H. Austin, *Letters* (5) 599.

48   9 Aug. 1844 letter to T. Curry, *Letters* (4) 172.

49   Byron 153, 154.

50   Jean-Paul Aron, *The Art of Eating in France: Manners and Menus in the Nineteenth Century*, trans. Nina Rootes (London: Peter Owen Ltd., 1975) 39.

51   19 July 1842 letter to T. Beard, *Letters* (3) 273.

52   21 July 1842 letter to T. Beard, *Letters* (3) 276.

53   8 July 1850 letter to T. Beard, *Letters* (6) 126.

54   30 Jan. 1843 letter to C. Stanfield, *Letters* (3) 433.

55   13 March 1842 letter to J. Forster, *Letters* (3) 125.

56   *Letters* (3) 125n. The Dickenses saw Mr. Leslie again in 1856 when he was living in Paris and later at the last Academy dinner in London: 5 July 1856 letter to W. Irving, *Letters* (8) 151.

57   Miss Leslie's cookery book was first published in 1837 with 41 editions when it was updated in 1851, see Janice B. Longone's introduction to *Miss Leslie's Directions for Cookery: An Unabridged Reprint of the 1851 Classic* (Mineola, NY: Dover Pub., Inc., 1999) ix–xv.

58   Leslie 134. Miss Acton's recipe on page 329 is very similar.

59   27 July 1848 letter to L. Watson, *Letters* (5) 377.

60   28 July 1848 letters to T. Beard and P. Cunningham, *Letters* (5) 379, 380.

61   Beeton iii.

62   24 Dec. 1852 letter to M. Lemon, *Letters* (6) 834.

63   Newlin (1996) 140.

64   Dodd (1856) 328.

65   Dodd (1856) 325, 326.

66   James Payn, 'Our Back Garden', *Household Words* 18 (1858) 334–336.

67   Webster 395.

68   Edmund Saul Dixon, 'Poultry Abroad', *Household Words* 11 (1855) 399–402.

69   Dodd (1856) 317–319.

70   Webster 406; Beeton 112.

71   Charles Knight, 'Illustration of Cheapness. Eggs', *Household Words* 1 (1850) 158–161.

72 Knight (1850) 160.

73 Dodd (1856) 317–319.

74 Webster 394, 395.

75 Webster 396.

76 Dodd (1856) 321, 322.

77 *What Shall We Have For Dinner?* (1854 edition) 23.

78 20 July 1851 letter to F. Stone, *Letters* (6) 438.

79 [? Jan. 1839] letter to T. Mitton. Charles Smithson was a partner in the law office with Mitton and Dunn. He had acted on behalf of Dickens in 1838 and was later mentioned in the preface of the first cheap edition of *Nicholas Nickleby*: *Letters* (1) 427n, 492.

80 24 Dec. 1847 letter to Miss Coutts, *Letters* (5) 213.

81 Webster 396.

82 Edmund S. Dixon, 'Truffles', *Household Words* 12 (1855) 285.

83 Thanks to Barbara Wheaton for this information.

84 Newlin (1996) 135, 136.

85 2 Jan. 1840 letter to Messrs Bradbury and Evans, *Letters* (2) 1.

86 The gift was sent from Charles Elliot Norton. 26 Dec. 1851 letter to R. Sturgis, *Letters* (6) 562. The demand in London during the Christmas season was enormous, Dodd stated that no less than 2,500 geese, 1,000 ducks, and 500 turkeys were slaughtered and shipped from Boston alone for the 1855 holiday: Dodd (1856) 322, 323.

87 27 Oct. 1841 letter to C. Hunt, *Letters* (2) 413; 3 Feb. 1844 letter M. Wheeler, *Letters* (4) 39.

88 30 Oct. 1841 letter to J. Hudson, *Letters* (2) 415.

89 3 Sept. 1850 letter to C. Dickens, *Letters* (6) 162.

90 Bernard Darwin, 'Country Life and Sport', in *Early Victorian England* (London: Oxford University Press, 1934) 252–254; Dodd (1856) 326, 327.

91 Dodd (1856) 327.

92 Richard H. Horne, 'The Cow With The Iron Tail', *Household Words* 2 (1850) 145–151.

93 Dodd (1856) 119, 120, 299.

94 Peter Quennell, ed., *Mayhew's London* (London: Pilot Press, 1949) 127, 128.

95 [unknown] Browne and Henry Morley, 'Perfectly Contented', *Household Words* 14 (1856) 214.

96 1 March 1850 letter to M. Lemon, *Letters* (6) 50, 51. Referring to the play *Used Up*, which they performed together, Dickens's note chided him about Farmer Wurzel's activities: 'How's Corn? – You are a protectionist, of course. – Pigs looking up at all? – Sheep lively? – Anything new concerning Calves? – Mangel Wurzel now. How's *that?*'

97 26 Aug. 1849 letter to H. Austin, *Letters* (5) 599.

98 Dodd (1856) 293.

99 Dodd (1856) 293.

100 Charles Dickens, *David Copperfield* (chapter 27), in Edward Guiliano and Phillip Collins, *The Annotated Dickens*, vol. 2 (London: Orbis Book Publishing Co., Ltd., 1986) 274, 275.

101 Harriet Martineau, 'Butter', *Household Words* 15 (1852) 344–349; Dodd (1856) 302–308.

102 Dodd (1856) 302–308.

103 Dodd(1856) 289–291.

104 1 June 1840 letter to T. Beard, *Letters* (2) 77.

105 Condiments and sauces could be purchased in London along with more exotic items from Fortnum & Mason or Crosse & Blackwell who had been in business for over 150 years, or from Harrods which had opened several years before Catherine first published her book: Sarah Freeman, *Mutton and Oysters: the Victorians and Their Food* (London: Victor Gollancz Ltd., 1989) 11–13.

106 C. Anne Wilson, *Food and Drink in Britain: From the Stone Age to the 19th Century* (Chicago: Academy Pub., Co., 1991) 296.

107   Two recipes were written for Harvey Sauce. First make Quin Sauce: 'Pound green walnuts in a mortar, squeeze out the juice though a strainer and let it stand to settle. Pour off the clear, and to every pint of juice add one pound of anchovies, one drachm each of cloves, mace, and Jamaica pepper, bruised. Boil together till the anchovies are dissolved, strain it off, put in a good handful of shalots and boil again. To every pint of the above, add half a pint of the best brown vinegar.' To every three ounces of Quin Sauce, add 'soy one ounce, cayenne one drachm, brown vinegar two ounces.' The second recipe for 'Another' Harvey Sauce is easier. 'Two glasses of claret and two of walnut pickle, with four of mushroom catsup, six pounded anchovies with their pickle, and six shalots pounded, and half a glass of soy, black and cayenne pepper. Simmer all slowly by the fire, strain, and when cold bottle for use': *English Woman's Domestic Magazine* 6 (1858) 94, 95.

108   The root represented one of the most profitable items raised by market gardeners in the 1800s. Since the plant thrives best in soft, sandy loam, it could be dug in autumn, preserved through the winter in boxes of dry sandy soil under sheds or in cellars, and used fresh when needed: J.C. Loudon, *Encyclopædia of Gardening*, (London: Longmans, Green, & Co., 1878) 875.

Notes to Chapter IX, pages 268–288.

1   Peter Atkins, 'The Production and Marketing of Fruit and Vegetables, 1850–1950', in *Diet and Health in Modern Britain,* Dereck J. Oddy and Dereck S. Miller, eds. (Croom Helm Ltd., 1985) 102–133.

2   Edmund Saul Dixon, 'My Garden Walks', *Household Words* 11 (1855) 601, 604.

3   *The Encyclopædia of Gardening* recommended raising cabbages of the early heading sorts, hardy German and Scots greens, early potatoes, parsnips, turnips, carrots, onions, leeks, peas, beans, and kidney beans, and a plant or two of celery (not blanched), thyme, mint, chives and other the sweet herbs in the small plots. A few rhubarb plants (for tarts) and shrubs which could be trained along walls such as gooseberry, black and red currants 'ought never to be omitted'. Heavy bearers among the small trees, particularly baking apples, plums, and winter bergamot pears, Loudon advised, would provide seasonal fruit for the table: Loudon 1226–8.

4   6 March 1839 letter to T. Mitton, *Letters* (1) 523. The cottage Dickens found for his parents was in Alphington, a mile from Exeter. The property had 'on the ground floor a good parlour and kitchen, and above, a full-sized country drawing room and three bedrooms – in the yard behind, coal-holes, fowl-houses, and meat safes out of number; in the kitchen a neat little range; in the other rooms good stoves and cupboards – and all for £20 a year taxes included.'

5   The Dickenses' gardener was paid a total of £15 on Dec. 7th and 17th, *Letters* (1) 646.

6   Shaw 235; 12 March 1841 letter to D. Maclise, *Letters* (2) 230–232; 13 March 1841 letter to T. Latimer, *Letters* (2) 232–234.

7   18 Feb. 1841 letter to J. Forster, *Letters* (2) 214.

8   23 July 1848 letter to T. Talfourd, *Letters* (5) 376.

9   [11 Aug. 42] letter to J. Forster, *Letters* (3) 308.

10   Charles and Mary Cowden-Clarke, *Recollections of Writers* (New York: Charles Scribner's Sons, 1878) 316.

11   [30 June 1841] letter to J. Forster, *Letters* (2) 317; 15 July 1842 letter to Mrs Cohen, *Letters* (3) 271.

12   20 May 1845 letter to T. Mitton, *Letters* (4) 314.

13   H. T. Taverner, 'The Favourite Flower of Dickens', *Dickensian* 3 (1907) 55.

14   6 Oct. 1851 letter to Wills, *Letters* (6) 509.

15   9 Sept. 1851 letter to W. Wills, *Letters* (6) 480. Mr Wood ran the Bedford Nursery on Hampstead Road, 7 April 1852 letter to M. Lemon, *Letters* (6) 637.

16   19 Sept. 1851 letter to F. Stone, *Letters* (6) 486.

17   The lilacs were blown down in a gale, 9 May 1856 letter to Mrs Dickens, *Letters* (8) 113, 114; 31 May 1855 letter to F. Stone, *Letters* (7) 636.

18   13 Aug. 1856 letter to Miss Burdett Coutts, *Letters* (8) 177.

19   1 Mar. 1857 letter to Sir Joseph Paxton, *Letters* (8) 292.

20   3 Aug. 1857 letter to Sir Joseph Paxton, *Letters* (8) 400.

21   Gad's Hill Place catalogue of sale for August 10, 1870, pp. 3–9.

22   Atkins 110–113.

23   George Dodd, *The Food of London: A Sketch of the Chief Varieties, Sources of Supply, Probable Quantities Modes of Arrival, Processes of Manufacture, Suspected Adulteration, and Machinery of Distribution* (London: Longman, Brown, Green, and Longmans, 1856) 152.

24   Atkins 111.

25   Atkins 103, 104.

26   Mitton lived in Lampton, near Hounslow, *Letters* (8) 587n.

27   Atkins 105.

28   Loudon 777–811.

29   Atkins 104, 105.

30   Otto von Wenckstern, translated for 'English Cookery', *Household Words* 13 (1856) 116.

31   William May Thomas, 'Market Gardens', *Household Words* 7 (1853) 409.

32   Atkins 114.

33   Atkins 114.

34   Atkins 118.

35   Dodd 368, 370, 371.

36   William May Thomas, 'Covent Garden Market', *Household Words* 7 (1853) 507.

37   Thomas (1853) 511.

38   Atkins 115.

39   Dodd (1856) 393, 394.

40   Thomas Webster, *An Encyclopædia of Domestic Economy* (London: Longman, Brown, Green, & Longmans, 1852) 460.

41   Loudon 856.

42   Webster 471.

43   Mrs Beeton, *Mrs. Beeton's Every Day Cookery and Housekeeping Book* (1865, facsimile ed. NY: Gallery Books, 1984) 67, 68.

44   *Letters* (4) 710.

45   Webster 471, 472.

46   Maisie Steven, *The Good Scots Diet: What Happened to It?* (Aberdeen: Aberdeen University Press, 1985) 13.

47   [16 Aug. 1841] letter to Dickens from D. Maclise (MS Henry E. Huntington Library, acc. #108); *Letters* (2) 360n.

48   Eustace (Grenville) Murray and Henry Morley, 'In Praise of Salad', *Household Words* 4 (1852) 406–408

49   Henry Morley, 'Justice to Chicory', *Household Words* 6 (1852) 408.

50   Loudon 811, 872, 873.

51   T. W. Hill, 'The Dickens Dietary: V Cookery and Cooks', *Dickensian* 38 (1942) 197.

52   Charles Dickens, *Martin Chuzzlewit*, Chapter 49 (Maryland: Penguin Books, 1968) 829.

53   Kenneth F. Kiple and Kriemhild Coneè Ornelas, eds., *The Cambridge World History of Food* (Cambridge: Cambridge University Press, 2000) 1870.

54   Loudon 885.

55   John Capper, 'Rice', *Household Words* 11 (1855) 522–526.

56   Capper 522

57   Jean-Paul Aron, *The Art of Eating in France: Manners and Menus in the Nineteenth Century*, trans. Nina Rootes (London: Peter Owen Ltd., 1975) 97.

58   Webster 463.

59   Henry Morley, 'A Dish of Vegetables', *Household Words* (5) 221, 222

60   Redcliffe Salaman, *The History and Social Influence of the Potato* (Cambridge: Cambridge University Press, revised edition 1985) 162–164.

61   Alexis Soyer, *The Modern Housewife or Ménagère* (London: Simpkin, Marshall, & Co., 1850) 238, 239.

62   Salaman 162–164.

63   Ellen Messer, 'Potatoes White', in *The Cambridge World History of Food* 192, 193.

64   Salaman 317.

65   James S. Donnelly, *The Great Irish Potato Famine* (Stroud, Gloucestershire: Sutton Publishing, 2001); Cormac Ó Gráda, ed., *Famine 150: Commemorative Lecture Series* (Dublin: University College Press, 1997); E. Charles Nelson, *The Cause of the Calamity: Potato Blight in Ireland, 1845–1847, and the Role of the National Botanic Gardens* (Dublin: Government Stationery Office, 1995); John Percival, *The Great Famine: Ireland's Potato Famine 1845–1851* (London: BBC Books, 1995).

66   24 March 1847 letter to E. de la Rue, *Letters* (5) 43.

67   *Letters* (5) 43n.

68   George M. Young, *Early Victorian England 1830–1865* (London: Oxford University Press, 1963) 3, 4.

69   5 Jan. 1848 letter to W. Alison, *Letters* (5) 224.

70   Morley (1852) 222.

71   Eliza (Lynn) Linton, 'The Growth of Our Gardens', *Household Words* 18 (1858) 21.

72   Soyer 328, 329.

73   Salaman 164, 165.

74   Salaman 170.

75   Dodd 377.

76   8 Dec. 1842 letter to J. Welsh from Mrs Carlyle: Leonard Huxley, *Jane Welsh Carlyle: Letters to her Family, 1839–1863* (New York: Doubleday, Page & Co., 1924) 63.

77   Eliza Acton, *Modern Cookery In All its Branches* (London: Longman, Brown, Green, & Longmans, 1845) 360–362.

78   William Wills, 'A Good Plain Cook', *Household Words* 6 (1850) 139–141.

79   Jennifer Davies, *The Victorian Kitchen* large print ed. (Oxford: Clio Press, 1991) 116

80   Edmund Saul Dixon, 'What Mushrooms Cost', *Household Words* 7 (1853) 594–597.

81   Dixon (1853) 594.

82   Dixon (1853) 594.

83   Eliza Leslie, *Miss Leslie's Directions for Cookery: An Unabridged Reprint of the 1851 Classic* (Mineola, NY: Dover Publications, Inc., 1999: reproduction of the 1863 printing of the 1851 edition of *Miss Leslie's Complete Cookery: Directions for Cookery*) 176; Beeton 201, 202.

84   Loudon 891.

85   Webster 83.

86   Webster 483.

87   Edmund Saul Dixon, 'Truffles', *Household Words* 12 (1855) 284, 287.

88   Acton 322.

89   10 March 1848 letter to J. Ellis, *Letters* (5) 261.

90   Beeton 346, 347.

91   John Wright, *The Fruit Grower's Guide* (London: J. S. Virtue & Co., Ltd., nd) 328.

92   Edmund Saul Dixon, 'My Garden Library', *Household Words* 12 (1855) 370, 371.

93 Webster 487; Wright 315.

94 Webster 486.

95 Wright 319.

96 Webster 487.

97 Beeton 7.

98 Webster 912.

99 Acton 387.

100 Webster 504.

101 Davies 128, 129.

102 Davies 126; Webster 504.

103 22 October 1835 letter to K. Hogarth, *Letters* (1) 79.

104 *The Cambridge World History of Food* 1779.

105 *The Cambridge World History of Food* 1779; see also note 65 to chapter VII, above; Mrs David suggested the sauce originated in Cornwall.

106 Webster 502, 503.

107 Webster 502, 503.

108 Webster 504.

109 Dodd 379–80.

110 Edmund Saul Dixon, 'Strawberries', *Household Words* 18 (1858) 63, 64.

111 William May Thomas, 'Covent Garden Market', *Household Words* 7 (1853) 511.

112 Webster 504.

113 Webster 490, 491.

114 Webster 491.

115 Webster 491.

116 Hannah Glasse, *The Complete Confectioner* (London: I. Pottinger and J. Williams, 1770) 211, 212.

117 Acton 429.

118 Webster 493.

119 Dodd (1856) 391.

120 Webster 493, 494.

121 Webster 507, 508.

122 28 Sept. 1851 letter to Miss Eden, *Letters* (6)499.

123 Webster 495, 496.

124 Webster 495.

125 Murray 348.

126 Webster 505, 506; Hannah Glasse in *The Complete Confectioner* provides a recipe to preserve barberries on page 72 as well as hawthorn jelly on page 87.

127 J.W.T. Ley, ed., *The Life of Charles Dickens* by John Forster (London: Whitefriars Press, Ltd., 1928) 156.

128 Wright 488.

Notes to Chapter X, pages 289–302.

1 Hannah Glasse, *The Compleat Confectioner; or, The Whole Art of Confectionary Made Plain and Easy* (London: I. Pottinger and J. Williams, 1770) 253.

2 According to Webster, in 1643 the English began manufacturing sugar on St. Christopher's and Barbados, and on Jamaica in 1656. With the introduction of coffee and tea in England, the increased demand for sugar began, although sugar-candy had been imported from Venice well before then. Maisie Steven, *The Scots Diet: What happened to it?* (Aberdeen: Aberdeen University Press, 1985) 72.

3   27 March 1858 letter from W. Wills to his wife, *Letters* (8) 538n.

4   Thomas Webster, *An Encyclopædia of Domestic Economy* (London: Longman, Brown, Green, & Longmans, 1847) 720–725.

5   Webster (1847) 720.

6   Webster (1847) 720–725.

7   Webster (1852 edition) 723, 724.

8   Dodd (1856) 428, 429.

9   Mayhew recorded a variety of 'sweeties' made of treacle for sale in the 1849 London market including 'hard-bake', 'almond toffy' [sic], 'halfpenny lollipos', 'black balls', and the cheaper 'bulls eyes', and 'squibs'. Peter Quennell, ed. *Mayhew's London: Being Selections from 'London Labour and the London Poor'* (London: Pilot Press, 1949) 135.

10   Edmund Saul Dixon 'Beet-Root Sugar', *Household Words* 24 (1853) 569.

11   Eliza (Lynn) Linton 'The Growth of Our Gardens', *Household Words* 18 (1858) 22.

12   Alexis Soyer, *The Modern Housewife or Ménagère* (London: Simpkin, Marshall, & Co., 1850) 405.

13   *Letters* (4) 709–711.

14   20 Dec. 1852 letter to J. Leech, *Letters* (6) 830.

15   Davies 78, 80.

16   *Letters* (4) 710.

17   Sara Paston-Williams, *National Trust Book of Traditional Puddings* (Vermont: David & Charles Inc., 1983) 35.

18   The blancmange recipe highlights another aspect of databasing the menus for the frequency with which Catherine used the dishes given in the recipes. Inconsistencies in editing are evident: rice blancmange was also referred to as 'ground rice pudding' and 'cold ground rice pudding' in the bills of fare, but must not be confused with another dessert she called simply 'rice pudding'.

19   The recipe Catherine gave is technically the preparation for rice flummery since it is dependent on the rice flour to thicken the pudding enough to mould. 'Margaret Dods' makes a point that whole rice is used in rice blancmange (and it is congealed with isinglass). By 1865, Mrs Beeton's work refers to the rice flour preparation as rice blancmange and the term 'flummery' appears to be on its way out. 'Margaret Dods' (Christian I. Johnstone), *The Cook and Housewife's Manual, a Practical System of Modern Domestic Cookery and Family Management*, 5th ed.(Edinburgh: Oliver and Boyd, 1833) 356; Mrs Beeton, *Mrs. Beeton's Every Day Cookery and Housekeeping Book* (1865, facsimile ed. NY: Gallery Books, 1984) 286.

20   Peter Brears, 'Transparent Pleasures – The Story of the Jelly: Part One', *Petits Propos Culinaires* 53 (1996) 9.

21   Beeton 165.

22   Processors removed the air bladder from species of sturgeon (or sometimes large carp), and soaked it for several days in frequent changes of water to remove all traces of fish tissue. The bladder was then split, and the exterior was attached to boards to dry in the sun. When the layers of pure isinglass could be carefully detached from the inside of the bladder, the dried tough thin sheets were wrapped in linen, and pressed to keep them from contracting. From ten to twenty-five sheets, weighing between one pound to one and a quarter pounds in total, were produced from each fish. Commercial packets of isinglass were carefully wrapped in linen bags, covered with a rush-padding, and sealed in lead for transport. The industry in the United States used heated rollers to process the bladders extracted from species of cod or hake, and were sold in long strips. In the mid-1850s, the Canadians were beginning to experiment by processing their native sturgeon. Inferior products, usually from India, resulted from poor techniques and the isinglass they sold was in rolls or threads that had a characteristically fishy smell: P. L. Simmonds, *The*

Commercial Products of the Sea: Marine Contributions to Food, Industry, and Art (New York: D. Appleton and Co., 1879) 238–256.

23 Carrageen was named for the town with the same name near Waterford, Ireland: John Robertson, 'The Purple Shore', *Household Words* 14 (1856) 391–395.

24 Peter Brears, 'Transparent Pleasures – The Story of the Jelly: Part Two 1700–1820', *Petits Propos Culinaires* 54 (1996) 34.

25 Otto von Wenckstern (translated from a German newspaper) 'English Cookery', *Household Words* 13 (1856) 116.

26 May Byron xliii.

27 With the revival of plum pudding as a holiday treat perhaps several common misconceptions about the dessert should be addressed. Despite the name, there are no plums in the pudding. While prunes (dried plums) originally may have been among the fruits that gave the ancient mixture its name, they were eliminated well before the Dickenses' time. Rehydrated raisins (sultans) were often referred to as plums in Victorian recipes, as they were in Knight's article. Examples of other popular sweets, like Plum Bolster (Spotted Dick) and Plum Cake, contained dried fruit, mostly currants and raisins, but no fresh or dried plums.

28 Quennell 131.

29 Charles Dickens, (stave 4) *The Christmas Carol* (1843).

30 Venetia Murray suggests that mince pies were distributed during the holidays as a long-standing tradition that was 'a cross between a tip for services rendered' and the later exchange of Christmas cards, *An Elegant Madness: High Society in Regency England* (New York: Viking Penguin Books, Ltd., 1999) 189.

31 T.W. Hill, 'The Dickens Dietary, Part V: Cookery and Cooks', *Dickensian* 38 (1942) 205.

32 Alexis Soyer, as above, 409, 410; and in *The Gastronomic Regenerator: A Simplified and Entirely New System of Cookery* (London: Simpkin, Marshall, & Co., 1847) 634.

33 Dods 368.

34 Jennifer Davies, *The Victorian Kitchen,* large print ed. (Oxford: Clio Press, 1991) 82.

35 This is the date that baking powder was commercially available in the United States: James Trager, *The Food Chronology: A Food Lover's Compendium of Events and Anecdotes from Prehistory to the Present* (New York: Henry Holt & Co., 1995) 855.

36 Davies 63.

37 Eliza Acton, *Modern Cookery In All its Branches* (London: Longman, Brown, Green, & Longmans, 1845) 493.

38 According to Ann Hagen, puddings using bread to contain fresh fruit represented an archaic tradition, *Handbook of Anglo-Saxon Processing and Consumption* (Middlesex: Anglo-Saxon Books, 1992) 58.

39 Adrian Bailey ed., *Mrs. Bridges' Upstairs Downstairs Cookery Book* (New York: Simon & Schuster, 1974) 139, 140.

40 George Dodd, *The Food of London: A Sketch of the Chief Varieties, Sources of Supply, Probable Quantities Modes of Arrival, Processes of Manufacture, Suspected Adulteration, and Machinery of Distribution* (London: Longman, Brown, Green, and Longmans, 1856) 421–423.

41 Sophie D. Coe and Michael D. Coe, *The True History of Chocolate* (London: Thames and Hudson, 1996) 241–243.

42 In contemporary cookbooks the term 'cocoa' was used for both chocolate and coconut (often listed as 'cocoa nut') sometimes causing confusion. Meg Dods reserved the term for coconut, saying 'Cocoa is a favourite flavouring ingredient in the Colonies for puddings, &c. It is thought to give the laurel-leaf flavour, and has no pernicious quality', 348. Soyer's index and topic sections in *The Modern Housewife* presents another example. In addition, he coined the term 'Cho-ca' as the 'scientific composition of chocolat and café': Soyer

(1850) 25, 26, 411.

43   Eliza Lynn (Linton) and William Wills, 'Common Cookery', *Household Words* 13 (1856) 43.

44   [1] April 1844 letter from T. Hood, *Letters* (4) 87n.

45   Henry G. Wreford, 'Macaroni-Making', *Household Words* 17 (1858) 163.

46   Elizabeth David, *English Cooking Ancient and Modern 1: Spices, Salt, and Aromatics in the English Kitchen* (Harmondsworth: Penguin Books, 1970) 100–103.

47   Jean-Paul Aron, *The Art of Eating in France: Manners and Menus in the Nineteenth Century*, trans. Nina Rootes (London: Peter Owen Ltd., 1975) 97.

48   J.C. Loudon, *Encyclopædia of Gardening* (London: Longmans, Green, & Co., 1878) 871, 872.

49   Dodd (1856) 377.

50   Dudley Costello, 'Lobsters', *Household Words* 9 (1854) 568, 569. In one recipe, Costello combined finely chopped lobster meat with the liver seasoned with salt, mace, and cayenne. The mixture was held together with eggs, rolled into balls, and then fried to a delicate brown colour. His recipe for butter lobster is not for the squeamish. The uncooked lobster meat was removed from the shell, minced, and then poached in Madeira, vinegar, grated nutmeg, salt, and pepper before being 'deluged with melted butter cunningly flavoured with anchovy' and enriched with egg yolks.

51   Dodd (1856) 311.

52   Webster (1852) 390–392.

53   Dodd (1856) 314.

54   *Letters* (4) 710.

55   Beeton 72.

56   Edgar Johnson, *Charles Dickens His Tragedy and Triumph*, vol. 2 (New York, Simon & Schuster, 1952) 750; Thomas Wright, *The Life of Charles Dickens* (London: Herbert Jenkins Ltd., 1935) 223; *In Windsor* Magazine, Dec. (1934) 23.

Notes to the Epilogue, pages 303–305.

1   Malcolm Morley, 'The Theatrical Ternans', *Dickensian* 55 (1959) 115.

2   'Personal', *Household Words* 42 (1858) 1. Dickens wrote to Arthur Smith, who had managed his reading tour, and gave Smith permission to show the statement to anyone who wished to see it: 25 May 1858 letter to A. Smith, *Letters* (8) 568. Consequently, Dickens's statement was printed in American and British newspapers, and subsequently referred to as 'The Violated Letter' by Dickens. It began: 'Mrs. Dickens and I have lived unhappily together for many years. Hardly any one who has known us intimately can fail to have known that we are, in all respects of character and temperament, wonderfully unsuited to each other. I suppose that no two people, not vicious in themselves, ever were joined together, who had a greater difficulty in understanding one another, or who had less in common....For some years past Mrs. Dickens has been in the habit of representing to me that it would be better for her to go away and live apart; that her always increasing estrangement made a mental disorder under which she sometimes labours – more, that she felt herself unfit for the life she had to lead as my wife and that she would be better far away. I have uniformly replied that we must bear our misfortune, and fight the fight out to the end; that the children were the first consideration, and that I feared they must bind us together "in appearance"', The 'Violated' Letter, 25 May 1858, *Letters* (8) 740, 741.

3   24 June 1858 letter from Mrs Martineau to Henry Bright: Valerie Sanders, *Harriet Martineau Selected Letters* (Oxford: Clarendon Press, 1990) 153–155. In a letter two years later, Martineau wrote: 'I have for some time wanted to say two things to you. – You

sympathised in what I said when Dickens put away his wife. In the summer I had much conversation about Mrs. D. with her trustee, – chosen by Mr Dickens himself. This gentleman (Mr Evans) says Mrs D. is absolutely free from the offences charged against her in her husband's letter; & that Mr D's temper was so ferocious to her that his nearest friends could not bear to go to the house. Mrs D. is now cheerful, – kindly treated by her son, son-in-law, & married daughter. Dickens is wretched, & in an awful temper, so that he has hardly a friend left': 8 Nov. 1860 letter from H. Martineau to H. Bright, Sanders 184, 185.

4   Catherine Dickens's letters, housed at the Charles Dickens Museum archive, serve as examples of her activities.

5   An unflattering account of a 10 March 1860 dinner party at Thackeray's home, may reflect Bigelow's prejudgment of Catherine Dickens and the rawness of the situation: John Bigelow, *Retrospective of an Active Life* (New York: Baker & Taylor Co., 1909) 263–265. Dickens was at odds with Thackeray after hearing that he revealed Dickens's infatuation with the young actress in an impulsive attempt to quell the rumour that Dickens was involved with his sister-in-law: Gordon Ray, *Thackeray: The Age of Wisdom* (New York: McGraw-Hill Book Co., 1958) 276–279.

6   Lillian Nayder, 'The Widowhood of Catherine Dickens', *Dickens Studies Annual* 32 (2002) 286–289.

7   Nayder 286–289.

8   Catherine Dickens's letters were ultimately given to her daughter's physician in 1899, with the additional request that the British Museum prohibited publication until after the death of the surviving siblings, Gladys Storey, *Dickens and Daughter* (London: Frederick Muller, Ltd., 1939) 163–165. Although some of the letters were published, with Catherine's permission, by her daughter and sister, the most complete set was published in book form by Walter Dean in *Mr. and Mrs. Charles Dickens His Letters to Her* in 1933. The forward was written by Katey (Dickens) Perugini.

INDEX

Wreford, Henry, 299
Wright, John, 283
What Shall We Have For Dinner?
   authorship of, 77ff.
   methods of cookery utilized in, 84ff.
   publishing history of, 77ff.
   recipes, 94ff.
   seasonality of menus in, 87ff.

Yapp, K.F., 200
Yarrell, W., 224
yeast, 95, 96, 296
Yonge, Lady, 182

Zeller-Baden wine, 195